THE GAY GENIUS

The Life and Times of Su Tungpo

BY

LIN YUTANG

WILLIAM HEINEMANN LTD

MELBOURNE :: LONDON :: TORONTO

FIRST PUBLISHED 1948

PRINTED IN GREAT BRITAIN
AT THE WINDMILL PRESS
KINGSWOOD, SURREY

THE GAY GENIUS
The Life and Times of Su Tungpo

To

Adet, Taiyi, and Meimei

CONTENTS

*(A section of illustrations appears
following page 18)*

vii

CONTENTS

Book Three: MATURITY
(1080–1093)

Book Four: YEARS OF EXILE
(1094–1101)

APPENDICES

PREFACE

THERE is really no reason for my writing the life of Su Tungpo except that I want tó do it. For years the writing of his biography has been at the back of my mind. In 1936, when I came to the United States with my family, I brought with me, along with a carefully selected collection of basic Chinese reference books in compact editions, also a few very rare and ancient editions of works by and about this poet, for which all considerations of space were thrown overboard. I had hoped then to be able to write a book about him, or translate some of his poems or prose, and even if I could not do so, I wanted him to be with me while I was living abroad. It was a matter of sustenance of the spirit to have on one's shelves the works of a man with great charm, originality, and integrity of purpose, an *enfant terrible,* a great original mind that could not conform. Now that I am able to apply myself to this task, I am happy, and this should be an all-sufficient reason.

A vivid personality is always an enigma. There had to be one Su Tungpo, but there could not be two. 'Definitions of a personality generally satisfy only those who make them. It would be easy to pick out from the life and character of a man with such a versatile talent and colourful life a conglomerate of the qualities that have endeared him to his readers. One might say that Su Tungpo was an incorrigible optimist, a great humanitarian, a friend of the people, a prose master, an original painter, a great calligraphist, an experimenter in wine making, an engineer, a hater of puritanism, a yogi, a Buddhist believer, a Confucian statesman, a secretary to the emperor, a confirmed wine-bibber, a humane judge, a dissenter in politics, a prowler in the moonlight, a poet, and a wag. And yet that might miss the sum total of what made up Su Tungpo. I can perhaps best sum it up by saying that the mention of Su Tungpo always elicits an affectionate and warm admiring smile in China. For more than other Chinese poets', Su Tungpo's personality had the richness and variety and humour of a many-sided genius, possessing a gigantic intellect and a guileless child's heart—a combination described by Jesus as the wisdom of the serpent and the gentleness of the dove. Admittedly, this is a rare combination, shared only by a few born upon this earth. Here was a man! All through his life he retained a perfect naturalness and honesty with himself. Political chicanery and calculation were foreign to his character; the poems and essays he wrote on the inspiration of the moment or in criticism of something he disliked were the natural outpourings of his heart, instinc-

ix   A* tive and impetuous, like "the bird's song in spring and the cricket's chirp in autumn", as he put it once; or again they may be likened to the "cries of monkeys in the jungle or of the storks in high heaven, unaware of the human listeners below". Always deeply involved in politics, he was always greater than politics. Without guile and without purpose, he went along singing, composing, and criticising, purely to express something he felt in his heart, regardless of what might be the consequences for himself. And so it is that his readers today enjoy his writings as those of a man who kept his mind sharply focused on the progress of events, but who first and last reserved the inalienable right to speak for himself. From his writings shines forth a personality vivid and vigorous, playful or solemn, as the occasion may be, but always genuine, hearty, and true to himself. He wrote for no other reason than that he enjoyed writing, and today we enjoy his writing for no other reason than that he wrote so beautifully, generously, and out of the pristine innocence of his heart.

As I try to analyse the reasons why for a thousand years in China each generation has a crop of enthusiastic admirers of this poet, I come to the second reason, which is the same as the first, stated in a different way. Su Tungpo had charm. As with charm in women and beauty and fragrance in flowers, it is easier to feel it than to tell what elements it is composed of. The chief charm of Su Tungpo was that of a brilliant genius who constantly caused worries to his wife or those who loved him best—one does not know whether to admire and love him for his valiant courage, or stop him and protect him from all harm. Apparently there was in him a force of character that could not be stopped by anyone, a force that, started at the moment of his birth, had to run its course until death closed his mouth and stopped his laughing chatter. He wielded his pen almost as if it were a toy. He could be whimsical or dignified, playful or serious, very serious, and from his pen we hear a chord reflecting all the human emotions of joy, delight, disillusionment and resignation. Always he was hearty and enjoyed a party and a good drink. He described himself as impatient in character and said that when there was something he disliked, he had to "spit it out like a fly found in one's food". When he disliked the verse of a certain poet, he characterised it as "the composition of a Shantung school-teacher after sipping bad liquor and eating tainted beef".

He made jokes on his friends and his enemies. Once at a great court ceremony, in the presence of all the high officials, he made fun of a certain puritanical neo-Confucianist and stung him with a phrase which made the victim smart, and for which he suffered the consequences. Yet what other people could not understand was that he could get angry over things, but never could hate persons. He hated evil, but the evil-doers did not interest him. He merely disliked them.

Since hatred is an expression of incompetence, he never knew personal hatred, because he did not know incompetence. On the whole, we get the impression that he played and sang through life and enjoyed it tremendously, and when sorrow came and misfortune fell, he accepted them with a smile. That is the kind of charm which I am trying to describe in my lame and halting fashion and which has made him the favourite poet of so many Chinese scholars.

This is the story of a poet, painter, and friend of the people. He felt strongly, thought clearly, wrote beautifully, and acted with high courage, never swerved by his own interests or the changing fashions of opinion. He did not know how to look after his own welfare, but was immensely interested in that of his fellow men. He was warm, generous, never saved a penny, but felt as rich as a king. He was stubborn, garrulous but witty, careless of his speech, one who wore his heart on his sleeve; versatile, curious, profound, and frivolous, romantic in manners and classicist in letters, a Confucianist as a father, brother, and husband, but a Taoist under his skin, and a hater of all shams and hypocrisy. He was so much better a writer and scholar than others that he never had to be jealous, and he was so great he could afford to be gentle and kind. Simple and unaffected, he never cared for the trappings of dignity; when he was shackled with an office, he described himself as a harnessed deer. Living in troublous times, he became the stormy petrel of politics, an enemy of a fatuous, selfish bureaucracy and a champion of the people against their oppressors. With the successive emperors as his personal admirers and the empresses as his friends, Su Tungpo managed to be demoted and arrested, and to live in disgrace.

The best saying of Su Tungpo and the best description of himself was what he said to his brother Tseyu:

"Up above, I can associate with the Jade Emperor of Heaven, and down below I can associate with the poor folks. I think there is not a single bad person in this world."

So he had reason to be joyous and unafraid, and went through life like a whirlwind.

The story of Su Tungpo is essentially the story of a mind. He was a Buddhist in metaphysics, and knew that life was a temporary expression of something else, an eternal spirit in a temporary carcass, but he could never accept the thesis that life was a burden and a misery—not quite. At least for himself, he enjoyed every moment he lived. Metaphysically he was Hindu, but temperamentally he was Chinese. Out of the Buddhist faith to annihilate life, the Confucian faith to live it, and the Taoist faith to simplify it, a new amalgam was formed in the crucible of the poet's mind and perceptions. The maximum span of human life was only "36,000 days", but that was long enough; if his search for the elixir of immortality was in vain, still every moment of life was good while it lasted. His body might die, but his spirit in the next incarnation might become a star in heaven, or a river on earth, to shine, to nourish, and to sustain all living. Of this living, he was only a particle in a temporary manifestation of the eternal, and it really did not matter very much which particle he happened to be. So life was after all eternal and good, and he enjoyed it. That was part of the secret of the gay genius.

I have not burdened the text with footnotes, but have taken care to make only statements which can be backed by sources, and have as far as possible used the original words, though this may not be apparent. As all the sources are in Chinese, footnote references would be of no practical value to the great majority of readers. A general statement of the sources will be found in the Bibliographical Appendix. To prevent readers from floundering in Chinse names, I have eliminated those of the less important persons, or sometimes indicated only their family names. It is necessary also to refer to a person consistently by one name only, where a Chinese scholar had four or five. In spelling Chinese names, I have abolished the atrocious "hs" and substituted "sh", because this is the only sensible thing to do. Some of the poems I have translated into English verse, and some I have had to paraphrase into prose on account of the literary allusions which would make the translation grotesque and unpoetic, and the meaning obscure without lengthy comments.

LIN YUTANG

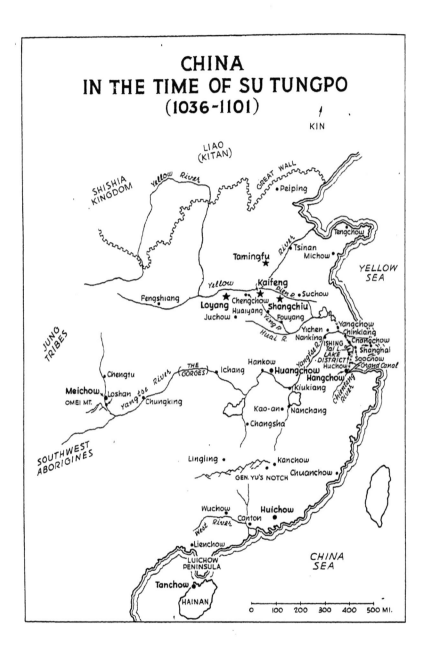

CHINA
IN THE TIME OF SU TUNGPO
(1036-1101)

KIN

LIAO
(KITAN)

SHISHIA
KINGDOM

Yellow River

GREAT WALL

• Peiping

Pien R.

Tengchow

• Tsinan
Tamingfu ★   Michow •

YELLOW
SEA

Yellow   Kaifeng
Fengshiang •   ★ • Suchow
            ★ Chengchow ★
Loyang   Huaiyang Shangchiu
Juchow •   Fouyang
                      Yichen • Yangchow
              Huai R. Nanking • Chinklang
JUNG   Changchow
TRIBES   ISHING Tai L. • Shanghai
                         LAKE Soochow
         THE   DISTRICT Huchow
• Chengtu   River (GORGES) Ichang   Hankow • Huangchow Grand Canal
Meichow   Hangchow
OMEI MT. Loshan • Yangtse Chungking   • Kiukiang
              • • Chungking   Chientang River
                    Kao-an • Nanchang
                    • Changsha
SOUTHWEST
ABORIGINES
            Lingling •   • Kanchow
                            Chuanchow •
              GEN. YU'S NOTCH

      Wuchow   Huichow
        •   Canton •
      West River •
        • Lienchow
        LUICHOW   CHINA
        PENINSULA   SEA
    Tanchow •

    HAINAN

0   100   200   300   400   500 MI.

BOOK ONE

CHILDHOOD AND YOUTH

(1036–1061)

Chapter One

LITERARY PATRIOTIC DUKE

IT is really not so difficult to know a man dead a thousand years ago. Considering how incomplete our knowledge usually is of people who live in the same city with us, or even of the private life of the mayor, it seems sometimes easier to know a dead man than a living one. For one thing, the living man's life is not completed, and one never knows what he is going to do next when a crisis comes. The drunkard reforms, the saint falls, and the pastor runs away with a choir girl. A living man has always so many "possibilities". Then, too, the living man has secrets, and some of the best secrets usually come out long after the man is dead. That is why it is so difficult usually to judge a contemporary, whose life is too close to us. Not so with a dead poet like Su Tungpo. I read his journals, his seventeen hundred poems, and his eight hundred private letters. The question of knowing or not knowing a man has nothing to do with being his contemporary. It is a matter of sympathetic understanding. After all, one knows only those whom one really understands, and one completely understands only those whom one really likes. I think I know Su Tungpo completely because I understand him, and I understand him because I like him. The question of liking a poet is always a question of taste. I think Li Po reached a greater height of sublimity and Tu Fu reached a greater stature in his total impression as a poet great by all the standards of greatness in poetry—freshness, naturalness, technical skill, and compassion. But without any apology, my favourite poet is Su Tungpo.

For me the great personality of Su Tungpo today stands out more sharply and fully etched against his life and writings than that of any other Chinese writer. There are two reasons for the clearness of the mental portrait of Su Tungpo in my mind. First, it comes from the brilliance of Su Tungpo's own mind, stamped upon every line he wrote, like the black lustre of ink in the two original bamboo paintings by Su that I have seen, which still glistens as if it were applied only an hour ago. This is a curious phenomenon, as in the case of Shakespeare, too. The vitality of Shakespeare's lines, coming straight from a sensitive and generous mind, remains fresh today. In spite of the labours of generations of research scholars, we still know extremely little about his external life; yet we feel some four hundred years after his death that we know the recesses of his mind by the power of emotion he injects into his writing.

The second reason is that there is a more complete record of Su

4 THE GAY GENIUS

Tungpo's life than of other Chinese poets. The material exists in various historical records of a long and colourful political career, in his own voluminous writings, both poetry and prose (close to a million words), in his journals, autograph notes, and private letters, and in the tremendous gossip about him as the most loved and admired scholar of his times, which has come down to this day in the form of journals and memoirs by his contemporaries. For a century after his death, there was not an important book of memoirs which did not have something to say about the poet. The Sung scholars were great keepers of diaries, notably Szema Kuang, Wang Anshih, Liu Chih, and Tseng Pu; or indefatigable writers of memoirs, like Wang Mingching and Shao Powen. Owing to the imbroglio over Wang Anshih's state capitalism and the heat and excitement of the political battles that extended through Su Tungpo's lifetime, the writers preserved the material for the period, including dialogues,* in more than usual abundance. Su Tungpo himself kept no diary; he was not the diary-keeping type—it would have been, for him, too methodical, too self-conscious. But he kept a journal, which was a collection of dated and undated items on particular trips, thoughts, men, places, and events. Other people were busy keeping memoirs of what he said and did. His letters and his postscripts were carefully preserved by his admirers. As a first-rate calligraphist very much sought after, he had the habit of writing a poem on the spot or of recording a thought or a comment and giving it away to a friend after a wine dinner. Such brief notes were carefully preserved and handed down to the friend's grand-children, or, in some cases, parted with for a very handsome sum of money. These casual notes contain admittedly some of Su's best writings. Some eight hundred of his letters and six hundred of his famous autograph notes and postscripts are preserved today. In fact, it was Su's popularity that started the fashion of collecting the postscripts and casual notes of other scholars after him, like Huang Tingchien, and publishing them in a volume. There was an art collector of Chengtu who, soon after his death, began to collect any autograph notes and intimate letters of Su Tungpo, inscribed them on stone, and sold rubbings from them as calligraphy.† The poem Su Tungpo wrote on a certain occasion was immediately circularised and repeated by heart among the scholars of the land. Innocent and honest, such poems of protest against the government's doings, at a time when all good scholars were hounded out of the capital, concentrated on him alone the fury of the ruling regime and almost cost him his life. Did he repent? Outwardly, in his banishment, to his less intimate friends he

* The dialogues in this book are based on actual records. See Bibliography, Section 1.

† The *Western Tower Scripts*, in thirty volumes. See page 243.

said he did, but to his best friends he said he did not and that he would do it all over again when the necessity came for spitting out a fly in one's food. Through these outpourings of his spirit, he found himself, to his sorrow, at the head of all decent-minded scholars of his time, and after a futile struggle with petty minds but great politicians, he went into his second exile outside civilised China in the island of Hainan, somewhat fatalistically and with great peace of mind.

It is natural, therefore, that the life of this man should be the centre of literary gossip and honoured with profound reverence, especially after his death. For Western analogies, Li Po may be compared to Shelley or Byron, a literary meteor that burned itself out in a short spectacular display. Tu Fu was like Milton, a devout philosopher and a good old man, writing in a profusion of apt, learned, and archaic metaphors. Su Tungpo was for ever young. He was as a character more like Thackeray, in his politics and poetic fame more like Victor Hugo, and he had something of the exciting quality of Dr. Johnson. Somehow Dr. Johnson's gout is exciting to us even today, while Milton's blindness is not. If Johnson were a Gainsborough at the same time, and also a Pope making criticism of current politics in verse, and if he had suffered like Swift, without the growing acidity of Swift, we would have an English parallel. The human spirit in Su Tungpo was mellowed, not soured, by his many troubles, and we love him today because he suffered so much.

There is a current Chinese saying that final judgment upon a man is possible only when the cover is nailed on his coffin. A man's life is like a drama, and we can judge a drama only when the curtain drops. There is this difference—a man's life is a drama in which the wisest and shrewdest actor does not know what comes in the next act. But real human life always evolves with an inevitability which only the best drama approaches. There is, therefore, a great advantage in writing the biography of a man of the past, where we can review scene after scene already completed, watching the inevitable development of events arising out of the necessity of outward events and inner temperament. After I had completed research on the chapters of Su Tungpo's life and understood why he had to do what he did, against his deep and sincere urge to forsake politics and retire, I felt as if I were reading the predictions of a man's entire life by a Chinese astrologist, clear, definite, inescapable. Chinese astrologists are able to plot the course of a person's entire life year by year, and are willing to put the whole prediction down in writing for a substantially higher sum than usual. But the hindsight of biographers is always better than the foresight of astrologers. Today, we are able to discern a clear pattern in Su's life with its many ups and downs, perceiving the same inevitability, but with the certainty that the different phases all came to pass, whether or not the fault was in the stars.

Su Tungpo was born in 1036 and died in 1101, twenty-five years before the conquest of northern China by the Kins and the end of the Northern Sung dynasty. He grew up under the best emperor of that dynasty, served under a well-meaning but over-ambitious one, and fell into disgrace when an eighteen-year-old idiot ascended the Dragon Throne. The study of Su Tungpo's life is, therefore, at the same time a study of national degeneration through party strife, ending in the sapping of national strength and the triumphant misrule of the petty politicians. Readers of *All Men Are Brothers* are acquainted with the quality of this misrule when good, honest men, in order to avoid tax-gatherers or evade the "justice" of rapacious officials, one by one took to the woods and became the much-beloved forest heroes of that novel.

At the time of Su Tungpo's youth there was a brilliant galaxy of scholars gathered at the court of the Chinese emperor. At the end of the dynasty there was none left. During the first persecution of scholars, and the purging of the censorate and packing it with under-lings by the illustrious state capitalist Wang Anshih, there were at least two dozen distinguished scholars and men of integrity who were will-ing to suffer for their convictions. During the second persecution, under the idiotic boy emperor, the good men were mostly dead or soon died in exile. This sapping of national strength had started in the name of "social reform" to prevent "exploitation by private capital", "for the benefit" of the always lovable common people of China, by an ardent believer in himself. Nothing is so dangerous to a nation's destiny as a misguided but opinionated idealist. Su Tungpo the poet and human philosopher pitted his common-sense against the logic of Wang Anshih the economist, and the lesson he taught and China paid for we still have not learned today.

In such ardent zeal for social reform Wang Anshih inevitably regarded any means as justifiable by the end, including purging of all dissenting opinion. A holy cause is always a dangerous thing. When a cause becomes holy, the means used to achieve it inevitably becomes vile. Such a trend of things could not escape Su Tungpo's perspicacious mind and was a little too much even for his sense of humour His path and Wang Anshih's crossed; their clash determined his whole career and the fate of the Sung dynasty.

Neither Su nor Wang lived to see the outcome of their struggle and the conquest of China by barbarian hordes from the north, although Su lived long enough to see the terrible results of the widely-publicised "social reforms". He lived to see that the "peasants" whom Wang had so "loved" had to flee their homes, not during famine or flood, but *in years of good crops,* when the officials put them in jail if they dared return to their villages, for failure to pay the loans and interest which the socialist regime had forced upon the peasants. And his voice cried to high heaven; he could not help himself. There were dishonest reporters who thought it expedient to maintain a strict silence on the bad features of the socialist regime, of which they could not be unaware, and to glamorise its virtues. The success of telling big lies, if the lies are big enough and repeated often enough, is not a modern invention. The eunuchs had to make their living. In such a way did irresponsible men play with a nation's destiny, as if they themselves could escape its consequences. Su Tungpo could at least keep his own soul and pay the price for it. The honest intentions of the Emperor were no excuse for his gullibility, for he was wrong, and Su Tungpo right, on the main issue. An iron rule was clapped over the people in the holy name of social reform. In the mad struggle for power, party fanaticism overruled patriotic interests, and the moral and economic fibre of the nation was consumed and weakened as Su Tungpo foretold, making the country an easy prey to a conqueror from the direction of Siberia. When petty men were ready to serve as puppets of a powerful neighbour from the north in the name of a "regional independent China" which owed allegiance to a foreign power, it was but right that the imperial dynasty should be extinguished and China should retreat south of the Yangtse River. When the Sung house had burned down, historians, walking among the charred ruins, began to survey the field and ponder, with self-important historical perspective, but a little too late, the causes of the catastrophe.

One year after the death of Su Tungpo, when the petty partisans were in power before they handed North China over to His foreign Majesty from across the Mongolian wilds, a historically important episode occurred. This was the establishment of the famous Yuanyu Partisans' Tablet, a symbol and a summing up of the struggles of the whole period. "Yuanyu" is the name of the reign (1086–1093) under which Su Tungpo's own party was in power, and the tablet was a black-list of 309 men, headed by Su Tungpo, of the Yuanyu regime. It banned for ever by imperial order these persons and their children from assuming office in the government. Descendants of the royal family were forbidden to marry children of the "Yuanyu partisans," and if there had been a betrothal, it was to be broken off by imperial order. A tablet containing the black-list was to be set up in all districts of the country; some of these still exist today on China's mountain-tops. It was a method of weeding out all opposition for ever, and, in the authors' minds, of committing these men to eternal infamy. Since China was turned over to the conquerors from the north by the social reformers, the effect achieved by these tablets was very different from what the authors had intended. For over a century, the children of the black-listed men boasted that their ancestors' names were included in the tablet. That is why the Yuanyu Partisans' Tablet became so famous in history. Actually, some of these ancestors did not deserve the honour, for in the zeal to weed out all opposition, the authors of the tablet included all their personal enemies, and black-listed some bad men as well as the good ones.

As the gods had decreed it, however, in January 1106 a comet appeared in the sky and the tablet established on the east wall of the Wenteh Palace was struck by lightning and split in two. There could not be a clearer indication of Heaven's displeasure. Emperor Huitsung was frightened, and in fear of the objection of the premier had the other tablet at the Tuan Gate secretly destroyed at night. On finding this out, the premier was greatly chagrined, but righteously exclaimed: "The tablet may be destroyed, but the names of these men shall be remembered for ever!" We know today that his wish was fulfilled.

The striking of the tablet by lightning started Su Tungpo's steadily increasing fame after his death. During the first decade all stone inscriptions bearing his handwriting or composition were ordered destroyed, his books were banned, and he was deprived of every rank he had held in his lifetime. A writer of this time noted down in his journal, however, that "the poems he wrote in exile are very popular. Although the court has increased the fine for possession of Su's works to 800,000 cash [or $800], the stronger the ban, the wider the poems spread. Scholars feel disgraced and are considered uncultured when they cannot recite his poems in company."

Five years after the lightning had struck, a Taoist priest reported to the Emperor that he had seen the spirit of Su Tungpo serving as the minister of literature at the gods' court in Heaven. The Emperor was still more frightened and hastily restored to Su the highest rank he had obtained in his lifetime, and later conferred one higher than he had ever possessed. By 1117 the imperial household, under the same emperor, was itself collecting Su Tungpo's manuscripts, offering as much as 50,000 cash apiece. The eunuch Liang Shihcheng paid 300,000 cash, roughly $300, a high price according to the then standard of living, for the inscription on the Stone Bridge of Ingchow (which had been discreetly hidden), and another man paid 50,000 cash for three words written by Su on the tablet of a scholar's studio. A brisk business was going on, and soon these precious manuscripts were in the palace or in the homes of rich collectors. When the Kin (Manchurian) barbarians captured the capital, they specifically demanded as part of the booty the works of Su Tungpo and Szema Kuang, for Su's name had spread to the northern tribes beyond China's border even in his lifetime. Some of the best of Su's paintings and manuscripts were carted north to enemy territory, together with two emperors who died there in captivity. (Huitsung had resigned in favour of his son.) Still hundreds of Su's manuscript items survived and were brought by their owners to the south.

Now that Su Tungpo was dead and the storms of passion over current politics were over, the emperors in the southern Sung dynasty, sitting in the new capital of Hangchow, began to read his works, particularly his state papers, and the more they read, the more they admired the intrepid patriotism of the man. One of his grand-children, Su Fu, was given a high office in consideration of his illustrious grandfather. All this leads to the final culmination of Su Tungpo's posthumous fame and position. By 1170 the filial emperor Shiaotsung conferred upon him the posthumous title of "Literary Patriotic Duke" and gave him the rank of Grand Imperial Tutor. The Emperor wrote what remains to this day the best tribute to his genius. The imperial decree and the Emperor's own preface to his *Works* stands at the beginning in all editions of Su's *Complete Works*. The imperial decree conferring upon him the title of Grand Imperial Tutor reads:

By Imperial Order: We come after the tradition of the hundred sages and seek wisdom in the Six Classics. While desiring to promote the culture of ideas, our thoughts turn back to the great one of the past. Although it is no longer possible to see him in person, we have the works of this great man before us. We desire to confer upon him the honour of an Emperor's teacher and exalt him to leadership among the scholars.

The deceased, Su Shih, formerly Minister of Education, Scholar of the Tuanming Palace, subsequently made Scholar of the Tsecheng Palace and posthumously titled Literary Patriotic Duke, cultivated the noble and upright spirit born in man and elevated to a higher level of understanding the tradition of the past. His scholarship was all-embracing, like the sea and the earth, and his words of advice were like the striking of jade and bells. In literary eloquence he can be compared to Mencius, and in political criticism he was not second to Lu Chih. At the nation's height of literary prosperity during Chiayu [reign of Jentsung] he was exalted to fame; during the confusing changes of Shining [reign of Shentsung] he submitted the principles for a lasting national prosperity. We sigh at the appearance of such a rare genius and are shocked at his suffering from his detractors. He was banished across the seas and mountains, but he remained the same man as if he were holding power at the court; he studied the past and the present and his mind comprehended the laws of the universe. What could not be taken away from him was his sturdy integrity, and what no man could confer upon him was his popular fame. In his lifetime he had no consideration for his own good, and posterity gave him his fair due after his death. So today everyone continues to speak of the scholar of Yuanyu, and every home possesses a copy of the works of Meishan. Three times over we have read his bequeathed works, and for a long time we have admired his high principles. We regret not being born at the same time with him in order to make full use of his talents as a counsellor of kings, but from generation to generation, the superior man's teachings ever grow from obscurity to popular acceptance.

We wish that your spirit could rise from the underground springs, so that the world might pay homage to your fame, and we pray that your talented soul will accept our Imperial favour. Su Shih is hereby specially given the title of Grand Imperial Tutor. His other titles may be kept as before.

Su Tungpo's peculiar position in China's history was, therefore, based on his courageous stand for his principles and opinions, as well as upon the charm of his poems and prose. His character and principles constitute the "bones" of his fame, while the charm of style and language forms the "flesh and skin" that embody the beauty of his spirit. I do not think that we can, at heart, admire a writer lacking in integrity, however brilliant and charming his writings may be. The imperial preface to Su's *Collected Works* emphasises the greatness of his "spirit", which distinguishes his works from mere "fine writing" and gives solidity to his fame.

But let us not forget that Su was principally a poet and writer. On this his reputation rests. His writings have a quality that is difficult to explain, much less feel in translation. A classic becomes a classic because the people in all ages recognise "good writing" as such. Ultimately, lasting fame in literature rests on the pleasure the writing gives to the readers, and who shall say in what way a reader is pleased? What separates literature from ordinary writing is the charm of sound and sense and manner which pleases the spirit. That a classic pleases all men in all ages and survives temporary literary fashions must come of a quality that we may call *genuineness*, like that of precious gems which survive all tests. "Literature is like genuine gold and good jade," Su wrote to Shieh Minshih. "They have an intrinsic value independent of fluctuating prices."

Yet what is that "genuineness" which accounts for its quality of wearing well? Su expressed his opinion on writing and style as clearly as anyone ever put it. "Roughly, [good writing] is like the sailing of clouds or flowing of water, moving forward where it is natural to move forward, and stopping where it must stop. From the natural flow of thoughts and language arises its wayward, abundant charm. 'An expression lacking literary beauty cannot survive very long,' said Confucius. Again he said: 'All you ask of writing is that it *expresses* well.' One may think that if the aim of writing is merely to express something well, it may be lacking in literary beauty. That is not so. Only one person in a thousand or ten thousand can appreciate an intangible, elusive idea, or the essence of a given situation, and make it clear to himself. It is still more difficult to communicate it by hand or mouth to others, which is what we mean by expressing it well. When one can do this, he can do anything with his pen. Yang Shiung loved to clothe a simple, insipid thought in high-flown, difficult phraseology, just because he knew that if he did not, the thought itself would be shown to be quite commonplace. That is the trick of the so-called petty journeyman writers." In this definition of style, Su Tungpo aptly describes his own process of literary composition, moving and stopping like "sailing clouds and flowing water", and he gives away all the mysteries of composition and rhetoric. There are no rules on when to go on and when to break off. The charms and wayward beauty come by themselves if the writer's thoughts are beautiful and he only can express them truthfully, genuinely, and well. They are not something laid on the writing. Simplicity, naturalness, and a certain freedom which comes from mastery of expression are the secrets of a good style. When such qualities are present, and the writing is not insipid, we have genuine literature.

Anyway, pleasure given was a characteristic of all Su's writings. Most pleased of all was the author himself in the act of writing. "The happiest moments of my life," Su said to his friend one day, "are when, at the time of writing, my pen can express all the intricacies of my thoughts. I say to myself: 'There is no greater pleasure in this earthly life than this.'" Much the same was its effect on his contemporaries. Ouyang Shiu said that whenever he received a new composition by Su, he remained happy for the whole day. An attendant upon Emperor Shentsung told people that whenever the Emperor's chopsticks stopped in the middle of his eating, it was sure to be Su Tungpo's memorandum that he was reading. Always whenever a new poem reached the court, even during the period of Su Tungpo's exile, the Emperor would praise it before the other ministers with sighs of admiration. But it was also these sighs of admiration on the part of the Emperor that frightened the ministers and kept Su in exile so long as this emperor lived.

Once the poet defended the power of giving pleasure as literature's own reward. In the last years of his life he sometimes wanted to throw away his brush and stop writing entirely, since it was writing that had brought him all his trouble. A friend and admirer, Liu Mien, edited his works and wrote to him about it. In his reply to Liu Mien he said: "I have fallen upon evil days because of my writing, and sometimes I wish to black out my intelligence, which unfortunately cannot be done. My youngest son, Kuo, is beginning to write more beautifully than ever. During my hours of boredom, living overseas, sometimes Kuo shows me one of his compositions, and I am happy for days and enjoy my food and my sleep better. This shows that literature is like gold and jade or precious stones, which have an intrinsic value of their own that cannot-be denied." In the pleasure it gives to the author during his free creative activity, and in the happiness it gives to its readers, literature justifies its own existence.

Su possessed an unusually generous talent, which broke all boundaries and seemed to know no limitations. His poems were always fresh, not like Wang Anshih's, which occasionally attained perfection. Su did not have to attain such perfection. Where other poets were limited by poetic diction and conventional themes, Su could write a poem on massage at a bath-house, and he could incorporate slang and make it sound well in a poem. Always it was that extra something which others could not do that compelled admiration from his fellow craftsmen. His chief contribution to a special form of poetry, the *tse*, confined hitherto to yearnings of the lovelorn, was that he could turn the metre into a vehicle for discourse on Buddhism and philosophy, and he succeeded in this almost impossibly risky task. Usually he wrote a little better and a little faster than others, for he often had to compose poems after dinner with people looking on. His thoughts were fresher and his analogies and allusions more appropriate than those of other poets. Once at a farewell dinner given him at Huangchow, a female entertainer came up and asked him to write a poem on her shawl. Now he had not heard of this entertainer, Li Chi, during his stay at Huangchow. He asked her to grind the ink and took up the brush and wrote a simple beginning:

Four years has Tungpo lived at Huangchow,
Strange that he never mentioned Li Chi.

Then he stopped and went on talking with his guests. It was, in the opinion of those present, a rather flat beginning, and besides, the poem was not finished. Su went on eating, chatting and laughing. Li Chi came up again and asked him to finish it. "Oh, I almost forgot," said Su. He took up the brush again and dashed off the second half of the quatrain:

Exactly like Tu Fu of the West River;
Of the best flower, begonia, he sang the least.

It fitted perfectly in rhyme and tone, and in effect the poem was like a little gem, written as usual with the poet's effortless grace. It gave a very subtle compliment to the girl, and Li Chi thereby became immortal in literature. The technical restrictions in Chinese poetry were many, requiring a high skill in the use of allusions and in the writing of a poem with the same rhyme words as those used in a poem written by a friend. Somehow, Su's rhyming was more natural, and his allusions, upon close examination, were found to suggest deeper implications. In prose his pen commanded a wide range of powers, from the most dignified pure prose in the simple style of the ancient classics to charming chatter in the style of the familiar essayists. It is difficult to choose between the two. That is why he was acknowledged a master.

Su Tungpo, therefore, ranks as a major poet and prose writer of China. In addition he was a painter and calligraphist of the first order, a distinguished conversationalist, a great traveller. Quick to comprehend Buddhist philosophy, he constantly associated with monks, and was the first poet to inject Buddhist philosophy into Confucianist poetry. He made a good guess that the dark spots on the moon were the shadows of mountains. He pioneered in a new school of painting, the "scholar painting" which makes Chinese art unique. He opened up lakes and canals, fought floods, built dams. He picked his own herbs and was a recognised authority in medicine. He dabbled in alchemy and was interested almost to his last days in his search for the elixir of immortality. He pleaded with the gods and argued with the devil— and sometimes won. He wanted to wrest the secrets of the universe, was half defeated, and died with a laugh.

Were the word not so much abused today, we would say he was a great democrat, for he associated with all manner of men and had for his friends emperors, poets, cabinet ministers and retired farmers, pharmacists, wineshop-keepers, and illiterate peasant women. His best friends were poetic monks, unknown Taoists, and those poorer than himself. He loved official honour and yet was happiest when the crowds did not recognise him. He established good water systems for Hangchow and Canton, founded orphanages and hospitals, instituted prison physicians, fought infanticide. During the aftermath of the social reforms he worked passionately and single-handedly at famine relief, against the colossal obstruction of bureaucracy. It almost seems he was the only man concerned over the widespread famine and the roaming refugees. Always he was the champion of the people against the government and worked for the forgiveness of debts to the poor until he got it. He wanted only to be himself. Today it may be said that he was truly a modern man.

IF you go up the Yangtse River, beyond Hankow, past the famous
gorges into the westernmost province of Szechuen, and further follow
the river past Chungking to its origins, you will come to a giant stone
Buddha, three hundred and sixty feet high, carved out of a mountain
cliff on the bank. Here at the western border of the province and at
the foot of the giant Omei Mountain, the highest in China, is Loshan,
called Kiachow in the days of Su Tungpo. At this point the Min River
flows into the Yangtse. The Min River, coming down from the north-
western mountains of the western aborigines, rushes down in a big and
deep torrent and, joining another river coming down from the Omei,
makes a straight dash for the Giant Stone Buddha of Loshan, where
the river then turns gradually south-east and then east to flow directly
into the China Sea. Lying in the shadow of the eternally cloud-covered
peaks of the Omei, and some forty miles north of Loshan, is the town
of Meishan, in Meichow district, made famous in China's literary
history as the home of the most distinguished literary family in China.
This was the Su family, also known as the "Three Sus". The father
was Su Shün, who gave birth to two illustrious sons, Su Shih (Tungpo),
and Su Cheh (Tseyu). Together the father and sons account for three
of the "Eight Great Prose Masters of the Tang and Sung Dynasties."*
    At Loshan, then as now, a traveller could go up the Polikiang, or
Glass River, in a junk to Meishan. The river received its name from
its colour, for it was a deep crystal blue in winter, while in summer the
torrents coming down from the mountains turned it into a murky
yellow. The river was a branch of the Min River, and as Meishan lay
halfway between Loshan and the capital of the province, Chengtu,
travellers who wanted to go to the capital had to pass through the
town. You would go up in the junk until you saw the Moyishan, or
Frog's Jowl Hill, standing directly over the stream. It was a low, round
hill like those we see around Kiangsu. Here was Meishan, the home
town of the Sus. Thanks to the engineering genius of Li Ping, who
lived at the end of the third century B.C., there was a perfect water
control and irrigation system, maintained and kept working for over a
thousand years; it made this whole region of western Szechuen into a
perennially fertile plain, free from floods. The little hill stood against
a vast plain of rice-fields, orchards, and vegetable gardens, dotted here
and there with bamboo groves and curiously dwarfed palm trees. You

* Of these eight masters, six are important figures in this book. Besides the
"three Sus," the other three are Wang Anshih, Ouyang Shiu, and Tseng Kung.

entered the city from the south and went up the clean stone pavements into the heart of the city.

It was not a very big town, but it was comfortable for a place of residence. A poet of the twelfth century reported that the streets were kept very clean and that Meishan was famous for its lotus flowers in May and June. The cultivation of the lotus flower had grown into an industry, for dealers from the neighbouring cities obtained their lotus flowers from this place. As one went up the streets, one passed many ponds on the roadside covered with these flowers, whose fragrance filled the air. At Shakuhang one came upon a middle-class home. Entering the gate, one faced a green painted screen which shut out the view of the interior from the passers-by. Behind the screen, a medium-sized house with its courtyards appeared. Somewhere near the house stood a tall pear tree, and there were a pond and a vegetable patch. In the little family garden there was a great variety of flower and fruit trees, while outside the wall stood a grove of hundreds of bamboo trees.

It was the year 1036, thirty years before the Battle of Hastings. On December the nineteenth, a baby boy was crying and kicking in his swaddling clothes. Since the first son had died in infancy, he was the eldest son of the family. And here, as the baby was doing nothing in particular or doing what every baby does, we may take time to look around at the family. But first something must be said about this birthday, lest we but add to a certain confusion plaguing Chinese biographies abroad. A Chinese baby is "one year old" the moment he is born, following the general pattern of everyone's desiring to reach venerable age as quickly as possible. On the next New Year's Day, when all people advance their age one year, he is "two years old". According to the Chinese reckoning, therefore, as compared with Western reckoning, a person always counts himself two years older before his birthday and one year older after that date in any given year. In this book, ages are given according to the Western reckoning, without taking into consideration a person's exact birthday. In the case of Su Tungpo, however, a little more exactness is required. As he was "one year old" the day he was born, on December nineteenth, he would be "two years old" already on the following New Year's Day—when he was hardly two weeks old, actually. As his birthday came toward the very end of the year, he was actually always two years younger than he would be according to the Chinese reckoning.

The second thing to be said about the birthday is that he was born under Scorpio. According to the poet himself, this explains why he ran into so many troubles all his life and was a target of rumours, both good and bad, which he did not deserve—a fate similar to that of Han Yu, who was born under the same star, and who was also sentenced to exile for his opinions.

On the central panel of one of the rooms in the house hung a portrait of a certain fairy by the name of Chang. The father of the baby, who was now twenty-seven and going through the greatest spiritual crisis of his life, had seen this portrait at one of the markets and had got it by offering a jade bracelet for it to the dealer. He had prayed to this fairy every morning for the last seven years. His wife had given birth to a girl several years ago and to the boy who died in infancy. He had always wanted a boy, and now his wish was granted. He must have been happy; and yet we know that he was suffering from a sense of terrific shame and torment.

It was a fairly well-to-do family, owning lands and perhaps richer than the average middle-class family. There were at least two maid-servants, and besides, the family was able to afford a wet nurse for Su Tungpo and his elder sister. When the younger brother was born, they were able to hire another wet nurse, and these two nurses remained according to Chinese custom for the rest of their lives with the children they had brought up to maturity.

At this time of Su Tungpo's birth, the grandfather was still living and was sixty-three years old. In his young days he had been a tall, handsome man, hale and hearty, given to drink, big-hearted and generous. One day when Su Tungpo was the acknowledged first scholar of his time and was acting as secretary to the emperor, he moved into a new residence close to the palace. Some of his close friends and admirers came to visit him, and as it happened to be his grandfather's birthday, he began to tell them certain amusing incidents about this curious old man. He was wholly illiterate, but a rather extraordinary personality. At that time they were living out in the country and owned large tracts of land. But instead of storing up rice in the way everybody did usually, he exchanged it for unhusked rice and stored it up to the amount of thirty or forty thousand bushels in his granary. People could not understand why he was doing this. Then a famine came, and the grandfather opened the granary and began to distribute the unhusked rice first to his own immediate family and relatives, then to his wife's relatives, then to the tenant farmers, and then to the poor of the village. Now people understood why he had accumulated the unhusked rice—it would keep for years, whereas husked rice would spoil in wet weather. Being carefree and well provided, he would often pick up a wine jug and go about with his friends to sit on the grass and enjoy himself. They would laugh and drink and sing, to the amazement of the usually quiet and well-behaved peasants.

One day during a carousal an important piece of news arrived. His second son, Su Tungpo's uncle, had passed the imperial examinations. There was another family in the neighbourhood whose son had also passed the same examinations. This was the family of Su Tungpo's mother, the Chengs. As the two houses were then connected by marriage, it was a double occasion for joy. The Chengs, however, were a very rich family, belonging to the landed aristocracy, and had long ago prepared for this celebration, while Su's grandfather had not. The son knew his father and had himself sent, along with the announcement, the official cap and gown and the ceremonial hand tablet, together with an armchair and a beautiful teapot. The news arrived when the grandfather was very drunk and was holding a large chunk of beef in his hand. He saw the red button on the official cap peeping out from the luggage bag and knew what it meant. Still under the influence of liquor, he took the official message, read it aloud to his friends, and gaily dumped the chunk of beef into the bag along with the announcement and the cap and gown. Having called a village boy to carry the luggage, he rode on a donkey into town. It was the happiest moment of his life. The people in the streets had heard the news and laughed at the sight of the drunken old man on donkey-back with the curious luggage following behind. The Cheng family thought it a disgrace; but Su Tungpo says only the intelligent scholars appreciated its beautiful simplicity. This grand old man was also a free-thinker. One day, in a drunken fit, he went into the temple of a particular god and smashed the idol into pieces. He had developed a special hostility towards this god, who was very much feared by the populace of this district, or more probably a special hostility toward its soothsayer, who extorted money from the believers.

Su Tungpo did not inherit from his grandfather his capacity for wine, but he did inherit his love for it, as we shall have occasion to see later. The intellectual brilliance of this illiterate old man, which lay dormant in his blood, was to blossom forth in all its power and glory in his son's sons. That extra energy of mind and body, that bigness of heart, and underneath it all the strong integrity of purpose were there in the grandfather. The Su family rose from the land, as all other distinguished families rose, by the law of infinite variations and natural selection. We have no indications of the mental qualites of Su Tungpo's mother's family, but a fortuitous combination of the blood of the Sus and the Chengs somehow produced the literary genius.

Apart from this, there was no great influence of the grandfather over the poet's literary life except the fact that his personal name was "Shü". It was most embarrassing for a writer, for this word meant "preface", and Su Tungpo, being a renowned scholar, had to write many prefaces. As it would have been sacrilegious for him to use the word preface, he called his prefaces forewords (*yin*) throughout his works. This taboo against mentioning one's parent's or grandparent's name was a very ancient custom which sometimes produced embarrassing results. It is particularly irritating when personal names of fathers happen to be

very common words. In the voluminous tomes of Szema Chien, t'
greatest historian of China, we cannot find the word *t'an,* meani
"talk" or "conversation", because that was the historian's father's p
sonal name. There was a man by the name of Chao T'an—he h
arbitrarily to change his name to Chao T'ung. In the same way t
author of the *Later Han History* had to avoid the personal name
his father, T'ai, and today we cannot find that word in all its hundr
and twenty volumes of verbiage. The personal name of the father
the poet Li Ao happened to be the common word meaning "now'
thus the poet had always to use an archaic word for the contemporary
moment. The same thing resulted from the taboo with respect to the
personal names of the emperors of a ruling dynasty. A candidate f
the state examinations was expelled if his name contained a wor
identical with any of the personal names of the preceding emperors c
the dynasty. As it happened, the emperors of a dynasty were usua'"
known by their reigns or their posthumous titles, so that many schol
did forget about the emperors' personal names and were expelle
Sometimes an emperor would fail in this way himself, as no one alwa
remembers his ancestors' names back for ten generations. In a momer
of forgetfulness an emperor once named a new pavilion and the
suddenly realised that he had used a tabooed word—the name c
his ancestor. No sooner was the name conferred than it had to b
changed.

Su Tungpo's father, Su Shün, was a reticent man, and as far as h
political ambitions were concerned, he died disappointed, although h
hopes for literary and official honours were realised in the persons c
his two sons before he died. Possessing a high intelligence, severe i
temperament, independent in mind, and crotchety in character, Su
Shün was not a man easy to get along with. He is known to this day
as the one great scholar who did not seriously begin to study until he
was twenty-seven. This is usually pointed out to young children as an
example to prove that with determination and industry, success always
awaits a man; though a bright child might deduce the opposite conclusion that one did not *have to* begin to study in childhood. And the
fact is, Su Shün had full opportunity to learn to read and write in childhood; it seems that there was enough ruggedness in this individual to
resist coercion and resent the formal education of those times. We
know that many brilliant children do. It cannot be true that he did
not learn to read and write at all in childhood, but rather that he completely wasted his childhood years. Yet, he made enough impression
as a young man for the Cheng family to be willing to make him their
son-in-law. Equally amazing is the fact that, starting at the late age of
twenty-seven, he did achieve such a high literary fame, a fame which
was by no means totally eclipsed by his brilliant sons.

SU TUNGPO

Portrait by Li Lungmien. From a copy owned by Weng Fangkang.

"Gathering of Scholars at Western Garden" (home of Prince Wang Shien) in the year 1087, from a late copy, probably Ming, of the original painted by Li Lungmien and described by Mi Fei. An earlier and more faithful copy by Chao Mengfu exists in the Palace Museum, Peiping. Many copies were made of this famous painting of a famous gathering. Present were three Sung painters and Su Tungpo's disciples. In the copy above, Huang's position has been changed. Chang Lei was originally kneeling on the ground instead of sitting. The figures of Chao Puchih, Cheng Chiahui, and two others are missing. The three illustrations that follow are details from this painting. (See page 242.) *Courtesy Metropolitan Museum of Art.*

Li Chihyi

Su Tungpo

Prince Wang's
Concubines

Tsai Tienchi

Prince Wang Shien

Chang Lei.

Huang Tingchien   Li Kunglin (Lungmien)

Su Tseyu

Chen Pishü

Wang Chungchih   Chin Kuan

Mi Fei

BAMBOOS by Sun Tungpo

Inscription reads: "Recluse of Tungpo. Painted in March, first year of Shaosheng [1094]." *Collection of Mr. M. C. Tsai, Shanghai*

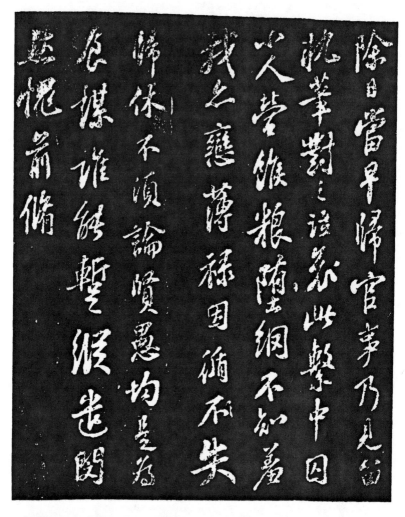

除日當早歸 官事乃見留
執筆對之泣 哀此繫中囚
小人營餱糧 墮網不知羞
我亦戀薄祿 因循不知失
不休不須論 賢愚均是為
誰能暫縱遣 卷卷前獺

Su Tungpo's calligraphy was famous and widely collected by connoisseurs, and many volumes of it are to be found in Chinese libraries. Most of them are rubbings from stone inscriptions; to preserve the living quality of the handwriting the highest special skill and the finest stone are required. One of the best examples is that shown above, which is a Sung rubbing taken from a stone inscription of the famous poem which Su Tungpo wrote on New Year's Eve, 1071, when, as a magistrate at Hangchow, he had to sentence to prison men arrested for smuggling salt. The translation appears on page 128,

From Western Tower Scripts, *owned
by Governor Tuan Fang* (1861-1911).

"Lady Su Hui and Her Verse Puzzle" by Chiu Ing, showing interior of Chinese house and ladies' costumes, as imagined by a Ming artist. Lady Su Hui was a poetess of the Su clan in the fifth century who won back her husband's love by an intricate verse puzzle. *Courtesy Metropolitan Museum of Art.*

"Lady Blossom," poetess of the tenth century in Su Tungpo's province, by Chiu Ing. Su Tungpo rearranged one of her poems and put it into a song. Lady Blossom was queen of Szechuen when it was an independent kingdom. *Courtesy Metropolitan Museum of Art.*

About the time when his son was born, he began to take himself seriously, regretting rather late, but with a sharp sense of remorse, the wasted years of his youth. He must have been bitten with shame to see that his own brother and his wife's brother, and his two sisters' husbands, had all passed state examinations and were going out as officials. Such a state of affairs might not affect a mediocre person, but to one gifted with the mental powers that he showed in his *Complete Works,* the situation must have become unbearable. In his sacrificial prayer to his wife on her death, he afterward indicated that she had prodded him along, for the wife, Su Tungpo's mother, was a very well-educated woman. The grandfather, however, had said and done nothing about the son, who to all intents and purposes appeared to be nothing better than a stubborn, erratic, loafing genius. When friends asked him why his son did not study and why he had done nothing about it, he replied placidly, "I am not worried", suggesting an enormous confidence that his brilliant but erring son would himself realise the mistake in due time.

The people of Szechuen were, even in those days, a hardy, argumentative, self-reliant, and largely self-governing race, retaining, as people of remote districts or colonies often do, certain ancient customs and habits and culture. Thanks particularly to the invention of printing in this province a century earlier, a sudden impetus had been given to learning, and in Su Tungpo's day a fairly high percentage of officials, or successful scholars, came from this province. Its general level of scholarship was higher then than that of the provinces now named Hopei and Shantung, for at the imperial examinations candidates from the latter provinces often failed in poetry. Chengtu was the centre of culture, famous for its fine letter paper, Szechuen brocade, and beautiful monasteries. There were gifted courtesans and talented beauties, and in the centuries immediately preceding Su Tungpo it had produced at least two famous women poets. In their writings the scholars still held to the early Han tradition of simple austerity of style as against the decadent, ostentatious style prevalent elsewhere at the time.

Then, as now, the people of that province were given to arguments and eloquent disquisitions. Even in middle-class society, conversations were often studded with learned instances and clever allusions, and had an air of archaic refinement to those from the outside provinces. Of this inborn eloquence and this determination not to be worsted in an argument, Su Tungpo had a fair share. Not to mention his arguing several times with the devil, his state papers were distinguished for clarity and forcefulness of presentation. Both Su and his father were attacked by their enemies as resembling the sophists of the Warring Kingdoms, and were praised by their friends as having the style of

Mencius, with Mencian eloquence and aptness of analogy. Szechuen people should make good lawyers.

It is for this reason that the people of Meichow acquired the reputation of being "difficult to govern". Su Tungpo once defended it thus: the people here, as different from the people of less cultivated regions, could not be easily bullied by a magistrate. The gentry kept law-books in their homes and "did not regard it as wrong" to be thoroughly conversant with the laws and statutes. These scholars tried to live according to the laws and wanted to hold the magistrates to them also. If a magistrate was good and just to the people, they would on his termination of office make a portrait of him and worship him in their homes and remember him for fifty years. But, like modern children at school upon the arrival of a new teacher, they had a game of their own to play. When a new magistrate arrived they would test him, and if he "knew his onions", they would let him alone. But if he was in any way officious or overbearing, he would have a hard time of it. As Su explained, they were hard to govern only when the magistrate did not know how to handle them.

In addition to a certain ancient quaintness in their local customs and habits, the people of Meichow also had developed a kind of social aristocracy. The well-known old families were classified as "A" and "B", and called *chiang ching* or "river squires". The squires would not marry their children to other families, however rich and powerful, if they did not "belong". There was also a well-developed custom of co-operation among the farmers. In the second month of each year the farmers would start work on the fields. By the beginning of April the time came for weeding. The farmers would come together by the hundreds and work collectively at this chore. They chose two leaders for command, one in charge of the hour-glass and the other in charge of a drum, and they started and stopped the day's work according to the drum signal. Those who arrived late, or those who were slack, were fined. Farmers who had proportionately more land but·fewer farm hands had to make up for it by contributing money to the general fund. At harvest-time, the villagers came together and made a grand festival of it. They broke the earthenware "hour-glass" and with the money from the fines and the assigned dues bought mutton and wine to celebrate the harvest. The ceremony was preceded by a sacrificial offering to the god of agriculture, and the people ate and drank and made merry before they dispersed to their homes.

Chapter Three

CHILDHOOD AND YOUTH

WHEN Su Tungpo was a child of between eight and ten years, his father went to the capital to take his chance at the imperial examinations. After his failure, he travelled abroad as far as the modern Kiangse Province, and the mother took over the personal instruction of the child at home. There is an incident recorded both in the official biography of the poet in the *Sung History* and in the long tomb inscription written by the poet's brother. The mother was teaching the young son a chapter in *Later Han History*. As a result of terrible misrule the government had fallen into the hands of eunuchs; and the scholars rebelled against the rule of the intermediate sex. Corruption and graft and extortion, and arbitrary arrests, were the order of the day, for the local magistrates were all underlings and protégés of the eunuchs. Courting death for themselves, the good scholars time and again impeached the ruling clique. Repeated waves of reform and protest followed repeated inquisitions. The scholars were subjected to bodily torture, persecuted, and murdered by imperial decree.

Among this group of upright scholars was a fearless young man by the name of Fan Pang, and it was his life that the mother and son were reading. The story was that after repeated persecutions and escapes, the end came. The imperial courier bearing the message that sentenced Fan Pang to death had arrived. As bearer of the unhappy news, the good courier shut himself up in the *yamen* and wept. The magistrate himself was a good man, too, and had high respect for the scholar. He offered to lay down the magistrate's seal and, instead of carrying out the arrest, flee with him, but Fan Pang refused, saying that it would involve his old mother and condemn her to the life of a fugitive from justice. Confiding the care of his mother to his younger brother, he went to say farewell to her. In this decision not to escape the mother concurred, and she said to him: "I had hoped for you a long life and a good name, but since you cannot have both, I prefer that you have a good name." So they parted, and in going, Fan Pang said to his young son: "If I should advise you to do wrong, I know that this would not be right, but if I should advise you to do right, you see I have done no wrong."

The young Su Tungpo looked up to his mother and asked her: "Mother, if I grow up to be a Fan Pang, will you permit it?" And his mother replied: "If you can be a Fan Pang, can I not be Fan Pang's mother?"

*   *   *   *   *

The young child entered school at the age of six. It was a fair-sized school with over a hundred pupils, all of whom studied under a Taoist priest. The brilliant young mind quickly distinguished itself, and among the great number of pupils Su and another child were the most praised by the teacher. This other pupil, Chen, later also passed the state examinations but became a Taoist with the ambition to become "an immortal". Quite late in his life, Chen was preparing to go up to Heaven, and he came to pay a visit to one of his friends. The friend gave him food and money. He went out and distributed the food and money to the poor and then sat down in Taoist fashion outside the gate, ready to depart from this earthly life by starvation. Some days later, to all intents and purposes, he had breathed his last. The friend, therefore, called his servants to remove the corpse. However, it was New Year's Day, and the servants complained at having to remove a corpse on such an auspicious day. Thereupon the dead man said: "Never mind, I will carry myself." He got up, walked to the country, and died in a more convenient place. Such is the factual manner in which many of the Taoist recluses were supposed to have "ascended to Heaven".

As a child Tungpo interested himself in other things besides study. After school, he would come home and peep at the birds' nests. His mother had strictly forbidden the boys and maidservants to catch birds, as a result of which, in a few years' time, the birds knew that they would not be molested in this garden and some came to build their nests on a branch low enough for the child to see. Su Tungpo remembered particularly a small bird with wonderful bright plumage that came and visited their garden for days.

Now and then, an official would pass by the town and pay them a visit, since Tungpo's uncle was already an official. There would then be a hullabaloo in the family and the maidservants would run about barefooted to pick vegetables from the garden and kill chickens to prepare a dinner. Such visits of the officials produced a deep impression upon the child.

He played with his cousins on the mother's side. He and his younger brother would visit the village fairs or dig in the vegetable garden. One day the children dug up a beautiful stone slab with a wonderful lustre and having delicate green veins in it. They struck it and it gave out a clear metallic tone; they tried using it as an ink slab, and it served the purpose very satisfactorily. Ink slabs had to be of a special porous stone, absorbing and retaining moisture well; they had a great deal to do with the art of calligraphy. A specially good one was always highly valued by a scholar, since it was an object upon his desk with which he had to do most of the day. The father gave the child this slab, which he kept until he grew up, and upon which he carved a special inscription. This was considered a good omen for his rise in *belles-lettres*.

If we believe the records, he is supposed to have penned some extra-ordinary lines at the age of ten. Two of these lines are found in his amusing tale of "The Cunning Mouse". It is a short piece describing how a little mouse, when found trapped in a bag, had pretended death, and then worsted his captors when thrown upon the ground. Also at about this time his teacher was reading a copy of a long poem describing the galaxy of illustrious scholars then living at the court. The young pupil looked over the teacher's shoulder and began to ask questions about these scholars. They were names great in China's history, for in Su Tungpo's childhood China was ruled by perhaps the best emperor of the dynasty, who was a patron of literature and the arts. There was peace in the country and peace with the barbarian hordes on the north and north-west, the Kins, the Liaos, and the Shishia kingdom, which had been a constant source of trouble. Under such a regime, good men held office and a number of literary talents had arisen to grace the court with their presence. It was then that the child first heard of the great names of Ouyang Shiu, Fan Chungyen, and others, and he was deeply inspired. Happily, these are about all the revelations we have of the poet's childhood. Though Su recorded many of his adult dreams and unfinished poems written during his dreams, there are no unwitting remarks for the modern biographer to build, with a mixture of interpretation, intuition, and fantasy, into a fabric of the poet's sub-conscious neuroses. Su Tungpo mentioned no diapers or constipation.

At the age of eleven he entered the secondary school in serious pre-paration for the official examinations. To meet the official tests, the students had to cover in their reading all the ancient classics, history, and poetry, and selected prose. Naturally they had to commit the classics to memory, and recitation in class consisted in repeating the passages by heart, with the student's back turned towards the teacher to prevent him from looking at the book lying open on the teacher's desk. The more ambitious ones would memorise whole chapters from the histories. It was not only the contents and information that were important but also the language and phraseology, which were to be-come elements in a writer's vocabulary. The use of a famous phrase or of an allusion without indicating the source aroused an aristocratic and egoistic pleasure in the learned reader. It was a kind of coterie language; the reader conceived a respect for the writer for writing it and for him-self for understanding it. It worked by suggestion and the association of ideas, and was always more effective than an explicit statement that lacked the charm of suggestion.

This memory work was hard and strenuous toil. The traditional method was for the student to go over a printed history book, which was never punctuated, and try to punctuate the passages as a means of making sure that he had completely understood them. But the most ambitious of all would do the really hard thing by copying the whole of the classics and dynastic histories once over by hand. This was actually what Su Tungpo did in his student days. Considering the severe canons of Chinese prose and poetry, and the constant allusions to names and incidents and metaphors used in the standard histories, such a method had distinct advantages. For after copying the whole book word by word, one began to know that book in a way that no amount of reading would give him. This labour served Su Tungpo well in the future, for when pleading with the emperor or drafting an edict for him, he was never at a loss to quote historic examples, used by scholars in those times as "cases" are used by lawyers today. Besides, in copying, he could practice his calligraphy.

Before the invention of printing this copy work was necessary, but in Su Tungpo's time the commercial printing of books had been in existence already for about a hundred years. The invention of printing from movable clay types had been made by a certain Pi Sheng, an ordinary business-man. The method was to have individual types for characters made of a special clay which hardened after carving; these were set on a metal tray prepared with a coating of resin. When the types had been set in line, the resin was heated and a flat sheet of metal was used to press upon the assembled type and give it a perfectly even surface. After printing was done, the resin was heated again; the types came off easily from the metal tray, to be cleaned and put in place for the next job. However, the method of printing from wood blocks, each block representing two pages, continued to be the one in popular use.

While Su Tungpo and his brother Tseyu were storing away this immense knowledge of literature and the classics, their father had failed at the examinations and had come back home. The civil service examinations went by set standards and formulas. Like a Ph.D. thesis, they required conformity to certain standards, a certain amount of drudgery, a good memory of facts, and normal intelligence. Too much intelligence or originality might be a hindrance, rather than an aid, to success at the examinations. Many brilliant writers, such as the poet Chin Kuan, could never pass them. In the case of Su Shün, his weak point may have been versification; tests in poetry required a passable virtuosity and aptness of phraseology, and Su Shün was chiefly interested in ideas. Since, however, an official career was the only road to honour and success and almost the only profession outside teaching open to a scholar, the father must have come home despondent.

It was the custom for young people to read aloud while their father lay on a couch and listened to their voices reciting the classics, said to be one of the most pleasant and musical sounds ever heard upon this earth. In this way the father was able to correct any errors in pronunciation, which was full of traps for the uninitiated. As Ouyang Shiu, and Su Tungpo himself later, lay and listened to their sons' recitation, so Su Shün lay now on the couch listening to the musical flow of his sons' voices, his eyes fixed on the ceiling, approximately in the state of mind of a hunter who had shot his last arrow and missed the deer, and it was as if he was refashioning new arrows and sending forth his sons to shoot that deer yet. Something in the boys' eyes and their voices, as their tongues rolled so smoothly over the syllables of the classics, told him that they would succeed, and his hope recovered and his wounded pride was healed. The probability is that the adolescent brothers had already outstripped their father, from exact memory of history to excellence of penmanship. One of Su Tungpo's disciples later said that Su Shün had a greater natural talent but that Su Tungpo was the more profound scholar. The father had not yet given up all ambition for an official career, but he would have been an idiot had he not already grasped the certainty that his two sons would pass the examinations though he had failed. This is not said in any disparagement of the father, for we know that he guided his two sons in the direction of purity of style and of a serious concern with history and government, through the study of the laws of prosperity and decay of a period.

It was lucky for Su Tungpo that his father had always stood for simplicity of style in contrast to the precious, ornate manner prevalent at that time; for when later the young scholar went up to the capital to take the examinations, the minister of education and chief examiner, Ouyang Shiu, had determined to start a reform of the literary vogue by failing all candidates who indulged in pedantic nonsense. This pedantic style may be described as a continual piling up of abstruse phrases and obscure allusions in order to "beautify" one's composition. It would be difficult to find one simple natural line in such compositions. The great fear was that things should be called by their right names and a line might be left unadorned. Su Tungpo described such pathetic writing as "building up each sentence by itself and using each word by itself" without reference to the total effect—like the opulent jewels worn on an old lady's arms and neck at an opera _première_.

The home atmosphere seemed just right for the growing up of an adolescent with a strong literary bent. The library was stacked with books of all kinds. The grandfather now was a different person; on the merit of his second son's having become an inspector in the finance ministry, the old man had also received an official rank, that of "counsellor" at an imperial court of justice. Such ranks were purely honorary, their chief merit being that of enabling an official to refer to his father as "the Counsellor" or "the Commodore", although he might never have seen a court or a ship in his life. It seemed at times that to die with some title on his epitaph was all that a man lived for—if one could not live as a gentleman, he at least hoped to die like one. And if he happened to die too soon, before securing such honours, there was always the convenient device of posthumous titles. Particularly in the Sung dynasty, even for the regular officials, one's title had little to do with one's actual post. Readers of the tomb inscriptions of the Su family may be misled into thinking that the poet's grandfather was a counsellor at a court of justice and also an imperial tutor, and that his father was a tutor to the prince, honours conferred upon them when Su Tseyu became a vice-premier. As a matter of fact, neither had ever held such an office in his lifetime. Su now had an uncle who was an official and two aunts who were married to husbands holding government offices. Both his paternal and maternal grandfathers held official ranks, one honorary, as we have just pointed out, and the other actual.

But the most important member of his family who grew up and studied with him and with whom his life was to be most closely connected was his younger brother, Tseyu. The love and devotion between these two brothers and their constant loyalty to each other through all vicissitudes of fortune was a theme song of the poet's entire life. They comforted each other in sorrow, helped each other in distress, and dreamed about each other and wrote poems to each other as a form of communication. Even in China the beautiful love between the two brothers was something quite unique. Tseyu was of steady, phlegmatic temperament, with practical sense, and somehow he managed to attain eventually a higher position than his elder brother. Although they shared the same political views and followed the same ups and downs through their entire political careers, Tseyu was the more hard-headed one and often helped his brother with wise counsel. Perhaps he was less headstrong; perhaps, being less brilliant and not enjoying such a singular reputation as his elder brother, he was considered less dangerous by their political opponents. At this period Su Tungpo acted not only as a fellow student but also as a teacher to his brother. He wrote in a poem: "In my youth I knew Tseyu as a child, gentle and bright. I regarded him not only as a junior fellow student, but also as a clever pupil." And the younger brother wrote in Su Tungpo's tomb inscription: "I had knowledge from you, my brother. You cared for me as an elder and guided me as a teacher."

At this point it is convenient to state the various names of the three Sus. In accordance with ancient custom, a Chinese scholar has several names. Besides the family name he has a legal personal name (*ming*) with which he signs his own signature in all letters and official registrations. He has a courtesy name (*tse*) by which he should be addressed orally and in writing by his friends. The usual way of addressing a person formally is by his courtesy name without his family name, with "Mr." added to it. In addition many scholars adopt special poetic names (*hao*) on various occasions as names for their libraries or studies —names that are often used in their seals, and by which they are popularly known once they become famous. Others are sometimes referred to by the names of their collected works. A few who rise to a position of national importance are referred to by the name of their home town. (A Chinese Wendell Willkie might have been known as "'Indiana Willkie", and F.D.R. would have been entitled to be called "Hyde Park Roosevelt". A great many eminent officials received also a posthumous honorific title.

Su senior's personal name was *Shün;* his courtesy name, *Mingyun;* and the poetic name by which he was commonly known, *Laochuan,* which came from the name of his family cemetery. The elder son was *Su Shih;* his courtesy name was *Tsechan,* and his poetic name, *Tungpo.* This last comes from his poetic title, "Recluse of Tungpo", the name he adopted for himself when he was living in banishment on the Eastern Slope (*Tungpo*) of Huangchow. This in time became the name by which he was and is popularly known all over China. Chinese records usually refer to him as "Tungpo", without "Su", or sometimes as "Mr. Tungpo". His complete works sometimes go by his posthumous title of *Wen Chung Kung* or "Literary Patriotic Duke", the title conferred on him by the emperor about seventy years after his death. Poetic critics sometimes refer to him with great respect by his home district: as Su *Meichow.* The younger brother's name was Su *Cheh,* his courtesy name *Tseyu;* in his old age, living in retirement, he styled himself "the Old Recluse on the Bank of the Ying River". He was therefore sometimes referred to in Chinese works as Su *Yingpin,* and sometimes as Su *Luancheng,* Luancheng being the title of his collected works and of the district of the remote ancestry of the Su family, situated near Chengting, south of Peking, whence the family had come to live at Meichow two hundred years earlier.

As one Chinese name per person is more than enough for the Western reader to follow, I shall always call the father *Su Shün,* the elder son *Su Tungpo,* and the younger son *Su Tseyu,* following the prevailing Chinese practice. The confusion arising from so many names adopted by one scholar takes up a great deal of the time of a student doing research in Chinese history. In Su Tungpo's time at least eight persons had the same name, *Mengteh,* which meant that the person's mother, before she conceived, had dreamed that she had a boy.

When Tungpo was sixteen, there was an episode which put a heavy strain on the relationship between the father's and the mother's family, and which reveals something of the father's character. As often happens in Chinese families, the father had married Su Tungpo's elder sister to a first cousin in the mother's family. We cannot know details at this late date, but we know that the young bride was unhappy in the Cheng family. Perhaps she was persecuted by her husband's relations. Anyway, she soon died and under circumstances that stirred up Su Shün's indigation. It seems the girl's father-in-law was a thorough scoundrel. Su Shün wrote a poem couched in bitter words and blaming himself for his daughter's death. He then did an unusual thing. He compiled a family genealogy, had it inscribed in stone, and erected a pavilion over it. To celebrate the occasion, he gathered the entire Su clan, before whom he intended to read a public denunciation of his wife's family. After the members of the clan had poured wine offerings to the dead ancestors, Su said to the clansmen that a "certain" person in the village, meaning his wife's brother, represented a powerful family; that he had brought moral chaos into the village; that he had driven out the orphan child of his own brother and monopolised the family property; that he had placed his concubine above his wife and indulged in licentious pleasures; that the father and son caroused together and the women's behaviour was scandalous; that they were snobs, "confusing the wealthy with the nice people"; that their beautiful carriages dazzled the eyes of their poor neighbours, and their money and official connections were able to influence the court; and finally, that "they are the scoundrels of the village. I dare not tell this to all the villagers, but I say it to the people of our own clan." The father undoubtedly offended his wife's family for ever, but he was prepared to sever all connections with them, and he told his sons never to have anything to do with their brother-in-law. For more than forty years after the incident neither Su Tungpo nor his brother had any contact with their brother-in-law, Cheng Chihtsai, although they maintained cordial relations with the other cousins after their father's death. The challenge to the powerful clan and the tone of the public denunciation show in the father something of the impetuosity and intolerance of evil that were characteristics of the poet in his later career.

The mother was very unhappy over the incident. She, too, felt great sorrow over the loss of her young daughter. It is difficult to surmise whether, in this family conflict, she stood for her own dead daughter or for her maiden family. The mother was, as we have said, a well-educated woman, her father being an official who had risen to a fairly high rank at the capital. For all we know, she may have rebelled against the snobbery of her family, or at least against the debauchery of her brother. She was broken-hearted and her health rapidly declined.

Charming legends very generally accepted in China credit Tungpo with having a very talented, if not beautiful, younger sister. She is

reputed to have been a poet, and to have married Chin Kuan, a very
well-known poet and a protégé of Su Tungpo. Stories are told of how
she kept away the bridegroom from her chamber on the wedding
night until he had completed a couplet she had set for him to finish.
It was an extraordinarily difficult task and the poet bridegroom was
in despair, pacing up and down the court-yard frantically, until Su
Tungpo helped him out. Other stories tell of how the two lovers
exchanged the most fanciful kinds of poems with words arranged to
be read backward and forward and in a circle. In such stories Su
Tungpo was reported to have said to his sister: "If you were a man,
you certainly would have become more famous than myself." One
would like to believe these stories. Unfortunately there is no historic
basis for them. In the hundreds of letters and records in Su Tungpo's
works and those of his brother, with many mentions of Chin Kuan, I
have not been able to find the slightest indication that they were ever
related. Nor was it once mentioned in the dozens of memoirs written
by scholars of the period that Su Tungpo had a younger sister. Moreover, Chin Kuan never saw Tungpo until he was twenty-nine and
married, and Su's younger sister, if she was born at all, would have
been around forty when Chin Kuan met Su. The legends grew up
very much later and are usually connected with stories which made
good after-dinner conversation. But the existence of such popular
legends merely shows how the personality of Su Tungpo captured the
imagination of the Chinese people.

Tungpo, however, had a younger cousin-sister, who was his first love,
and for whom he showed very tender feelings till the end of his days.
She was his first cousin on the father's side. When his grandfather
died, Tungpo's father returned from his trip abroad, and so also did
his uncle with his family, to attend the funeral ceremony. The cousins
therefore had much chance of seeing and playing with one another.
According to Tungpo she was "good and intelligent and kind". Since
they both bore the same family name, marriage was out of the question, as would not have been the case had she been a first cousin on the
mother's side—that is, had she borne a different family name. In time,
the cousin was married to one Liu Chungyuan. Later, in his travels,
Tungpo had occasion to visit her at Chinkiang at her home for three
months. During his stay he wrote two poems that are difficult to
explain except as love poems addressed to her.* No writer of the period
and no research student of Su Tungpo's life ever mentioned this special
relationship, because no one would. However, when he was living in
exile in his old age and heard of this cousin's death, he wrote to her
son that he felt as if "a knife had been thrust into his heart". After
his return from exile, when he was passing through Chinkiang, where

* See pages 143-5.

her grave lay, he made an effort, though he was very sick at the time, to go and sacrifice to her spirit and the spirit of her husband. The day after, when some friends went to call on him, he was found to be lying in bed and shaking with sobs with his face turned towards the wall.*

* See pages 307, 338-9.

Chapter Four

THE EXAMINATIONS

W HEN Su Tungpo and his brother were adolescents and almost ready to take their examinations, inevitably the marriage question came up. If they went up to the capital unmarried and if they passed the examinations, they would be spoken for by families having grown-up daughters anyway. At this time there was the custom of *chuo-hun* ("catch marriage"): rich merchants at the capital with unmarried daughters were on the look-out for the announcement of the results of the examinations, and were ready to negotiate financial settlements on successful bachelor candidates. The time of the civil service examinations was also the busy season of the matrimonial market. It was far preferable, from the parents' point of view, to have their sons married to girls from their own town, born of families they knew. As was the general custom, it was all properly arranged by the parents. Tungpo was going on his eighteenth year when he married Miss Wang Fu, aged fifteen, of a family living at Chingshen, some fifteen miles to the south, on the river. His younger brother was married the following year at the age of sixteen to a girl two years younger. These were early marriages, though not uniquely so.

In principle, early marriages, though not quite as early as those of the Su brothers, tend to save the young people a great waste of time and energy and emotional confusion in trying to select and attract a desirable match. It was most desirable for the young people to have their love and romance settled and out of the way. In China, the system of parents' support of daughters-in-law made it unnecessary for young people to postpone marriage, and it was perhaps just as well for a girl to love a man who was already her husband as to love one who was not yet married to her, though to an incurably romantic society the latter seems more exciting. Anyway, the Su brothers were happily married. It is not by any means implied that mistakes were not made by parents in arranging their children's marriages, or that a higher percentage of happy marriages ensued; all marriages, however arranged, are a gamble and an adventure upon an uncharted sea. The prescient parent or fortune-teller who knows exactly how his son's marriage is going to turn out, even if arranged by him, does not exist. In an ideal society where marriages are made in a blindfold game in a dark forest, participated in by unmarried men and women between the ages of eighteen and twenty-five, but where social ethics and community life are stable, the percentage of happy marriages may still be the same. Men, whether at the age of eighteen or fifty-eight, select their mates,

with rare exceptions, still on the basis of sexual selection designed by
nature, while women attract, but do not select, on the same basis. They
make more of an attempt to approach an intelligent choice, and this
alone prevents a modern marriage from completely resembling the
amorous mating of animals. The advantages of the system of arrangement by parents are merely that it is simpler, more efficient, less wasteful of time, and allows a much greater freedom and wider range of
choice. All marriages are contracted in heaven but made on earth and
by the men and women who have to make it *after* they come away
from the altar.

Soon after the younger son's marriage, therefore, the brothers and
father set out for the capital. They had first to go to Chengtu, the
capital of the province, where they came into contact with Chang
Fangping, a very high official who later was almost like a father to
Su Tungpo. Their father also hoped to obtain a position of some kind.
He was now about forty-seven, but he had worked hard since his return
after his failure at the examinations. In that period he had produced
an important work on the principles of government, war, and peace,
showing great depth and originality, which should bring him the attention and respect of the scholars at the capital. There were at the time
possible channels for one to receive an office on special recommendation
of some high minister of state. He submitted his works to Chang
Fangping, who thought very highly of them and was ready to appoint
him a teacher at the district college of Chengtu. But Su senior was not
content with a "mere post as a college teacher". Eventually, overcome
by his enthusiasm, Chang was persuaded to write a letter of introduction to Ouyang Shiu, the first writer of the land, although he was
not on very good terms with him. Another friend, by the name of Lei,
also wrote a letter of introduction, speaking of the eldest Su as having
the "talent of a counsellor of kings". Armed with these letters to
Ouyang Shiü and Mei Yaochen, the father and sons went up to the
capital by a land journey of over two months, passing through the high
mountain ranges of northern Szechuen and Shensi.

In May of 1056 the three Sus arrived at the capital and put up at a
Buddhist temple, awaiting the tests that were to come in the autumn.
These were the preliminary tests given by the ministry of education
selecting candidates for the spring examinations to be held under the
personal supervision of the emperor. Of the forty-five candidates from
Meichow, both brothers were among the successful thirteen. Having
nothing more to do than to wait for the palace examinations in spring,
the father and sons stayed to look over the city and get an introduction
to society. Su Shün now submitted his works to Ouyang Shiu, the
highly respected and loved leader of the scholar class. The genial-
mannered Ouyang Shiu had unusually white long ears and a short

upper lip which revealed his gums when he laughed. He was not particularly handsome to look at, but to meet this dean of letters and receive his favour was the dream of all aspiring scholars. Ouyang Shiu had won the love of the *literati* because he had always regarded it as his duty to discover and encourage young talent. He received Su Shün cordially, and through him Su senior was invited to privy councillor Han Chi's home and introduced to the high-ranking officials. But with his aloof and somewhat self-important manner, Su Shün failed to make a good impression on the government leaders.

The young brothers spent their time looking at the gay streets, eating at the famous restaurants, and standing in the cold watching with great admiration the renowned ministers passing by in their carriages. The Sung dynasty had four capitals, of which Kaifeng, in modern Honan, was the chief. Kaifeng, then called the Eastern capital ("Tungking", which in Japanese would be pronounced "Tokyo") consisted of an outer city, thirteen miles in circumference, and an inner city seven miles in circumference. The city had twelve gates, provided with double and triple traps against enemies, and on top of the city wall "horse heads" resembling gun emplacements were constructed at regular intervals. As the capital was situated on a low-lying plain without strategic protection, save that on the north it was protected by the long stretch of some two hundred miles of the Yellow River, along which the modern Lunghai Railway now runs, a well-thought-out plan of military defence had been devised.

On the west at Loyang, about a hundred and thirty miles away, was the Western Capital, which was established as a bulwark guarding the approach from the north-west through the strategic Tungkuan Pass. On the east, at Shangchiu, some eighty miles away, was established another military anchor, the Southern Capital. There was no fear of invasion from the south. On the other hand, during the first half of the tenth century, barbarian tribes from the north had invaded China. There was a war lord then who had set up a separate government and was able to defy the rest of China by pledging allegiance to a strong dictatorial foreign power lying in the direction of Mongolia. Shih Chingtang became the son of the Siberian emperor, though he declared that he loved China and was concerned for the peace and welfare of the people. He called himself the "Sonny Emperor", while he addressed the Siberian as "Daddy Emperor". While he lived and broke up China's unity, he won the plaudits of foreigners. Particular care, therefore, was taken to prevent a repetition of such a separatist regime, because, whether in ancient or in modern China, there are always enough "patriots" willing to serve as puppets of a foreign government in the name of the common people of China so long as they can keep themselves in power. The fact that the "son" of a foreign dictator was thrown out of power and died of shame and frustration did not prevent the rise of another puppet, Chang Pangchang, in the twelfth century; and the fact that Chang was thrown out when he had served his purpose did not prevent still another "patriot" in the sixteenth century, Wu Sankuei, from leading his army, armed by a foreign power, inside the Great Wall to crush the Chinese government. The Northern Capital, therefore, was established at Tamingfu in southern Hopei, guarding against the approach of a Mongol potentate from the north.

The city was the metropolis of China, kept in imperial grandeur, where the wealth and talent and beauty of the nation gathered about the court. All around the city ran a moat a hundred feet wide, planted on both banks with elms and willows, revealing the white parapeted walls and vermilion gates behind. Four rivers flowed through the city, running mainly east and west, the most important being the Pien River, which carried all the river traffic and food supplies to the capital from the south-east plains of Anhuei and Honan. Water gates on these rivers were closed at night. Inside the city, the great avenues were provided with guard posts every hundred yards. Painted and carved wooden bridges spanned the rivers running through the city, while the most important one in front of the palace was built of carved marble, elaborately designed. The palace occupied the centre of the city, beginning in the south with a long stretch of stone and brick wall below the Shüanteh Tower, with an elaborate bas-relief of dragons and phœnixes, while above showed the glittering roofs of the palaces, made with glazed tiles of variegated colours. Around the palace on four sides were the main streets, named by the four points of the compass. On the west of the palace stood the premier's office, and the office of the military privy council. In the southern outer city, outside the Red Sparrow Gate, stood the national college and imperial temples. The streets swarmed with pedestrians, officials' horse-carriages, bull-carts, and sedan chairs, which were the general mode of travel, while a few small two-wheeled carts were pulled by men—prototypes of the modern rickshaw. The women in the bull-carts travelled with their screens let down. It was the peculiarity of the imperial city that no one was allowed to go about bare-headed, and even the humblest fortune-teller tried to dress like a scholar.

The time for the palace examinations came. Ouyang Shiu was nominated by the emperor to be chief examiner, together with a number of distinguished scholars as judges. The approach to this most critical moment of a scholar's life was always filled with keen excitement, tense hope, and a nervous fear of failure. It was the moment to which all his years of grinding labour and hours of burning the midnight oil were supposed to lead. The candidates had to get up in the middle of the night and come to the palace at dawn, bringing their cold meals with them, for they would not be able to leave until the examinations were over. During the examinations, they were shut up in cubicles under the supervision of palace guards. There was a rigorous system to prevent bribery or favouritism. The candidates' papers were recopied by official clerks before they were submitted to the examiners, to avoid recognition of their identity by their handwriting. In the recopied papers the writers' names were taken out and kept on file. While the candidates were let out after the examinations, the judges themselves were shut up within the palace and forbidden to have any contact with the people outside, usually from late January till early March, until the papers were properly graded and submitted to the emperor. The candidates were examined first on questions of history or principles of government. There was a second examination on the classics, and finally, after the successful ones had been graded, there was one—under the direct supervision of the emperor—on lyrics, descriptive poetry (*fu*), and again, essays on politics. Emperor Jentsung was especially anxious to recruit good talent for his government and took a personal interest in these tests. He sent out the subjects for the papers by his own personal servants, and sometimes, to avoid leakage, changed them at the last moment.

Both the Su brothers passed with high honours. Tungpo wrote a paper which Ouyang Shiu later showed to his colleagues and admired for days. It dealt with the principle of simplicity and leniency in the administration of a country, which was Su Tungpo's basic philosophy of government. However, there was an unfortunate mistake. Ouyang Shiu was so delighted with the brilliant style and content of the paper that he thought it must have been written by Tseng Kung, his friend. In order to avoid criticism he shifted it from the first to the second place, and thus Su Tungpo came out second in the examinations. On April 8, 1057, Su passed the examinations, and on April 14, at the age of twenty, was officially decorated a *chinshih*, almost at the head of 388 successful candidates. To obtain such an honour meant that one became at once nationally known as one of the first scholars of the land.

It was typical of the brilliant young man, however, that he took some liberties with history and invented a dialogue in his paper. He was developing the theme that in giving rewards one should rather err on the side of generosity, and in punishment one should give every benefit of the doubt to an offender lest an innocent man be killed. In the time of Emperor Yao, he wrote, a man was about to be condemned to death. "Three times the minister of justice said: 'Let him be killed!' and three times Emperor Yao said: 'Let him be pardoned!'" The dialogue read very well, and it seemed to support an **authentic story** that the sage emperor was willing to use a bad man and give him a chance to prove his talent. The judges read the story, but dared not question it, because it amounted to their admitting not having read it somewhere in one of the obscure ancient texts. So Su Tungpo was passed. After the examinations one day Mei Yaochen, one of the judges, said to him:

"By the way, where does that story occur about Emperor Yao and the minister of justice? I can't quite recall where I read it."

"I invented it," the young scholar confessed.

"You did!" said the old judge.

"Well, that was what the sage emperor would have done, wasn't it?" replied Su Tungpo.

To pass an examination under a certain examiner was to place a scholar under heavy obligation to him for recognition of his talent, and establish a permanent relation between the two as "master" and "disciple" (*menshia*). The candidates went up to pay their respects to their master and the chief judges and wrote them letters of gratitude. Ouyang Shiu was the authority on literature. He could make or unmake a scholar by a word of praise or blame. A writer of the time said that the scholars did not know the fear of punishment or the joy of promotions, nor did they value the gift of life or fear the doom of death, but they did fear the opinion of Ouyang Shiu. Imagine, therefore, the effect on the young poet when Ouyang Shiu said to one of his colleagues: "On reading Su Tungpo's letter, somehow I perspired all over with joy. My old person must give place to this young man and let him rise to the top." When such a statement was made by Ouyang Shiu, the whole capital heard about it. Ouyang Shiu was also reported to have said to his own sons: "Mark my word, thirty years from now nobody will talk about me." This prediction came true, for in the first decade after Su Tungpo's death, nobody was talking about Ouyang Shiu, but everybody was talking about Su Tungpo and reading him in secret, when his works were banned.

Just as he was about to begin his official career, Tungpo's mother died. It was such an important event according to Confucian custom that even a premier had immediately to retire and go into a twenty-seven-months' period of mourning before he could return to office. Tungpo's eldest sister had died several years earlier, and thus when all the men of the family went away to the examinations, the mother was left alone with the daughters-in-law. She died without hearing the good news from the capital. Hurriedly the father and brothers set out for home, to find the mother gone and the house in very bad condition, with the fences broken down and the roof leaking, "like the home of a refugee".

After the proper ceremonies they selected a site for the family cemetery at Old Man's Spring, at the foot of a mountain slope. The spring was so named because, according to the people of the district, on clear moonlight nights an old man with white hair and a beautiful face 'could be seen sitting or reclining on the bank; but upon the approach of people he would disappear into the water. Later Su Shün was buried in the same grave, and it was from the name of this place, Old Man's Spring, that he was popularly known as "Laochuan".

In his sacrificial prayer to his wife's spirit Su Shün said: "I know your heart as a mother did not wish your children high official honours, but that they might be renowned in literature. When I was young I wasted my talent; I knew that in your heart you were concerned lest I should die unknown. With a sigh, I decided to reform, and it is thanks to you that I have this day. . . . In your grave I have opened two chambers that I may share the tomb with you when I die. . . . Alas, I am old and alone in this wide world; after your death, who will give me good advice? I am going back to our old home to make improvements and alterations in our house. If your soul has not perished, come and visit us."

The twenty-seven months of compulsory hibernation were the happy days of Su Tungpo's youth. The brothers were living with their young wives. Tungpo often visited his wife's home at Chingshen, which was in beautiful mountain country with streams and deep ponds and Buddhist temples on high mountain-tops. An air of mystery and romance and legends hung over the region. Su Tungpo often visited the temples or enjoyed picnics and drinking parties on the banks of the river near the Juitsao Bridge with his wife's uncles and cousins. On summer evenings he sat outside their cottage eating melon seeds and hard fried beans. It was a big household: there were his wife's father, Wang Chieh, and her two uncles and their families. Among the cousins in the Wang family, some thirty in number, there was one girl, known as "Miss Number Twenty-Seven", who was destined to become a part of his life.

Meanwhile Su senior was waiting for his appointment. He was eligible for office at this time because mourning for a wife was not an impediment to holding an office, as mourning a mother was. High officials at the capital had promised help, but he had been waiting for over a year and no news had arrived. Finally an imperial edict came, asking him to go up to the capital and submit himself to special examinations. This threw the old man into consternation. By that time he had developed a phobia about all examinations. He wrote a reply to the emperor declining to go, giving old age and poor health as his excuse. But in his letter to a friend he said: "I do not necessarily want to be an official, nor do I decline on principle to be one. . . . Why should I, at this dignified old age, submit myself to the disgrace of being judged by official examiners and become a laughing-stock of others? . . . I have already submitted my works to Ouyang Shiu. If he considers them good, why should there be further examinations? If he cannot believe the best that I have written, how can he rely upon the tests of a day?" In another letter, to a high official, Mei, he said: "I have never been able in my life to conform to the standards of the judges, and that is why I have not succeeded to this day. . . . I remember how when I was young and preparing to go into the examination hall, I got up at midnight, packed up my rice and cakes, and stood at dawn before the Eastern Palace Gate. Then we filed in together and sidled up to our respective seats and cowered over our desks. Every time I think about that scene, my heart shudders. . . ."

By June of the following year, 1059, he received another order from the government, a repetition of the first. There was no mention of any special exemption from examinations; but nothing else would satisfy him. The government leaders should believe in him—take it or leave it. He was not going to be quizzed like a schoolboy. So a third time he declined. He was already about fifty, he wrote to say. What could he do at this stage for the country? A scholar, after all, wants to go into the government only to do something for the country, or else he should live as a poor humble scholar. If he should decide to go into the government now, he would neither gain an opportunity of serving the country nor enjoy the distinction of being a great recluse. But, he concluded, it was summer already, and his sons' mourning period would be over by the next month; he would go with them to the capital again. He hoped to see the officials then and talk over the situation. The tone of the whole letter suggests that he really did not mind going into the government even at the age of fifty, provided these influential people arranged that his papers would not be graded by the examiners like those of school children.

In fact, Su senior was prepared to leave his Szechuen home for ever, now that his wife was dead. It was clear that he belonged at the capital. His two sons had obtained official degrees and the next step was, therefore, to see what openings there would be in the way of government positions for them, if not for himself. Hardly two months had passed after the regular mourning period when the father and his sons set out once more for the capital, this time with the young wives. Proper preparations had been made for the spirit of the deceased mother. Su Shün had had images of six bodhisattvas made and placed in two carved and gilt wooden niches, to be set up at the Hall of Buddha Julai at the Paradise Temple. These six bodhisattvas were: the Goddess of Mercy; the God of Wisdom; the Ruler of the Skies; the Ruler of the Earth; a saint specially in charge of pacifying souls who were victims of injustice in human life; and a celestial guide for all the wandering spirits. Immediately before their departure, Su Shün formally presented these images to the temple and went to say farewell to the spirit of his dead wife. The prayer ended with the words: "I have done these things in the hope that your soul, if it is still conscious, will either go up to Heaven or float around in the upper or the lower regions in complete comfort and ease, just as I myself am going to roam over the world in complete freedom."

Chapter Five

FATHER AND SONS

THE father and sons and sons' wives were now ready to set out for the capital. It was to be a different journey from the one they had taken previously. Their literary ambitions had been vindicated, their success in official careers was almost assured. As they were moving their home to the capital, they took the voyage down the Yangtse instead of going by land through the north-west. It would be a journey of eleven hundred miles, about seven hundred miles by water and four hundred by land, beginning some time in October and ending in February of the next year. There was no great hurry, and as the women were with them, they took their time, drinking and playing cards while on the boat and enjoying the beautiful scenery on the way. The brothers' wives had never been outside their home town. They knew they were travelling with *chinshih* scholars for their husbands, but they could hardly be aware that they were in a family of three prose masters of the dynasty, one of them a major poet. The brothers made verses all the way—but all scholars versified in those days, to record a scene or a sentiment, as we write letters today. Tseyu's bride came from an old family of Szechuen, the Shihs. Young Mrs. Su Tungpo was by position and age the senior. She was the practical, sensible, able sort, with whom it was easy for her sister-in-law to get along. Besides, the old father, the head of the family, was with them; nothing short of obedience and complete harmony would be considered good form. She saw that of the three men, her husband was decidedly the excitable, irrepressible, talkative one. Tseyu was taller, thin, and not as robust as his brother, while Tungpo, born with very prominent cheek-bones and a well-proportioned jaw, was handsome and had a more·muscular build. With them was her baby boy, the first grandson of the Su family, born within the year. That was all good and proper. It would have been slightly embarrassing if the baby had been born a year earlier, for it would have meant that the young poet had indulged himself during the first year of mourning for his mother. The Sung neo-Confucianists might look askance at such a regrettable lapse from austere filial piety.

Embarking at Kiachow, where the Great Stone Buddha was, the young couples set out on a voyage of hope; keen, enthusiastic, confident. "Leaving our home town far behind, we look forward to the vast horizon beyond." Szechuen was the largest province of China, the size of Germany, and closely connected with the history of the Three Kingdoms. It took them a month to come to the eastern border

40

of the province, where the Yangtse Gorges begin and where cities and towns and temples on mountain-tops reminded them of the warriors and Taoist saints of long ago. The brothers went up to visit Shientu, the "Fairies' City", where an ancient Taoist saint had lived before he went up to heaven. One of the earliest poems by the young poet, about a legendary white deer, a companion of the Taoist, already bore witness to the elevation of his spirit.

> The unremitting wheels of time turn round,
> And we to this terrestrial life are bound.
> The fairy went to his celestial home
> And left his deer upon the sainted mound.
> The homeless deer now sadly gazed afar
> At where, cloud-capped, the Elysian City lay.
> I hear at night this creature of the forest
> Come wandering and cry on river's bay,
> While myriad pines are sighing in the wind,
> So near the ancient Master's hallowed place!
> Oh, where are you, night-crying deer? Alas!
> Among the woods I cannot find a trace.

The Yangtse Gorges, majestic in their beauty and exciting in hazards for the travellers, are a stretch of two hundred and twenty miles of the river where the torrents swirl in and out through the rocky precipices, with hidden rocks beneath the water, requiring a great dexterity on the part of the boatmen. The gorges annually claim their toll of shipwrecks and travellers' lives, for this is a big, deep river, and those who sink are lost. But the gorges are also, in their majestic, awe-inspiring beauty, unsurpassed anywhere in China and by very few places in the world. They are also the reason why Szechuen has always been considered practically a kingdom by itself, naturally protected by the gigantic mountains on its eastern border and by these narrow gorges, impenetrable by an enemy.

While going up the gorges was a strenuous task for the boatmen, with perhaps sixty or seventy boat hands tugging a little junk against the swift current by long ropes slung across their shoulders, the voyage down was always more dangerous, the boat being carried forward by the force of the current and guided only by the extreme skill of the boatman at the rudder. This dangerous long stretch is known as the Three Gorges: the Chutang Gorge and the Wu Gorge in Szechuen, and the Shiling Gorge above Ichang in Hupeh. Each of these consists of a series of dangerous rapids alternating with whirlpools and torrents that pass between sharp cliffs rising several hundred feet high straight from the water.

The thrills and dangers began at Chutang, conveniently indicated by a group of rocks which sometimes stood up thirty feet above water and sometimes were partly submerged, as the water rose and fell according to the seasons. It was winter, a difficult time for navigation. Because of the narrow passage, the difference in the level between the summer flood-tide and the dry winter could be as much as a hundred feet. The boatmen usually watched the level of the water at this group or rocks in the middle of the river. These rocks, called Yenyu, took their name from the appearance of swirling waters which, breaking against them, formed spray like the misty, tremulous hair of women. When completely submerged, they formed a vortex even more dangerous for the sailors. There was a local proverb: "When Yenyu appears like a horse, down the Chutang do not pass; when Yenyu becomes an elephant, up the Chutang do not ascend." But the saying really did not help much because of the varying nature of the river-bed; it was desirable at one place for the water to be low, and at others to be high, all depending on the height of the hidden rocks under the water. At a certain point, if there was a sudden storm, the boatmen would wait for days for the water to recede to its safe level before they proceeded. Still, through these gorges people went and were willing to risk their lives for money or for fame, as the Su brothers were doing now. All a traveller could do was to confide the care of his soul to God, because there was nothing else he could do about it. People usually offered a prayer at the beginning of the gorges and another prayer of thanks at the end, in whichever direction they were travelling, and consequently the gods at the more dangerous sections of the voyage were always well provided with wine and beef.

One of Nature's wonders, the gorges provided the proper setting for strange tales and legends of fairies living on the mountain-tops. Just before coming to the entrance to the Chutang Gorge, there was the "Spring of the Holy Mother". This was a small crevice in the rock on the bank, responsive to the sound of human voices. Whenever a traveller went up to this crevice and shouted loud enough: "I am thirsty!" the spring would give forth water to the amount of exactly one cup and then stop. A man who wanted a second cup had to shout again.

The Sus asked the blessing of the gods and proceeded down the river. As it was dangerous for boats to travel too closely together, it was the custom for one boat to pass at least half a mile below before another boat started. When officials were travelling, soldiers were stationed at proper intervals with red flags in their hands to give the signal when the boat in front had safely passed a dangerous point. As Su Tungpo described it:

Entering the gorge, the river seemed blocked in front.
Then from the cliffs a cleft appeared like Buddha's niche.
The swirling waters began to leave their wide expanse,
And narrow themselves into a deep abyss.
The winds bellowed through the cliffs,
And the clouds spewed forth from the caves.
Overhanging cliffs whistled in the high winds,
And twining vines glistened in resplendent green.
Bamboo groves stood over rocks, dripping with cold verdure,
And rhododendrons dotted the mountainside.
Falling cataracts spread a shower of snowy mist,
And strange rocks sped past like horses in fright.

Now and then they sailed past lone cottages, and saw, silhouetted high
up against the sky, some country lads cutting wood. The bare huts of
the cottagers bore witness to their extreme poverty; their roofs were
made of wooden boards, without tiles. As Su was reflecting on the
toil of human life, his attention was arrested by a grey falcon circling
at ease and in freedom in the sky without a thought for the morrow,
and he wondered whether the honours and emoluments of office were
worth the fetters of a civilised life. The falcon became a symbol of
the emancipated human spirit.

Now they entered the famous Wu Gorges, a stretch of fifty miles.
Here the mountains rose in height, the cliffs closed in, and the river
narrowed. The daylight changed into the dusk of an eternal dawn.
Gazing up from the boat, the travellers could see only a tiny ribbon
of blue which was the sky. Only at high noon could they see the sun
for a moment, or at night only get a glimpse of the moon when it was
at its zenith. Strange monoliths rose straight from the banks, while
the peaks were usually hidden in clouds. As the clouds, driven by the
high winds, constantly shifted and changed, the peaks at the awe-
inspiring heights changed their shapes also, making a moving picture
beyond the power of portrayal by artists. One of these peaks, the Fairy
Girl, had the shape of a nude female form and had become the most
famous one of the twelve since a poet of the third century B.C. celebrated it in a passionate, imaginative poem. It was clear that here
up on the mountain-tops, where the heaven and the earth met in an
eternal interplay of winds and clouds, the *yang* and the *yin*, or the
male and the female, principles had achieved a union, and today the
"rains and clouds of the Wu Mountains" remain a literary euphemism
for sexual union. The air itself seemed filled with fairies and sprites
frolicking in the clouds. For a moment, Su Tungpo's young rationalism
asserted itself. The legends carried a logical contradiction. "People
are only little children. They like to talk about spirits and ghosts," he

said. "The ancient tale of Ch'u is pure fiction. The fairies do not have a sex life."

But the old boatman began to tell.him stories, how in his young days he used to climb the highest peaks, bathe in a mountain pool, and hang his clothes on a branch to dry. There were monkeys on the mountains, but as he went up to the great altitudes, the bird-calls and the monkey-cries stopped, and there was nothing but silence and the mountain wind. The tigers and wolves did not go up there and he was completely alone and unafraid. At the temple to the Fairy Maiden there was a special variety of bamboo whose soft branches bent low and touched the ground, as if in worship of the fairy spirit. As the wind moved, the branches swayed and kept the stone altar always clean, like a servant of the goddess. Su Tungpo was touched. "Perhaps one can become a fairy after all. The difficulty lies in forgetting human desires." Throughout his life Su Tungpo, like his contemporaries, was quite open-minded about the possibility of meeting fairies and becoming one himself.

When they entered the Wu Gorges, "divine birds" began to follow the boat. These ravens were doing no more than what every bird of sense would do. For several miles above or below the Fairy Girl's Temple, they spotted a boat coming and followed it all the way to pick up food from its passengers. The latter usually made a game of it. They tossed up cakes into mid-air and watched with delight how the ravens swooped down and picked them up without fail.

Naturally, these regions were uninhabited and uninhabitable. The Sus passed through the East Dashing Rapids, where the water surged and billowed and tossed the boat about like a dry leaf in a small whirlpool, and when they thought they had gone through the worst, they came upon the even more dangerous Roaring Rapids. Strange monster rocks lined the shore and extended to the middle of the stream. Then they came to a place whose name, to be intelligible, can only be translated as "the Jar of Human Herrings", meaning a place where many travellers had lost their lives, like a kettle of dead fish. This was a giant boulder occupying four-fifths of the river, narrowing it down to a small passage and forcing the boat going down to take a precipitous curve. Any traveller surviving the sudden dip around the Jar of Human Herrings would feel towards the old boatman as towards his second father.

Coming out of the Wu Gorges, they soon arrived at Tsekuei and began to see shabby huts dotting the bank at different levels. It was a very small town, with no more than three or four hundred families, situated on the sharp slope of the hill-side. The inhabitants were extremely poor, and yet considering the exciting beauty of the place, which must enter into men's souls, it was not altogether unreasonable that this half-civilised remote village should have produced two major poets, a famous queen, and another famous woman in history. As is generally the custom with mountaineers, the men and women carried their loads in a barrel or basket swung on their backs; but it was mostly the women who did the carrying. This was tiring for their muscles, but, as we know, was always good for their figures. The unmarried girls distinguished themselves by wearing a high coiffure in two joined buns, decorated with as many as six silver pins sticking out on both sides and a large ivory comb, the size of one's palm, at the back.

But the travellers had passed only two of the gorges, and the worst was yet to come. About thirty years before, there had been a landslide which threw sharp-edged rocks into the middle of the stream, and made it impossible for navigation. River traffic had been stopped at this point for about twenty years until a narrow passage had been opened. This place was, therefore, called "the New Rapids". At this point Su Tungpo and his family were held up for three days by a snow storm.

> Lying huddled in the night, I slept like a frozen turtle,
> But I was the first to know that it was snowing outside.
> In the morning I discovered a vast expanse of white,
> And the cold wind was shaking the tree-tops.
> The green hills were like a youth transformed,
> Overnight covered with white hair and whiskers.
> The atmosphere of warmth had descended to the river,
> And the gurgle of the stream had been silenced on the bank.
> Up in the air the flakes fluttered without choice of direction,
> And down they came and spread and disappeared
> Over the wide river and the empty wastes.
> But entering the boat their fluffy footsteps were light;
> Like engraved flowers they rested on one's clothing.
> Could it be that God had carved these one by one?
> Extravagantly these were broadcast and filled the valley;
> Alas! Who held this mighty power in his hands? . . .
>
> I see the mountaineers carrying their load of fuel;
> They would not know of the pleasure of warm wine and
>   song. . . .
> The poet's frozen brush is hard and ready to break,
> And the peasant girl is weaving at night uncurtained.
> A recluse is treading in the icy cold in his sandals,
> And the wind blowing at his hood makes him look like one
>   of God.

A poor monk is clearing the snow before his doorstep,
And the cold liquid is frozen below his nose. . . .

What does the traveller in the boat want?
He wants a hunting horse to dash through the winds.
While a cold rabbit is hiding in the grass,
A lone falcon swoops down like a fierce host.
Ah, to boil venison in water from broken ice!
Though I cannot drink, I will raise the cup high.
The people of Ch'u are known for hunting;
I will follow whoever leads the hunt.
Let the snowflakes flutter and swirl round my face;
I will take up my brush and make of them a worthy poem.

The natives of this place profited from the natural hazards. They made a business of salvaging wrecks and selling the boards for repair of other ships. They also profited in the way of all resort towns from trade with the tourists, who were often compelled to remain there for days. The torrents were such at this point that the boat usually had to be relieved of all its load and the passengers preferred to walk on land for their health.

From Tsekuei on, the back of the Giant Buffalo was visible on the distant horizon, towering above the tops of the nearer mountain ridges. For they were now entering a section dominated by the giant Yellow Buffalo Mountain. The rocks here were so strange that the Yellow Buffalo seemed to be led by a cowherd in blue, wearing a farmer's hat on his head, as the silhouette of the mountain was etched against the distant sky. The local saying here described the dominating appearance of the Buffalo as follows: "In the morning you start from the Buffalo and at night you stop at the Buffalo. For three mornings and three nights you do not get away from the Buffalo." The women here were of fair complexion and tied scarves with black polka dots on their heads. The landscape vied in its beauty with that of the Wu Gorges, even surpassing it in the opinion of some travellers. It was the kind of landscape that we usually see in Chinese paintings, with monoliths of unbelievable shapes standing against the horizon like a stone screen designed by God, or a group of stone giants, some with bended heads and some on their knees, offering their prayer to heaven. On the river-banks were formations of rock strata designed to impress men with Nature's grandeur. Here a massive bluff with a flat surface would stand like a giant sword-blade sticking its point into the bank. Some distance below, before they were quite finished with the dangerous section of their voyage, they came to the Frog. The Frog was a great flat boulder with a striking resemblance to a frog's head, with water lripping down into the river like a crystal screen from its mouth. The colour of the boulder was a mossy green, and the Frog's back was covered with little globules. At the tail end there was a stone cave from which came the clear gurgling sound of a spring. Some scholars, going up to the capital for their imperial examinations, would collect water from the Frog's mouth and use it to grind ink for their examinations.

Not far past the Frog the temporary spell of Nature's fury spent itself, the drama of rocks and water came to an end, and below Ichang the landscape changed into one of peace and quiet. The setting sun shone upon a low plain of rice-fields and cottages with chimney smoke, reminding the travellers that they had come back once more to a habitable world. According to custom, the travellers congratulated one another on their narrow escape and their good fortune in remaining alive. The boatmen were rewarded for their labours with pork and wine, and everybody was happy and grateful. Looking back, the travellers felt as if they had lived through an unbelievable dream.

At Kiangling they left the boat and began the land journey by cart towards the capital. By the time they had ended their voyage, the brothers had already composed a hundred poems. These were published in a separate volume entitled *The Southern Voyage*. Yet some of the best poems Su Tungpo wrote were composed on the land journey, which concentrated on music and tone and atmosphere alone, and were rich in rhythm and variety of form. At Shiangyang he wrote "songs" or boatman's ditties, like the "Song of the Eagle", recalling the story of Liu Piao, and the "Song of Shangtu", recalling the story of Meng Ta, who lost his control of a rich district through two incompetent officers:

> On the wind-swept terrace stands a handsome knight.
> His sad song melts into the autumn forest's moan.
> Some maidens attentively listen unobserved;
> They learn the tune but cannot imitate his tone.
>   O knight! what ails you?—Two idiot lads
>   Have lost a golden city and silvery plain,
>   Well guarded by the White Horse and Phoenix Hill!
>   The kingdom's lost, though land and water remain.
> To what avail do I distress myself?
> The bream are hard to catch in this deep cold.
> The people on the bank listen and pass by,
> But the burden of my song cannot be told.

The Su family arrived at the capital in February. They bought a house and garden, about half an acre, near the Ichiu Gate, far away from the busy streets. There were tall old locust trees and willows around the house, and the rustic atmosphere suited the family of poets very well. Thus settled, the father and sons waited for official appointments, which usually were a long time in coming. The brothers passed yet two other examinations, one for ministry posts in the capital, and the other, more important, for "frank criticism" of the administration. Emperor Jentsung, anxious to secure good talent, ordered this special examination to encourage the spirit of public criticism, and all scholars could apply upon the recommendation of some minister and upon the merits of special works submitted. On the recommendation of Ouyang Shiu, both the brothers applied and passed, Su Tungpo receiving a grade given to only one other person in the Sung dynasty. He also submitted a collection of twenty-five historical essays, some of which have remained favourite prose selections for schools. Later, the wife of the Emperor told people that Jentsung had said: "Today I have secured two future premiers for my descendants."

Happily, the father was appointed an examiner of scripts in the department of archives, *without examinations,* according to his wish, and later was given a post in a bureau to compile a history of the lives of the emperors of the dynasty. It was a writer's job and he accepted it gladly. But then the question came up how truthful these lives of the emperors should be, the emperors being the ancestors of the reigning ruler. Su Shün took the view that this was strictly a historian's job and a historian should not gloss over the faults even of one's ancestors. There was a dispute. In a paper preserved in his *Collected Works* today, Su Shün said: "I hear that some colleagues have petitioned to Your Majesty, saying that the ancestors may have had personal blemishes, but that if they were no concern of the state, these should be struck off the records. . . . We are not establishing a code of ceremonies or moral conduct for the future generations to follow. It is a historian's duty to record all that they did, regardless of good and bad, to the end that posterity may learn of the truth. If it is the intention of the court to present and preserve idealised, complimentary portraits of the ancestors, I cannot regard this as part of my duty. The author of *Han History* recorded all that happened. If we now emulate his example, we shall be able to show that their personal weaknesses were easily outweighed by the great things that they accomplished, and we shall have a record that the future generations may regard as honest and reliable."

The reputation of the three Sus as scholars and writers had now steadily risen. They were friends of the most famous writers of the land, their poems and essays were greatly admired, and the family was already known as a literary phenomenon. The brothers were just

over twenty, and youth sometimes acted as a handicap for a genius.
Vivacious, irrepressible, ambitious, Su Tungpo felt like a thoroughbred impatiently pawing the ground, ready to break into whirlwind speed to conquer the world. But he had a silent partner, Tseyu,
and an old father, deep in intellectual penetration, uncompromising
in spirit, and socially aloof in character, who held the pair of thorough-
breds in check.

BOOK TWO

EARLY MANHOOD

(1062–1079)

Chapter Six

GODS, DEVILS, AND MEN

IN spite of Su Tungpo's brilliant record, he had to start from the bottom. Late in 1061, the sixth year of the reign of Chiayu he was given the rank of a councillor of justice and the office of an assistant magistrate at Fengshiang, with the power of countersigning reports and official communications with the court. In the previous Tang dynasty, the country had suffered from decentralisation, and at the end the dynasty had fallen as a result of rebellion among the provincial governors, who were often princes of royal blood. The Sung dynasty, therefore, tried to correct this evil by centralisation, concentrating its army around the capital and devising a system of checks and controls for the magistrates in the provinces. Magistrates' terms of office were usually three years, so that they were constantly shifted around. The system of having assistant magistrates with the power of counter-signing official memorandums was a part of this set-up. Tseyu also had been appointed to an assistant magistracy at Shangchow; but their father's work was at the capital, and one of the brothers had to stay, as it was unimaginable to leave the widowed father living alone. Tseyu therefore declined the appointment. After he had seen Tungpo and his family as far on their way to his post as Chengchow, a distance of forty miles, the two brothers parted for the first time in their lives, and Tseyu returned to live with his wife and father for the three years while Tungpo was away. Tungpo watched his brother riding on a thin horse in snow outside the West Gate of Chengchow, his head bobbing up and down above the sunken road, until he could see him no more. And in his first poem letter to his brother Su Tungpo wrote:

"Why is it that I feel like being drunk without wine? When your horse turned back home, my heart went home with it. I knew you were thinking of our parent, but now what am I to do with myself? I went up the slope and turned back for a last look, and saw your black hat bobbing up and down beyond the ledge. I was sorry that you were so thinly clad in this weather, riding on a skinny horse in that declining moonlight. A few passers-by came my way singing and laughing, and the servants wondered why I looked so sad. I know that there must be parting in this life, and I fear the months and years will too quickly pass over us. Remember, my brother, whenever you sit in the lamplight on a cold evening, how we promised each other that one day we shall sleep in opposite beds

53

and listen to the rain in the night. Keep this in mind, and don't let us be carried away by our official ambitions."

This idea of "sleeping in opposite beds listening to a storm at night" was found in the poem of a Tang poet to his brother, and it became a pledge between these brothers and an ideal of the happy life that they planned to live together when they were able to retire. Twice later, when the brothers met together in their official careers, they reminded one another of this promise in their poems.

Mail from the capital to Fengshiang took only ten days, and the brothers sent each other regularly one poem a month. From these poem letters we are able to read Su Tungpo's restlessness of spirit during the beginning of his official career. The brothers often *ho,* or "echoed" each other's poems; to "echo" a poem is to answer it with another one using the same rhyme words. It was a good test of poetic skill, for the rhyming had to be natural, and this was one of the accomplishments of all scholars in ancient China. People looked for surprising, or delightful, or refreshing turns of thought, expressed with the prescribed rhyme words, and the lines had to have natural sequence. As in a crossword puzzle, the difficulty increased the delight when the rhyming was done with ease and without effort. In one of these earliest "echo" poems, written to Tseyu, Tungpo revealed already a complete mastery. Having to write a poem where the first two rhyme words had to be "snow" and "west", Tungpo wrote:

> "To what can human life be likened?
> Perhaps to a wild goose's footprint on snow;
> The claws' imprint is accidentally left,
> But carefree, the bird flies east and west."

It remained one of Tungpo's best poems. The flying bird was a symbol of the human spirit. In truth, the events and doings of Su Tungpo we are reading about in this book are but the accidental footprints of a great spirit, but the real Su Tungpo is a spirit, like a phantom bird, that is even now perhaps making dream journeys among the stars.

Fengshiang is near the Wei River in the western part of Shensi province. The whole Wei valley is filled with historic sites and names connected with ancient history, for Shensi is the cradle of Chinese civilisation. Owing, however, to constant troubles with a very strong neighbouring kingdom, the Shishia, situated in what is now northern Kansuh, there was a heavy drain on the man-power and wealth of the people, and the country was very poor. In the first year after his arrival Su Tungpo built a little house and garden as the deputy-magistrate's official residence, with a pond in front, a very good garden planted with thirty-one varieties of flowers, and a pavilion at the back.

Now he was well settled and without too much official responsibility as an assistant magistrate. He was free to travel, and he made trips to the mountains east and south for days. Once his official duty called for extensive travel in the neighbouring district on an inspection tour to settle outstanding cases of crime quickly and to release as many prisoners as he could. Nothing could have suited him better, and he roamed through the mountains of Taipo, the temples of the Black Water Valley, and the birthplace of the founder of the Chou dynasty. Sometimes there was nothing to do, and he would go as far as the famous Chungnan Hills near Sian, to look at a precious manuscript or an original painting by the famous portrait painter Wu Taotse, owned by one of his friends.

Su Tungpo was young and restless. For the first time he was completely on his own, living with his young wife and baby. Now that he had tasted the first flavour of official life, it did not seem so wonderful as he had pictured and dreamed. Living away from the excitement of the capital, the position of a deputy magistrate in an outlying district countersigning documents and trying lawsuits rather bored him. Now and then he would feel very lonely, but at other times, seeing the moonbeam in his wine goblet, he would be elated.

In his years of immaturity, he had need of the advice of his wife. Mrs. Su seems to have had far better practical sense than he. She admired her husband, it is true, for she realised that she had married a famous, young, handsome poet. When a brilliant poet lives with a woman of plain common-sense, however, it usually turns out that the wife rather than the husband shows superior wisdom. Always in marriage there is the continual play of the opposite and complementary forces of man and woman. Knowing Tungpo's very forthright and sometimes impetuous nature, she felt not so much the need of admiring him as the duty of taking care of him. Su Tungpo had sound sense in big things and no sense in little things; but life usually consists of the many little things and the big things are usually few and far between, and Tungpo the husband listened to his wife. Mrs. Su reminded him that he was now living for the first time without the guidance of his father. Su believed in everybody, but his wife was a better judge of men. She would stand behind the screen and listen to the conversations between her husband and his visitors. One day, after a guest had left, she said to him: "Why did you waste your time talking with that man? He was always watching what you were going to say in order to agree with you."

She warned him against superficial friends who were a little too demonstrative, and whom he had befriended on his famous theory that

there was not a bad person in this world. To the end this seemed to be
his trouble; he could not see faults in others. His wife said to him: "Be
careful of those people. A friendship which is too quickly formed never
lasts." Tungpo admitted that her advice turned out to be true. She
had learned this wisdom, I think, from the accepted Chinese saying:
"The friendship between gentlemen is mild, like the taste of water"—
it has no exciting flavour, but one never grows tired of it. Sincere
friendship is never demonstrative. Really good friends don't write
letters to each other, for in the complete trust of each other's friendship no one needs to write. And after a few years of parting, they
meet again and find the friendship as true as ever.

Su Tungpo was the type that was unhappy and bored when he had
nothing to do. A drought, however, was threatening to come over the
land there. It had not rained for a long time, and the farmers were
desperately worried over their crops. There was nothing to do except
to pray for rain, and it was the magistrate's duty to do it. Su Tungpo
was suddenly aroused into activity. Something was wrong somewhere,
for the gods were angry, and the farmers were going to suffer if rain
did not come immediately. He had a very good case to present to the
gods. In this he could not possibly fail and he was ready to plead for
the farmers before the gods with all the eloquence in his command.
And he did.

On the south of the Wei River there is a high mountain range,
generally known as the Tsinling Mountains, and in this range the
highest and best-known peak is the majestic Taipo. On top of the
Taipo Mountain, in front of a Taoist temple, there was a little pool
where lived the God of Rain, a "dragon" who could disguise himself
in the form of any small fish. Su Tungpo went up to this temple and
prayed. He pleaded for the farmers, but, like a good lawyer, he tried
to make the Dragon God see that a drought or famine was not to the
god's own interests. After flattering the god a little, he said in the
official prayer: "There has been no rain or snow since last winter.
Thou knowest well that the people's lives depend upon their crops. If
it doesn't rain now, there will be a famine; the people will starve and
be forced to become bandits. This is not only my personal duty as a
magistrate to prevent; as a spirit, thou shouldst not stand quietly by
and do nothing about it. His Imperial Majesty has conferred upon thee
the different honours, and we have kept up the sacrifices, all for this
day when we may need thee. Wilt thou please listen and fulfil thy
obligation to His Majesty?"

Coming down from the Taipo Mountain, he went on to visit various
places, particularly one that he had missed on his previous trip. He had
offered the prayer on the seventh day of the month, and, returning to

the town, he found that there was a slight shower on the sixteenth, but not enough to satisfy the crops or the farmers. He searched for the reason and was told that prayer at the Taipo Mountain had never failed, but that since the god had been made a count by a Sung emperor, prayers to him no longer worked. Su looked up a volume of *Tang History* and discovered that in the previous dynasty the Mountain Spirit of Taipo had been created a duke. The spirit had been in fact degraded in rank and was probably displeased on this account. Immediately, he drafted for the chief magistrate a memorial to the Emperor asking that the Mountain Spirit of Taipo be restored to his previous rank as a duke. Then he and the chief magistrate took a ceremonial bath and sent a special messenger to inform the spirit of what they had done in the way of securing a higher rank for him, and also to bring back a basin of the "dragon water" from the pool.

On the nineteenth, Su Tungpo went out of the city to welcome the arrival of the basin of "dragon water". The whole country population was excited, for in the success of this venture they were all concerned. Several thousand people had come from all over the countryside and there was a great hubbub. The "dragon water" had not yet arrived. But a huge sheet of dark clouds had overcast and darkened the sky. The people waited a long time and still it did not rain. Su Tungpo went into town again and prayed at Chenshing Temple with the chief magistrate, Sung. On his way, he saw a column of cloud coming very low over the ground and spreading in his direction. Borrowing a basket from one of the farmers, he caught some of this cloud in the basket and shut it as tightly as he could. The poem prayer he addressed to this cloud when in the city says: "Now I am going to let you return to the mountain-tops. Pray do not embarrass us, the officials." After the prayer, he and Sung came out of the city again. As they reached the suburb there was a sudden gush of cold wind. The flags and pennants and tassels of spears waved violently in the air, and from up in the heights the clouds descended like a herd of wild horses. There was a rumble of distant thunder. At this point, the basin of "dragon water" arrived. Su and Sung went up to receive the basin and after setting it up on a temporary altar, said a prayer to it, which is preserved along with his other prayers in his *Works*. As if in answer to the prayer, the showers came and spread all over the countryside. Two days after, there came another heavy rain lasting three days, and the wilting stalks of wheat and corn stood up again.

Now there was great joy all over the country, but the poet was the happiest of all. To commemorate this joyful occasion, he gave the pavilion at the back of his official residence a new name, the "Pavilion of Joyful Rain", and wrote an inscription on it. This inscription is one of the favourite prose selections from Su Tungpo for use in schools because it is simple in language and typical of Su Tungpo's character, happiest when he was sharing the happiness of the common people.

A sequel to this episode was that the god on the Taipo Mountain was promoted and appointed a duke by the Emperor. Both Su and Sung went up again to the mountain on this occasion and offered their thanks and their congratulations. In July of the following year there was another drought, but this time the prayer was not answered. Disappointed, Su Tungpo went to Panchi to pray to the spirit of a famous man, Chiang Taikung, who is still a very popular god among the common people of China today. He had been a great and wise old man, living in the twelfth century B.C., who, in legend, was reputed to have fished with a hook and line three feet above the water. What the beautiful legend seems to say is that Chiang was a kind and fair person, and if a fish jumped three feet out of the water to be caught by his hook, it was the fish's own fault.

There is no record whether the prayer to Chiang Taikung was answered. But that is no reason for believers in any god, whether it be Buddha or a magic old stump, to doubt the efficacy of prayer. It can never be proved that prayer is not efficacious because, according to Buddhist teachings, something can always be wrong with the man saying the prayer, usually his lack of complete faith. All gods must answer prayers, or humanity would not be interested in them. Besides, prayer is based upon one of the deepest instincts in man. To pray, or to have the attitude of prayer, is, after all, the important thing; whether it is answered or not is secondary.

Anyway, Su Tungpo, as a magistrate in different districts, continued to pray for rain whenever the occasion required it. He knew he was doing the right thing. He believed in the essential justice of the Creator and in His reasonableness. Since he believed in the existence of spirits, he could not but believe also that a spirit would do its best to help relieve suffering and bring happiness and justice into human life. For if reasonableness is the highest human attribute, surely God must be reasonable too, and open to persuasion and a fair argument. But in some of his later memorandums on natural calamities, Su pointed out also, in the orthodox Chinese fashion, that prayers were useless unless at the same time the government gave the people relief from its own oppressive measures. Such is the Chinese religion of common-sense which made a writer in the earliest classic say: "Consult the oracles after you have made up your mind what to do." After knowing all the stupid things the Chinese have done, such sayings as this restore my confidence that the Chinese are, after all, truly great thinkers.

I am almost tempted to say that the spirit of Su Tungpo represents the Element of Fire, for all his life he was fighting floods and drought and was always preoccupied with a city's water supply and with canal systems and drinking wells wherever he went. The symbol of fire is also appropriate because it was a life distinguished by an expansive spirit, or *esprit;* in simple words, his temperament and his whole life were like a leaping flame, giving life and warmth wherever it went and also destroying certain things on its way.

This leaping flame, according to the record, twice argued with the devil. For Su went safely upon the assumption that not only the gods, but also the devil, should be open to a forceful onslaught of his logic. He hated anything that did not make sense, and even the devil should be made to see the sense or nonsense of what he was doing. Devils may be sometimes forgetful or confused, but if by Su Tungpo's eloquence they could be made to see the folly of what they were doing, they could also be stopped.

Once, walking along a mountain road on his return from Fengshiang to the capital, he was passing Paihua Mountain. One of his guards was suddenly possessed of the devil and began to take off his clothes one by one while on the road, until he was completely naked. Su Tungpo ordered that they put his garments on him by force and have him bound, but the clothing came off again. Everybody said that the Mountain Spirit must be angry and that the soldier was possessed. Su, therefore, went up to the temple and addressed the spirit as follows:

"Dear Mountain Spirit, I am paying thee a visit because I happen to be passing this way. When I passed here last time, I did not ask anything of thee and now, when I am returning, I am asking nothing for myself. I have, however, a guard who is possessed of the devil and the people say that thou art angry. I do not know whether this is true or not. He is only a small, insignificant being in thine eyes, not worthy of the manifestations of thy spirit. If this man had committed some great crime unknown to others, I would not know what to say. But if he has committed only small offences, such as negligence of duties or discourtesy, or perhaps if he has stolen food or dress, thou shouldst not bother thyself with these small things. It seems to me that thou, the spirit of a mountain, dost control a vast district, and in this vast district there are a great many rich and powerful persons who commit much greater offences and violations of the law. Is it not preposterous that thou darest not to manifest thyself against the rich and powerful, but showest thy anger against a humble soldier? I am only a small official, dependent upon the service of my little retinue, and when one of them is ill, there is nobody to do his work. Wilt thou not please forgive him? I am a stupid and straightforward person, and am therefore telling thee frankly all this."

As soon as Su Tungpo left the temple after finishing this prayer, a gust of wind blew right into his face. Soon it developed into a squall blowing up pebbles and sand into the air and blinding the travellers. Su Tungpo said to his followers: "Is the spirit getting angrier still? I am not afraid of him." He went ahead on his journey and the storm blew fiercer than ever. Only one man with his immediate luggage followed him, while the others and the horses tried to seek shelter, for they found it impossible to proceed. Someone advised him to go back to the temple and to apologise to the Mountain Spirit. "My fate is controlled by God in high heaven," Su Tungpo replied. "If the Mountain Spirit chooses to be angry, let him be angry. I shall proceed. What can the spirit do to me?" Then the storm abated and blew over, nothing else happened, and the soldier was cured.

Always believing in matching his wits against the unseen spirits, Su Tungpo once drove a sharp bargain with the devil himself. Years later, when he was a high official living at the capital, the wife of his second son, who was a granddaughter of Ouyang Shiu, one night was also possessed of the devil, after childbirth. The young daughter-in-law assumed the personality of a dead woman and said to those present: "My name is Tsing and my surname Wang. My coagulated spirit has not been able to disperse and I have remained a ghost around this place for a long time." Su Tungpo said to the possessed woman: "I am not afraid of ghosts. Besides, there are plenty of priests at the capital who can drive out an evil spirit, and they can drive you out, too. Don't be so stupid! Apparently you died because you were a stupid woman, and now that you have died, you still want to create trouble." Then he explained to the ghost some Buddhist ideas about human spirits, and told her: "Now go quietly away, and tomorrow at dusk I shall say a prayer to Buddha on your behalf." The ghost then put her palms together and said: "Thank you, Your Excellency," and the daughter-in-law recovered. The next day after sunset he wrote a prayer to a buddha and prepared an offering of incense and wine and meat and sent the ghost away.

Soon after, however, a child of his second son said that he had seen a thief running about the house, looking very dark and thin, and clad in a black dress. Su told his servants to search the house, but could find nobody. Then the wet nurse suddenly fell on the floor and screamed. Su went to see her and the wet nurse shouted:

"I am that dark, thin person in a black dress! I am not a thief, I am the house ghost. If you want me to depart from the person of the maid-servant, you must invite a sorceress."

Addressing the ghost, Su said firmly: "No, I won't do it."

"If Your Excellency won't do this, I will not insist," replied the ghost in a modified tone, "but can I have a prayer in my favour?"

"No," Su said.

The ghost began to come down in her terms and asked in a still softer tone if she might have a little wine and meat, but Su Tungpo was still adamant. Over-awed by the infidel, the ghost would now be satisfied with the burning of a little prayer money. The poet still refused. Finally the ghost asked only for a glass of water, and Su Tungpo said: "Give it to her." After drinking the water, the wet nurse fell upon the ground again and soon recovered her consciousness. But her breasts dried up thereafter.

There was an episode during his Fengshiang period of which Su Tungpo seemed a little ashamed and which he did not like to talk about in later life. So far, he had got along beautifully with his superior, Sung, who was an old friend of his family. When a new chief magistrate arrived, however, there came a change. The new magistrate, one Chen, was an old soldier and a stern disciplinarian, dark and muscular and with a sharp glint in his eyes. He came from Su Tungpo's home district and was inclined to look upon him as a young upstart. Chen had an unusual and creditable official record. Once he arrested a corrupt monk of Changsha with many powerful connections and handed him over to justice, to the amazement of the people of the district. Another time he arrested more than seventy sorcerers who preyed upon the ignorant populace, and he compelled them to return to their homes as farmers. At the same time he demolished certain temples given over to immoral practices. It was said that when his soldiers were commanded to stand still, they would do so even when arrows from the enemy were falling thick from the sky.

It was such a person that Su Tungpo now had for his superior. All the military and civil officials bowed their heads in his presence, but in the case of Su Tungpo, as we can well surmise, two uncompromising characters were brought face to face. Often in an argument hot words were exchanged. Su Tungpo was both young and brilliant, and it was difficult for a brilliant young man who had very definite ideas of his own to bow to external authority. Probably the chief annoyance to Su Tungpo as a writer was the fact that the chief magistrate again and again would correct and mutilate Su's drafts of official communications. As a means of showing his displeasure, Chen often would not receive him when he called, and sometimes kept him waiting long enough for Su to take a nap. The quarrel between the two eventually went so far that Chen sent a report to the capital on Su Tungpo's insubordination.

The opportunity soon came for Su Tungpo to have his revenge. The chief magistrate had erected an open terrace inside the official residence, where, in his leisure hours, he could go up and get a better view of the

surrounding country. For what reason we do not know, Chen asked Su
Tungpo to write a piece, to be inscribed on stone, in commemoration
of this terrace. It was too good a temptation for the young poet to
resist: he had to have his fun. A text prepared for stone inscription
was meant for posterity; it should be solemn, elegant, and even poetic..
Obviously he could not make direct attacks on Chen, but he knew
he could aim little shafts of fun at the old man and get away with
it. And so today the "Record on the Terrace for Stepping on the
Void" reads:

"Since the terrace is situated at the foot of the southern hills, it
would seem that every day one would eat and sleep and live in close
association with the hills, but His Honour the Chief Magistrate was
unaware of their existence. When His Honour Sire Chen was walk--
ing around in the garden one day, he saw hill-tops showing above
the trees like the knotted hair of passengers walking outside the wall,
and he declared: 'This is strange indeed!' His Honour ordered a
square pond to be dug in the front part of the garden, and with the
dug-up earth he built a terrace to the level of the house roof, so that
future visitors of this terrace would not be aware that they were
standing on a high place but the hills would seem to meet their eyes
on the level. 'Let this terrace be called the Terrace for Stepping on
the Void,' said His Honour. He told this to his junior colleague, Su
Shih [Su Tungpo], and asked the latter to write an inscription fo·
the terrace. Su Shih replied to His Honour and said: 'Who can tel
how and when the things of this life rise and decay? When the
place was a stretch of wild country, exposed to the dew and frost,
and foxes and snakes made their homes therein, who would suspect
that one day the Terrace for Stepping on the Void would be erected
at this place? Since the laws of rise and decay go on in a continual
cycle, who can tell but one day this terrace may once more become a
stretch of wasteland and barren fields? Once I went up to the terrace
with His Honour and looked around. On the east we saw the prayer
temple and springs of Emperor Mu of Chin, on the south we saw
the halls and terraces of Emperor Wu of Han, and looking to the
north we saw the Jenshou Palace of Sui and the Chiucheng Palace of
Tang. I thought of the days of their glory, their magnificence and
everlasting solidity, greater a hundred times than this terrace. Yet,
after a few centuries, travellers over these ruins found only broken
tiles and rubble, and mounds covered with brambles and fields of
corn. How much more must this be true of the present terrace?
And, if even the solid structure of a terrace cannot last long, how much
more deceptive are the successes and failures and the ever changing
fortunes of human affairs, It would indeed be a mistake for some

people to pride themselves on their present good fortune. For we
know that there are things in this life which last for ever, but this
terrace is not one of them.' "

If Su Tungpo had been older, his tone would have been mellower and
his shafts better concealed. As it is, the inscription, containing such a
calm contemplation of the ruin of the terrace it was supposed to celebrate and the innuendos about an old man never hearing of the hills
outside the city where he lived, is certainly unique in the literature of
inscriptions. But the old man was also big enough to take it. This time
he ordered the text to be inscribed on stone without any corrections.

As may be seen, Chen was really not a bad person at heart. After the
two parted their ways, Su came to see this and made amends. One of
the constant obligations of a writer who became famous was to write a
tomb inscription for a man upon the request of his sons or relatives.
Tomb inscriptions containing expected and rather hackneyed eulogies
of the deceased were of no literary value, besides always bordering on
dishonesty. The writing of such a tomb inscription was sometimes
called by the ancients "flattering the dead". Still, it was a social obligation that a writer often found hard to decline. On this point Su Tungpo
made a rigorous rule for himself and carried it out; he would not write
a tomb inscription even upon the request of a prince. In all his life he
wrote only seven tomb inscriptions, each for a very special reason, when
he really wanted to say something. He also wrote one for this chief
magistrate years later. It was the longest he ever wrote except that for
Szema Kuang. For in the end the two men gained a high respect for
each other.

One must mention here Chen Tsao, the chief magistrate's son, who
became Su Tungpo's friend for life. Chen Tsao loved drinking, riding,
fencing, and hunting, and was a great spendthrift. Su Tungpo met him
one day in the mountains when Chen Tsao was hunting with two
soldiers on horseback. A magpie had suddenly appeared in front of
him and his horsemen failed to shoot it down. With a curse the young
hunter dashed out from his hiding-place in the thicket and brought the
bird down with his first arrow. Something in the face of that young
man attracted Su Tungpo to him. Later, Chen's father was sentenced
to death on account of allegedly receiving a bribe when serving in
another place. The story goes that when Su Tungpo was about to be
banished, Chen Tsao was at the time living in retirement in Huangchow. Remembering the quarrel Su Tungpo had had with Chen's
father, Su's enemies banished him to this place with the idea of placing
him at Chen Tsao's mercy. Perhaps Chen Tsao might want to avenge
his father, and Su's enemies would be technically guiltless. As a matter
of fact, Su had nothing to do with the father's death, and Chen Tsao

turned out to be Su Tungpo's best friend during his long years of banishment at Huangchow.

Another "friend" Su Tungpo met, Chang Chun, was destined to blight his later career. Chang Chun, who later became a vicious political enemy, was then a young magistrate serving in a district nearby in the same province. We have no record whether Mrs. Su had advised him against Chang Chun, but the latter was brilliant, hearty, of the type Su Tungpo liked. The story has often been told how Su Tungpo predicted Chang Chun's future. On a trip to Loukuan, the two friends went deep into the mountains and on to the Black Water Valley, where they came to a chasm. A small wooden plank served as a bridge across the chasm, with a deep current churning perhaps a hundred feet below, enclosed by the straight rocks of the canyon. A very courageous man himself, Chang Chen made a bow to Su and proposed that he go over the wooden plank and leave a writing on the wall of the cliff on the opposite side, as tourists often do. Su Tungpo declined, but Chang Chun went over the bridge alone with great nonchalance. Gathering up his gown, he took hold of a suspended rope and descended the sheer cliff to the bank of the stream, where he wrote five big characters on the rock: "Su Shih and Chang Chun visited this place." Then he returned in as leisurely a fashion as if nothing had happened. Patting his friend on the back, Su Tungpo said: "One day you are going to commit murder." "Why?" asked Chang Chun, and Su Tungpo replied: "One who can take his own life in his hands can also kill others." Whether Su Tungpo's prediction was correct or not, we shall see later in the story.

Except for a brief period when he was aroused to great activity again when Emperor Jentsung died, and was put in charge of supervising the transportation of timber from the mountains of western Shensi to build the Emperor's mausoleum, Su was not particularly happy with himself. He grew very homesick. In the autumn of 1063 he wrote to Tseyu: "When I first came, I learned to countersign the signatures, and now I have learned even to preside at a law court. Every day I carry on the daily duties, without asking what they are for. Before a scholar obtains an office, he worries about obtaining it, and if after obtaining it he worries about losing it, what is to be the end of such a life? Now I feel like a tired traveller on a journey, coming upon a clear stream midway. Though I cannot shake off the dust of the road, I would like to have a dip in the stream. I was going away to the southern brooks, where I could hear the bird's song in spring, but official duties tied me down, and now already autumn begins. Every day I receive rush orders for timber, and as a magistrate I have to draft even more farm hands. Who would dare to complain about service to the Emperor? But the people's hard life is an official's shame. I see hundreds of workmen lugging one piece of lumber, and yet at every step forward they have to pause for rest. The rations are barely enough to keep their stomachs filled. That leaves no time to worry about other things. I am glad that the work is now over, and I wish my vessel were made of better clay. Soon there will be high winds in September, and I am going to roam on the western hills, to let one day of happiness make up for a life of toiling days."

In December, 1064, he was relieved of his post. His wife's elder brother had come from Szechuen to stay with them, and the family returned to the capital in January of the following year. Usually, at the end of three years' service, a local official was put through a review of his records, called *mokan*, literally meaning "the grind". On the basis of such a review an official would receive recommendations for other appointments. Now that Tungpo was back, Tseyu could be relieved and he very soon departed to serve as a magistrate at Tamingfu up in the north, then called the Northern Capital or "Peking", but actually over a hundred miles south of the present Peiping.

The new emperor, Ingtsung, had heard of Su Tungpo's fame and wanted to make an exception of him and promote him at once to the post of a *hanlin* serving as secretary to the Emperor in charge of drafting edicts. Premier Han Chi opposed this step and advised the Emperor that, for the good of Su Tungpo, the young poet should be allowed to mature his talents and not suddenly come into a position of such high eminence. The Emperor then suggested that perhaps he might be put in charge of recording the official proceedings of the palace. Again the premier objected, saying that such a post was too close to that of an imperial secretary. He recommended some post in the cultural and educational departments and suggested that Su Tungpo be submitted to the regular tests for such a post. "We give a test," said the Emperor, "only when we do not know a person's real talents. Why should we test Su Tungpo?" But the premier had his way, Su was put to the tests, and again he passed and was given a post in the department of history. In this department, officials took turns working in the imperial library, and Su Tungpo was delighted at the opportunity of looking at the rare books, manuscripts, and paintings in the imperial collection.

That year, in May, Su Tungpo's wife died at the age of twenty-six, leaving him a son six years old. His father said to him: "Your wife has followed you and lived with you without being able to enjoy success with you. You should bury her together with her mother-in-law." On the tenth anniversary of his wife's death, Su wrote an exquisite poem revealing his sentiments about her, full of a strange, ghostly beauty and a haunting music which unfortunately cannot be reproduced.

Ten years have we been parted:
The living and the dead—
    Hearing no news,
    Not thinking
    And yet forgetting nothing!
I cannot come to your grave a thousand miles away
To converse with you and whisper my longing;
And even if we did meet
    How would you greet
        My weathered face, my hair a frosty white?

                          Last night
I dreamed I had suddenly returned to our old home
And saw you sitting there before the familiar dressing-table
We looked at each other in silence,
With misty eyes beneath the candle-light.
May we year after year
    In heartbreak meet,
    On the pine-crest,
    In the moonlight!

His wife's death was followed by that of his father in April of the next year, 1066. Su Shün had completed his work on the *Lives of the Emperors* of that dynasty. As was expected, both brothers immediately resigned from their offices. They carried the father's and Mrs. Su Tungpo's coffins home a thousand miles by land and water to be buried at their home town in Meichow. Their friends showered them with funeral gifts.

With the coffins, they had to take a boat down the rivers of Anhuei and then go up the Yangtse. The brothers took a long time going home, trying perhaps to satisfy their yearning for travel on the way, and they did not arrive at Meichow till April of the following year. The construction of their father's tomb had been completed by the father himself, and all they needed to do was to lay the coffin in the chamber provided for it next to that for his wife. However, Su Tungpo liked to do big things, and on the mountain slope he planted thirty thousand pine seedlings, hoping that one day they would grow into a great pine forest.

Again a period of compulsory hibernation followed until the twenty-seven months of mourning were over, in July, 1068. Before they returned to the capital, two things had to be done. Following his father's example in setting up buddhas in honour of his mother, Su Tungpo had a temple erected in his father's honour. In this temple he placed a portrait of his father and four extremely precious paintings of buddhas by an old master, Wu Taotse, which he had acquired at Fengshiang. The temple was erected at the cost of one thousand dollars, of which the Su brothers contributed fifty, the rest being provided by the monks.

The second important thing Su Tungpo did after the mourning was over was to remarry. The bride was his wife's first cousin, daughter of Wang Chieh. Ten years earlier, in the period of his mother's mourning, Su Tungpo had returned home and had often visited his wife's home at Chingshen. Junchi, then a girl of ten or eleven, frequently saw him in her house. On their outings and picnics she was excited about this young man who had gained the highest honours in the imperial examinations. Now she was a girl of twenty, and she was Su Tungpo's choice, since his parents were dead. The match was probably instigated by her brother, who had become devoted to the poet. Being eleven years her husband's junior, and adoring him with complete surrender, she seems to have let her husband have everything pretty much his way. She was unable to make him save money to the end of his days. Less capable than the first wife, she was also of a gentler disposition, yielding and always content. She was to be the poet's companion during the most active period of his life, bringing up her cousin's son and her own sons, and sharing with him all the ups and downs of fortune that came in alternate succession in his life. Against the man's curious adventures of the mind and spirit, it was enough that a woman remained sane and normal and stood as a constant reminder of beauty, health, and good-ness. With his mind darting about in all directions, absorbed in new interests and occupied with a world of ideas, with his leaps of high gaiety and deep anguish, many times did he wonder at the serenity of woman that enabled human life to be carried on.

In December, 1068, the Su brothers with their families returned to the capital by land, after entrusting the care of their parents' cemetery to their cousin Tse-an and a good neighbour, one Yang. Neither of the brothers ever visited their home again, for soon after their arrival at the capital they were swept into the centre of a political storm. Their later official duties took them to almost every province of China except their own.

Chapter Seven

EXPERIMENT IN STATE CAPITALISM

THE Su brothers arrived at the capital in 1069, in the second year of Shining, in the reign of Shentsung, the "Divine Emperor". From that year on, China was to be plunged into a wave of new social experiments amid political storms whose concussions were felt to the very end of the Sung dynasty. This was the last of China's experiments in state capitalism, though by no means the first. In the four thousand years of China's history, four great political experiments in totalitarianism, state capitalism, socialism, and drastic social reforms were attempted, and each of these failed miserably. The most successful one was the Fascist totalitarianism of the philosopher Shang Yang, whose theories were effectively carried out by the first emperor of Chin, the builder of the Great Wall (third century B.C.). The outstanding two principles of this early fascist theory were the glorification of war and soldiery and the promotion of agriculture, but the two were really one because Shang Yang believed that peasants made the best soldiers and that all business-men and traders of the bourgeois class should be suppressed as far as possible. As is well known, the powerful military machine built up and developed according to these doctrines enabled Chin to establish a dictatorship over all China; but as soon as such a theory of government was applied to the whole of the Chinese Empire, it dramatically collapsed within a few years.

Two other drastic reforms were attempted under Emperor Wu of the Han Dynasty and under Wang Mang, in the second century B.C. and the first century A.D. respectively. The first, following the finance theory of state capitalism of Sang Hungyang, successfully enriched the Emperor's treasury for his extensive wars, but was rescinded because it ended in a near rebellion; the second, under the usurper Wang Mang, ended when the usurper was overthrown. That Wang Anshih failed now in the fourth experiment is, therefore, no surprise. But in each of these four great new experiments, the idea started from an original thinker who was willing to make a complete break with the past and who combined the strength of his convictions with great determination of character. It is an interesting fact that Wang Anshih was an admirer of the fascist philosopher Shang Yang and wrote a poem pleading for a better understanding of this man. At the same time it must be noted that never was a totalitarian theory advanced, in ancient or modern days, without the basic appeal that it was for the good of the state and of the common people. How many political crimes have been committed in history in the name of "the people", the modern reader can well appreciate.

Wang Anshih was a curious man, extraordinary in mind and character. He was an industrious student, a good scholar except in his abominable philology, and certainly a major poet. Unfortunately, he combined a Messianic sense of mission with a deplorable lack of tact and inability to get along with anyone but himself. He was at the same time unquestionably an unpractical idealist. If by idealist we mean a man who was negligent of his food and appearance, Wang Anshih was certainly one. He achieved a certain notoriety by his dirty dress and his unshaved and unkempt appearance. Su Shün characterised him in a rhetorical flourish as "dressed in a barbarian's robe and eating the food of pigs and dogs", and said that "he discussed history and poetry with a convict's unshaven head and unwashed face." Whether Wang Anshih loved that distinction or not we do not know, but it is easy to believe that a man so absorbed in his ideas was naturally negligent of his external looks. The story is told that he never changed his gown. One day some of his friends went with him to a bath-house at a temple. The friends stealthily left a clean robe while he was in the bath and wanted to test whether he would find out his dress had been changed. Wang Anshih came out of his bath and put on the new robe, totally unaware of what his friends had done. Anyway, he had put on a robe.

Another day, his friends reported to Wang Anshih's fat wife that her husband loved shredded venison.

"I don't believe it," said his wife, greatly surprised. "He never pays any attention to his food. How could he suddenly love shredded venison? What makes you think so?"

"We know because at the dinner he did not take food from the other dishes, but finished all the shredded venison."

"But where did you put that dish?"

"Right in front of him," was the reply.

The wife understood, and said to his friends: "I tell you what. You have some other kind of food put in front of him tomorrow and see what happens."

The friends, therefore, changed the position of the dishes the next day and put the shredded venison away from him and watched him eat. Wang Anshih began to take food from the dish next to him and did not know that the deer meat was upon the table.

The story is also recorded how Wang Anshih studied all night when he was serving on a magistrate's staff at Yangchow. The chief magistrate then was Han Chi, who later became premier. Wang would read all night and doze off in the chair towards dawn. On waking up he would find that he was late and then rush to the office without washing his face or combing his hair. Han Chi noted his appearance and, thinking that he had indulged himself all night with women, gave him a piece of advice.

"Young man," he said, "I should advise you to make the best use of the years of your youth and apply yourself to studies."

Wang Anshih stood there without giving any explanation, and on departing told his friends that Han Chi did not appreciate him. Later, as Wang's fame as a scholar steadily grew, Han changed his opinion of him and accepted him as a follower, which Wang rather resented. As it happened, the year Wang accepted a high office at the capital was the year in which Han Chi quitted his office as prime minister. Wang also diligently kept a diary, running to seventy volumes, and in this diary he often put in the remark that "there is nothing to Han except his fine looks".

But there is more to this strange man than his unkempt appearance. For about two decades before his rise to power, what made him most talked about was his repeated refusal to accept promotion to an office at the court. It is hard to believe that he did this for the sole purpose of earning fame, for from his twenty-first year, when he passed the examinations, to his forty-sixth, when he came into power—that is, during the most active years of his manhood, a period of twenty-five years—he steadily declined appointments and always preferred to serve as a minor magistrate in the outlying provinces. It was during the reign of Jentsung, a very good period when all distinguished talents who could do so gathered at the court. The more Wang Anshih refused an offer of a good post, the more his fame grew. Finally it got to the point where all the officials at the court were dying to have a look at this man. For besides distinguishing himself by his literary compositions, he had proved himself an able administrator as a magistrate. He had built dams, reformed schools, established loans for the farmers, and put into practice some of his new social ideas. It was a good administrative record and the people liked him. Enticements for him to come to the capital were without avail, and it was not until he was offered a job on the board of finance that he was attracted to the capital, in 1060. It is clear that this man was primarily interested in economics and finance and felt he could do most for the country along this line. Then his mother died and he had to retire; but even after the mourning period was over, when he was called to the court again, he refused the offer and remained away at Nanking.

This period of his self-imposed obscurity is difficult to understand, for the man certainly believed that he had great things to do for the country when the time came, and it would have been logical for him to have built up his official career during the period of his manhood. Perhaps the competition of great scholars at the capital was too great for him, for there were certainly older, better, and sounder scholars, such as Fan Chungyen, Szema Kuang, Ouyang Shiu, Tseng Kungliang, and others, who were inclined to look askance at any radical reforms and who commanded sufficient popular prestige to discourage any young man with newfangled ideas. Wang Anshih bided his time. But I think psychologically there was another reason. A man of Wang's temperament had to be the boss wherever he was, and when serving as a magistrate in an outlying district, he was the big frog in a little puddle. Again and again, when he was in the capital holding some office for a short time, he quarrelled with his colleagues and upset everything. He wanted to change the rules and run things in his own way. Wu Kuei and Chang Fangping both recalled such experiences of difficult co-operation with him as a colleague or even as a junior official.

In 1060, therefore, he had come to the capital as a rather strange phenomenon. He had written good prose and poems. He had original ideas and was a good talker. The high-ranking old officials such as Fu Pi and Wen Yenpo had the best opinion of him, and even Ouyang Shiu liked him. Here was a singular man beneath whose strange appearance lay talents and character the officials could not quite fathom. Among the few people who saw through Wang Anshih's character and considered him a great danger to the country were Su Shün and his old friend Chang Fangping. The latter had worked with him as a colleague in supervising certain local examinations, had dismissed him and never talked with him again. He must have told Su Shün about his experiences with Wang in his early days. The two, therefore, intensely disliked Wang, the more for what they considered his affectations in dress and habits. Ouyang Shiu had introduced Wang to Tungpo's father, and Wang himself was desirous of making the acquaintance of the Sus, but Su senior refused to see him. When Wang's mother died, of all the invited guests, Su Shün refused to attend the funeral and wrote the famous *Pien Chien Lun,* or "Essay on the Hypocrite", one of the most popular essays for school reading today.

In this essay Su Shün started by pointing out how difficult it was to know a man's character and how often even clever people were deceived. Only the quiet observer could see through a man's character and foretell his future development. He quoted an ancient scholar who was able to foretell about Wang Yen when the latter was a brilliant young man distinguished for his appearance, and another great general who was able to foretell about Lu Chi, who was more or less responsible for bringing an end to the Tang dynasty. Lu Chi was a scheming person of great ability but so fearfully ugly that, in receiving him, the host had to dismiss all his female entertainers for fear that the

women would be shocked or would offend him by ill-concealed titters
But, says Su Shün, each of these separately would not have beer
enough of a personality to ruin an empire, had it not been for the
weak-minded emperors under whom they came into power. Now
however, a man had appeared who combined the ugliness and scheming ability of a Lu Chi and the eloquence of a Wang Yen. "Here is a
man who discourses on Confucius and Laotse and lives the life of the
famous recluses, who associates himself with disgruntled persons and
establishes a group for mutual admiration which declares to the world:
'A sage has arrived!' His cunning and his dark scheming mind lead
him towards strange ways." Such a person could deceive the most dis-
cerning ruler and be a great danger to the state if he should ever come
into power. "It is natural for a man to want to wash his face when it
is dirty and to send his filthy garments to the laundry. Not so with
this man! He wears a barbarian's robe and eats the food of pigs and
dogs and discusses poetry and history with a convict's unshaved head
and unwashed face. Now is this natural? A man who does not act
according to common human nature must be a great hypocrite and a
scheming intriguer." Su Shün hoped that his prophecy was wrong,
that he could be like a good general who defeats an enemy before the
battle. But, he said: "If my prophecy goes wrong, people will think
that these words are exaggerated and the man himself will complain
of his fate. Nobody then will be aware of the calamity he could have
brought upon the nation. But if these words come true, the country
will be plunged into a dire calamity, and I shall be honoured as a wise
prophet—a sad consolation indeed!"

Whether Wang's strange habits were an affectation or not it is impossible to decide; but when a person overdoes a thing, people are
inclined to suspect there is an element of conscious self-advertisement
in it. If we may believe Shao Powen, Emperor Jentsung had the same
suspicion. One day, at an imperial dinner given for the ministers, the
guests were to catch their own fish for dinner from a pond. Before
the dinner, fish-bait, in the form of little pills, was laid out on gold
plates on the table. Wang was not interested in fishing and began to
eat the fish-bait from the table and finished the plate. The next day,
the Emperor said to the prime minister: "Wang Anshih is a fake. A
person may well eat one pill by mistake, but no one will in a state of
absent-mindedness finish them all." According to the story, that was
the reason why Jentsung never liked Wang. In Wang's private diaries,
he was also particularly hard against Jentsung.

In view of later developments, Su Shün was right. Somehow in all
countries, cranks and crackpots and schizophrenics have always believed that slovenliness is the mark of genius and that the best assur-
ance of immortality is the refusal to dress like a gentleman. There is

also a curious notion that filth and squalor imply contempt for material surroundings and therefore high spirituality, the logical conclusion of which is that heaven must reek with stinking angels.

When this essay was written, Su Tungpo said that both he and his brother thought the condemnation too extreme. Only Chang Fangping heartily approved. However, very soon Su Tungpo's contemporaries were to find out how true the prediction was; and the essay survives to this day, revealing the uncanny insight of the old father.*

Very soon after he assumed office on the board of finance, Wang Anshih tried to test the political ground under him. Emperor Jentsung was ruling at this time, and Wang submitted to him a long memorial on governmental policies, running to about ten thousand words. In this document he enunciated the basic principles of his financial reform, the principles of "using the nation's power to produce the nation's wealth, and using the nation's wealth to provide for the nation's expenditure". He said that since the beginning of the dynasty, the government had suffered from insufficient revenue, and this resulted from the lack of a good financial and economic policy. Such a policy had not been thought of only because there were no men great enough to deal with the problems. The men in power at the time, he said, were not "great" enough for this job, nor did he think that there were other talents in the country who could be called into power. He cleverly pointed out that in making radical reforms, one should connect them with the practices of the ancient kings so that people would not regard them as a radical departure from the past. But then, he said, in following the tradition of the past, one should not copy the methods of the ancient kings, but rather their intentions, which were, after all, only for the good of the people, no matter how the policies differed. On the whole, it was a very well-written and well-organised treatise on political reforms, covering every aspect of government, including finance, civil service, and even education.

If Wang Anshih wanted to test his political ground, he found that the ground yielded under his feet. After reading the long memorandum, Emperor Jentsung laid it aside and let it sleep. During the short four-year reign of the following emperor, Ingtsung, Wang was once recalled, but again he declined office. Historians usually give the reason that he felt uneasy because he had advised against the nomination of Ingtsung as successor to Jentsung, who had died without an heir.

Meanwhile, Ingtsung's son, who was to succeed him, was living at

* Incorporated in a tomb inscription of Su Shün, written by Chang Fangping. Some scholars who wish to defend Wang Anshih try very hard to prove that this piece was a forgery, by pointing out that it was not included in Su Shün's works. Su Tungpo's own testimony, however, confirmed its genuineness.

the capital as crown prince; he later became the emperor Shentsung, under whose regime Wang Anshih came to power. While he was the crown prince, Han Wei, a great admirer of Wang Anshih, was his secretary. Han would express certain views on government, and whenever the Crown Prince liked them, he would say: "This is not my own opinion, but that of Wang Anshih." The Crown Prince, therefore, developed a very high opinion of Wang, and hoped one day he would be able to utilise his great political talents. In 1067, as soon as he ascended the throne at the age of twenty, he had Wang appointed chief magistrate at Nanking, and in September again promoted him, to the rank of a *hanlin* scholar. Wang was in constant communication with his friend and was convinced that now his opportunity had come. Contrary to his previous practice, he accepted the post at once. But he delayed coming to the capital for seven months.

"This Anshih has always declined an appointment and refused to come to the capital in the previous reigns," said Emperor Shentsung. "Some people thought he was impudent, and now again he does not come, giving illness as his excuse. Is he really ill, or is he fishing for a better post?"

At this time there was great jealousy between two veteran officials, Tseng Kungliang and Han Chi. The latter had served successively as premier and privy councillor under three emperors and was becoming too powerful. In his endeavour to shake Han Chi's position, Tseng Kungliang hoped to find in the person of Wang Anshih a powerful ally for himself. He assured the Emperor that Wang had the true calibre of a prime minister and that His Majesty should believe in him. On the other hand, another high official, Wu Kuei, who had known Wang Anshih intimately, warned the Emperor that if Wang should ever be given power he would plunge the whole country into chaos.

Finally, in April, 1068, Wang Anshih, having been assured of the Emperor's attitude, appeared at the capital and was ordered to go into imperial audience with special permission to "speak out of rank"; i.e., without observance of protocol.

"What is the most important thing to do in a government?" asked the Emperor.

"To choose the right policy," answered Wang.

"What do you think of Emperor Taitsung of Tang?" asked the Emperor again, referring to the most beloved emperor of that dynasty.

"Your Majesty should take the Emperors Yao and Shun, and not merely Tang Taitsung, as your standard. The principles of Yao and Shun are really very easy to put into practice. Because the scholars of the latter days do not really understand them, they think that the

standards of such a government are unattainable." (Yao and Shun
were the emperors idealised by Confucius, ruling China in the semi-
legendary era of the twenty-third and twenty-second centuries B.C.)

The Emperor said with some satisfaction, but modestly: "You are
expecting too much of me. I am afraid I cannot live up to your high
expectations."

But then there came a time for Wang Anshih to have a private
audience with the Emperor alone, when the other officials had been
dismissed. Here was a great chance for Wang Anshih.

"Sit down," said the Emperor. "I want to have a long talk with
you." His Majesty then began to ask him why two famous emperors,
one of them Tang Taitsung, had to secure two famous scholars as their
premiers to run the government. One of the two premiers mentioned
was none other than Chuko Liang, probably the most renowned and
capable administrator in history. Again Wang Anshih brought the
discussion around to the topic of the legendary emperors of three
thousand years ago. Wang said that he preferred to talk of the able
assistants of the emperors Yao and Shun. "Chuko Liang is not worth
talking about in the opinion of the best minds." Chuko Liang's
political genius consisted in proceeding step by step towards a definite
goal, which hardly suited, the impatient, self-confident wizard of
finance.

"Your Majesty," continued Wang, "is now reigning over a vast
empire with a huge population. After a century of peace, with so many
scholars all over the land, is it not strange that no worthy men have
arisen to assist Your Majesty in the government? The reason must be
that Your Majesty has no decided policy and has not shown confidence
in men. Though there may be great talents living at present, like those
who assisted Emperors Yao and Shun, they will soon lay down their
office because of obstruction by petty politicians."

"There are petty politicians in every regime," said the Emperor.
"Even in the reigns of Yao and Shun there were the famous Four Evil
Monsters."

"Exactly," Wang agreed. "It was because the emperors Yao and
Shun knew the four wicked ministers for what they were and had
them killed that they were then able to accomplish what they did.
If the four evil ministers had remained at court to carry on their
machinations and intrigues, the good and able ministers would have
left, too."

Shentsung, the "Divine Emperor" was duly impressed. He was only
twenty, and like all young men was very ambitious and wanted to
make his country strong and prosperous. He was a good and just
man and he had a round and well-proportioned face like those of his
imperial ancestors. It was not until after Shentsung that the emperors

of the Sung dynasty began to show distinctly degenerate traits in their physiognomy. His young enthusiasm was fired by the high expectations that Wang Anshih had entertained of him, and from that conversation on, the young emperor was ready to go through fire and water to carry through this man's political doctrines, even if it cost him all the other ministers—which was what happened. Somehow' images of the "Four Evil Monsters" appeared in the young emperor's mind whenever the wise old ministers offered counsel and advised caution against Wang Anshih's proposed reforms.

In February, 1069, when the Su brothers arrived at the capital, Wang Anshih was appointed a vice-premier. The next two years were to see an exodus of all the old ministers from the court, the purging of the imperial censorate and the packing of it with Wang Anshih's own underlings. No sooner had Wang assumed office than he began to sweep the whole governmental household with a wide new broom., Protest followed protest and the whole officialdom was thrown into a deep turmoil. There was great and outspoken opposition from all ministers of proved ability and respected character. The young emperor could not understand it. Wang Anshih managed, however, to make him see the turmoil and the uproar in the light of a desperate struggle between the Emperor himself and the wicked ministers who dared to oppose his will.

"Why all this hubbub?" asked the Emperor. "Why is it that all the great ministers, censors, and scholars of the court are lined up against the new reforms?"

"You should understand," said Wang Anshih, "that Your Majesty is trying to follow the great teachings of the ancient emperors, but in order to do this you have to overcome the reactionaries. It is inevitable, therefore, that there will be a struggle for power between Your Majesty and the reactionaries. If they win in the struggle, the government will be in their hands, and if Your Majesty wins, then the power of the government will rest in the hands of Your Majesty. These selfish men are trying to obstruct the will of Your Majesty in carrying out the great teachings of the ancient emperors. That is why there is all this hubbub."

Given the earnest desire of an ambitious young ruler to make his country powerful and strong, and a premier who had an overweening confidence in his own political and financial theories, the stage was set for launching the radical reforms of Wang Anshih. The motives of such reforms cannot be questioned. It is perfectly true that the Sung dynasty, coming after fifty years of disunity and internecine strife, had never known a strong government. Besides, the Shishias, the Kitans (later called the Liaos), and the Kins had been making constant inroads into China's northern border. Brief wars with these northern tribes were followed by temporary treaties of uneasy peace. The terms of the treaties were humiliating to a Chinese emperor, for while some of these kingdoms acknowledged the emperor, it was not they but the emperor who had to give annual contributions in silver and silks to the northern tribes, running anywhere from a hundred thousand to a quarter of a million dollars a year. This acted as a tremendous drain on the imperial treasury. The domestic administration had always been lax, and the government was constantly running into financial deficits. Wang Anshih believed that he was a great financial wizard who could raise money for the imperial treasury by juggling with the systems of taxation and conscription. I believe that the desire to build China into a powerful state and to increase the prestige of the empire through wars of conquest in the north-west were prime factors in influencing the young emperor Shentsung in Wang Anshih's favour, for Wang's administration was characterised by several wars started by China with the northern tribes, some victories and one disastrous defeat. In order to carry on wars, the Emperor needed money, and in order to have money, the country's financial system had to be reorganised. Yet, without ever questioning the sincere motives of the reformer, we shall see how these reforms, financial and economic in character, produced the most grievous consequences of a different nature.

Soon after Wang Anshih had arrived at the capital, Szema Kuang had an argument with him in the Emperor's presence which seems to sum up the fundamental opposition of the two sides. The imperial treasury was actually impoverished at this time, and during an important ceremony at the worship of Heaven in spring, the Emperor wished to dispense with the customary gifts of silver and silks to the officials, thus saving some money for the imperial household. This started an argument between Szema Kuang and Wang Anshih. Wang Anshih maintained that the national treasury was impoverished only because the officials did not understand finance.

"What you mean by finance," countered Szema Kuang, "is only increase of taxation and levies from the people."

"No," said Wang Anshih. "A good financier can increase the government revenue without increasing taxation."

"What nonsense! After all, a nation possesses a definite amount of wealth, and this wealth is either in the hands of the people or in those of the government. No matter what measures you carry out or by what names you call them, they can only mean taking away part of the wealth of the people and giving it to the government."

The Emperor was inclined to agree with Szema Kuang, and for a month or two the measures were held in abeyance.

Without being an economist, one is safe to accept the general thesis that the two factors in a nation's wealth are production and distribution. To increase a nation's wealth, one must increase its productivity or have a better distribution of goods. In Wang Anshih's day, however, increase of production was out of the question, since there was no means of industrialisation. Therefore, all that a financial wizard could do would be in the line of distribution. Since Wang was primarily interested in enriching the national treasury, increase of the nation's wealth strictly meant the increase of the government's revenue. Wang saw clearly that the rich merchants and landlords were making money in a system of free enterprise, and he could not see why the government should not take away the profits from free enterprise and run business and make the money itself. The conclusion was inevitable. The terms he used were actually strikingly modern. He wanted to stop "monopoly" (*chienping*) by capital; he wanted to equalise wealth by "taking it away from the rich and giving it to the poor"; he wanted to prevent the peasants from borrowing from landlords at high interest. It would be a great and charitable measure on the part of the government to lend money to the peasants during spring planting and have them return the money when the crops were harvested. Wang Anshih was able to convince the Emperor that all these measures were "for the good of the people"; but history records that, after a period of hesitancy, the thing that decided him on launching the loans was the argument of a certain minor official that with an investment of half a million dollars the government stood to earn a quarter of a million dollars in interest per year, since there were two crops and the twenty or thirty per cent interest could be collected twice a year.

Without going too much into the details of the various reforms, which were started in 1069 and ended disastrously about eight years later when both Wang Anshih himself and the Emperor were thoroughly sick of them and of each other, we may give a brief summary of these measures.

The most important and the best known were nine in number, which I have for the sake of convenience arranged in three groups. There were three state capitalist enterprises, three new taxes, and three systems of registration for a complete regimentation and control of the people. The three state capitalist enterprises were: a government bureau for national trade, a bureau for government stores in retail trade, and the famous loans to the farmers with an official interest of twenty per cent and an actual interest of thirty per cent (i.e., plus application and registration charges). The three new taxes were the draft exemption tax, the excise tax, and the income tax. The systems of registration were the organising of all citizens into groups of ten families for military draft (the *paochia*), and the re-registration of land and of horses. In general, all these measures suggest the tendency to economic collectivism of modern days.

The state capitalist enterprises began in July, 1069, with the establishing of a bureau for national or interprovincial wholesale trade. Convinced of the great profits to accrue to the government, the Emperor allocated a sum of five million dollars in cash and thirty million bushels of rice as capital with which the government would take over the interprovincial trade in goods and raw materials. Immediately this system ran into practical difficulties. In February of the same year a bureau of economic planning was established, charged with the duty of studying the plans and programmes before promulgation. Among the staff of the planning bureau was Su Tungpo's brother, Tseyu. In his memorandum Tseyu pointed out that when the government took over the national trade, free enterprise would at once be paralysed, for local dealers would be handicapped in competition with the government. It was inevitable that the government and the business-men would be treading on each other's toes. Moreover, he denied that the imperial treasury stood to gain. While private business worked through an established system of credits and other arrangements, the government lacked these facilities. It must first set up a big staff with high salaries and beautiful office buildings. It would not be doing business according to supply and demand but instead would make transactions on the merit of commissions, distributing favours and contracts according to personal connections. Tseyu argued that, short of forcing down the price of its purchases by official pressure, through sheer bureaucratic incompetence the government would buy at a higher price than independent business-men were able to get. Therefore it stood to lose.

This so-called government wholesale trade was, therefore, stopped for a year's further study; then the government came out with a modified programme under a new name. The division between wholesale and retail was not a hard and fast one, and trade bureaus in charge of the large government-run stores were established in big cities such as Chengtu, Canton, and Hangchow Another government grant of a million dollars from the national treasury and $870,000 in the local currency of the capital was allocated for the development of these trade bureaus. The reasons advanced for their establishment were that "the country's goods had fallen into the hands of capital monopolists" and that "the prices of goods fluctuated from time to time because of capitalist manipulations; in order to rule the country peacefully, one should take away the wealth from the rich and give it to the poor". A very capable official was put at the head, and the more profits he was able to report to the government, the more capable he was considered to be. This Lu Chiawen became a kind of trade dictator of the country, having monopoly control of the small business-men. The rules of the trade bureau at the capital, for instance, were that the small traders were to become affiliated members of the bureau; that these small traders could pool their goods with the bureau's assets, or that the government would provide the capital for purchasing stocks for the stores run by them; that in case traders wished to liquidate their business and hand over the goods to the government bureau they would be permitted to do so; that they could use part of their goods as security for cash advances from the government, for which they were to pay an interest of ten per cent per half year or twenty per cent a year; that others not connected with the bureau would also be permitted to sell their stocks to it at prices fixed by the government; and that, finally, all imperial purchases, by whatever department, would be transacted through the trade bureau.

The government's absorption of small business was one of the worst features of the regime, and private business came almost to a standstill. In a few years trade and commerce actually decreased so that the government revenue was affected to an alarming degree, in spite of the theoretical high profits. The Emperor found himself, to his great disgust, degenerating in the eyes of the people into a petty pedlar selling fruits, ice and coal, calendars, and straw mats. In the end it was the scandal connected with the trade bureau at the capital and the excise tax that reached the ears of the imperial household and caused the Emperor to put a stop to the most unpopular features of the reform.

But the most widely known of the new reforms in this regime was the farmers' loans, and to this day when people speak of Wang Anshih's reforms they always think first of these loans. It was a measure that affected every village of the empire and precipitated the biggest political battle among the ministers at the court. In itself the plan was good and sound, suggesting the idea of a farmers' bank. While serving as a young magistrate, Wang Anshih had made loans to the farmers during spring planting and collected them with interest when the harvest was in. He had found that this was a real help to the farmers because in a local administration he could see to it that the farmers came to borrow money only in actual cases of need, and upon proper personal investigation. In Shensi the local authorities also tried this scheme with success, and it was from the practice started in Shensi that the farmers' loans received their Chinese name of "seedling loans".

In a good year, when the authorities were sure of good crops, they made loans to enable the farmers to purchase equipment and seedlings for their wheat-fields; and when the harvest came, they were able to collect grains for the army with an advantageous interest. In the words of the bureau of economic planning: "It is proposed that the money and grain from the price equalisation granaries be loaned to people upon application, following the example of Shensi province. They may be asked to pay an interest of twenty per cent, which they will pay together with the capital during the collection of the summer and autumn taxes. People who wish to repay the loans in cash in place of grain may be permitted to do so. In case of natural calamities, they may be permitted to delay the repayment until a good year comes. Thus not only will the people be able to tide over famine and drought, but through these loans they will be spared the necessity of borrowing from the rich exploiters at double interest before their harvest is in. Besides, the stocks of wheat and grain are now usually kept in the price equalisation granaries for a long time and sold to the people only when the prices have gone up, and this system benefits only the idle rich who live in the cities. It is proposed now that such sales and purchases be organised and unified within each province, so that price stabilisation may be better carried out and the farmers enabled to plant their farms without being exploited. All this is for the benefit of the people and without profits to the government. It is in accordance with the principles of the ancient kings in giving money to the people and assisting the farmers."

How such a beautiful and innocent plan turned out to harass and destroy the lives and homes of the farmers for whose benefit it was conceived, we shall see later. It should be explained, however, that this new measure started as a continuation of the old system of the price equalisation granaries and gradually replaced it. From the very beginning of this dynasty, such granaries had been maintained in different districts by the government to stabilise the price of grains. In years of good crops, when low prices hit the farmers hard, the government bought up the surplus wheat and rice. Conversely, in bad years, when the prices of grain went up, the agencies poured the grain into the market to force the prices down. It is true that the agencies were not always kept up to their highest efficiency, for many officials did not bother to buy up grain when it was cheap. But even in 1066 the published figures of the price equalisation granaries showed that they had bought from the people 5,014,180 bushels of grain and sold 4,711,570 bushels during that year. Now, when the money and stocks of the granaries were used as capital for the farmers' loans, the normal operations of the granaries were naturally stopped.

The heart of the matter was that the subscription of the loans inevitably became compulsory. Intolerant of opposition, Wang Anshih had to succeed. He had to show the Emperor that the loans were a great success and were welcomed by the people. He would not hear of slackness in selling them. He could not understand why the farmers should not want the loans, and when loans were not sold up to the quota, he flew into a rage. He began to promote officials who showed a good record, and to punish the slackers. As each official was looking out for his own career, his most important concern was to make a good report. The incentive for personal competition was very much like the selling of government bonds in modern days. When the officials knew that they would be cashiered and degraded for "blocking reforms" if they did not sell up to their quota, it was inevitable that loans began to be allocated by official pressure, by what Wang was pleased to call the "energetic" officials. Every family had to borrow from the government, and everybody had to pay thirty per cent interest for a period of three months. There were good officials who knew what harm these loans were causing the poor people and the certainty of their being put in jail for failure to repay capital and interest. These took the government at its word and announced to the public that these loans, according to the imperial decree, were strictly "voluntary"; and they were prepared to be degraded for "blocking reforms" when the day of reckoning came.

In the draft exemption tax also, there was a great discrepancy between official intentions and actual practice. This was probably the best reform put through by Wang Anshih, and it was this measure which Su Tungpo alone defended against his own party, when the latter was in power and was determined to wipe out each and every one of Wang Anshih's reforms.

For a long time the people of China had been subjected to conscription for military service. The proposal was that the people should pay a tax in place of the conscription. In other words, it meant replacing a military draft system by a standing army of hired and paid soldiers. However, from a careful study of the rules of this draft exemption, one cannot escape the conclusion that the government was primarily interested in the revenue from the tax, and whatever benefit it had in relieving the people from military draft was nullified entirely by the *paochia* system, which was even worse as a form of compulsory draft. After careful deliberation for over a year, the regulations were published. They provided that families which had been exempt from the military draft were also compelled to pay the draft exemption tax; for example, widows, families without children or with only one son or with children not of age, and nuns and monks were compelled to pay the tax under a different name, called "the draft-aid tax". Moreover, twenty per cent was added to the regular tax over and above district draft quotas, nominally to provide against the bad years when the people might not be able to pay. With the money collected from this tax, soldiers and other employees of the government were to be hired. Just as Su Tseyu had pointed out in the case of the farmers' loans that the people would be put in prison and whipped for default, so Szema Kuang pointed out now exactly what happened later, that people who had no cash to pay this tax in autumn and summer—when all the other taxes came—would be compelled to sell their grain, kill their cows, and cut down trees in order to obtain the cash. Moreover, in the preceding system of military draft, the people took turns serving for a period of years, whereas in the new system the people were compelled to pay for exemption every year, including years when they would not have to serve.

Together with the new excise tax and the income tax, this draft exemption tax must be viewed principally as a new means to raise revenue from the people, rather than to relieve them of the draft for service, since the people were drafted for military training under another name, the *paochia*. The excise tax was a tax on the profits of business-men, based on an examination of their books. The income tax was not an income tax in the modern sense. I call it income tax here because it was a system of compulsory registration of a citizen's income and property as a basis for allocation of the other taxes. It was like the income tax also in the sense that the people had to make returns of their income and property, under pain of defrauding the government. In the fight over this reform it was stated that after the order was issued, there was "not a chicken or a pig on a farm, or an inch of soil, or a beam or rafter in a roof" that was not reported and registered with the government. This last measure, instituted in 1074, was short-lived because Wang soon went out of power; and even before its suspension Su Tungpo refused to enforce it in the district under his control on the ground that it was illegal.

What gave the lie to Wang Anshih's desire to relieve the people from military draft, professed in the preceding draft exemption tax, was the *paochia* system. This is clear because both the new *paochia* system and the draft exemption tax were promulgated in the same month, December, 1070. The government took away the burden of military service from the people with one hand by making them pay for the "exemption", and put it back on the people with the other. The *paochia* was a system for collective guarantee under the law of families living in the same neighbourhood. Each ten families were organised into a *pao*, and each fifty families formed a great *pao*. The members of a *pao* were to be collectively responsible in cases of harbouring criminals and thieves; and in cases of such crimes as murder and rape they were bound to report the circumstances to the court. Able-bodied persons in each great *pao* were to be organised into a company for military drill and training, a family with two able-bodied males contributing one, and a family of more than two males contributing more in proportion. These were to leave their farms for drill every fifth day, the five-day period being the ancient equivalent of the week, dividing a month conveniently into six periods. Thus instead of taking the sons of the families to the army as in the regular draft system, this reform brought

the army right into the village. But Wang Anshih was a great propa-
gandist; he knew that by giving a thing a new name, he made it cease
to exist. "Conscription was abolished."

Besides this collective registration and regimentation of the people,
there was also a new and compulsory registration of the farmers' lands
as a basis for the new taxes, and a system of farming out the government's cavalry to be cared for by the farmers. Like all other collectivistic systems, Wang Anshih's administration could not leave the
people alone. In its anxiety to take good care of them, the government
had to know exactly what the people did and what they possessed. Like
all other collectivistic systems also, this regime found it impossible to
govern without secret agents, which were instituted in the year 1072,
luckily after Su Tungpo had left the capital. Nor was it able to operate
without bringing under control the imperial censorate, the equivalent
of the modern press, and packing it with the party's underlings who
were willing to follow strictly the party line. Again, Wang Anshih
considered it necessary to control the thoughts and ideas of the scholars.
Like Wang Mang of the ancient days, and like the modern Hitler, he
had the idea of one state, one belief, and one leader. Like Hitler, he
exploded in fits of temper when he encountered opposition; modern
psychiatrists might classify him as a paranoiac.

What showed the "paranoid" character of the man, and what all
historians and critics agree to have been his one inexcusable act, was
not any of his political or socialistic ventures, but his setting up himself now as the one and only interpreter of the classics. As Wang Mang
re-edited and falsified the ancient classics, so now Wang Anshih wrote
his own interpretation of three Confucian classics and made it the
official guide to thinking, to replace all the great commentators of the
past. Wang was a fairly good scholar, but not good enough to replace
the great masters of the past, such as Cheng Shüan, Ma Yung, Lu
Tehming, and others. To do this was both an abuse of his official power
and an insult to scholarship. The examination papers were usually
upon passages from the classics, and candidates' interpretations had to
conform. Setting up this new standard, therefore, meant that every
scholar of the land had to study and absorb what Wang Anshih said
on every topic, from principles of government and Buddhist-coloured
Confucianism to the etymology for "quail", "owl", and "pheasant".
After leaving the capital, Su Tungpo had once to supervise a local
examination, and wrote a poem recording his disgust with the deadening uniformity of thought and ideas expressed by the candidates in the
papers.

Like his philology, Wang's *New Commentaries on the Three Classics,*
often savouring of Buddhist ideas, showed more originality than sound
scholarship. He believed, however, that in the interpretation of the

ancient ideas and political systems, whatever he thought was so must therefore be so. These *Commentaries* were so bad that they were soon forgotten after his death, and no copy has been preserved. But while he was in power, they were the bible of the scholar candidates at the examinations; the slightest variation from the interpretation of the premier was enough to disqualify a paper. Particularly it showed offence to scholarship to have the compilation of the *Commentaries* made in only two years; the work was formally started in March, 1073, with the help of his young son and a political henchman, and published in June, 1075. This hurried piece of work was set up as the orthodox interpretation of Confucianism, and as Wang changed his mind about the interpretations, new versions were published for the benefit of the scholar candidates, who knew their lives depended on keeping abreast of the revisions.

This is not the place to discuss Wang Anshih's scholarship, a subject rather painful for Su Tungpo because he was by far the sounder scholar. But it may be mentioned that Wang Anshih's "etymology" was indescribably funny, as all amateurish etymology is. Besides the *Commentaries on the Three Classics,* the great rage among the scholars of the time was the fashion for discussing etymology started by Wang Anshih. This "etymology" was really a study of the structure and origin of the written characters, not by the comparative method, but by the lively use of one's fancy. Wang believed this to be his most original and lasting contribution to learning and continued to work on it in his old age, completing it in twenty-five volumes. Western scholars can understand how easy it is to compose twenty-five volumes on etymology once the scholar lets his imagination go without checking it by scientific methods—the methods used, for instance, by Han and Ching dynasty scholars. For "fanciful etymology" can be spun out of pure fantasy at the rate of a dozen a day. It was easy and it was a great deal of fun to try to read into the composition of a Chinese character all sorts of reasons why a particular combination of certain components should come to be the symbol for a certain meaning. Some fifty items of Wang Anshih's etymology have survived to this day, chiefly as after-dinner pleasantries. Many jokes that passed between Su Tungpo and Wang Anshih hinged on these "etymologies".

Su Tungpo loved to use the method of *reductio ad absurdum*. There is a Chinese word meaning turtledove. It is composed of two elements, "nine" and "bird". Clearly the element "nine" is phonetic, because both "nine" and "turtledove" are pronounced *chiu*. Wang Anshih, however, ran riot over the phonetics of the elements in his desire to make something interesting out of their meaning. Su Tungpo one day, in the course of a chat, asked Wang Anshih: "By the way, why is the word turtledove written with the elements nine and bird?" Wang was stumped. "I can tell you why," said Su Tungpo. "The Book of Poetry says [in a poem of satire]:

> 'O turtledove! O turtledove!
> He has seven young.'

The seven young, plus their two parents, make nine, don't you see?" The character for "waves" or "ripples" is written with the classifier radical designating water, and a phonetic component which happens to denote skin. It struck Wang's fertile imagination that the character for ripples was so constructed because "ripples were the skin of water". Su Tungpo met him one day and wittily remarked: "If so, then the word for *slippery* must be constructed that way because it means the *bones of water*." (The phonetic component in this case happens to mean bones.) Wang Anshih violated the very elementary principles of the structure of the Chinese literary symbols. The way he mutilated a "root", riving it in half and misconnecting it with another component, as he did in the character for "rich" (*fu*), would make any philologist weep.

Some Chinese scholars of later days, following Western ideas of collectivism, have tried to rescue Wang Anshih from historical infamy and revise his reputation upward by showing that his ideas were essentially "in conformity with modern socialism".* Among those who took up the defence of Wang Anshih was a great modern scholar, Liang Chichao. It would be possible to argue the pros and cons of Wang's socialistic ideas, but Wang's socialistic regime must be judged by its results. The facts are that in place of "private monopoly" the state set up its own monopoly; small business-men were thrown out of jobs, and farmers, unable to repay the compulsory loans or keep up the interest, sold their wives and children or fled, and their neighbours who were made guarantors of the loans fled with them or sold or mortgaged their properties. The country jails were full, every district government found thousands of closed mortgages and confiscated properties on its hands, and lawsuits filled the courts. It was a misrule that would have ruined any dynasty, even if there were no foreign invaders. In 1074 an imperial edict said that business was at a standstill and people were thrown out of their jobs; and another edict in 1076, which stopped the loans, said that many were jailed and flogged for failure to repay them. In a memorandum sent in June, 1090, some twenty years later, when he was trying to salvage the economic wreckage left of the countryside and begging for restoration of con-

---

* For the argument advanced in defence of Wang, see brief statement in Section K, Bibliography.

fiscated properties and forgiveness of all debts of the poor, Su Tungpo wrote:

"Since the order to return the confiscated properties, the people are overjoyed. They have said to me that since they were driven out from their homes and business, parents have been separated from their children and wives from their husbands, living the life of homeless, wandering refugees. Since the establishment of the trade bureaus and government stores, all means of livelihood of the people have been taken over by the government. The small traders, deprived of their normal trade, were forced to join up with the government trade bureaus and compelled to mortgage their goods and properties to obtain immediate cash at a high interest. When the loans matured and they were not able to repay, they were fined double interest. Gradually their debts piled higher and higher, and more and more people were put in jail together with their families."

For the first few years, however, Wang Anshih was able to keep the Emperor in the dark about the terrible conditions by adroit propaganda, insisting he had the "people's support" for his "agrarian programme" and painting a totalitarian regime as a "democracy"—a confusion of terms strangely reminiscent of modern days. Then as now, whether a people love a regime or not can be judged only when a despotic regime is no longer in power. Sincere in his desire to learn the truth, the Emperor sent out his own reporters. But knowing that the reforms were popular with the Emperor himself, the eunuchs and dishonest reporters always reported to the Emperor that the people loved the reforms, and that upon the arrival of the tax commissioners, the "people cried with joy", which was literally true, as far as a staged reception was concerned. The terrible conditions of the people after a few years of Wang Anshih's regime were at last revealed to the Emperor in the form of pictures submitted by a curious, obscure palace gatekeeper, a very daring man.

Standing at the gate, this official, Cheng Shia, saw the hordes of refugees who had fled from the north-east and were swarming the streets of the capital. Knowing that pictures spoke louder than words, Cheng Shia conceived the idea of making pictures of these poor farmers and presenting them to the Emperor. Here was a picture of the refugees, half clad and starving, travelling on the highway in a blinding storm. There was a picture of half-naked men and women eating grass roots and tree bark, and others working in chains carrying bricks and firewood to sell to pay the taxes. Upon seeing the pictures, the Emperor shed tears. It was this dramatic presentation, which we shall come to later, coupled with the appearance of a spectacular comet and a landslide on a sacred mountain, that made the Emperor suspend many of the "reforms".

Chapter Eight

THE BULL-HEADED PREMIER

A POLITICAL storm now blew and started a conflagration that burned down the house of Sung. It started with a fight between the state capitalist Wang Anshih, the "Bull-headed Premier", and the opposition, which comprised the entire officialdom, a generation of men selected and nurtured for government leadership in the atmosphere of intellectual freedom under the wise emperor Jentsung. It is necessary to understand the nature of the political battle because the party strife shadowed Su Tungpo's entire life.

One of the earliest extant copies of Chinese vernacular literature, presaging the advent of the novel in China, was a short story entitled "The Bull-headed Premier" (*Yao Shiangkung*). It is a collection of short stories in the vernacular of Sung dynasty times, recently discovered, and it shows that soon after Wang Anshih's death he was known by this nickname in· folk literature. The tragedies of the political strife arose from the defects of character of a man who was unable to take good advice and unwilling to admit a mistake. Friends' opposition to Wang Anshih only increased his determination to carry through his policy. Determination of character, we are told, is a great virtue, but a qualification is necessary: so much depends upon what a man is determined to· do. It is entirely possible that Wang Anshih, remembering the homely adage he had heard as a schoolboy that determination was a key to success, mistook mulish obstinacy for that desirable virtue. In his lifetime Wang Anshih was known among the *literati* as a man of "three not-worths"—"God's anger is not worth fearing, public opinion is not worth respecting, and the tradition of the ancestors is not worth keeping." It was a label given by Su Tungpo.

The "Bull-headed Premier"·brooked no opposition from any quarter, friends or foes. Being a good talker and able to persuade the young emperor of his programme for building up a strong state, he was determined to carry his socialistic programme through. This implied the silencing of opposition in general, and the silencing in particular of the imperial censors, whose official duty was to criticise the policies and conduct of the government and act as the ·channel of· public opinion". It was the basis of Chinese political philosophy that a good government "kept the channels of opinion open" and a bad government did not. It was therefore natural that, having begun with questions of the new measures themselves, the fight very soon surged around a more fundamental issue, the issue of freedom of criticism and dissent.

It was a fight in which Wang the premier won the first bout; but from then on, all the officials of the country were lined up in two camps, locked in party strife which went on until the end of the dynasty. The ⁄reform measures were modified or suspended after only a few years, but the schism which developed had far graver consequences for the country.

In this political battle at court the issue was known as a fight between "reactionaries" and "progressives", terms which appeared again and again in the literature of that period and which Wang Anshih was very fond of using. For him, anybody he disliked or anybody who disagreed with him was a "reactionary" (*liushu*, conservative philistine), while he and his followers were the "progressives" or "reformists" (*tungpien*). The premier charged all critics with malicious intent to block his reforms. On the other hand, the opposition charged that he "regarded the fair criticism of people as reactionary and all who differed from him as corrupt". As Liu Chih formulated it: "One party regards the other as 'reactionary' and the other regards the ruling party as 'rebels against all established values'." As the premier began to purge all the imperial censors who spoke up against him, the more important charge of the opposition was that he wanted to "shut up the mouths of all people"; i.e., muzzle all free criticism of the government.

The Chinese Government had never perfected a machinery of party rule with recognised rights and responsibilities of the party in power and the opposition. There was no counting of votes, show of hands, yeas and nays, or any other form of establishing majority opinion. The Chinese at any meeting merely discussed matters and somehow agreed upon a decision. In principle and practice, criticism of government policy was allowed and encouraged. The opponents might overthrow the cabinet, or might beg to retire. When a bitter factional feud took place, it was the custom to send the opponents away from the court to hold different posts in the country. Even under Jentsung and Ingtsung, famous leaders of government like Fan Chungyen and Ouyang Shiu had been dismissed to temporary obscurity, and had then returned to power. In this way one party came to power and another went out.

The bickerings and dissensions at the court now were increased by the peculiar Sung system of government, which centred no clear-cut responsibility on one man as prime minister. The cabinet was more like a state council, with the emperor holding the balance of power. The government consisted of a complicated, cumbersome system of interlocking departments with duplicating functions, so that the final decision always rested with the emperor himself. The so-called "premier" (*shiang*), a social term, went by the complicated title of "General Control Head of the Chancellery and the Imperial Secretariat", and there might be two vice-premiers. The general set-up was as follows:

Two Councils	Three Departments	Six Ministries
PRIVY COUNCIL (military) (*president* and *vice-president*)		
STATE COUNCIL	1. Chancellery, or Premier's Office (*chancellor*)	
ADMINISTRATIVE COUNCIL (*premier* and *vice-premier*)	2. Imperial Secretariat (*chancellor*)	1. Civil Service
		2. Interior
	3. Executive Board (*chancellor*)	3. Education
		4. Army
		5. Justice
		6. Public Works

The board of finance was entirely separate, directly responsible to the emperor. There was an independent imperial censorate, besides the censors within the three departments, as well as other various boards and bureaus useful chiefly for conferring nominal titles. Usually the "premier" was concurrently head of the chancellery and of the imperial secretariat. The heads of the three departments and of the military privy council together formed the state council and were called state councillors (*chihcheng*). Later Shentsung tried to simplify the system by drastic changes aiming at better-defined functions: the imperial secretariat was to *deliberate,* the premier's office (chancellery) to *promulgate,* and the executive board to *execute* government orders; but the same confusion and divided responsibility continued to exist.

Wang Anshih was at first only a vice-premier; but, backed by the Emperor, he went ahead with his programme over everybody's head and made all decisions at home with Lu Huiching and Tseng Pu. This seemed an ideal situation for embroiling the state councillors before the Emperor. The issues were mainly two, the farmers' loans and freedom of criticism by the censors. On one side were all the veteran officials, men of tried ability, constituting a majority so overwhelming as to suggest unanimity, and on the other, one man, Wang Anshih, backed by Emperor Shentsung, and a rather curious conglomeration of new and unknown petty, ambitious, energetic but scheming politicians. For convenience of reference, and in order not to encumber the text with too many names, the following table of the more important personages in the conflict, showing the amazing alignment of forces, may be useful:

DRAMATIS PERSONÆ

IN POWER

WANG ANSHIH, "the Bull-headed Premier"
SHENTSUNG, an ambitious emperor

Two Henchmen

TSENG PU, energetic politician
LU HUICHING, a notorious character who double-crossed WANG

Four Rascals

LEEDING, a man who concealed his mother's death; later, court prosecutor of SU TUNGPO
-DUNQUAN, great turn-coat, served HUICHING and WANG alternately
SUDAN, with DUNQUAN, impeached SU TUNGPO
WANG FANG, son of WANG ANSHIH

Great Horde of Office-Seekers
(As in any other age)

SHIEH CHINGWEN, brother-in-law of WANG ANSHIH
TSAI PIEN, son-in-law of WANG ANSHIH
CHANG CHUN, later enemy of SU TUNGPO
LU CHIAWEN, trade dictator in WANG'S regime

THE OPPOSITION

Elderly Statesmen (ex-premiers, privy councillors, etc.)
SZEMA KUANG, leader of the opposition, great historian
HAN CHI, veteran leader
FU PI, old minister
LU HUEI, fired first shot
TSENG KUNGLIANG, weak character
CHAO PIEN
WEN YENPO, friend of everybody

Su and Close Friends

CHANG FANGPING } elderly statesmen, "like "uncles" to SU
FAN CHEN
OUYANG SHIU
SU TUNGPO
SU TSEYU, Tungpo's brother
FAN CHUNJEN, a great man
SUN CHUEH, tall, fiery
LI CHANG, stocky
LIU SHU, quick-tempered

Wang's Former Friends

LU KUNGCHU, called "Handsome Beard", brilliant scholar
HAN WEI, from powerful Han family
CHENG HAO, neo-Confucianist, elder of the famous "Cheng brothers"

Wang's Two Brothers

WANG ANLI
WANG ANKUO

D*

Independent Critics

LIU CHIH, later enemy of SU
SU SUNG
SUNG MINCHIU } "three secretarie of Shining"
LI TALIN
Other Censors
CHENG SHIA, "the little man
with the big role", small gate-
keeper who overthrew WANG
ANSHIH

The highly unbalanced alignment of forces is both tragic and amusing. Looking down the list, one cannot help wondering at the unhappy knack of Wang Anshih for alienating his own friends, and the
heavy price the Emperor was willing to pay to keep Wang in power,
since all those in opposition were cashiered, dismissed, and punished.
In the end, Emperor Shentsung had to dismiss Wang Anshih, Lu
Huiching, and Dunquan, too. His dream of a strong, powerful state
vanished, and he was content to govern in a vacuum of mediocrities.
If good judgment of men is an attribute of divinity, it would seem that
the posthumous title of the emperor, *Shentsung,* or "Divine Ancestor",
was a gross misnomer.

The tragedy of Wang Anshih comes from the fact that he was not
in any way self-indulgent or corrupt himself, and that his hand was
forced. To carry out anything so radical as his state capitalism programme, he knew he had to override all opposition. Perhaps that was
why he had bided his time so long. He had a vision, and his wagon
was hitched to that starry vision, not of a happy, peaceful and prosperous nation, but of a rich, strong, and powerful state, expanding its
borders north and south. God had willed that the Sung dynasty was to
be great and expansionist, like the Hans and the Tangs, and he, Wang
Anshih, was the manifest Man of Destiny. But there is not one "Man
of Destiny" who does not appear slightly pathetic in the contemplation
of future historians—a man caught in the prison of his ambition, a
victim of his own dream, which grew and expanded and then burst
like a bubble.

Despising all the "conservative philistines", he not only alienated
the good old ministers, but even lost Han Wei and Lu Kungchu, who
were his best friends. Han Wei, we remember, was the friend who had
turned Shentsung's heart and hopes towards Wang Anshih when the
former was crown prince. When these friends disagreed with him on
the manner in which he carried out his projects, he had no hesitation
in banishing them from the court. Deserted and alone, he took in and

promoted unknown and unqualified men who were smart enough to agree with him and use him for their own purposes. To make it easier to distinguish the three notorious characters, I have given them a more familiar spelling: Leeding, Sudan, and Dunquan. Leeding was a man who concealed the news of his mother's death to avoid going out of office, a daring offence in Confucian society. Dunquan is remembered by posterity as the author of the famous saying: "Let them all laugh who want to laugh; a good official post is mine." But the arch supporters of Wang Anshih were two extremely active and persuasive talkers of great scheming ability, Tseng Pu and Lu Huiching, particularly the latter, who eventually double-crossed Wang Anshih in an effort to supersede him. The collapse of this eight-year regime was summarised by a contemporary as follows: "Huiching sold out Wang Anshih, Wang Anshih sold out the Emperor, and the Emperor sold out the people." When Huiching stooped to publishing Wang's private letters to alienate him from the Emperor, Wang was overthrown, and in his old age he used to spend his fury over the turn-coat friend by scribbling the word "Fukienite" a few times every day, Fukien being the province from which Huiching came. When Su Tungpo met Wang Anshih in Nanking after the regime was over, and rebuked him for starting wars and persecuting scholars, Wang replied that Huiching was responsible for all the doings. This is hardly a plausible defence, since it was Wang himself who insisted on dealing harshly with all opposition, and since the institution of espionage at the capital against critics of the government was established during the period when Huiching was in retirement in mourning for his father, between April 1071 and July 1073.

Otherwise, the two leaders of the opposite factions, Wang Anshih and Szema Kuang, while uncompromising in their fight over government policies, were both sincere in their convictions and above reproach in their private lives. Neither was ever accused of corruption in money matters or of looseness of morals, while Ouyang Shiu was at least alleged to have had some affairs in his private household.

Once Wang Anshih's wife, Wu, had bought a concubine for her husband. When the woman was presented, Wang asked, in surprise: "What is that thing?"

"The Madame has asked me to serve you," replied the woman.

"But who are you?" asked Wang again.

"My husband," replied the woman, "was working with the army in charge of a boat-load of government rice. The boat sank and he lost the whole cargo. We sold all our property to restore the loss but still could not make up the amount. And so my husband sold me to pay for the balance."

"How much were you sold for?" asked Wang.

"Nine hundred dollars."

Wang Anshih sent for her husband and bade the woman go back to him, telling him to keep the money:

The same thing happened to Szema Kuang, for he, too, had a concubine against his wish. In his younger days he was serving as a deputy magistrate and his wife had not yet produced a son for him. The chief magistrate's wife presented him with a concubine, but Szema Kuang ignored her. Thinking that it was because of her own presence, his wife one day asked the girl to wait till she was out of the house and then dress up and go into his study at night. When Szema Kuang saw the girl appear in his room, he said in surprise to the girl: "How dare you come here? The Madame is away," and he sent her away. Both men were more interested in carrying out their policies than in personal power, and Wang Anshih certainly had no regard for money. While he was premier, as soon as his salary was received, he turned it over to his brothers to spend it any way they liked.

Szema Kuang, who towered intellectually and morally above his generation, fought a clean-cut battle of principles from the beginning to the end. He and Wang Anshih stood at opposite poles on government policy. In the words of a contemporary: "Wang Anshih refused to be premier unless the new policies were carried out, and Szema Kuang refused to be vice-privy-councillor unless the new policies were abolished."

Not only did Szema Kuang rank with Fan Chungyen as one of the two most respected prime ministers of Sung dynasty; he was, besides, author of the monumental comprehensive history of China up to the Sung period, the *Tsechih Tungchien* or *Mirror of History*, in 294 volumes, with thirty volumes of appendix on sources and comparative material, a work sound in scholarship and masterly in judgment and style, which became the pole star to which all history writing in China after him must be orientated. The first draft (*changpien*) was several times the number of volumes. He used to work at it steadily, filling ten feet of paper copying notes every day, and his manuscripts were said to fill two whole rooms. The gigantic work occupied the author for twenty-five years.

What started the final fight was the issue of the farmers' loans. After months of deliberation by the bureau of economic planning, the "Regulations for Seedling Loans" were promulgated in September 1069. Forty-one high commissioners were sent out to the provinces to push through the new plan. It soon became apparent that the loans could not be voluntarily sold to the people as had been intended. The question for the high commissioners, then, was whether they wanted to come back and report that their mission had been a failure or to force the loans on the people and report a great success. The government preferred to lend money to the rich for better guarantees, but the rich were not in particular need of money. Some poor people were in need of money, but the government had to have guarantees of their ability to repay. Some of the commissioners therefore devised a system of allocating the loans to the people according to their financial standing, down to the poorest farmers. But the poor can be too poor to borrow; only the rich can borrow money, which is the essence of sound modern banking and finance. To make sure that the loans were repaid, the government made their richer neighbours stand guarantors for the poor. One of the commissioners reported that the people "cried for joy" when they were offered the loans. Another commissioner, who was not willing to force the measure on the people, came back with a different report. Censors impeached the successful commissioner for "forcing" the loans on the people, which was clearly against the intention of the original edict. Wang Anshih went to the censorate office and said to the officials: "What are you people trying to do? You impeach one commissioner who is energetic in carrying out the reforms, while you say nothing of the other who is slack in his duties."

Han Chi, who was serving at Tamingfu as governor of Hopei, had seen how the loan plan worked in the country, and he submitted a memorial which gives the best picture of how the loans were being distributed. In contrast to Su Tungpo's vehement outburst, here was a well-considered and well-worded, matter-of-fact report to the Emperor by a retired premier who had served the country in the highest capacities. In the paper he said that even the poor people of the lowest class were assigned a denomination, while the richer classes were asked to subscribe more. The so-called farmers' loans were also enforced among the city people and were sold among the landlords and "monopolist exploiters" whom it was the intention of the new measure to supplant and suppress; the loans were, therefore, defeating their own purpose. For every dollar borrowed, the people had to pay back $1.30 after a few months. However energetically the government denied that it was lending money for profit, people would not believe it. Han pointed out that it was impracticable to prevent the forcing of loans and depend on voluntary subscription, for the rich would not borrow and the poor, who would, could not offer guarantees; therefore, in time, it would be necessary to make the guarantors pay for the loans. And since the high commissioners were anxious to please the authorities at the court, while the lower officials dared not speak up, so Han said, he found it incumbent upon him as an old faithful servant of the court to bring the facts to the Emperor's attention. He asked for the suspension of the new measure, the recall of the tax commissioners, and the restoration of the price equalisation granaries on the old basis.

"Han Chi is a faithful minister," said the Emperor, discussing this memorandum with Wang Anshih. "While serving in the country, he still has not forgotten about the imperial house. I thought the loans were for the benefit of the people and did not realise that they were doing so much harm. Besides, these seedling loans were intended for the farming districts. Why do they sell them in the cities?"

"What's the harm?" replied Wang Anshih quickly. "If the people in the cities want the loans, why not let them have them?"

There was, therefore, a long exchange of letters between Han Chi and the court, and the retired premier specifically pointed out that what the state-capitalist of the Han dynasty had done in squeezing the life blood of the people in order to fill the emperor's war chest could hardly be considered a measure to "enrich the country".

This shook Wang Anshih's position, and the Emperor began to think of suspending the loans. Wang Anshih heard about it and asked for sick leave. In referring to Wang's request for leave, Szema Kuang used the phrase, "the scholars are in a boiling rage and the people of the country are in an uproar". The high ministers discussed this situation, and Chao Pien, who was still for Wang, said that they had better wait until Wang's leave was over. That very night Tseng Kungliang, a cabinet member, had his son tell Wang Anshih secretly of the impending change, and asked Wang to cancel his leave. Following Tseng's secret tip, Wang did cancel his leave and appeared at the court again, and was able to persuade the Emperor that the opposition was merely trying to "block His Majesty's reforms".

Not knowing what to think, the Emperor now sent two eunuchs to the country to report on the situation. The eunuchs, however, knew on which side their bread was buttered, and came back with the report that the loans were "popular" with the people and that "there was no compulsion". Wen Yenpo, an old official, objected and said to the Emperor: "Do you believe two eunuchs, but will not believe Han Chi, who has served as a premier in three successive regimes?" But the Emperor believed his own reporters and was strengthened in his determination to go through with the new measure. How often a few irresponsible or ignorant reporters who do not understand what they are talking about can affect the development of events and influence the national policy of a country! If the castrated men had had the manliness to tell the truth, the course of the Sung dynasty would have taken a different turn at this time. What happened to those two eunuchs when the truth was revealed to the world we do not know. They had reported what the Emperor wanted to hear. When times changed and it was no longer the fashion to talk about these wonderful "agrarian reformers", they could keep sheepishly quiet.

Szema Kuang, Fan Chen, and Su Tungpo carried on their fight together. Szema Kuang had had a good opinion of Wang Anshih, and he enjoyed the great confidence of the Emperor. When the Emperor asked him about Wang Anshih, he said: "People's criticism of him as a hypocrite is perhaps extreme. But he is unpractical and terribly stubborn." However, he had had a hot debate with Wang Anshih's henchman Huiching during a class in history for the Emperor, so much so that the latter had to break up the dispute and tell the parties to calm down. Wang Anshih had therefore begun to dislike Szema Kuang as opposed to his policies. Now while Wang was so briefly on sick leave, the Emperor wanted to make Szema Kuang vice-president of the privy council. Szema Kuang declined the office, saying that his personal position was of no concern whatsoever, and that the important thing was whether His Majesty was going to stop these new policies. Nine times Szema Kuang submitted these memorandums. The Emperor replied:

"I am asking you to be a privy councillor in charge of military affairs. Why do you keep on declining the office and talking about these things which have nothing to do with the army?"

"But I have not yet accepted the military post," replied Szema Kuang. "So long as I am in the imperial secretariat, I must bring these things to your attention."

When Wang cancelled his leave, his position was strengthened and he degraded Szema Kuang into the position of a treasurer in the secretariat. Twice Fan Chen rejected the imperial edict carrying this new appointment, and the Emperor, thus being defied, with his own hand handed the edict to Szema Kuang. Upon this, Fan Chen begged to resign his position in the imperial secretariat and was permitted to do so. With the restoration of Wang Anshih to power, Han Chi also begged to resign as governor of Hopei, retaining only his district office as magistrate at Tamingfu. Naturally, this also was granted.

Su Tungpo was getting hot under the collar. He had so much to say and he had to say it. As may be expected, he was much more forthright than the others. He was then only thirty-two, and his position in the department of history was a low and strictly literary, non-administrative post. He wrote two letters to the Emperor, in February 1070, and February 1071. The letters were long, exhaustive, eloquent and minced no words. They were like those occasional modern editorials which arouse immediate national attention. He opened his first letter with a direct attack on the farmers' loan. He told the Emperor that the entire nation was turning against him, and warned him not to rely on power to suppress the people. Quoting Confucius, he said:

"If the people of the country are rich, does a ruler ever have to worry about his private wealth? . . . I do not know, when Your Majesty speaks about enriching the country, whether you are speaking about enriching the people or enriching your own purse.

"In all things, great and small, one should not depend on force, but must observe reason and the nature of things. For in all things done according to reason one is bound to succeed, and in all undertakings against reason one is doomed to fail. Now Your Majesty has compelled the farmers to pay you high interest, and you have entered into competition with business-men for profits. Is this in accordance with nature, and do you wonder that it has failed? . . . If Your Majesty has the welfare of the people truly at heart, the people would show confidence in you despite all rumours; but if you are going only after revenue, the people can hardly be convinced by words. If a judge receives presents from a defendant and lets himself be influenced in his decision, people will say that he has been bribed; and if a man takes what does not belong to him people will call him a thief. That would only be calling a thing by its right name. Now, you are receiving twenty per cent interest from the farmers' loans, yet you insist that you are not making these loans for interest. How are the people to believe you? . . . A man is condemned by his acts and not by what he professes to do. . . . All this commotion is because the whole country is coming to believe that Your Majesty is looking for the revenue, while you maintain that you are working only for their good. While you insist that you are totally disinterested, the whole world thinks that you are avaricious."

He advised the Emperor on a course of caution.

"Sometimes a man falls from a horse in his youth and never dares to ride again all his life. . . . Bent on a mad rush for drastic reforms, you have started the farmers' loans, instituted the draft exemption tax, started the national trade bureau, shifted the army units. You are determined to carry these through against all criticism, but should you find out the error, then, when you have good policies to carry out in the future, you will have lost all self-confidence. . . . Your Majesty started the reign with the high hopes of youth, gifted with high intelligence and determination, and if your ministers should fail to advise you now to take the path of steadiness and caution, you would be like a man dashing over dangerous terrain in a light coach on a dark night with the coachman lashing the horse. Might it not be far better if Your Majesty would ease the reins, feed the horse, and wait patiently till the dawn, when you could travel on safe highways in broad daylight?"

The Emperor was greatly mistaken, Su Tungpo warned, if he thought he was going to succeed by reliance on his arbitrary power. Officials had been degraded and dismissed; there was talk of restoring severe punishment by bodily mutilation. He went on:

"Now the court is torn by dissension, for which there must be a cause. Instead of seeking the cause, Your Majesty intends to overcome opposition by force. But since history began, force has never been able to suppress the people. In ancient days, scholars were threatened with knives and saws in front and the boiling pot behind, but that did not stop them from voicing their convictions. Your Majesty has not yet killed any minister. So far you have only dismissed those who oppose your policy. I hardly think Your Majesty will have the heart to imitate the example of the Chin dictator and kill men for gossiping in the streets, or revive the party inquisitions of Han. Do you suppose scholardom will be frightened and silenced? The more men you banish from the court, the more will rise in protest. . . . If Your Majesty intends to change the code of punishment and do the extreme, how will you prevent a rebellion?

"There is not a man in the country whose heart is not turning against the government, and not a tongue which is not talking ill of the regime. Does this sound like the beginning of a great reign when the Emperor and his ministers work in complete harmony for the good of the state? The ancient saying has it: 'A hundred people cannot be wrong.' Now it is not only a hundred people, but the entire nation which is voicing the same opinion, and yet Your Majesty persists in your course against the opposition of the entire nation. I really do not know what to say. The *Book of Songs* says:

'Like unto a drifting boat,
None knows where it is heading.
Restless I lie upon the pillow,
'For my heart is bleeding.'

I hope Your Majesty will consider these humble words of mine, although I know I am courting death by this memorial.
Your humble servant,
Su Shih"

The issue that deeply stirred all officialdom was Wang's purge of the censorate. From the very beginning, Wang Anshih frightened the entire court, not so much by his drastic and extensive economic plans and policies as by his arbitrary habit of cashiering all censors who criticised them. The right to criticism of public policies was challenged. The foundation of the governmental structure was being undermined. A sensitive spot in the body politic had been touched. All officialdom was dismayed, and friends began to desert him.

The issue of the purge of the censorate was in itself enough to cause the withdrawal of support and the resignation of the government leaders. The imperial censorate was an old institution in the Chinese government, whose purpose was to represent public opinion and constantly check and criticise the ruling regime. It was held as essential to a good government that free criticism should be made readily available to the emperor so that the state of public opinion could be properly reflected. In consequence of its position, the censorate had tremendous powers and responsibilities and could overthrow an administration when the censors attacked it hard enough. It was a somewhat lax and not too well defined method for bringing about changes in the government personnel and policies, acting in somewhat the same way as the modern press. The difference in ancient China was that there was no legal protection for the censorate or for the rights of the opposition, but only the established tradition that a "good" emperor should be liberal towards criticism; whether he cared for such a good reputation was up to the emperor himself. If he did not choose to exercise moral restraint, he could constitutionally degrade, punish, torture, or kill the censors and their entire families. Many did so. The censors were placed in the impossible position of having the official duty to admonish both the government and the emperor himself without any constitutional protection of their personal liberties. But as in modern times there are always editors with a sense of responsibility to the public who are brave enough to defy a totalitarian regime at the risk of imprisonment and death, so there were always censors who braved corporal punishment, flogging, and even death to carry out their duties to the people. This is particularly true of the Eastern Han and the Ming periods, when there were censors who, having written their protests against a vile premier and knowing that they were only courting death, hanged themselves before they sent in their letters of protest. These censors went up to battle like soldiers; as soon as one fell, another rose to take his place. Good emperors who loved a good name would be careful in their treatment of these censors, earning great fame and popularity for themselves, but bad administrations were anxious to silence the censors just as modern dictators find it necessary to muzzle the press.

Wang Anshih had started his administration with great expectations from the elder statesmen.

Huei fired the first shot at Wang Anshih, describing him as "a hypocrite and a sinister character destined to bring the country to the brink of catastrophe", even Szema Kuang was surprised. As they walked together to a class in classics to be given to the Emperor, Lu revealed to Szema Kuang what he was going to do that morning, and showed him the memorial concealed in his sleeve.

"But what can we do? He is so popular," said Szema Kuang.

"You, too!" replied Lu Huei, shocked.

Lu Huei was dismissed from his post, and the purge began.

Now a spark set the court politics on fire. There was the case of a woman who had attempted murder of her husband but had only succeeded in wounding him. The woman had confessed her intent of murder, and the highest officials disagreed on the proper punishment. The case had therefore been standing for over a year. Szema Kuang wanted to settle it one way, and Wang Anshih wanted to settle it the other and insisted on carrying it through. The punishment was embodied in an imperial decree, but the censor, Liu Shu, rejected it for reconsideration, as the imperial censors often did. A second censor defied Wang's will, and Wang impeached him through one of his underlings. This then brought the fight into the open.

The imperial censors were aroused. The question was whether they were to be free to prosecute their duties, or whether one by one they were to be politically disposed of. Several of the censors sent a joint impeachment of Wang Anshih and asked for his recall. Wang Anshih was angered and wanted to put them in jail. Szema Kuang and Fan Chunjen opposed this on principle, and eventually six censors were sent out to distant provinces to sell wine at the government stores. Upon this, Fan Chunjen took up the fight. He demanded that the order dismissing the censors be rescinded—and was dismissed himself. The next to fall was Tseyu, Su Tungpo's brother, who had consistently opposed the farmers' loans and the national trade bureau. Two months later the good old premier Fu Pi resigned, warning that in any political fight the good men were bound to lose, while the bad politicians were bound to come out on top. For good men fought for principles and bad men fought for power, and in the end both would get what they wanted, by the good men's quitting and the bad men's staying. He predicted that with this trend of affairs, the country would soon be plunged into chaos.

The court was now thrown into an uproar. The bureau of economic planning was instituted in February 1069, the national trade bureau in July, and the farmers' loans in September. In the course of a few months public opinion towards the new administration changed from great expectations to doubt, doubt gave place to confusion, and confusion to anger and fear.

Things were happening fast now. The months of March and April 1070 saw a wholesale purge and packing of the censorate. The two censors who fell next were Wang's personal friends, men who had helped him to power and on whom he had depended for support. Tall, fiery, eloquent Sun Chueh, who was also Su's lifelong friend, had challenged Wang on his claim that the currency bureau of the Chou dynasty, established in the twelfth century B.C., had lent money to people at the rate of twenty-five per cent interest. Still hoping for his support, Wang sent him out on a court investigation, again demanded by the Emperor, into the persistent rumours that the loans were being "forced" on the farmers even in districts close to the capital. Sun came back and honestly reported that there was compulsion, which Wang regarded as a "betrayal" of friendship—so Sun was dismissed. The more important case was that of "Handsome Beard" Lu Kungchu, son of a premier, and a man of great learning but few words. In their earlier days Wang and Lu had divided literary honours and the admiration of scholars. Lu had helped Wang to power, and in return Wang had made him chief of the censorate. Now Lu asked in a petition to the Emperor, somewhat too pointedly for Wang's comfort: "How is it that all public opinion has suddenly become 'reactionary', and how is it that the great and able ministers of yesterday have suddenly become the 'corrupt' men of today?" Wang drafted the edict of dismissal himself in words which showed something of the temperamental character of the man. In their days of friendship, Wang Anshih had said to the Emperor: "A man of Lu's ability simply has to become a prime minister some day." Now he compared Lu to one of the "Four Evil Monsters" under the ideal emperors Yao and Shun.

What alienated his former admirers more was that in the same month Wang appointed two disreputable characters to replace the censors he had dismissed. The appointment of Leeding as a full-rank censor aroused a great fury in the censorate. Leeding had neither passed the official examinations nor acquired the necessary civil service standing, and he was known to have concealed the news of his mother's death and failed to observe the rites of mourning. In Chinese eyes, this is tantamount to degenerating into a beast. Wang promoted him to this post because Leeding had come up from the country and had reported that the farmers' loans were "extremely popular" with the people; Wang had introduced him to the Emperor to make the report in person. This aroused the ire of the censors. At the same time Wang made Shieh Chingwen, his brother-in-law, also a censor. To secure promotion, Shieh had married his sister to one of Wang Anshih's brothers. Three imperial secretaries rejected the edict of appointment—which brought about the dismissal of these three from their office. The other remaining censors then took up the issue. Chang Chien

demanded the recall to power of the dismissed censors and the cashiering of Leeding and Huiching, known as the power behind Wang
Anshih. When Chang Chien went up to the premier's office to press
his case, he found Wang Anshih in a curious state of mind. The latter
listened to him without saying a word, but was laughing behind a fan
held before his face.

"I do not doubt," said the censor, "that you are laughing at me for
my stupidity. But you should be aware that there are many more
people in the country who are laughing at you."

Another important censor to fall at the same time was Cheng Hao,
the elder of the two "Cheng brothers", great neo-Confucianist
philosophers of the Sung dynasty. Cheng Hao had co-operated with
Wang intimately in the early days of the reforms. Now he also went
to the premier's office to fight the case out with Wang personally. The
latter had just read his memorandum, and the caller found him in a
state of uncontrollable rage. Philosophically, the neo-Confucianist said:
"Look here, my friend, we are not fighting over personal or family
affairs; we are discussing the affairs of the country. Can we not talk
in a calm and dispassionate manner?" By all Confucian standards,
Wang lost face and felt ashamed of himself.

Within a few weeks the purge of the censorate was complete. With
the six censors who had been cashiered in the previous year, the total
of dismissed censors was now fourteen, eleven in the censorate and
three in the palace. Szema Kuang warned the Emperor in unmistakable terms. Only three persons, Wang, Tseng Pu, and Lu Huiching,
were for the new reform measures, and the entire court was against
them. "Is His Imperial Majesty going to make up the government and
the nation with these three persons?" Han Chi and Chang Fangping
had quit in February; Szema Kuang had refused a post as privy
councillor and was degraded in the same month; Fan Chen had left
in anger. In September the vacillating Chao Pien, the cabinet minister
who had for a time been inclined to favour the new regime, now
decided to resign. He to pointed out that "the farmers' loans and the
appointment of tax-commissioners are by comparison small matters, but
the choice of the right men to assist the Emperor in his government is a
matter of far greater consequence." A few months later, aged, fatalistic,
imperturbable Tseng Kungliang, who had ascribed Wang's rise to
power to "God's will", resigned in disgust, giving old age as his excuse,
but in reality partly under fire from the critics. By December 1070,
Wang Anshih was formally made premier and was placed in an un-
challenged position at the head of the whole government. In June of
the following year Ouyang Shiu resigned all his posts in the government and went to live in retirement.

*   *   *   *   *

Su Tungpo now wrote his famous nine-thousand-word letter to the Emperor, and was prepared to be dismissed. He and Szema Kuang and Fan Chen had carried on the fight together, but Szema and Fan had quitted in disgust and anger. Fan Chen, later related to Su Tungpo, had served in the imperial secretariat under the last two emperors. Fat and soft in appearance, he had the strength of steel in his character. When he left, he said in his letter of resignation: "Your Majesty is disposed to take frank criticism, but your minister obstructs it; Your Majesty loves the people at heart, but your minister is oppressing them in practice." The Emperor showed this letter to Wang Anshih during a court audience, and Wang's face blanched. Some of those close by reported that they saw his hands holding the letter shaking with rage.

Szema Kuang had been sent to an outpost in Shensi in September 1070. He had been slow to give up. It was after three exchanges of earnest if bitter letters with Wang that the complete break came. The Emperor was still hoping for him to return to the court, for he had repeatedly told the other ministers that he felt safe from committing bad blunders so long as Szema Kuang was by his side. Again and again the Emperor called him to the capital, and Szema Kuang refused. He had said enough. If the Emperor could not be dissuaded from riding on the stubborn mule to perdition, his duty was done. When he decided to quit altogether and live in retirement, his anger was unrestrained. He wrote to the Emperor: "Whoever agrees with Anshih is right, and whoever disagrees with Anshih is wrong. Those who lick Anshih's spittle are the 'loyal ministers', and those who oppose his policies are the 'scheming intriguers'. . . . I have disagreed with Anshih, and am therefore both wrong and a 'scheming intriguer' in Your Majesty's opinion. I ask for your decision. If my crimes are like those of Fan Chen, allow me to lay down my office as you allowed Fan Chen to do. If my crimes are worse, exile or sentence me to death, and I will gladly accept my fate."

From now until the Emperor's death, sixteen years later, Szema Kuang was to shut himself up completely to devote himself to the monumental history already begun nine years before. Later, when Emperor Shentsung had dismissed Wang Anshih and wanted to call Szema Kuang back to power, his one reply was still, was the Emperor ready to reverse his economic policies? Thus the two poles of political thought stood, each unmoving and immovable to the end. Yet in the first year of the next emperor, when Wang Anshih died and Szema Kuang was on his death-bed, the order he gave as premier then was: "Wang Anshih was not too bad a person. His only fault was his stubbornness. Let him be buried with all the honours the court can give."

Su Tungpo's nine-thousand-word letter to the Emperor is important as embodying his political philosophy, and as indicative of his personal temperament and style, a mixture of wit, learning, and intrepid courage. Angered polemics alternate with cool, lucid reasoning. Now he was despondent, bitter, sharply critical and uncommonly forthright; now he was arguing, citing examples, quoting from Mencius, Confucius, and the histories to bolster his thesis. Adroit, sincere, and convincing, it was written with profound emotion and sorrow at the state of affairs. In his audience with the Emperor in January, His Majesty had praised a memorial by him on educational reforms and asked him for "straight criticism . . . even of His Majesty himself". Su Tungpo took him at his word. It was his last desperate effort to make the Emperor change his mind, when all high officials had left and all chances were against him. He knew that he would be dismissed, if nothing worse happened.

The two most important points for the modern reader are the Mencian principle that the ruler derives his power from the people, and the defence of free criticism on the principle of dissent in politics. Su Tungpo warned the Emperor, a ruler is ruler, not by virtue of a mythical "divine right" of kings, but by the support he derives from the people. Let the king beware!

"It is said in the *Book of History*, 'In ruling over the people, I feel as if I were holding six horses with worn-out reins.' This means that no one in the nation is in a more precarious position than the emperor himself. When the emperor and the people come together, they are ruler and subjects; when they detest each other, they become foes. But the line of division, determining whether the people go with the ruler or against him, is extremely tenuous. He who is able to command the support of the millions becomes a king, while he who alienates their support becomes a solitary private individual. The basis of the ruler's power lies, therefore, entirely in the support of the people in their hearts. The relation of the people's support to the ruler may be likened to that of the roots to a tree, oil to the lamp, water to the fish, rice fields to the farmer and capital to the business-men. A tree dries up when its roots are cut; the lamp goes out when the oil is gone; fish die when they leave the water; farmers starve when deprived of their rice fields, and merchants go bankrupt when they have no more capital. And when an emperor loses the support of the people, it spells his ruin. This is an inexorable law from whose consequences no ruler can hope to escape. From ancient times such has been always, the danger confronting a ruler."

But how was the ruler to obtain the support of the people unless he permitted the free expression of opinion? Su Tungpo went on to develop what I consider the most important point in the memorandum. This was the principle of disagreement in politics, as embodied in the system of the imperial censorate. For, according to Su Tungpo, the maintenance of a good regime depended very much upon the healthy operation of political opposition. Democracy itself is predicated upon the principle of disagreement among parties. In modern times I am sure Su would have opposed the principle of unanimity in the United Nations Security Council as being essentially antidemocratic. He knew that at least since Chinese Adam no two persons have ever completely agreed, and that the only alternative to democracy is tyranny. I have never yet found an enemy of democracy who is not a tyrant in the home, in the country, or in world politics. Su Tungpo went on:

"Sun Pao has well said: 'The Duke of Chou was a great sage and the Duke of Shao was a great genius, and yet history records they seldom agreed with one another at court.' There was, too, Wang Tao of the Chin dynasty, who may be considered truly a great minister. But when at dinner the guests approved of whatever he said, Wang Shu was displeased. 'No one is a sage; you cannot always be right,' said Wang Shu, and the minister thanked him for the advice. If Your Majesty wants everybody to think the same thought and express the same opinion and the whole court to sing the same tune, everybody can do it. But should there be in the government unprincipled men serving along with the rest, how will Your Majesty expect ever to find it out?"

No one, I believe, stated the reasons for the existence of the censorate and the principles underlying it so clearly as Su Tungpo in this letter. The issue of a free, unfettered, fearless censorate was the issue of a free public opinion.

"It appears to me that when the atmosphere for free criticism prevails, even mediocre people will be encouraged to speak up, but when such freedom is destroyed, even the best people will be inclined to hold their tongues. I fear that from now on the pattern may be set and the censors will become no more than the flunkeys of the cabinet ministers, with the result that the Emperor will stand in complete isolation from his people. Once the system has been destroyed, anything may happen. . . . One cannot, furthermore, escape the conclusion that when there are no fearless critics of the government in times of peace, there will also be no national heroes willing to die for the country in times of trouble. If you do not permit your people even to put in a word of criticism, how do you expect them to die for the country when trouble comes?"

He compared the state of public opinion of the present with the past.

"I remember hearing in my childhood from the elders that the censors always reflected faithfully the public opinion of the country; what the public praised, the censors also praised, and what the public disliked, the censors condemned. . . . Now the country is in an uproar and grumblings are heard on every side; it should not be difficult for Your Majesty to gauge what the state of public opinion is like."

Su developed the *raison d'être* of the censorate by a comparative study of different systems of government in the different dynasties. Here he showed himself as a great advocate, scholarly in manner, cogent in reasoning, penetrating in insight.

"From a study of the governmental systems of the ancient times, we see that there was always the question of balance of power between the central and the provincial governments. In the Chou and Tang dynasties the system inclined toward decentralisation, while in the Chin and Wei it inclined toward centralisation. The result of over-centralisation was that a few corrupt men close to the court were able to make the emperor their tool for power, while the result of over-decentralisation was that the provincial governors became too powerful and sometimes raised the banner of rebellion. A great statesman shows foresight by providing against the causes of corruption and decay while a country is yet at its height of prosperity. . . . In comparison with the other dynasties, it [the present dynasty] may be described as inclining towards a centralised system of government. I do not presume to know what the founders of this dynasty, the Imperial Ancestors, had in mind as the means to check the dangers of over-centralisation. But it seems to me the establishment of the Imperial Censorate was meant as such a safeguard. . . . Since the founding of the Sung house, never has an official censor been severely punished. . . . When there was important information concerning the country, everyone was free to speak up, regardless of his rank. If it concerned the personal character and morals of the emperor, he always listened with attentive respect; if it concerned important government policies, the cabinet ministers held themselves ready for questioning. This was carried to such an extent in the regime of Jentsung that it was derisively said of the cabinet ministers of the time that they were merely servants of the censorate carrying out their orders.

"Now there is a deep purpose in the establishment of the system of the censorate, of which people are not usually aware. It is true that what the censors suggest may not be always right, but it is of the greatest importance that these critics should be given complete freedom and great responsibility, not merely as a matter of form, but for the very definite purpose of checking the rise of selfish men to power and of safeguarding against the danger always inherent in a strongly centralised government. Before a bad minister comes into power, it is a comparatively easy thing for the censors to stop him; but after he is entrenched in his position, it may take an army to overthrow him, and then it may not always succeed. . . . I hope Your Majesty will ponder deeply the purpose and meaning of this institution of government critics, and keep it alive for the protection of Your Imperial Descendants. There is in my mind nothing more important for maintaining the proper functioning of the government than this institution."

Su Tungpo warned the Emperor against reliance upon his power to cow the people into submission. Again he referred to the growing rumour of restoration of punishment by bodily mutilation. Hundreds of years earlier, various forms of mutilation had been used in the punishment of criminals, including branding, cutting off noses, cutting off legs, and castration. These inhuman punishments were abolished after the second century B.C., except castration, which was abolished around the year 600 A.D. It is to the credit of Su Tungpo that he prevented the restoration of such cruelties by these two letters. The gossip was increasing.

"Even Your Majesty and the few ministers close to you have heard of these rumours. You have disregarded them by saying: 'Why should I worry about these rumours when there is no basis to them?' While it is true that such rumours may not all be correct yet they must have sprung up for good reasons. A man must be greedy before he is accused of being a thief, and a man must be loose in his morals before he is accused of immorality with women. . . ."

Business had been paralysed, Su pointed out, and prices had gone up; from the near-by provinces to distant Szechuen, rumours were rife and the people were in an uproar; even deep in the mountainous districts a wine monopoly had been established; monks and nuns had been arrested and deprived of their property, and soldiers' and officials' pay had been cut.

"You have established the bureau of economic planning, which is for the purpose of securing revenue. You have sent out over forty tax commissioners, whose evident objective can only be to raise money for the government. It is useless for a man to ride out to the

forests with a pack of greyhounds and announce to the world: 'I am
not going hunting,' or for a man to go with a fish-net to the lakes and
declare: 'I am not going fishing.' It would be much better to stop
the rumours by throwing away the fish-nets and sending home the
hunting dogs."

He trusted that the Emperor would be able to see clearly for himself
that there was dissension and strife in the country. He should be able
to deduce from the resignation of all the able ministers what the state of
public opinion was like. After repeating most of the arguments against
the current reforms, he drove home the idea that in carrying out these
economic policies, the Emperor had already forfeited the people's
support and public opinion was against him and against the regime.

The letter was received in silence. In March, Su followed up with a
third letter. The Emperor had in the interim issued an edict forbidding
compulsory allocation of loans, but he was not ready to put a complete
stop to these measures. Quoting Mencius, Su said this was like a
chicken thief who said he was now ready to reform, and would steal
only one chicken per month. What aggravated the situation was that
in his capacity as magistrate at the capital, an office he had held since
January 1071, he gave out as subject for the local examinations "On
Dictatorship", which angered Wang Anshih greatly.

Promptly, Su Tungpo was cashiered. Just as he predicted, although
the Emperor might take his advice kindly, the politicians could get him
in trouble by some framed-up charge. The brother-in-law and flunkey
of Wang Anshih, Shieh Chingwen, set the wheels of the law moving
against Su Tungpo. There was now a rumour that while he was carrying his father's coffin home in the long voyage back to Szechuen, he
had made unwarranted use of government guards and had bought
furniture and porcelain and possibly smuggled salt for profit. Officials
were sent out to the different provinces along the route which the Su
brothers had travelled to collect data from boatmen, soldiers, and
custom officers. Su Tungpo probably did buy a lot of furniture and
porcelain, but there was nothing illegal about it. The couriers came
back and reported that they could not find anything, and they certainly
would have if they could.

In his letter to his wife's brother, who was at this time living back at
Szechuen, Su wrote: "Miss Twenty-Seven [Mrs. Su] is doing well and
recently a son has been born to us. . . . I have been a thorn in the sides
of the authorities for a long time. Let them investigate all they want.
I know they will only make fools of themselves. You may have heard
of the rumour, but do not worry on my account."

When Szema Kuang was in the capital before proceeding to his home in Loyang, the Emperor said to him:

"It seems to me Su Shih has not a good personal character. Perhaps you have made a mistake in your high opinion of him."

"Are you referring to the charges against Su?" replied Szema Kuang "I know the man better. Your Majesty is aware that this Shieh Ching-wen is a relative of Anshih and the charge was instigated by Wang himself. Besides, though Su Shih may not be perfect, is he not better than Leeding, the beast who concealed his mother's funeral?"

According to his official standing Su should now have been made a full magistrate, which the Emperor had intended to do. Wang Anshih and Shieh Chingwen objected and made him deputy magistrate in a near-by district; however, the Emperor changed it and appointed him deputy magistrate of the beautiful city of Hangchow. Against the charge of the censor Su Tungpo did not even bother to write a defence. He let the investigators do their work, while he proceeded with his family to Hangchow.

Chapter Nine

THE EVIL THAT MEN DO

THERE was peace at the court now, the peace of death. By the time Su Tungpo left the capital with his family, all the brilliant scholars of the famous reign of Jentsung had been disposed of and had dispersed out into the country. Ouyang Shiu was living in retirement at Fouyang in Anhuei. The great friend of the Su family, Chang Fangping, was living at Huaiyang, in Honan.

Tseyu, the year before, had been appointed a teacher in the district college at the same place. There is something curious about Tseyu; less headstrong than his brother, he had always, without compromising his integrity, nevertheless been able to look out for himself and to choose a safe and obscure position, living in the company of some great scholar. Later, when Chang Fangping retired and moved to Shangchiu, then called Nanking, or "Southern Capital", Tseyu had himself appointed to a post there also, and in the following years Su Tungpo always stopped at Chang Fangping's house on his way to and from the capital, asking and getting advice from him as from an uncle. Szema Kuang and Lu Kungchu were now to spend the following years in quiet retirement at the "Western Capital" in Loyang. Lu Huei fell ill and was about to die, but before he died, he sent a conundrum for the Emperor to solve.

"Your Majesty:

"Since my departure from the court I have fallen ill. There was really nothing wrong with me, but I had a bad doctor, and was forced to take all kinds of drastic medicines and strange prescriptions. In time I developed a paralysis of the limbs, and my movements are no longer free. But I suspect there is deeper trouble at the heart of the whole system, for I feel a revolt from within. Now the disease has developed to such a point, what can I do? Although my own person is not important and I do not mind dying, still I am mindful of the fact that I am a member of a house, entrusted with the duty toward my ancestors, and I am greatly worried about my descendants."

The good old premier Fu Pi was not yet able to live quite at peace. He had been degraded to a magistracy at Pochow, and had not been dutiful in selling the loans to the farmers. Besides, he had the audacity to write to the Emperor that "if this state of things keeps on, soon wealth will be concentrated at the top and the people will be scattered below." It was a great chance for one of Wang Anshih's men,

Dunquan, who now suddenly sprang into great activity, to serve his master. Dunquan proposed prosecuting Fu Pi for blocking reforms, and the old minister was deprived of his high ranks and transferred to another district as magistrate. But Wang was dissatisfied and said to the Emperor that Fu Pi had committed crimes similar to those committed by the Four Evil Monsters, and if he were merely deprived of his ministerial honours, how could other traitors be warned and stopped from following in his footsteps? The Emperor refused to listen to Wang's advice, and permitted Fu Pi to keep his small job. On the way to his new appointment Fu Pi passed the Southern Capital and called on Chang Fangping.

Regretfully the old premier said to Chang: "It is so difficult to know a man's character."

"You mean Wang Anshih?" replied his friend. "I did not think it was so difficult to know *him*. I once served with him on the board of a local examination and he started to upset everything. I dismissed him from my staff and never talked with him again." The old premier felt ashamed of himself. He went on his way, and in his old age he used to gaze at the roof and sigh in silence.

Just before Su Tungpo left, there was a riot at the capital. The *paochia* system had been enforced during the previous winter. Military training of the conscripted men was going on in the villages. Suspicious of this training, and thinking that the conscripts would soon be taken from their homes to fight wars with the northern tribes, the villagers near the capital staged a demonstration. The trouble also arose from the fact that the farmers were asked to provide their own military equipment, which really consisted only of bows and arrows. Fathers and sons wept together, and there were villagers who chopped off their fingers or their wrists in order to evade the draft. Through this riot Wang Anshih was to lose his last remaining friend, Han Wei, for as magistrate of the district he reported the riot and asked that the military training be delayed till late winter when the farmers would no longer be busy with their crops. For this even Han Wei was dismissed.

It took a visible demonstration of God's anger and the curious gatekeeper of the palace to put Wang Anshih out of power. In 1073 there was a landslide on the sacred mountain Huashan. Thrown into consternation, the Emperor, according to custom, moved to another palace as a sign of respect for God, and ordered poorer food to be served for his dinner. Besides, from the summer of 1073 to the spring of 1074 there had been no rain; the Emperor was deeply worried and did not know what to do. He questioned Wang Anshih about it, and the latter replied:

"Floods and droughts are natural calamities; they occurred even in the regime of the ideal emperors Yao and Tang. All we need to do is to carry on with a good government."

"That is exactly what I am afraid of," replied the Emperor, "that we have not been carrying on a good government. I hear so many complaints about the excise tax. Everybody at the court has heard about it, including the Empress and the Empress Dowager."

Another cabinet minister, Feng Ching, was present, and he said: "So have I heard also."

"Why, I've never heard anything," replied Wang Anshih. "Mr. Feng hears all about these grumblings because all the disgruntled persons flock around him."

Now the little man destined to play the big role appeared. It was Cheng Shia, the gatekeeper who had made paintings of the refugees.* Along with these paintings of the victims of the administration working in chains to cut down trees and obtain cash to pay back the government loans, he now sent a brief note to the Emperor.

"Your Majesty:

"It has been the custom after the successful completion of military campaigns to have paintings made to celebrate the victories. No one, however, has submitted to you paintings of the hardships and sufferings of the people, paintings that would show families being separated and refugees roaming over the countryside. Your servant has stood at the Anshang Gate and daily watched these scenes, and has had a panoramic picture made of them. These show only one hundredth part of what I saw, but I know that even you will shed tears when you see them. Imagine, therefore, those who see the reality in the provinces! If Your Majesty will look at these pictures and take my suggestions for abolishing reforms, if it does not rain within ten days, you can behead me on the execution ground outside the Shüanteh Gate as a punishment for lying to Your Majesty.

"Your humble servant,

"Cheng Shia"

The Emperor took the scroll of paintings to his sleeping quarters. He showed them to the Empress and other members of the royal household. It was the Emperor's grandmother† who first spoke:

"I hear that the people are suffering from the draft exemption tax and the farmers' loans. I do not think that we should change the tradition set by the ancestors."

*See page 87.

† It was the rule that when an emperor's grandmother was living, she, rather than the emperor's mother, was the empress dowager. In relation to the emperor's mother, she was mother-in-law, and in relation to the imperial household, she was the eldest. This empress dowager was the wife of Jentsung, not of Ingtsung.

"But these are for the benefit of the people and were never intended to oppress them," replied the Emperor.

"I know that Wang Anshih has great ability," said the Empress Dowager, "but he has made too many enemies. For his own good I think you had better temporarily suspend him from office."

"I find," replied the Emperor, "that among all the courtiers only Wang Anshih is willing to shoulder all the responsibilities."

The Emperor's brother, Prince Chi, was standing by. He said: "I believe you should think over what Grandmother has just said."

His Majesty flew into a rage. "All right, all right!" he cried. "I don't know how to run the government. You take over."

"I didn't mean that," said Prince Chi.

For a moment there was an awkward silence. Then the Empress Dowager said: "Wang Anshih has brought on all this trouble. What are you going to do about it?"

The next morning Wang Anshih was dismissed, although Huiching and Dunquan remained. The Emperor decided to suspend the excise tax, the farmers' loans, the draft exemption tax, the *paochia* system, and the registration of land, a total of eighteen measures in all.

It began to rain. Truly God was pleased!

But Wang Anshih's hour was not yet over. There was a technicality by which the gatekeeper was impeached. When he first submitted the scroll through the regular channels, the palace officials had refused to accept it on the ground that, as a minor official, he had no qualifications to communicate with the Emperor. Cheng, therefore, had gone to an imperial courier station outside the capital and, telling the courier that it contained urgent military business, had asked him to dispatch it immediately on horseback. On this technicality of illegal use of the courier system, Cheng Shia was tried at the censor's court.

History does not record the result of the trial. But we find that in January of the following year Cheng Shia sent up another painting album to the Emperor, entitled *The Story of Righteous and Corrupt Ministers*. It was the story of certain famous good ministers and evil geniuses of the Tang dynasty, and while no direct reference was made to the men of the present regime, the story of what these evil geniuses did in a previous dynasty bore unmistakable resemblance to the acts of the men in power. If there was any possible ambiguity, the legend in the paintings had provided against it. Along with the album, Cheng also submitted a memorial recommending a good man to be the prime minister, since Wang Anshih had already been dismissed. Huiching was now in power, and Dunquan had already switched his allegiance from Wang Anshih to him. The two, therefore, succeeded in banishing Cheng Shia to remote Kwangtung.

Before his departure a certain censor came to visit him and said: "It is wonderful of you to keep up the fight when all the censors are gagged. It almost appears that the censorate's responsibility for criticising the government has now devolved upon the shoulders of a palace gate-keeper." Thereupon the censor handed him a package of two volumes of collected reports against those in authority that had accumulated in the office of the imperial censorate, saying: "I consign these data to your care." But Huiching obtained this news through his efficient spy system, and now he sent Sudan to overtake Cheng Shia on the way and search his baggage. With the two volumes of reports which contained all the names of people who had ever criticised the administration, Huiching, Dunquan, and Sudan proceeded systematically to prosecute these critics, one by one, and put them in jail. Huiching wanted to sentence Cheng Shia to death, but was prevented by the Emperor, who said: "Cheng Shia is not thinking of himself but of the country. I admire his courage and honesty. He should not be punished too severely." So Cheng Shia was permitted to go on to his place of exile.

A certain Huang, after Su Tungpo was dead, obtained a wonderful manuscript by Su Tungpo, which contains one of his famous sayings. "It is easier to stand poverty than success, easier to stand hard work than leisure, and easier to stand a pain than an itch. If a man can take success well, be happy in leisure, and stand an itch, he must indeed be a man of great principles." Every revolutionary party shows its best strength and unity before it comes to power, but after achieving power and weeding out opposition, it begins to crumble and split from internal strife. There is no question that the desire to overthrow someone in power brings out some of the best instincts in human nature and the power to rule others brings out the worst. As long as things were going well and everybody had a good job, Dunquan and Huiching and Tseng Pu were too busy to quarrel among themselves. As soon as Wang Anshih was out of power and things began to go wrong, the gang soon fell out with one another.

Long before this happened, the seeds of internal decay had been planted. Wang Anshih's son hated Huiching and Huiching hated Tseng Pu. Dunquan, who ran with the hare and hunted with the hounds, was going to have a very busy time. Wang Anshih was un-fortunate in his one remaining son. Brilliant, erratic, and cruel, the son was responsible for many of the mischiefs of this administration.* Now that he was grown up, he had taken charge of the family's finances and his uncles could no longer have a free time with Wang Anshih's money. The arrogant son of an all-powerful premier, he

* He also suspected his wife and believed that his son was not his own. Wang persecuted his wife and she died very young.

thought he could achieve distinction by abominable manners. There is a story that once the neo-Confucianist philosopher Cheng Hao was having a conference with Wang Anshih at his home in the early days of the reform. The son appeared with dishevelled hair and bare feet and carrying a woman's scarf in his hand, walked right up to his father and asked what they were talking about.

"Why, I am discussing with Mr. Cheng the new measures which are being criticised by the other ministers," Wang replied.

The son plumped down on the mat where they were sitting and said with a laugh: "All we need to do is to cut off the heads of Han Chi and Fu Pi, and there will be no more opposition."

How much Wang was to suffer for his son we shall see soon. It was not a very pleasant household, for there were the two uncles who had all along disapproved of Wang's doings and who had particularly warned Wang against the double-crosser, Huiching. Confucius once said that one should "banish the lewd music of Cheng and keep away from the fawning flatterer." So one day when Wang Anshih was having a conference with Huiching and his brother Ankuo was playing a flute outside, the premier shouted to his brother: "Will you banish the lewd music of Cheng?" His brother shouted back: "Will you keep away from the fawning flatterer?"

Now the clique was worried about the future. Huiching, however, had not given up all hope, and he now saw his chance to rise to power in Wang's stead. There are certain people in this world who can turn on the tears at will, and Huiching and Dunquan went to the Emperor and "wept before him" in the most touching manner. The thought of what was going to happen to the country gave them great distress. With their gift of persuasion they were able to turn the Emperor back on his old course, and Huiching was made the prime minister.

Now the quarrelling really began. The trade dictator of the country, Lu Chiawen, was at this time impeached. Reports of the abuses and extortions of the trade bureau had of course reached the Emperor's ears, and he asked Wang Anshih, who was still in the capital, about the matter.

"Chiawen has always followed the official regulations rigorously, and therefore he has made many enemies. That is why he is being attacked," Wang Anshih replied.

"But," said the Emperor, "the government receives actually very little revenue from the excise tax. Besides, I don't like the idea of selling fruit and ice and coal. It is undignified for Our Imperial Government."

"Your Majesty," said Wang Anshih, "should not bother yourself about such trifles. These are things for the small officials to worry about. You should concern yourself only with the major policies of the government."

"Even so," replied the Emperor, "why is it that everybody at the court regards it as an oppressive measure?"

"Please give me the names of those persons," Wang Anshih replied.

We need not go into the details of this dirty squabble. What happened was that the trade dictator in his powerful position had begun to defy the board of finance and had insulted one Shüeh. Tseng Pu began to side with the latter and attacked the trade dictator, who was removed from office. Huiching and Tseng Pu were appointed to investigate his case. The two men had always heartily disliked each other, both being in a position relative to Wang Anshih similar to the position of Stalin and Trotsky under Lenin. In the course of the investigation Huiching began to attack Tseng Pu, and Tseng Pu began to attack Huiching, and Tseng Pu was overthrown.

This was only the beginning of the trouble. Huiching was left the sole head of the government. He not only took the occasion of Cheng Shia's case to dismiss Wang Anshih's brother Ankuo, but with the help of the ubiquitous Dunquan tried to implicate Wang Anshih himself in a local rebellion in Shantung, motivated by a prince. Wang Anshih was charged with complicity in the plot because he was a friend of one of the members of the rebellion. There was another cabinet minister, also nominally a premier, who could not get along with Huiching, and he hoped to get Wang Anshih back to the court to check Huiching. He sent a secret message to Wang Anshih, besides asking the Emperor to cashier Huiching and make Wang Anshih prime minister once more. The charge of rebellion was a serious one, and Wang made the trip from Nanking to the capital in seven days.

Wang Anshih had really nothing to do with the plotting of the rebellion, and he was again made premier in February 1075. It was a little awkward for Dunquan, who now lost no time in turning against Huiching and coming over to Wang Anshih's side. In order to bribe himself back into Wang's favour, he decided to sell out Huiching. Without the knowledge of Wang Anshih himself, Dunquan plotted with Wang's son to prosecute Huiching for extortion of 5,000,000 cash from a merchant at Huating; and the court had Huiching dismissed and appointed a magistrate. Dissatisfied with the easy escape of Huiching, Dunquan and the trade dictator, Lu Chiawen, reopened the prosecution and had Huiching detained in the prison of the imperial censorate awaiting trial.

One after another the members of the once powerful administration fell into disgrace. Dunquan was no exception. Still as energetic as ever, he had seen that Huiching had fallen and observed that the Emperor was growing tired of Wang Anshih himself. With his great genius for scheming, he thought the next men to serve would be Wang Anshih's son and son-in-law. He submitted a petition to the Emperor asking for their promotion. But both Wang Anshih and the Emperor were tired of Dunquan's turn-coat tactics, and instead of being grateful, had him dismissed from the court. Dunquan began now to "lose faith in human nature"!

It was then that Huiching, while awaiting trial, dealt the final blow to Wang Anshih. He had kept all these years some private letters of Wang for blackmail purposes, and now he submitted these to the Emperor, accusing Wang of plotting behind the Emperor's back, for several of the letter contained the words: "Do not let His Majesty know about this." The Emperor was thoroughly sick of the whole mess, and now the revelation of these private letters made him really angry with Wang for the first time. Wang scolded his son severely for recklessly attacking Huiching without his knowledge. The son evidently did not know that Huiching had kept these letters and had a secret hold on his father. Regretting his rash step, and mortified at being scolded by his father, the son fell ill and soon developed a malignant ulcer on his back. Wang Anshih had always been a believer in Buddhism. He tried monks as well as doctors, but was not able to save his son's life. Fang's death was a deep blow to the old premier. Thoroughly disillusioned politically and about human life in general, he felt tired and begged to resign. The Emperor allowed him to retire from his office in October, 1076, but retaining some of his highest ranks. He was by no means in disgrace. Years later, he was seen in the Nanking countryside, riding his donkey and mumbling to himself.

Chapter Ten

THE TWO BROTHERS

SU TUNGPO left the capital with his family in July 1071, to take up his post in the beautiful city of Hangchow on China's south-east coast. For the next eight or nine years he served successively at Hangchow, Michow near Tsingtao, and Suchow in Kiangsu. This was the period of his great activity as a poet, and he wrote beautiful songs, songs of sadness, of humour, and of anger. Innocently and with a carefree, almost childish abandon he sang of what he felt in his heart, and in the end it was these songs of sadness and of anger against the ruling authorities that brought him into trouble.

His brother Tseyu was working as a poor college professor at Chenchow, then called Huaiyang, a city lying about seventy or eighty miles to the south-east of the capital and on the direct route of Su Tungpo's journey. As he always did later, he took this opportunity to spend as much time as he could with his brother and he stayed over seventy days. His son was twelve years old and he had a baby of one year, but his brother had a big family with many children. The quiet Tseyu just kept on producing children until he had three sons and seven daughters, whom Su Tungpo helped to marry off. Su Tungpo gladly agreed with his brother's plea to stay with them until the mid-autumn festival was over. Tseyu was very poor and they were living in a small low building, and Su Tungpo used to make fun of his brother's height.

"Bending his head, he reads the classics and history,
Straightening, his solid head strikes the roof."

Their old friend Chang Fangping, the retired elderly official, was living in the same city and they had frequent wine dinners together. Chang was a great drinker, his capacity being one hundred cups. According to himself, Tungpo had a much smaller capacity, but he felt that was no reason for his abstaining from wine. Ouyang Shiu, too, was a great drinker—but Chang Fangping was able to outdrink him, for when Chang began to drink, he did not say to his guests how many cups they were going to drink, but how many days. "Yet," says Su Tungpo, "I don't envy the great drinkers. I get drunk after a couple of cups, but don't I enjoy it just as much as you people do?"

Enjoying these months of leisure and family reunion, the two brothers often went boating on Willow Lake or walking in the suburbs of the city, discussing politics, domestic affairs, and their future. One day

when they were walking together in the country and discussing the
political condition of the country, Tseyu gave his elder brother a piece
of advice. Su Tungpo's one great fault was his habit of always speaking his mind before guests or in writing. The times were bad, and
Tseyu knew his brother all too well. As he did later after Tungpo's
release from confinement, Tseyu put his hand across his mouth, which
was to tell him to keep still henceforth.

The two brothers were different in temperament and appearance.
Tseyu was taller, and had a plumper, rounder face, with plenty of loose
flesh round his cheeks, while Su Tungpo had a more muscular build,
with the right proportion of bone and muscle. As far as we can judge
from his portraits, he was about five feet seven or eight, had a big face
with very prominent cheekbones and an imposing forehead, extremely
long, brilliant eyes, a well-proportioned chin, and a beautiful, tapering,
long, mandarin beard. The most revealing was his sensitive, mobile,
full-powered lips. It was a face which flashed and glowed with human
warmth, quickly changing its expression from hearty fun to a pensive
look of thought-drunk fantasy.

"I know," said Su Tungpo to his brother, "that I am always careless of
my speech. When I feel something is wrong, it is like finding a fly in
my food, and I just have to spit it out."

"But you've got to know the people you are talking to," said his
brother. "Some people you can trust, and some you cannot."

"That's my weakness," Su Tungpo agreed. "Perhaps I am too confiding in nature. Regardless of whomever I am talking with, I like to
unburden my whole inside."

He told his brother that when he had sent the letter to the Emperor,
he was truly afraid for his life. One of his friends, he said, was also
worried. This was Chao Tuanyen,* who had come to visit him, and
who, having passed the examinations in the same year with him, was
often referred to as of the "same class", in the same sense as modern
college graduates of the same year.

"But I told Chao I had passed the special examination under Emperor
Jentsung," Su Tungpo went on, "and that I was at once regarded by the
high officials as a friend. And the Emperor had accepted my advice. If
I did not speak up now, who would? I told Chao that what I was really
afraid of was that I might be killed. Chao remained silent and looked
very grave. Then I said to him: 'It's all right. If the Emperor wants
to kill me, I shall take it without regret. But there's one thing, I don't
want to give you the pleasure of seeing me dead.' And we both
laughed."

"Do you know something?" said the younger brother. "Do you notice
that when one has a day of leisure, it seems twice as long as other days?

* Father of Chao Puchih, who became Tungpo's disciple.

Therefore, if a man can spend all his days in leisure during a life of seventy years, he will practically have lived one hundred and forty. That's an easy way of achieving long life."

While the two brothers always agreed in their political viewpoints, and had taken an identical stand in politics, their characters were really different. Tseyu was steady, practical, reserved, and given to few words; Tungpo was volatile, expansive, loquacious, naïve and inclined to disregard the consequences of his actions. Tseyu was considered dependable by his friends and associates, while Tungpo often frightened people by his outspoken genius and his fun and frivolity. Among his close associates, Tungpo bubbled, joked, and made atrocious puns. He gave the practical people of the world the nervous feeling that at any moment he might tell the truth—as if a thing's being true were enough reason for telling it!

In literary style, too, there was a difference—the difference suggested by that between Henry and William James, Tungpo being William and Tseyu being Henry. By all the indications of their separate genius, William James should have written novels and Henry James treatises on psychology and philosophy. Nevertheless, the world stands to gain by the injection of William James's brilliance and humour into the usually dull textbooks on psychology and philosophy, and by the solid structure of Henry James's thoughts and observations on human nature in the field of fiction. Tseyu had not half the brilliance of his brother, but his writings had enough substance and depth to make him a major writer on his own merit.

Tungpo knew that his brother's advice was right, and if he had had the quieter temperament of his younger brother, he would have followed it. But it was not a question of what he thought, but what he felt. It is difficult to avoid the term *ch'i* when we discuss the character of Su Tungpo, for every critic of the poet mentions this Mencian word when he comes to summarise Su Tungpo's character. *Ch'i* is a common word meaning gas, air, atmosphere, spirit, force, drive, stored-up anger. In Mencius it was a philosophic notion akin to Bergson's *élan vital*, the vital, impelling force in a human personality. What distinguished greater personalities from lesser people was often the difference in the energy, drive, dash, and vivacity of such men. In Mencian philosophy it means the great moral impetus, or, more simply, the noble spirit of man that makes for good and righteousness, a spirit inherent in all men, either nourished and grown strong or weakened as one gets along in life. In the case of Su Tungpo it was synonymous with a great spirit, the spirit of man raised to the *n*th degree, big and strong and impetuous, demanding expression by its own vitality. It was this something tremendous in his spirit, a big, booming force, that Su's critics and admirers constantly spoke of. Mencius felt this force in himself, and described it as a spirit which, when sustained by justice and truth, fears nothing in the universe.

"What do you mean by the vital spirit?" one of the disciples of Mencius once asked.

"It is very difficult to describe," Mencius replied. "This spirit is tremendous and strong. If unobstructed and properly nourished, it will fill the whole universe. But it requires for its growth the steady pursuit of the sense of justice and truth. For without the sense of justice and truth, the spirit of man withers."

Given this vital, expansive spirit so characteristic of Su Tungpo's bubbling personality, he was constantly confronted with an ethical conflict, the duty to remain himself and keep up the fearless spirit born in man, and the other equally important duty of self-preservation. At different times in Su Tungpo's career the conflict became acute and usually the duty to remain himself won. I do not think it ever was very much of a struggle for Su Tungpo. The vitality of his great genius constantly demanded free and unfettered expression.

> "Beautiful lines come and will not be denied.
> How can I alter them as favours to friends?
> The apes and wild geese cry on mountaintops,
> Unaware of passers-by in the valley below."

So Tungpo spent the mid-autumn festival with his brother's family. It was a memorable mid-autumn, one which he recalled later with fond regret, and the only one which he could spend with his brother for the next six years. The parting was hard and Tseyu decided to accompany his brother as far as Yingchow (modern Fouyang), eighty miles down the river, where they again spent over two weeks together in the company of Ouyang Shiu. Still, the parting had to come. The night before Tungpo was to sail the two brothers spent together in the boat on the Ying River, sitting up all night discussing politics and writing poems to each other. The conclusion of their discussion on politics was summed up in a poem which Su Tungpo wrote and sent to Tseyu on his arrival at Hangchow.

> "One can see that further opposition is useless,
> And to repay the Emperor's favour is beyond one's power now."

A thought by Mencius came aptly to the brothers' minds: "To expect the highest of the ruler is to show the highest respect; to guide him with good advice and keep unprincipled men away from him is in accordance with duty; but if the ruler will not take the advice, he becomes a thief to his country." In fact, they realised the full truth of what Mencius said in that whole passage:

> Goodness of heart alone is not enough to govern a country, and laws alone without good men cannot be properly enforced. . . . Therefore it is said that to reach a high position, one must go up a hill, and to go down a valley, one must follow the stream. In the governance of a nation, it would be foolhardy indeed to depart from the principles of the ancient kings. Therefore only the kind-hearted man should be appointed to a high office; for an unkind man to assume a high position is merely to reveal his wickedness to the world. When a ruler does not follow the ancient tradition, the ministers upset the law, the court has no respect for truth, and workmen no longer follow the squares and compasses; when educated people violate their own principles, and the common people violate the laws, it will be sheer good luck if such a country can continue to exist. Therefore, I say, it is not a national calamity when the city walls are not fortified and the army is not properly equipped; it is not a national calamity when the farms are not cultivated and there is no financial reserve; but when educated people lose their manners and morals and the common people are not educated, then destroyers of society will arise and the country will soon perish.

That night Su Tungpo wrote two poems which reveal his state of mind:

> "The western wind fills the boat sails
> And my parting tears drop into the Ying.
> I know it is useless to delay the parting;
> Let's make the best of the remaining hours.
> Three times have we been parted in this life,
> But this parting is the hardest of all.
> You are so much like our deceased father,
> Quiet, reticent, but inwardly strong.
> To have few words is evidence of the blessed man,
> And inward possession [kai-shek] gives wisdom and strength.
> Among all the scholars of the land,
> You were the first and quickest to resign.
> Alas, I have been like a crazy man,
> Walking straight toward an unfenced well,
> Like a drunkard who totters and tumbles,
> But luckily wakes before the fatal fall."

In the second poem he writes:

"For a short parting, I can bear it well,
But for a long parting, tears wet my breast.
When we do not see one another,
Distances great and small are all the same.
Without parting in this human life,
Who would guess how much one really cares?
When I first arrived at Huaiyang,
You tossed the children who clung to my gown.
You knew then the sorrow of parting
And asked me to stay until the autumn came.
The autumn wind has now arrived and gone,
But this remembrance will always remain.
You asked when I would be coming back,
And I said: 'It will be three years from now.'
So parting and reunion go in a cycle,
And joys and sorrows pursue our way.
Talking about this I draw a long sigh,
For my life is like a spikelet in the wind.
With many sorrows, my hair turns white early.
Say farewell to the 'Six-One Old Man.' "

"Six-One Old Man" is the literary title of Ouyang Shiu. The image of the reed flower being blown about by the wind is a fit symbol of Su Tungpo's life, for, from now on, he was to be the stormy petrel of politics and was never to remain in one place for more than three years till the end of his life.

Early at dawn the next morning the brothers said farewell. Su Tungpo's deep attachment to Tseyu was really extraordinary. Later, in a poem he wrote to one of his best friends, Li Chang, he said: "Alas, I do not have many brothers; in all the world there is only Tseyu." When his three-year term of office at Hangchow was over, he asked to be transferred to Michow, just because Tseyu was then serving at Tsinan, which was close by in the same province of Shantung.

Chapter Eleven

POETS, COURTESANS, AND MONKS

HANGCHOW, then as now, was a magic city, sometimes called "Paradise on Earth". It was to be almost like a second home to Su Tungpo, who wrote upon his arrival:

> "Come, take from time the leisure's share you will.
> Semi-retirement is retirement still.
> Where better could I settle and find a home
> Than such a place with peerless lake and hill?"

It was like a second home to him not only because of the beauty of its hills and forests and lake and sea and its busy streets and magnificent temples, but also because he was very popular with the people and spent some of his happiest days there. The people had the gaiety of the south, with its songs and its women, and they loved this young famous poet just as poet, with all his dash and verve and insouciance. His mind was inspired by the beauty of the place, and his heart was soothed by its pliant charm. Hangchow won his heart and he won the hearts of the people of Hangchow. During his term of office as an assistant magistrate he was not able to do much for the people, but for them it was enough that he was poet; when he was arrested, the common people of the city set up altars in the streets to pray for his release. After he left, the soft beauty and warmth of the south continued to haunt him in his dreams. He knew he would go back. When he went back eighteen years later as governor of the province, he did so much for the city that he left a permanent halo around his memory at Hangchow, and it claimed him as its own. Today, almost a thousand years after the poet lived and sang there, as you go on the lake or mount the top of the Kushan Island or the Phœnix Hill or have a sip at one of the lake-shore restaurants, you hear your host, who is a native of Hangchow, repeating frequently the name "Su Tungpo—Su Tungpo." If you point out that the poet came from Szechuen, he will not like it. Why, he thought Su was born here and never went anywhere else in China except to the capital!

Su Tungpo and West Lake make a perfect combination in mood, vagrant charm and love and laughter. The poetry of the region and the poetry of the poet found in each other a perfect expression. It is not an easy thing for a town to find its poet, who can discover the living, changing, complex individuality of the locality and in a verse of four lines compress and express the essence, the spirit, and the beauty of the region. In what is justly considered the best poem on West Lake, Su compared it to the beauty of the days of Mencius; a "Miss West", who was just as beautiful when she was in a morning negligée, at home and familiar, as she was in full make-up. Both clear and rainy days added their charm to the immortal lake:

> "The light of water sparkles on a sunny day;
> And misty mountains lend excitement to the rain.
> I like to compare the West Lake to 'Miss West',
> Pretty in a gay dress, and pretty in simple again."

That was of course merely a figure of speech. "Miss West" looked at any time prettier with painted eyebrows than without them. It was Su Tungpo who embellished the fringes of the lake and gave them little touches with consummate art to make them natural. Today the Su Embankment stretching across the lake, the reflections in water of the enchanted isle, called "Three Ponds Reflecting the Same Moon", and the willow-fringed shore line bear testimony to his skill as a landscape architect. The West Lake of Hangchow and the "Little West Lake" of Yangchow are two places where the profound landscaping genius of China found perfect expression, where human art and skill improve but do not spoil. The artist first seized the natural design of the locality and saw it as a whole in its natural structure and composition. He merely added a few touches to tighten or smooth out, or to emphasise a contour here and there, and nothing more.

Su Tungpo arrived at Hangchow with his wife and children on November 28, 1071. The residences of the magistrates were situated on top of the Phœnix Hill, enjoying a full view of the Chientang River with its great fleet of seafaring ships on the south, and the West Lake, surrounded by cloud-capped mountains, dotted with temples and rich men's villas, on the north, while the waves of the bay lashed its shores on its east. There were two deputy magistrates at Hangchow besides the chief magistrate, for Hangchow was a big metropolitan city. The Su family occupied a building on the north side of the compound, which was the lake side. Immediately below the Phœnix Hill, and lying on a strip running north and south between West Lake and the Chientang Bay, was the city itself with its high walls, its bridges and canals. Mrs. Su was transported when she opened the window in the morning and saw beneath her the beautiful placid surface of the lake reflecting moving clouds and mountain-tops and villas. Before the day was well advanced, pleasure-seekers' boats filled the lake, and at night from their house on the hill she could hear the sound of flutes and songs. Certain sections of the city were more brilliantly illuminated than others, for there were fairs open every night until two or three in the morning. For the wife, particularly, there was an exciting variety of fancy foods, silks, embroideries, and fans, and for the children a great variety of candies and toys and rotating lanterns. The candy sellers of Hangchow in Sung times resorted to strange advertising tactics to attract the attention of the public. There were candy sellers who sold their wares on the roulette principle, others who dressed as white-bearded old men, and those who wore masks and danced and sang. Some sold candy floss, some blew candies into shapes of different animals, and some made "sand sugar", which is like maple candy. There is a book about the city life of Hangchow written at the end of the Sung dynasty about a hundred years after Su Tungpo and a hundred years before Marco Polo visited it, giving fascinating details of the streets, canals, the lake, the foodstuffs and popular amusements, and providing a more detailed picture of the city life of those times than is made in Marco Polo's description of the city. While Marco Polo mentioned the hunting of princes and the bathing of princesses on the lake shore and the great merchant fleets that plied between Hangchow ("Kinsai") and Chuanchow ("Zayton"), he was not familiar with the names of the sweetmeats, fancy bakery, and popular amusements. The long and almost old-womanish lists of fancy delicatessen food recounted again and again on the pages of this book by Wu Tsemu can drive any reader crazy.

Su Tungpo half believed that he had lived here in his previous incarnation. This is recorded in his own poems and in the journals of contemporaries. One day he was visiting the Shoushing Temple, and the moment he entered the gate he felt the scene was very familiar. He told his companions that he knew there were ninety-two steps leading up to the Penance Hall, which they found to be correct. He could also describe to his companions the buildings, court-yards, and trees and rocks at the back of the temple. We do not have to believe these stories of reincarnation, but when society believes in ghosts or in reincarnation, there are always many such first-hand stories and, like ghost stories, they cannot be conclusively proved or disproved. In Su Tungpo's time the belief in a person's previous existence was general and such stories were not uncommon. There was a story about the previous existence of Chang Fangping. One day he was visiting a temple and told people that he remembered he had been abbot at this place in a previous life. Pointing upstairs, he said that he recalled being occupied in copying a certain Buddhist classic in the attic, a work which was left unfinished. He and his friends went upstairs and found indeed an unfinished manuscript in a handwriting bearing a striking resemblance to Chang's writing. He took up his brush and began to copy from where he was supposed to have left off in his previous life. There was also the story told of one of Su Tungpo's best friends. Huang Tingchien, the great poet, told people that in his previous life he had been a girl. He suffered from body odour in one of his armpits. One night when he was magistrate at Fouchow, a little below Chungking in Szechuen, a girl appeared in his dream and said to him: "I am your previous self and I am buried in a certain place. The coffin is decayed and on the left side there is a big ant nest. Please have it removed for me." Huang did so, and the body odour in his left armpit disappeared thereafter.

As an assistant magistrate Su had no great responsibilities except presiding at court trials. This was something he heartily disliked, knowing that the people who had been arrested were chiefly those who had violated laws of the new regime, laws that he disapproved. Yet there was the law and he could not alter it. It is perhaps easiest to understand the mind and heart of Su Tungpo at this period by reading the poem he wrote on New Year's Eve when he had to try prisoners arrested for salt smuggling. The government monopoly had taken over the trade in salt, but the traders in the salt-producing area around Hangchow Bay refused to be driven out of business. The complete situation of salt smuggling was embodied in a letter by Su Tungpo to a cabinet minister. We are not concerned here with the objective conditions, but rather with the poet's attitude towards his fellow-men, for he saw no difference between himself and those on trial.

> "On New Year's Eve, I should go home early,
> But am by official duties detained.
> With tears in my eyes I hold my brush,
> And feel sorry for those in chains.
> The poor are trying to make their living,
> But fall into the clutches of the law.
> I, too, cling to an official job,
> And carry on against my wish for rest.
> What difference is there between myself
> And those more ignorant than I?
> Who can set them free for the time being?
> Silently I bow my head in shame." *

To Tseyu he wrote more intimately: "There are certain things which used to shame me, but of which I am no longer ashamed now. I sit facing the ragged prisoners and witness their flogging. When I talked with my superiors, my mouth said 'yes' but my heart said 'no'. What is the use of occupying a high position, while degrading one's character? My vital spirit has shrunk and withered, no longer what it used to be."

In another poem he spoke about the sufferings of the people under the *paochia* system, and described how the people screamed when they were whipped, and how even men's wives and children were put in jail.

* A facsimile of the original of this poem in the poet's own handwriting is reproduced in the beginning of this book.

It was the steady accumulation of lines like these which later, when he was arrested and tried, established his guilt as one trying to destroy confidence in the regime.

Meanwhile he enjoyed himself when and where he could. He tried to escape to nature, and nature was there at its best at his feet. His poetic spirit feasted upon the beauties of the neighbourhood. For not only the city itself and West Lake, but all the mountains within ten or fifteen miles of Hangchow became his favourite haunts. Starting from West Lake, the traveller could go in all directions, either following the north bank to the famous Lingyin Temple and reaching the top of Tienchu, or starting from the south bank, he could go to Kehling, stop over at Hupao, famous for its spring water, have his tea there, and return by following a beautiful winding mountain brook. In the city and the suburbs there were three hundred and sixty temples, usually on mountain-tops, where he could while away a whole afternoon chatting with the monks. An outing to these hills usually took a whole day, and he reached home late at twilight, when the street lights were already on. Passing the crowded and illuminated night fair at Shahotang, he would come home drowsy and half drunk, thinking up poetic lines and forgetting half of them.

"Suddenly rubbing my sleepy eyes,
I saw the brilliant lights of Hotang.
The milling people were clapping their hands,
And frolicking like young deer in the wilds.
I realised then that the simple joys of life
Could be enjoyed only by the simple men.
What is happiness in human life?
My ways, I fear, are all wrong."

Hangchow was gay and West Lake was enticing. The southern climate invited one to spend one's time outdoors in all seasons. In spring and autumn all Hangchow played on the lake. Even in winter on a snowy day there were pleasure-seekers who went out in boats to enjoy the landscape in snow. Particularly on great festivals, like the third day of the third moon, the fifth day of the fifth moon, the mid-autumn festival, the ninth day of the ninth moon and the birthday of a local god, the eleventh day of the second moon, the lake was filled with holiday-makers, and one had to engage a boat on the previous day. It was not necessary to bring food along because everything, including cups, saucers, spoons, and chopsticks, was provided by the boatmen. There were also boatmen who caught fish and sold them to people who could put them into the water again as a way of "accumulating merit" or laying up treasure in heaven for having saved living creatures, according to Buddhist teachings. It was quite possible that one and the same fish could save three lives from Hell, if he were caught three times and loosed three times.

Su Tungpo participated fully in the life on the lake. There were two kinds of parties, families enjoying themselves and others with sing-song, women. The lake was a place where the wives looked at the sing-song women with fear, and the sing-song women looked at the wives with envy. The sing-song women wished from the bottom of their hearts that they could be "liberated" and have homes of their own with growing children around them, like those wives. Su Tungpo sometimes went with his wife and children, and sometimes with his drinking official friends. He was versatile. He had at his command a pen which could produce such skilful, ornate, and technically excellent lines that they compelled admiration from fellow scholars, and he could write simple effortless lines that stuck in one's memory. With his family, he could sing:

> "The sound of chopping fish comes from the bow,
> And the fragrance of cooking rice issues from the stern."

With his fellow officials he wrote lines that delighted them in their gaiety:

> "The pleasure boats with oars of Wu have been painted,
> The dancing dress of new Yueh gauze is first being tried."

As soon as they arrived at the lake shore, the boatmen crowded around them and each asked them to take his boat. They would choose a small one, seating four or five people, or sometimes when there was a bigger party, one large enough to set a dinner-table in, and have food prepared by the boatwoman, who was usually an expert cook. These houseboats were elaborately carved and had gargoyles at the bows. On the lake there were other boats catering to the holiday-makers. Some boatmen sold chestnuts, melon seeds, stuffed lotus roots, sweetmeats, roast chicken, and fresh sea-food. Other boatwomen specialised in serving tea. Some boats carried entertainers who customarily drew up to the tourists' boats and entertained them with songs, light acrobatics, and provided slings and other shooting games.

Around them all lay the clear blue waters of the lake with a circumference of about ten miles, and in the distance beyond, clouds nestled against the mountain-tops, half concealing and half revealing them. The clouds gave variety to the mountains by lending them a changing shape, and the mountains housed the clouds by providing them a home of rest. Sometimes the air felt as if it were going to snow, and a low haze covered the foothills. Behind the haze, the pleasure-seekers could see here and there glimpses of pagodas and towers and catch the faint outlines of the distant hills. Or on a sunny day, the water was so clear they could count the fish in the water. In two delightful lines Su Tungpo gave an impressionistic colour picture of the boatmen's yellow turbans moving against the background of the green hills.

"Against the hills yellows turbans bob on gargoyle-head boats.
Along the streets blue smoke rises from sparrow-tail lamps."

Going ashore towards the mountains, they could hear the birds calling to one another in the deserted woods. A lover of travel, Su often roamed alone over the mountains, and scribbled poems on the rocks at the highest mountain-tops or near the head streams seldom visited by other tourists. He became a great friend of the monks in the temples, which he frequently visited. An old monk told the story after Su Tungpo's death that when he was a young boy serving at Shoushing Temple, he used to see Su come up the hill on foot alone on a summer day. There he would borrow a monk's couch and move it to a selected place under the near-by bamboo grove. Totally devoid of any sense of official dignity, he took off his jacket and shirt and slept bare-backed on the couch during an afternoon. The young acolyte peeped at the great scholar from a respectful distance, and saw something that nobody had been privileged to see. He saw, or thought he saw, seven black moles on the poet's back, arranged like the constellation of the Dipper. And that, the old monk said, was an evidence that he was a spirit sent down from the heavenly sphere to live merely as a temporary guest in this human world.

In a poem which he sent to Chao Tuanyen after he left Hangchow, Su Tungpo made a good summary of his habit of travel. Chao was going then to Hangchow as a commissioner, and Su Tungpo advised him what to do.

"The landscape of West Lake tops the world.
Tourists of all classes, intelligent and otherwise,
Find and appreciate each what he wants.
But who is there that can comprehend the whole?
Alas, in my stupid honesty,
I have long been left behind by the world.
I gave myself completely to the joys of hills and water—
Is it not all determined by God's Will?

Around the three hundred sixty temples,
I roamed throughout the year.
I knew the beauty of each particular spot,
Felt it in my heart but could not say it in my mouth.
Even now in my sweet sleep,
Its charm and beauty remain in my eyes and ears.
Now you come as a commissioner;
Your official pomp will insult the clouds and haze.
How can the clear streams and the purple cliffs
Reveal their beauties to you?
Why not dismiss your retinue
And borrow a couch from the monk,
Read the poems I inscribed on the rocks,
And let the cool mountain air soothe your troubled soul?
Carry a cane and go where you like,
And stop wherever seems to you best.
You'll find some ancient fishermen
Somewhere among the reeds. Talk with them,
And if they say wise things to you,
Buy fish from them and argue not about the price."

It seems from the literary records that Su Tungpo's preoccupation at Hangchow was with religion and women, or rather with monks and courtesans, and the two are more closely related than we think. In Su Tungpo the life of the senses and the life of the spirit were one, co-existing without conflict in a poetic-philosophical view of human life. With his poetry, he loved this life too passionately to become an ascetic or a monk, and with his philosophy, he was too wise to give himself up to the "devil". He could no more renounce women and song and pork and wine than he could renounce the blue waters and the purple mountain-sides, and at the same time he was far too profound to put on the garb of a shallow, cynical fop.

The best illustration of the attitude of the young and fun-loving poet is the story of how he tried to bring an austere priest and a courtesan together. Abbot Tatung was a severe old man of saintly character, and it was said that people who wanted to see him in his retreat had to take a ceremonial bath. Women were of course forbidden his chamber. Su Tungpo was one day visiting the temple with a party in the company of a show-girl. Knowing the priest's habits, the party stopped outside. Su knew the old priest well and felt a devilish urge to bring the woman in and break his monastic rules. When he went in with the show-girl to pay their respects to the old abbot, the latter was visibly displeased at the young man's impudence. Su said he would write a song of apology and make the show-girl Miaochi sing it, if the abbot would permit her to borrow the clapper used for beating time during the singing of litany. So Tungpo gave the girl these lines to sing:

> "Holy Father, I do not know what to say,
> Being not conversant with your way.
> May I borrow the door rapper and litany clapper?
> Kindly take this in a spirit of fun.
> A maiden's stolen glance should cast no blemish,
> Please, Your Reverence, be not so squeamish.
> For if you were my age, I might be all your rage..
> As it is, no harm is done."

It was strictly a one-man comic opera, and even the austere Tatung laughed. Su Tungpo came out with the girl and boasted to the others that they had learned a great "lesson in the mysteries".

It is not possible to separate monks from women, at least not in Chinese literature. The stories of monks are often stories of women and the stories of women are often stories of monks. For East and West, there is a secret grudge among lay people against a special class of celibates who announce to the world that they have no sex life and are different from the generality of mankind, and it is this secret grudge against celibates that underlies the popularity of the stories of Boccaccio. Besides, a monk's affairs with women make a better story than a business-man's.

As a judge, Su Tungpo had once to adjudicate a case involving a monk. There was a monastic brother at the Lingyin Temple, by the name of Liaojan, who frequented the red-light district and fell madly in love with a girl named Shiunu. In time he spent all his money and was reduced to rags, and Shiunu refused to see him any more. One night in a drunken fit he went to call on the girl again, and being refused admittance, he forced his way in, beat the girl, and killed her. The monk was therefore being tried for murder. In examining him the officers found on his arm a tattooed couplet: "May we be born together in Paradise, and not suffer the love pangs of this life!" After the completion of the investigation the evidence was submitted to Su Tungpo. Su could not resist writing the sentence in the form of a light verse:

> "Away from here, you bald-head daisy!
> In vain you took the vow of celibacy,
> Reduced yourself to this ragged shape
> By your unmonkish profligacy.
> By your cruel fists you killed your love.

What's illusion now, and what reality?
Your arm bears witness to love's longing,
This time you shall pay love's penalty."

The monk was sent to the execution ground and beheaded. Comic poems, such as the two above, written in the language of the day, quickly passed from mouth to mouth and added to the current gossip about this eccentric genius.

Among such stories there was a small collection of tales about Su Tungpo and his friend the pleasure-loving monk Foyin. At this period Su Tungpo had not taken up Buddhism seriously; it was only after he was forty, during his period at Huangchow, that he began an intensive study of Buddhist philosophy. But some of the monks of Hangchow became his best friends, and in time he gathered more and more friends among the monks of Chinkiang, Nanking, and Lushan as well. Among them, two at least, Huichin and Tsanliao, were poets and scholars worthy of respect. From the literary records, Foyin was not important. But he cut a romantic figure, and in popular literature he, rather than Tsanliao, became most frequently talked about as the friend of Su Tungpo.

Foyin had never intended to be a monk. Furthermore, he came from a wealthy family. According to one curious story, he was born of the same mother as Leeding. Apparently the woman was a loose character and had married three times, having three sons by three different husbands—quite a record in those days. When the Emperor gave an audience to Buddhist believers as a gesture towards Buddhism, Su Tungpo presented this man at court. Foyin tried to impress the Emperor with his ardent conviction in the Buddhist faith. The Emperor looked at him and saw a tall, handsome man with an unusual face, and graciously said that he would be glad to give a monetary grant, the so-called *tutieh*, to endow him in a monastery if he would join the church. Finding himself in a quandary, he could not but accept the Emperor's suggestion, and thus he had to enter a religious order. While he was living in Hangchow, legend says he used to travel with a whole retinue of servants and pack-mules, in a far from ascetic way of life.

Foyin was quite a wit. One of the better stories with a philosophic point told about these two men runs as follows. Su Tungpo was one day visiting a temple with Foyin. Entering the front temple, they saw two fierce-looking giant idols who were conceived as conquerors of the evil spirits and were placed there to guard the entrance.

"Of these two buddhas," asked Su Tungpo, "which is the more important?"

"The one who has a big fist, of course," replied Foyin.

Going into the inner temple, they saw the image of the Goddess of Mercy holding a rosary in her hand.

"Since the Goddess of Mercy is a buddha herself, what is she doing there telling the beads?" asked Su Tungpo.

"Oh," replied Foyin. "she is only praying to buddha like all the others."

"But which buddha?" asked Su Tungpo again.

"Why, the buddha, the Goddess of Mercy herself."

"Now what's the meaning of that? She is the Goddess of Mercy; why does she pray to herself?"

"Well," said Foyin, "you know it's always troublesome to beg from others—it is always easier to depend on oneself."*

They saw then a Buddhist prayer-book lying open on the altar. Su Tungpo found that a prayer read thus:

"A curse upon all poisons!
By the help of the Goddess of Mercy,
May those who use poison on others
Take the poison themselves."

"This is utterly unreasonable," said Su Tungpo. "Buddha is kind. How can she be expected to avert trouble from one person in order to give it to another? If that is so, then Buddha is not Love."

Asking permission to have the prayer corrected, he took up a brush and crossed out some of the lines to make it read:

"A curse upon all poisons!
By the help of the Goddess of Mercy,
May both the users of poison
And the intended victims be spared."

Many of the stories of clever repartee between Su Tungpo and Foyin were based on puns and are untranslatable. There is, however, the following.

The word "bird" had a dirty meaning in Chinese slang, and Su Tungpo thought to make fun of his friend with it. "The ancient poets," said Su Tungpo, "often placed *monks* opposite *birds* in a couplet. For instance, there is a couplet: 'Hearing a *bird* pecking at a tree, I thought it was a *monk* knocking at the door.' Again, another couplet says: '*Birds* perch on trees beside the pond, and a *monk* knocks at the gate under the moon.' I always admire the wisdom of the ancient poets in placing monks against birds."

"That is why," said Foyin, "I, as a monk, am sitting opposite you."

* The original word *chiu* means both "to beg" and "to depend."

These stories always show the monk as outwitting the poet. I have a suspicion that Foyin himself was the author of the stories.

The institution of courtesans in China dated back, according to known records, to Kuan Chung in the seventh century B.C., who regularised it in order to entertain soldiers. Even in Su Tungpo's time, there were state-owned courtesans, who continued to be known as "barracks entertainers", and others who were independent But a peculiar tradition had developed so that the higher-class courtesans, as distinguished from the common prostitutes, made their mark on literary history, some by being poets themselves, and some by being closely associated with the lives of the literary men. As a class, they were closely connected with the history of song and music and therefore with the changing forms of poetry. After a period of servile imitation at the hands of the scholars, when poetry had become no more than a string of outworn clichés, it was always the courtesans who introduced new forms and gave poetry a new lease of life. Music and song were their special domain. Inasmuch as the playing of musical instruments and singing were deprecated among family girls, the songs also tended to concentrate almost entirely on love and passion, which in turn was considered detrimental to the virtue of adolescent girls. The result was, the tradition of music and dance was carried through the centuries almost entirely by the courtesans.

In the life of the times of Su Tungpo, mixing with courtesans at wine dinners and official functions was a part of an official's life. No more opprobrium was attached to it than to the presence of Aspasia at men's parties in the time of Socrates. The courtesans were entertainers who poured wine for the guests and sang for the company. Many of them were gifted, and those who understood reading and writing and were accomplished in music and song were very much sought after by the scholars. Because women were excluded from the social parties of men, the desire for female company made the men seek gaiety in the company of the professional artists. Sometimes the flirtations were innocent, carried on in the teasing, suggestive atmosphere of a modern night-club, with the courtesans singing light, sophisticated, and genuine or fake songs of love, and making concealed or brazen insinuations about sex. The higher-class courtesans resembled the modern night-club artist also in that they had complete freedom to choose their men friends, and some had fabulous establishments of their own. Emperor Huitsung was known to leave his palace and woo such a courtesan at her home. However, the attitude towards courtesans was much more lax than it is today. The poets of Manhattan do not write love poems to chorus girls, at least do not publish them, but the poets of Hangchow did. The practice of writing poems in honour of certain courtesans was quite common, even among highly respected gentlemen. In this period we find that not only Han Chi and Ouyang Shiu left poems about courtesans, but even the austere premiers Fan Chungyen and Szema Kuang wrote this type of sentimental poetry. The great patriot general, Yo Fei, also wrote a poem concerning female singers at a certain dinner.

Only the strict, puritanical neo-Confucianists, whose code of life was summed up in the one word *ching* ("reverence", an equivalent of "fear of God"), highly disapproved. They had a more stringent code of morals, and a greater respect for the devil. Cheng Yi, who was Su Tungpo's political enemy, used to warn Emperor Tsehtsung, when the latter was only a child of twelve, about the lascivious charm of women. The young child was so sick of such warnings that when he reached eighteen, one woman alone convinced him that she was right and the puritan was wrong. Once one of Cheng Yi's disciples wrote two lines on his "dreaming soul going out of bounds" and visiting a woman in his sleep, and Cheng Yi cried in horror: "Devil's talk! Devil's talk!" Chu Shi, the great neo-Confucianist of the twelfth century, had the same horror of the seductive power of women. Once a good man, Hu Chuan, wrote two lines on the occasion of his pardon after ten years of exile: "For once let me get drunk to celebrate the pardon, with a girl's sweet dimpled face by my side." Chu Shi was moved to express himself as follows:

"Despite ten years' exile and tribulation,
The sight of a dimple caught him unaware.
Nothing should be more feared than this damnation.
How many lives are wrecked by woman's snare!"

In contrast, Su Tungpo took a more humorous view of sex. In his *Journal* he wrote, later, at Huangchow:

"Yesterday I went to Ankuo Temple with chief magistrate Tang Chuntsai and deputy magistrate Chang Kungkwei, and in the conversation we talked about the art of prolonging life. I said: 'All is easy except continence.' Mr. Chang said: 'Su Wu was a great man. He went to Mongolia, lived like a Mongolian, and went through all hardships without a grumble. He was quite a philosopher, wasn't he? Yet he could not help marrying a Mongolian woman and having children by her. It must be, therefore, more difficult to practice continence even in marriage. This thing is really difficult to overcome.' We all laughed at the remark. I am putting this down because there is a lot of sense in it."

All his life Su Tungpo took part at courtesans' dinners, and nine times out of ten had to write poems on shawls or fans by request of the entertainers.

"Oh, hush the night, each minute an ounce of gold,
While faintly floats the music of flute and song.
So fragrant the air, so cool the moonlit courtyard,
While darkly glides the silent night along."

Su wrote many sentimental poems about women, but he never wrote erotic poetry, as his friend Huang Tingchien did.

The Sung courtesans had popularised a new form of poetry, the *tse,* and Su Tungpo mastered it and transformed it from a metre for sentimental poetry of the lovelorn into a vehicle fit to express any thought or sentiment in his breast. One of his best *tse* was on the "Red Cliff", whose theme was the passing of great ancient warriors. Li Po and Tu Fu had sung three centuries earlier, and by their genius had made the Tang quatrain and double quatrain the regular verse patterns for a distinguished host of imitators. But these quatrain forms, uniformly of five or seven words to the line, with the inevitable two couplets in the middle, had become stereotyped. Every poet tried to evolve a new style. But the last nuance in observation of a waterfall or an egret or the shadows of willow trees had been discovered, and somehow the richness and emotional intensity of the Tang poets were gone. What was more serious, even poetic diction had become a repetition of hackneyed metaphors. Some of them were bad in themselves to begin with. Su Tungpo wrote in a preface to one of his poems on snow that he was determined not to use the word salt. After all, snow was a better word. The themes of Tang poetry had been overplayed, and the language too often deliberately harked back to lines by other poets, giving a secret delight to the learned reader who knew where that particular twist of thought and expression came from. It was the tracing of the expressions to their obscure sources that gave the greatest opportunity for the "commentators" to display their pedantry. As a rule, writers of the so-called commentaries on collected poems did not consider it part of their duty to elucidate the meaning or judge the quality of the poem, but contented themselves with pointing out the source of a particular expression.

The liberation of poetry from decadent inertia always came from the growth of a new form of poems popularised by the courtesans. The language was fresh and new, the Sung *tse* was closer to the vernacular than Tang poems, and the later Yüan drama was still closer to the vernacular than Sung *tse.* The *tse* was nothing but a song written to a given piece of music. People did not "write" *tse,* they "filled in"

the words to a known melody. Instead of lines of a uniform number
of syllables of Tang "regulated verse", there was a rich variety of
long and short lines, strictly conforming to the requirements of the
song.

In the time of Su Tungpo this new form of poetry was at the height
of its popularity. Through Su Tungpo, Chin Kuan, Huang Tingchien
and others of his generation, like Yen Chitao and Chou Pangyen, it
became *the* poetry of the dynasty. Su Tungpo, discovered it in Hangchow, fell it love with it, and from his second year in Hangchow
began to write a great number of verses in the metres of the songs. But
the *tse* had been strictly a form for sentimental love verse. Such poems
invariably sang of "fragrant perspiration", "gauze curtains", "dis-
ordered hair", the "spring night", "warm jade", "sloping shoulders", a
"willowy waist", "tapering fingers", etc. When and where such sentimental poetry bordered on the licentious depended entirely on the
poet's handling of the material. The difference between passion and
love is as difficult to establish in poetry as in real life. Invariably also,
like modern cabaret artists, the poets preferred to sing of heartbreak
and the pangs of love and the longing of the unrequited lover. They
sang of a woman secluded in her chamber, sadly longing for the absent
one, fondling her belt silently, or keeping lone company with the
candlelight. In fact, the whole feminine appeal was built around
woman's helplessness, her sallow cheeks, her silent tears, her *ennui*,
insomnia, "broken intestines", lost appetite, general lassitude, and every
form of physical and mental misery, which, like poverty, sounds poetic.
It would seem the word *suyung*, "lassitude", was almost voluptuous.
Su Tungpo not only became one of the acknowledged few great *tse*
masters of this dynasty; it was to his credit that he freed it, in his own
practise at least, from sentimental drivel.

There is no record that Su Tungpo became enamoured of any of the
courtesans. He enjoyed the gay parties and "fooled around" with
women enough to be a "good fellow", not enough to take a mistress.
Two of the women were especially close to the poet. Chintsao, a gifted
courtesan, was persuaded by him to free herself and become a nun.
Chaoyun, who became later his concubine, was then a girl of twelve.
We shall come to her later.

Today there is a Sung rubbing of a stone inscription in the handwriting of Su Tungpo which records a poem written by a courtesan.
It is called "The Dark Clouds Script" from the first words of a poem.
It tells the story that once a state-owned courtesan, Chou Shao, was
present at a dinner. She used to hold tea contests with the great tea
connoisseur and calligraphist Tsai Shiang, and won them. When Su
Sung passed through the town, the chief magistrate Chen Shiang gave
him a party with Chou Shao present. During the party Miss Chou

begged to be released from her profession, and the guest asked her to write a quatrain. The courtesan wrote the following, comparing herself to a caged parrot (the "snow-dress maiden").

> "See her turn her head and her sad feathers preen,
> Dreaming of her old nest where a home had been.
> Open the cage and set the snow-dress maiden free!
> She will say her whole life, 'Blessed be Kuanyin!' "

The other scholars also wrote poems about the occasion. Su Tungpo adds that the woman was then wearing white in mourning. Everybody was touched and she was released.

An official life such as this demanded a great deal of trust and understanding from the wives of the officials. However, the problem of being a good wife is principally the problem of finding a good husband, and conversely the problem of being a good husband is principally the problem of finding a good wife. Having a good wife is the best guarantee against a husband's going wrong. Mrs. Su knew she had married a popular poet and a genius, and she certainly did not try to compete with him in literary honours. She had made up her mind that her best job was to be a wife, a good one. She had now two babies of her own, and as wife of a deputy-magistrate she had a comfortable home and enjoyed certain social honours. She was still very young, between twenty-three and twenty-five. Her husband was brilliant, big-hearted, fun-loving, and—what a scholar! But he had so many admirers, men and women! Did she not see those women on the south side of the compound and those dinners at Wanghulou (Lakeview House) and Yumeitang? The new chief magistrate, Chen Shiang, a good scholar who arrived the year after them, certainly attended to a magistrate's social duties well, and the state courtesans were at their beck and call. There were Chou (Pin) and Lu (Shaoching), not really desirable company for her husband. The courtesans were accomplished, could sing and play stringed instruments, and some of them could write verse. She herself could not versify, but she understood these songs. They were growing familiar to her, for she heard her husband humming them. She would die of shame to sing them, for no respectable lady would. She felt really much more comfortable when her husband went to see the bare-footed monks, Huichin, Pientsai, and others, those old men with their adorable long beards.

It took her some years to know the depth of his character, a character with so many facets, so easy-going and yet at times so intense and strong-willed. She had learned by now one thing, that he could not be influenced, and certainly there was no way of arguing with him. On the other hand, if he wrote poems to courtesans, what of it? He was expected to. He had not taken fancy to any of the professional artists, and she had heard he had even converted one of the most famous courtesans, Chintsao, to become a nun. Chintsao had really remarkable intelligence, and from poetry to religion was only a short step. He really should not have quoted Po Chuyi's lines about the end of a courtesan's life to Chintsao. With her good sense and tact, Mrs. Su was not going to push her husband into a courtesan's lap the wrong way. Besides, she knew her husband was a man not to be stopped by wife or emperor. She did the smart thing—she trusted him.

As daughter of a *chinshih* scholar, she could read and write, but she was not an "intellectual". Instead she cooked the Meichow dishes and ginger tea that he loved. And how he needed attention when he was ill! If poet husbands sometimes were unusual, that was their privilege. The husband knew there were books to be read, thousands of them, and the wife knew there was a home to be built, children to be brought up, a life to be lived. For that, she was willing to put up with his famous snore in bed—especially when he was drunk.

Apart from that, he was certainly a curious man for a bedfellow. She must not disturb him in bed when she lay awake listening to his snoring. Before he fell asleep, he was fussy about tucking himself in properly. He would turn about and arrange his body and limbs and pat the sheet until he was well-placed and nice and cosy. If any part of his body was stiff or itchy, he would gently rub and massage it. But after that, order was established. He was going to sleep. He closed his eyes and "listened" to his respiration, making sure that it was slow and even. "And then I lie perfectly still," he said to himself. "Even when some part of my body itches, I do not make the slightest move, but overcome it by will-power and concentration. Thus, after a short while, I feel relaxed and comfortable down to the toes. A state of drowsiness sets in and I fall into sound sleep."

This really had something to do with religion, Su claims. The freedom of the soul does depend so much upon the freedom of the body. Unless one controls one's mind and body, one cannot control one's soul. This was to be a great part of Su Tungpo's occupation. After describing his way of sleeping to his two disciples, he continued: "Try my method, and you will find how good it is, but don't tell it to everybody. Remember this, wisdom comes from self-control. The awakening of the divine spark in men and knowledge of buddhahood begin with self-discipline. No one who does not achieve control of his mind can ever understand God."

Later Mrs. Su was to discover more variations of her husband's habits at night and dawn. Combing his hair with a fine comb and taking a bath were among the important occupations of the poet's life. For if there was one man in that period thoroughly devoted to speculation about the body and its internal functions and the study of medicinal herbs and teas, it was Su Tungpo.

She was sane and she was steady, which a poet usually is not. Her husband was often impatient, despondent, and moody. In contrast, Mrs. Su once said on a moonlight night in spring: "I like the spring moon much better. The autumn moon makes one too sad, while the spring moon makes everybody happy and contented." A few years later, at Michow, when they were very poor and Su Tungpo was greatly angered at the introduction of the new income tax, he was once annoyed by his children tugging at his gown and bothering him.

"The children are so silly," said Su.

"You are the silly one," replied his wife. "What good will it do you to sit around and brood the whole day? Come, I will make you a drink."

In a poem recording this incident, the poet said that he felt ashamed of himself, and the wife began to clean the cups and prepare warm wine for him. This, of course, made him very happy and he said that she was much better than the wife of the poet Liu Ling, who asked her husband not to drink.

But there was one corner of Su's heart, hidden from most, which Mrs. Su must have known about. That was his first love for his cousin, who to us, unfortunately, is nameless. Being the confiding soul he always was, Su Tungpo must have told his wife about it. His deep affection for the cousin afterwards lay buried in two poems that passed unnoticed by all students of the poet's works.

Su Tungpo did not stay all the time at Hangchow but took frequent trips south-west, west, and north. From November 1073 to March 1074, he went up to the neighbourhood of Shanghai, Kiashing, Changchow, and Chinkiang, which in the Sung dynasty were parts of the province of Chekiang. His cousin-sister was now married to Liu Chungyuan and living in the neighbourhood of Chinkiang. He remained in his cousin's home for three months, and although he versified a tremendous lot on this trip and wrote and travelled constantly in the company of his cousin's father-in-law, Liu Chin, he never once mentioned his cousin's husband or wrote a poem to him. He also wrote a poem about a family dinner at his cousin's home, and two poems on calligraphy to his cousin's two boys when they came to ask for his autograph. Su Tungpo had great respect for Liu Chin as a poet and as a calligraphist, and also thought a lot of his cousin's children. But the complete silence about the cousin's husband during this trip is hard to explain.

Two poems, written during this trip, suggest this special relationship with his cousin. One was a poem he wrote to Tiao Yueh, and the subject was declared to be reminiscent of a certain flower he had seen at the palace. It contained the following two lines:

> "Tired of seeking new beauties in the company of youth,
> I sit facing the palace flower and recognise its old fragrance."

He was not exactly sitting opposite that flower at that moment, for he was not in the palace. He was obviously describing himself when he said he was tired of youth's company; and as "flower" was the regular symbol for woman, the "old fragrance" could be a reference to an old love.

The reference is clearer in another poem, one he wrote to the chief magistrate of Hangchow, Chen Shiang. The subject stated was that by returning so late in spring he had missed the flowering season of the peony. (Titles of poems indicating the occasions were sometimes quite long.) It was true that by the time of his return to Hangchow the peony season would be over. Nevertheless, the references to a girl now married and become a mother are unmistakable, and there was no reason why in a poem on peonies he should make two clear references to belated courtship. In order to understand the references, it must be explained that there was a girl in the ninth century who wrote the following poem at the age of fifteen:

> "Spare not, my friend, the gold-embroidered gown,
> Miss not the years of youth—enjoy them now.
> Come, pluck the flower while to pluck is good,
> Wait not until you pluck the empty bough."

To "pluck the empty bough" was therefore to miss the courtship of youth. Furthermore, Tu Mu, a contemporary of this girl, wrote as follows:

> "It is my fault I should have missed the spring,
> Yet shall I fret because the flowers are gone?
> Late storms have blown the petals far away,
> On leafy bending boughs rich fruits are borne."

Ever since Tu Mu wrote this poem: "On leafy bending boughs rich fruits are borne" has become a common expression for a woman become a mother of many children, particularly because in the Chinese language the same word (*tse*) is used for "fruit" and "sons".

In his poem, where the thoughts seem to be disconnected, Su Tungpo specially used the phrases, the *gold-embroidered gown,* the *leafy boughs bearing fruit* and *plucking an empty bough.*

> "I'm ashamed to come home for I missed the spring bloom;
> See the generous green of the fruit-laden tree.
> If I'm lonely and changed, think kindly of my age;
> With your poems, I have passed this year's spring happily.
> I am now no more drunk in the morn in jade halls;
> But in gold-braid dress celebrate still the bare bough.
> From now on every year let us meet without fail,
> While I learn the fine art of the spade and the plough."

The song was neither appropriate to Chen Shiang nor to the peony, and on close examination bears no relation to the subject. A fruit laden bough is hardly appropriate for the peony. There was no reason why he should ask Chen Shiang to "think kindly" (*lien*) of his age. The pledge to see each other "from now on" was written for parting, not for one returning to see a colleague; and Su certainly had no idea of settling on a farm to live as Chen's neighbour. Above all, the reference to belated courtship of a mother of children must be considered strange, if it was really meant for Chen Shiang. It is true that in a Tang poem of this kind, where the middle two pairs are always couplets with nouns, adjectives, etc., in one line balanced by the same class of word in the other, sometimes such pairs in the middle are decorations for the verse, with the first and last couplets bearing the poetic message; nevertheless, a skilfully constructed Tang poem should have complete unity. Rarely would Su Tungpo write such a badly constructed poem with lines made merely to fill a vacuum. On the other hand, read as a message composed for his cousin, the poem has a unified thought and theme. The first line says he was ashamed to come home because he had missed the spring bloom, or the girl's youth. The second line makes a clear reference to her having children now. The third line asks for her sympathy and expresses his feeling of loneliness. The fourth line expresses the thought that he has had a happy spring this year, in her company. The third couplet then clearly expresses his regret at the belated courtship. The fourth couplet becomes easily intelligible. Su Tungpo at this time wrote a poem expressing his desire to settle at Changchow, which was not very far from the Lius' home. He did carry out his plans to buy a house and farm at Changchow, and it was here that he died.

I know that admirers of Su Tungpo will take issue with me for thus suggesting that he had a secret love for his cousin. Whether it casts a slur on his character or not, however, is a matter of opinion. Su Tungpo would have been condemned by the neo-Confucianists if it had been true and known. But cousins have often fallen in love since time began. Su Tungpo did not and could not defy the conventions by marrying his first cousin on the father's side who bore the same clan name, Su.

One poem which he scribbled on the wall of the monastery at Chiaoshan, during the trip to Chinkiang, is of particular interest to Western readers. Su Tungpo should have known of the Cinderella story, with the step-mother, step-sisters, missing slipper and all, which was contained in the writings of a ninth-century Chinese author.* But as far as I know, he was the first to put in writing the story of how an old man arranged his beard when he went to bed.

In a simple rhyme he told of a man with a long beard who never gave a thought of how he should arrange his beard in bed. One day someone asked him where he put his beard during sleep. That night in bed he became conscious of his beard. He first put it outside his quilt and then inside, and then outside again, and lost sleep the whole night. The next morning he got so restless that he thought the best way would be to cut it off. From the text of the poem, this seems to be a popular tale, not an invention of the poet himself.

It may be appropriate to mention here that Su was the originator of the parable of "The Blind Man's Idea of the Sun", written at Michow. Albert Einstein somewhere quoted this parable to illustrate the average man's idea of the theory of relativity.

"There was a man born blind. He had never seen the sun and asked about it of people who could see. Someone told him: 'The sun's shape is like a brass tray.' The blind man struck the brass tray and heard its sound. Later, when he heard the sound of a bell, he thought it was the sun. Again someone told him: 'The sunlight is like that of a candle,' and the blind man felt the candle, and thought that was the sun's shape. Later he felt a [big] key and thought it was a sun. The sun is different from a bell or a key, but the blind man cannot tell their difference because he has never seen it. The truth (Tao) is harder to see than the sun, and when people do not know it they are exactly like the blind man. Even if you do your best to explain by analogies and examples, it still appears like the analogy of the brass tray and the candle. From what is said of the brass tray, one imagines a bell, and from what is said about a candle, one imagines a key. In this way, one gets ever further and further away from the truth. Those who speak about Tao sometimes give it a name according to what they happen to see, or imagine what it is like without seeing it. These are mistakes in the effort to understand Tao."

* See *Wisdom of China and India*, page 940.

Curiously, this fable was used as testimony at his court trial. The charge was that he was ridiculing the scholars of the time for following blindly the commentaries of Wang Anshih on the classics.

Su Tungpo was too complex a character, too many-sided, to be understood easily. While he was too good a philosopher to be a puritan, he was also too good a Confucianist to be just a drunk. He understood life too well and valued it too highly just to squander it with wine and women. He was a poet of nature, with that peculiar wholesome mystic view of life which is always associated with a deep and true understanding of nature. No one, I believe, can live in close touch with nature and its seasons, its snows and rains, its hills and dales, receiving its healing powers, and have a warped mind or a warped view of life.

On the ninth day of the ninth moon, 1073, he refused to go to the drinking parties usually held on such a festival. Running away from his friends, he took a boat all by himself. Getting up before dawn, as was the custom on this festival, he went out to the lake and called on the two priests at Kushan. That night he sat alone in a boat on the lake, watching the lights from the windows of Yumeitang on the top of the hill, where his colleagues were enjoying themselves at one of those usually boisterous wine dinners. Writing to a colleague, Chou Pin, he said:

> "The high note of your poems suggests the mountain clouds.
> You would not fall drunk on a woman's breast!
> If you won't pierce the country green with your sandals,
> Why not watch the boat cut ripples on the blue?
> I remember the gambling and shouting of Yuan Yentao;
> But where is the angry, cursing General Kuan? *
> The sunset and the breeze are nature's free gifts,
> Come to the lake, and share the cool evening air!"

* Allusions, not to contemporaries, but to historic characters.

Chapter Twelve

POETRY OF PROTEST

IT is well to remember that even Hangchow was not all lotus and peonies. Su Tungpo could not always laugh and sing and stage one-man comic operas and go boating on the lake in the moonlight, for there were seventeen thousand prisoners in jail to be tried for debt and for salt smuggling, locust pests to be fought, the salt canal to be dredged, a famine to be investigated. In the hundreds of poems written by the poet at this time of his life, it is hard to find any dominant mood. He wrote comic and satiric verse, inspiring descriptions of landscape, sentimental poems of love, songs gay with laughter, and other songs bitter with tears. But underlying all his superficial frivolities and gaieties and cracking of jokes at the wine feasts, there was a spirit of restlessness, of despondency, of sorrow and even of fear. No one man reflected the feelings of his people more fully than Su Tungpo, and it was given to him to put into songs and words of beauty more richly and more fully what the other writers were trying to express. Yet, it is well to remember that Su Tungpo had come away from the capital to his post with a wound in his heart. There was a feeling of insecurity and of hidden grief over the trend of political events, a grief which touched his soul more deeply than others. As he beautifully expressed it:

"The wounded mallard folds its wings e'en though the wind is quiet,
The frightened rook sleeps lightly when the moon is clear."

One poem he wrote at Michow, addressed to Chiao Shü, sums up his general attitude in this time of prolific writing, between the years 1071 and 1076, at Hangchow and then Michow.

"Thirty-six thousand days comprise a human life.
Of this, old age and sickness occupy half.
And in this life, joy is attended by sorrow,
Laughter and song keep company with tears.
Without a why or wherefore, madly we plunge
Headlong like puppets or playthings of the gods.
Then in a while we laugh about the past,
All things blow over like a thunderstorm.
—Since I perceived this truth some time ago,
I have forsaken my merrymaking friends."

147

In another poem, addressed to Kung Wenchung, he revealed his inner contempt for the pomp of office.

> "By nature I am like a forest deer,
> With hardly the temper of the harnessed breed.
> Look at these gilded accoutrements,
> The jadeite buckles and the silken reins!
> Compelling admiration from onlookers,
> But meriting well my inner contempt. . . .
> Every man has his goal and aim in life,
> And I have always held to my belief.
> Others will laugh at what I am saying,
> But I expect the highest of you and me."

And so along with his songs of laughter we hear a voice of outcry and a sigh. We hear beyond the boom of the bittern the moaning of those in jail, and beyond the gurgle of water on the water-wheel the sad plaint of an old farmer's wife. Mixed with the noise of celebrations overlooking the lake, we hear a resigned voice complaining of his thin and greying hair.

Su Tungpo was unpredictable. He had the habit of beginning his poems in the most natural, simple and effortless manner, he would put in an allusion or two recalling ancient history, and from then on nobody knew what was going to happen, least of all the poet himself. Sometimes he gives us an amazing piece of contented inconsequentialities, a song without purpose, recording the curious impression of a moment, and then he may burst into bitterness, satire, or profound irony. There is no question that he was a master of both prose and poetry, written in the style of "sailing clouds and winding waters, going whither it wants to go and stopping whenever it is right to stop". It also may be said to be the style of an author who cannot help himself. At a time when free criticism was most resented at the court, it was a style definitely calculated to land the poet in trouble.

But Su Tungpo did not know what lines he was going to write next, and he did not care. With the prodigality of his genius, he would often write three or four or five poems in succession on the same theme and using the same rhyme words. There was a poem which started by describing the atmosphere of a day when it felt as if it were going to snow. And so he began:

> "It is going to snow,
> Clouds cover the loch,
> Towers and hills seem to be there, and seem not."

The friend to whom he sent it wrote back, and he replied with a second poem which begins like this:

> "Beasts are in the lair,
> Fish are in the loch,
> Once in the traps and snares, they return not."

The friend replied and he sent a third, which begins:

> "Eastwards lies the sea,
> Westwards lies the loch.
> Distant hills appear so dim, they appear not."

And in the fourth poem he began:

> "'Don't you see
> The Chientang loch?
> Today King Chien's palaces exist not."

In the second poem, he got into trouble, for then he was carried away by the thought of the fish and the beasts losing their freedom. From then on it was only a step in thought to go on and speak about the prisoners who were being flogged in prison and whose wives and children were sent to jail. These were long poems, and he had to start with the end rhyme words and build his thoughts around them. Two of the rhyme words were "fugitive" and "describe". While in one poem he said: "I write this poem in a hurry, like a fugitive," it was natural for him to say in the other poem: "In a famine year there is no way of sending the fugitives home." In using the rhyme word "describe", he said in one poem: "The setting sun and cottage smoke are difficult to describe"; but in the other poem about the prisoners, he also said: "It is easy to paint a stork, difficult to describe a tiger"—a clear reference to a rapacious government.

Su Tungpo was hardly the kind of man to deny that he was happy when he was, or to pretend that he was happy when he was not. Many of his friends kept up correspondence with him and they wrote poems to each other. Liu Shu was now at Kiukiang and so was Li Chang. Sun Chueh was at Huchow, only a short distance north of Hangchow. These were friends who had fought together against Wang Anshih's administration and were now serving in various capacities in the southeast. All of them felt disgust with the state of things, for at this time Wang Anshih was still in power, but being less headstrong, they kept their opinions to themselves. Han Chi and Ouyang Shiu were dead. Fu Pi and Fan Chen were living in retirement. Szema Kuang devoted himself to authorship, Chang Fangping gave himself to drink, while Tungpo's own brother was wise enough to keep his mouth shut. Tungpo was less tactful. It was just a question whether, when one actually saw the people suffering, one should express his feelings regardless of consequences for himself. Perhaps he never considered the question. And so along with poems of delight and wonder at pastoral beauty, he kept on writing about what was not so beautiful in the countryside. The poet was either mad or terribly in earnest. He knew that his lines travelled fast to the capital, and he did not care.

It would be interesting to take a close look at some of these lines which, as time went along, accumulated in sufficient volume to convict him of disrespect for the ruling regime. Taken separately, they were merely occasional comments, but together they were impressive as a collection of poetry of protest. A few examples will suffice. He wrote in the simplest language of the horrible scenes of people conscripted, to dredge a canal for salt boats. As an official supervising the work, he saw the workmen gather together at the sounding of the horn at dawn, and he said in so many words that "the men were like ducks and pigs, splashing about in the mud".

On his trip to Fuyang, south-west of Hangchow, he wrote a fresh and delightful poem on the clearing up of the sky, beginning as follows:

"The east wind knows that I am going home,
It stopped the sound of raindrops from the eaves.
The cloud-lined blue peaks lift their cotton caps,
And the morning sun hangs like a gong atop the trees."

But he could not help seeing things, and while he sang about how "the spring brought flowers into every village", he also wrote about the food of the farmers. They were eating bamboo shoots, and the bamboo shoots were good, he said, but they were not salted, for "they have not tasted salt for three months", because the government monopoly had killed the salt trade. Once he let himself go, he could not help telling how the young sons of the farmers took advantage of the farmers' loans, borrowed the money, stayed in the city and spent it all, and came home bringing no more than a city accent, for the government was clever enough to open wine-shops and amusement places right next to the loan bureaus.

On his trip north, near the Taihu Lake district, he saw his good friend, the tall, bearded Sun Chueh. As a connoisseur of painting and calligraphy, he wrote a piece on his friend's collection of famous handwritings; but in his poem he also said: "Alas, you and I stand alone in this world, stuffing our ears and steeling our hearts against all current affairs." While he wrote a beautiful poem on the gushing current of water coming up the water-wheels, he also wrote a poem called "The Sigh of a Peasant Woman".

> "This year the rice crop ripens late,
> Waiting for the sharp, dry winter wind to come.
> But the rains came when the frost was due,
> The sickle rusted and the rake was covered with mould.
> I cried my tears out, but the rains continued.
> How could I bear to see the ears lying in the mud?
> After waiting for a month living in a shack,
> The skies having cleared, I carted the crop home.
> With sweat on my red shoulders I carried it to town,
> The price was low and I begged to sell it like chaff.
> Careless of next year's hunger, I sold the cow
> To pay the tax and chopped the doors for fuel.
> The government wants tax in cash and not in kind;
> For wars in the north-west across a thousand miles,
> My sons are drafted."

Again, he was writing joyous songs for the surf-riders during the period of the Hangchow bore. It was the custom at mid-autumn every year at Hangchow for people to come from great distances and line up on the bank of the Chientang River and watch the coming of the bore, which steadily rose in height as it came in from the sea and entered the narrowing bay. Before the bore came, there was usually a marine display. It is not clear how they rode on the surf. While they were called by the name of "riders on the surf", *ta-lang-erh,* the impression was that good swimmers rode out in small boats with red and green flags on them to meet the oncoming bore. Su Tungpo wrote rousing popular songs for these surf-riders to sing, and spoke of the white foam swallowing up the red flags of the riders and the height of the surfs covering half the view of the Yueh hills. But he also wrote of his inner feelings after waking up from a drink in the early hours of the morning.

> "The affairs of men are in a turmoil.
> The lonely scholar's spirit is vexed.
> Why should the melody of the lute
> Be drowned in the noise of the kettle-drum?
> Three cups can drown ten thousand worries,
> And after waking up my spirit is cleansed. . . .
> Sleepless with the burden of my thoughts,
> I rise to see the lambent Milky Way.
> Over the railings the Dipper has turned low,
> And the bright Venus shimmers in the east."

One of the poems that got him into trouble was a subtle crack he made at the ruling authorities, by implication comparing them to owls. He was visiting the district of Linan in the company of Chou Pin. According to the story told later at Su's trial, a magistrate of Linan had drafted a proposal for simplifying the collection of the draft exemption tax. This magistrate had come up to Hangchow with his proposal, and now, returned home, told Su Tungpo his story.

"I was driven out by the owl," the magistrate said.

"What do you mean?" asked Su Tungpo, and the magistrate told him how he had gone to the city with the plan and submitted it to a deputy tax commissioner, and how the latter had him escorted out of the city under armed guards. So Tungpo asked to see his proposal and found that he had suggested a good simple system of collection.

"What do you mean by the owl?" asked Su Tungpo, and the magistrate replied:

"Well, this is a popular fable. One day a swallow and a bat were having a dispute. The swallow held that the sunrise was the beginning of the day, while the bat argued that sundown was the beginning. As they could not decide the matter, they went to ask the opinion of the wise phœnix. On the way, however, they met a bird who said to them: 'We haven't seen the phœnix lately. Some say he is on leave and some say he is taking a long nap. At present the owl is taking over the position in his stead. So there is no use your going to consult that bird.'"

In his poem written on this occasion, addressed to his companion Chou Pin, he said in a tone of resignation and great despondency:

"For years I have been going through a struggle,
And now I gradually feel the Master prevails.
I want to find a farm of five acres,
And clear all vexations from my breast. . . .
I have not yet been able to go my way,
But who will listen when I try to persuade?
I have always admired the upright ancients,
And I shall leave the rest to heaven's will. . . .
Why follow the example of the swallow and the bat,
And argue about the beginning of the day?"

In time, lines like these were carefully collected and scrutinized by those in power. There was no preaching of rebellion, no overt criticism, no declamation against those in authority. But such lines have the power of mosquito bites. They sting, they irritate, and they annoy; and if there are too many bites, they can thoroughly ruin one's sleep for the night. It was particularly annoying to have these poems published by one of Su's close friends, Prince Wang Shien, who was married to the Emperor's sister. At a time when verse was the popular form of communication of ideas, two clever lines of verse made better "quotes" than a windy memorandum. And Su Tungpo was enormously popular; his verse was repeated at scholars' parties. The day was coming when it was no longer possible to ignore Su Tungpo's voice.

In September 1074 his term of office at Hangchow was up. His brother was now serving only as a secretary at Tsichow, modern Tsinan, in Shantung province, and Tungpo had begged to be transferred to that province. His wish was granted, and this time he was appointed chief magistrate of Michow, which is near Tsingtao. He served at Michow only for two years, then was again appointed a chief magistrate, of Suchow, where he served from April 1077 to March 1079.

After saying good-bye to his friends in the monasteries on the northern and southern hills of Hangchow, Su started with his family on the way north. His wife had bought a very intelligent maid of twelve, by the name of Chaoyun, who was to become most important in the life of Su Tungpo.

Michow was a very poor district, growing principally hemp, dates, and mulberries, and the life here offered a striking contrast to that of Hangchow. The officials' salaries had been cut at this time, and in his preface to a descriptive poem, "Medlar and Chrysanthemum", Su Tungpo said: "After being in the service for nineteen years, I am becoming poorer every day and can no longer live as I used to. When I came over to be magistrate of Kiaochow, I thought at least that I would not have to starve, but the pantry is bare, and we have to live frugally. I often go out with a fellow magistrate, Liu Tingshih, along the ancient city walls, and pick the medlar and the chrysanthemum in the abandoned gardens and eat them. Then we feel our bellies and laugh."

With Wang Anshih out of office, Huiching was now in power and a new income tax was instituted. The allocation of the draft exemption tax was far beyond the ability of the people of the district to pay. Children were dying on the roadsides. One line in a poem Su wrote at this period spoke of his "going along the city wall with tears in my eyes" to bury the exposed corpses. In a letter he wrote years later, he mentioned the fact that he was able to save thirty or forty starving orphans and put them in homes.

It was a period when Su Tungpo was feeling sad and despondent, and, strange to say, it was when the poet was saddest that he wrote his best poems. That is, judged by Chinese standards, it was in this period that he reached complete maturity as a poet. The anger and the bitterness were gone, and there was only peace and resignation. Even his joys in the beauties of nature and the pleasures of the day were more mellow, indicating a clear difference from the youthful gusto and effervescence of his Hangchow days. He had steadily grown in his admiration for Tao Chien, the one great harmonious poetic spirit of China, and in the poem "On the Western Garden" his work cannot be distinguished from that of Tao. In this poem we see not only true peace and contentment but also a complete union with nature and a quiet delight in the sounds and colours of nature itself.

> "In the deep western room, I recline on a bed,
> Quite awake from a nap, yet the day seems so long.
> I feel tired for no reason and dazed though not drunk,
> But the wind from the grove sets right all that was wrong.
> Then I stroll in the garden, catch the sweet smell of grass,
> A pomegranate has burgeoned, the dates are so strong!
> The dove rests in the shade, idly folding its wings,
> And the oriole's gay golden throat trills a new song.
> On a cane, I observe the world's course and myself.
> All things prosper in turn; why should I hustle along?"

It was when the poet had reached this state of complete harmony with nature that he could write a poem like the following: "The Recluse Pavilion."

> " 'How can you pass such days of quiet and calm,
> While human life is sore beset with ills?'
> Last night I slept by the breezy northern window;
> This morn the crisp air fills the western hills."

From such a mystic view, he obtained a sense of spiritual freedom, a freedom which equalled that of the clouds travelling without aim and purpose over the mountain peaks. The poem "Cloud-Gazing Tower" reads as follows:

> "Through rain and shine, alternate night and day,
> Drifting at will and stopping as it may,
> The cloud has made the universe its home,
> And like the cloud's so is the gazer's way."

It is striking that Tseyu always made the occasion for Su Tungpo to write some of his best poetry. On his journey from Hangchow to Michow, thinking of his brother, Tungpo wrote a beautiful song in the metre of a *tse*, in this case set to the tune of *Shinyuanchun*:

"A lone dim lamp in a quiet room;
At the wayside inn a cock crows.
On a traveller's pillow lie unfinished dreams.
Declining moon gathers up its beams.
The morning frost covers the hills like a brocade,
Which sparkles with the pearly dew.
Human toil fills life's endless journey,
Freshened now and then with moments of joy.
Holding the reins in silence,
I thought of the myriad things that had gone by.

"I look back upon those days
When we stopped together at Changan,
Like the two Lus,
Both inspired by the high hopes of youth.
With a thousand words from our pens
And ten thousand volumes in our breasts,
We thought it not difficult to make our Emperor the best.
Whether to serve or to retire
Depends entirely now upon ourselves.
Why not fold our hands in our sleeves and leisurely watch?
May we remain forever in good health
And spend the last years of our lives at ease—
Over a contest of wine!"

It was in Michow, thinking of his absent brother, that he wrote what is considered the best poem on the mid-autumn by any poet. Critics say that after this poem was written, all the other poems on the harvest moon could be well forgotten.

"How rare the moon, so round and clear!
    With cup in hand, I ask of the blue sky,
'I do not know in the celestial sphere
    What name this festive night goes by?'
I want to fly home, riding the air,
But fear the ethereal cold up there,
    The jade and crystal mansions are so high!
Dancing to my shadow,
    I feel no longer the mortal tie.

"She rounds the vermilion tower,
Stoops to silk-pad doors,
    Shines on those who sleepless lie.
Why does she, bearing us no grudge,
    Shine upon our parting, reunion deny?
But rare is perfect happiness—

F*

> The moon does wax, the moon does wane,
>   And so men meet and say goodbye.
> I only pray our life be long,
>   And our souls together heavenward fly!"

The above poem, "Mid-Autumn Moon," composed in 1076 at Michow, was a *tse*, a song written to music, as has been explained. It may be interesting to analyse the tonal pattern and formal structure of such a poem. Like all Chinese poems, the *tse* uses word tones instead of accent as the basis of rhythm. The word tones are divided into two classes: First, the even and sustained tone, corresponding to English open syllables or syllables ending in liquid consonants (*l,m,n*) and second, the shifting (rising or dropping) and abrupt tones, corresponding in tonal quality to English syllables ending in stop consonants (*p,t,k*). The difference in tone between the two is roughly seen in that between *song* and *sock*, or between *seen* and *sick*, or very roughly between the end of a question and the end of a period. It is necessary to understand this tonal basis of Chinese poetry, which gives rise to its musical character. The Chinese language is essentially mono-syllabic; moreover, most of the time, auxiliary particles like *be, should, and, to, of, the, a,* which furnish a great part of the unaccented syllables in English poetry, are omitted. This brevity of the word gives a marked syllabic weight, convenient for the development of a feeling of the tonal scheme. The music of a Chinese poem therefore, whether in the loose "ancient style", or in the precise "Tang poem", or in the still more precisely regulated "*tse*", may be said to consist entirely in the subtle and varied contrast and counterplay of word tones. A basic rule, for instance, is that when a rhyme word is in a sustained tone, all the unrhymed lines must end in the opposite tones, and vice versa.

Taking "Mid-Autumn Moon" as an example, one may let "o" stand for the sustained tone and "x" for the shifting or abrupt tones. It is quite possible to get the tonal pattern as shown below by clinking a glass for an "o" and tapping the table for an "x", letting each letter represent one musical note in the pattern:

First Stanza		*Second Stanza*	
1. o x / o o x /		1. ( ) x o x / o	
x x / x o o /	R	x x / x o o /	R
2. o o / x x / o x /		2. o o / x x / o x /	
x x / x o o /	R	x x / x o o /	R
3. x x / o o / x x /		3. x x / o o / x x /	
x x / o o / o x /.		x x / o o / o x /	
· x x / x o o /	R	x x / x o o /	R
4. x x / x o x /		4. x x / o o x /	
o x / x o o /	R	o x / x o o /	R

It will be seen that all the rhymed lines ("R") at the end of each long phrase or sentence (four long phrases in each stanza) have essentially the same pattern (x x / x o o /), which is therefore the dominant musical phrase. The variations at the beginning of each long phrase and leading to the dominant phrase are arranged to give contrast to each other. The accent, contrary to that in the musical bar, is always on the last note of the bar; therefore, differentiation in tone on the last note of a bar is absolute, while some slight laxity is allowable in the first note of some bars. In this sense, the fourth long phrase is really a repetition of the first. Also, with the exception of the first long phrase, the second stanza is identical with the first in tonal arrangement. The first long phrase of the second stanza is quickened in pace and shortened into three bars with three notes to each bar, but on examination it discloses the same final dominant phrase.

Chapter Thirteen

THE YELLOW TOWER

EVEN for a genius like Su Tungpo, life began at forty. Su was now to enter his Suchow period, the period of the "Yellow Tower". Suddenly Su Tungpo found himself. For the first time in his life, he is revealed as a man of action, doing things and building things and occupied in the public activities which characterised his life from now on. So far, as an assistant magistrate at Hangchow, he had not been able to do anything constructive and important, and although he was given a full magistracy at Michow, it was a poor, remote district, giving no opportunity for the full expression of his administrative talent. He was later to be forced into a period of temporary retirement and political eclipse, after which emerged the full, round, mature, active, patriotic Su Tungpo that we know and people in China love, the Su Tungpo with a mellow humour, a friend and champion of the people and a great human spirit. But before his arrest and banishment, the magistracy at Suchow already gave proof of what Su Tungpo, the man of action, could do as an able administrator.

At the end of 1076 Tungpo was recalled from Michow, with an appointment to office at Hochungfu, at the south-western tip of Shansi province; and in January of the following year he set out for the capital by way of Tsinan, where his brother's family lived. Tseyu was not there, for great political changes were in the air. By now Wang Anshih, Huiching, Tseng Pu, Dunquan, and again Wang, had all fallen, one after the other, and nobody knew what was going to happen next.

Tseyu was a quiet but determined man. Su Tungpo had kept on sending memorandums on tax and draft reforms and had advised the Emperor against the income tax; but Tseyu, silent before, thought perhaps the time had come to strike hard for a complete change of government policy. Wang Anshih had been on his final way out in October, and Tseyu, without waiting for his brother, had gone right ahead to the capital with an important memorandum for complete reforms. His family had remained at Tsinan, and there Su Tungpo was greeted by his three nephews standing in the snow outside the gate. That night they had a great feast and the two brothers' families were happily reunited. Tsinan, a large city, provided a great change from Michow, and Su Tungpo remained there for about a month. It was not till about the tenth of February, 1077, that the two brothers' families reached the bank of the Yellow River near the capital. Tseyu had come

out to meet them some thirty miles north of the bank, and the two
brothers spent some good days together during the journey in the snow.
Tseyu brought the news that Su Tungpo's new appointment to
Hochungfu had been cancelled, and that he was appointed chief magistrate of Suchow.

A mysterious incident happened when they reached the capital.
Coming to the Chenchiao Gate, Su Tungpo was informed by the gatekeeper that he was not to be admitted to the capital city. This incident,
recorded by his brother, has never been satisfactorily explained. I do
not think it was the Emperor's will, but with the impending political
uncertainty, some officials probably wanted to make sure that he had
no chance to see the Emperor; and so far as we know, the Emperor
may not have known of this order himself. The brothers turned back
and put up at the home of their great good friend Fan Chen, in the
eastern outer city.

By this time Su Tungpo's eldest son, Mai, was eighteen and therefore ready to marry. Research students have never been able to verify
who the girl was. My opinion is that he married one of Fan Chen's
grand-daughters. In Su Tungpo's correspondence with Fan Chen and
his son, he referred to them repeatedly as relatives connected by
marriage. What that marriage was between the Su and Fan family
waits to be explained. Fan Chen was also from Szechuen, and Su was
staying at the time in Fan Chen's home. In the next two years Su
Tungpo also helped to marry off two of Tseyu's grown-up daughters
by selecting husbands for them. One was Wang Shih, brother of the
famous Wang Chiung (Tsekao) who, according to legend, actually
"married a fairy",* and the other was a son of the famous bamboo
painter, Wen Tung.

After his son's wedding Su Tungpo went east with his family to his
post at Suchow, in modern Kiangsu. Tseyu, too, was going with his
family as a deputy magistrate to Shangchiu, the Southern Capital; and
after leaving his family there with Chang Fangping, he continued the
journey with his brother to Suchow, where he remained three months
before returning to his family.

Suchow was not only a big city, it was a place of the greatest strategic
importance, holding control of the mountainous regions in southern
Shantung. In past dynasties wars had always been fought around
Suchow, which today stands at the junction of the Tsinpu and
Lunghai Railways. It was also near a region to be made famous in the

* Wang Chiung personally confirmed the story to Su Tungpo. This became so
embarrassing to the man that later he changed his name. Wang first met his
wife in a supernatural vision, during his affair with a strange unknown woman,
but the wife denied that she was a fairy, or at least was totally unaware of her
previous existence,

next decades as the robbers' lair celebrated in the romance *All Men Are Brothers*. The city lay on a river, surrounded by two high mountains on the south, with deep, rapid currents flowing past the city below. It produced very fine granite, iron, and coal, which were exploited in Su Tungpo's days. Consequently the place was also famous for its knives and swords. He was delighted with the natural scenery and the variety of fish and crabs available, and called it a good place for a "temporary stay".

On August 21, three months after his arrival, a big flood reached Suchow. Wang Anshih had previously tried to dredge the Yellow River; but after spending over half a million dollars he had failed, and the chief engineer had committed suicide. The Yellow River now broke out eastward at a point some fifty miles north of Suchow and began to spread, flooding several hundred square miles. When the flood reached the city, it was held back by the tall mountains south of the city; and the water rose higher and higher, until in September it reached 28.9 Chinese feet. At one time the level of the water was higher than the city streets. Su Tungpo plunged into the work of saving the city. For weeks he did not go home, but stayed in a shack on top of the city wall supervising the strengthening of the outer wall. Well-to-do families were fleeing from the city, and Su Tungpo stopped them at the gate, begging them to remain for fear of starting a panic. "I am going to stay, so you had better, too," he said to them, and forced them back. This is not the place to go into Su Tungpo's architectural and engineering genius, but let it be said that he always worked with exact figures in all his engineering projects. While the swirling waters were threatening to overrun the south-eastern walls of the outer city, he was strengthening the base and increasing the height of the walls. The defence works that were thrown up against the flood were 9,840 feet long, 10 feet high, and 20 feet wide. For this he needed thousands of workmen. Splashing about in the mud, he went straight to the army camp and spoke to the commander. As this was the so-called Palace Army, under the direct control of the Emperor, he asked for their co-operation. The officers gladly responded, and said: "Since Your Honour has come out personally to supervise the work, certainly we should do our part." Meanwhile, preparations were made in the north to turn the water into an old abandoned course of the Yellow River, which had already changed its route many times in history. The waters threatened the city for forty-five days, but on the fifth of October the flood began to subside as the river found its old course and drained eastward towards the sea near Haichow.

The people were overjoyed and grateful for the saving of the city. But dissatisfied with the temporary dams, Su Tungpo sent a letter with detailed figures to the court, asking for money to build a stone city wall against future calamities. Waiting in vain for a reply, he modified his proposal and recommended the building of dams not with rock, but with strong timber reinforcements. In an official letter the Emperor then congratulated him on his great work, and in February of the following year, Tungpo was accorded a grant of over $30,000 and 18,000 bushels of rice, and provision for hiring 7,200 men to build a wooden dam along the south-east side of the city. On top of this outer city wall, following his love for architecture, Su Tungpo had a tower built a hundred feet high, which was called the Yellow Tower. Later this became the name of the collection of poems that he wrote during his term at Suchow, just as the Chaojan Terrace he built at Michow was used as the title of the collection of his poems written there.

The Yellow Tower was so called because of a belief in the old Chinese cosmogony. According to this system, all things in the universe are composed of five elements, gold, wood, water, fire, and earth. Each of these stands for a principle, such as hardness, growth, fluidity, heat, gravity, etc., principles which have a universal meaning and are supposed to apply not only to the physical universe but also to life functions and human character and conduct, applicable, for instance, to a matrimonial match. All life consists of the interplay of these five principles which overcome or reinforce one another, and each of the elements has a colour which is symbolic of that element. Curiously, yellow stands for the earth and black stands for water, and the yellow earth is supposed to overcome the black water by its power of absorption. The name given the Yellow Tower was, therefore, symbolic of the power to resist water.

On the ninth day of the ninth moon, 1078, there was a grand opening ceremony of the Yellow Tower. Su Tungpo was truly happy. The people had been saved from a flood, they had worked for over half a year at the building of the dam and the tower; and the tower belonged to the people of the city as a visible symbol of their security against future inundations. The whole town was present to witness the opening ceremony. There stood the Yellow Tower, a hundred feet high, on top of the East Gate, with flag-poles fifty feet high below. It was in the style of a broad pagoda, and the party went up to the top to get a view of the surrounding country. There was a heavy fog that morning, and as they looked out of the window and heard the squeaking oars of the boats passing below, they had the feeling of being on a ship at sea. Soon the sky cleared and they could see fishing villages in the distance and half a dozen temples scattered on the hill-sides below the jagged mountain peaks. The old people felt cold, and Su Tungpo asked them to have a drink of warm wine first. In the foreground, on the south, they saw the raised terrace that used to be the race-course but was now the site of a Buddhist temple. From this temple stretched the mile-long new embankment northward along the east city wall. They could hear in the distance the roaring torrents of the Lu Rapids and the Hundred-Yard Rapids, amidst the cackling of ducks and geese below. The ceremony ended with a grand dinner, with a full orchestra, for the invited guests.

Su Tungpo wrote a piece to commemorate the occasion and had it inscribed on stone. This tablet had a curious history. Later, when he was exiled and all tablets containing his handwriting were ordered to be destroyed, the magistrate of Suchow at that time merely dropped it into a moat near-by. After about ten years had passed, when the people had forgotten about the ban and the imperial household itself began to collect the poet's manuscripts, another magistrate at this place had the tablet hauled out of the moat again. Secretly at night he had several thousand copies of rubbings from the inscription made. After this had been done, the magistrate suddenly announced to his colleagues: "Why, I forgot! The law prohibiting Su's inscription has not yet been suspended and this inscription is still lying here. Let's have it destroyed." Naturally, the price of the rubbings shot up after the stone was destroyed, and the magistrate, Miao Chungshien, made a lot of money.

Su Tungpo was now very popular, not only because of his successful fight against the flood, but also because he had taken a personal interest in the health and welfare of the prisoners, something which was rarely, if ever, done by magistrates at the time. He had personally visited the prisons and for the first time had appointed prison physicians to attend to the sick. While there was a law punishing magistrates who had flogged prisoners to death, Su pointed out that there was nothing being done about prisoners who died of disease and bad care. As the prisoners were no other than the common people, he earned the deep gratitude of their relatives.

There were many small things that could be easily done if a man thought about doing them, but only Su Tungpo cared. He saw, for example, that there were many soldiers who deserted the army and became bandits, because of a preposterous system practically compelling corporals to go into debt when they were sent on a distant journey on official business without fees for travel. He had this corrected, and he was able to do this by setting aside only a few hundred dollars each year. He had forbidden gambling and drinking in the army, and in his letter to the Emperor was able to point out that the local army there was "the best disciplined of all those in that region, as the court inspectors have seen".

Su Tungpo's fame as poet had steadily risen, until he was now the acknowledged first scholar of the land. After Ouyang Shiu's death the mantle had passed to him. Scholars came to acknowledge him as

"Master". He had met two of his four famous disciples before, Chang Lei at Huaiyang and Chao Puchih near Hangchow. The other two, Chin Kuan and Huang Tingchien, who later became major poets of the Sung dynasty, now asked to be considered his disciples. The short, stocky Li Chang had come to visit Su in the spring and had constantly spoken of Chin Kuan and shown him Chin's verse. With Li Chang's introduction, Chin Kuan had come to see him that summer. This was the romantic poet who, according to legend, was married to Su Tungpo's younger sister. Not yet having a degree, but young, romantic, and carefree, Chin had many women friends. Later, when he died, a courtesan committed suicide for love of him. Here was a new voice in poetry, singing like a lark in spring. In his presentation to Su Tungpo, Chin said that "rather than be a magistrate ruling over ten thousand families, he would make the acquaintance of Su Suchow [Tungpo]". He compared him to a "unicorn in heaven", and asked: "Of all those born this side of the pole star, how many men are like him?"

Huang Tingchien, who later became the father of the Kiangse school of poetry, was a different type of man, scholarly and quiet. He did not come to visit Su, but wrote two poems in a tone of great humility to introduce himself, comparing Su Tungpo to a towering pine tree standing on top of a cliff, and himself to a tender plant grow-ing at the bottom of a canyon and aspiring to grow to the same height. Su had seen Huang's verse before, which he said had a solid content and depth and an elevation of poetic feeling "not seen for quite a few centuries". In his letter to Huang he said: "Why do you write such a humble letter as if you were afraid of me? I was wanting to have your friendship and was afraid that you might not accept me." Of the four disciples of Su Tungpo, Huang was the eldest, and in the talk of the time the names of Su and Huang were always coupled together. After Su Tungpo died, Huang became the greatest poet of his time, and people always spoke of him in the same breath with Su Tungpo. But to the end, Huang considered himself Su Tungpo's pupil. Huang, also, was introduced through Su Tungpo's closest friends, for he was a nephew of Li Chang and the son-in-law of Sun Chueh.

In September, another man who became closely implicated in the court trial of Su Tungpo's case came to visit him. Wang Kung was again another type. The grandson of a premier, he travelled with a whole cartload of the best wine from his own cellar because he would not touch wine bought from the shops. He also brought to Suchow his three concubines, Inging, Panpan, and Chingching. Su Tungpo joked about his concubines, and in the introduction to his poem on the Hundred-Yard Rapids he described Wang's exciting trip down the rapids in the company of women with dimpled cheeks, while Su himself stood in a feathered coat at the top of the Yellow Tower, watching them sailing below, looking like a fairy or like a Li Po reborn.

A fourth very important person came into Su Tungpo's life at this time, the great poet-monk Tsanliao, who was probably introduced to him by Chin Kuan. Curiously, throughout Su Tungpo's three-year stay at Hangchow, Tsanliao—living at a neighbouring town—had remained unknown to him. Tsanliao was too great a poet himself and had too much moral elevation to be a celebrity-hunter. He had only watched and admired Su Tungpo from a great distance. From now on Tsanliao was to become one of his closest and life-long friends.

It is possible to get a close glimpse of Su Tungpo at the mid-autumn festival that year. On August twelfth, a grandson had been born to him, and on this mid-autumn night he was feeling unwell and lonely. Six days after the festival, receiving a poem on the mid-autumn moon from his brother, he wrote one describing how he spent the night.

"Before the moon came up the mountain peaks were high,
A sheet of luminous white then blazed forth in the sky.
Before I finished a cup, the silver gate was opened,
Cloud clusters billowed in retreat like falling waves.
Who could wash the sparkling eyes of Father Heaven
But with a thousand lotions from the Silver Stream?
The moon now so serenely looks upon this earth,
And finds me cool, resigned, like an unruffled well.
In the south-west, meteors shoot across like bullets,
The white Spica used to shimmer bright in the east,
But scanning the eastern heaven, I cannot see it tonight.
Only roaming glow-worms vie in their fluorescent glow.
Who are there sitting on a boat on the ancient Pien?
A thousand lanterns scare the dragons in their lairs.
Out and in, the boats weave glistening chains of ripples,
Up and down, they float to the rhythm of the songs.
The fireflies flit and float against the distant hillside,
And the autumn wind sends up sparkles in the stream.
Too rapidly the moon declines and people disperse,
Coming home I ask for wine to have a look again.
The moon over the courtyard seems even more serene,
While crickets chirp among the grass covered with dew.
Lifting the beaded screen I find the inside silent,
Only my grandson is cooing before 'the window light.
At the Southern Capital be proud of your poverty;
How many men can sing about this autumn night?
Tomorrow at sunrise comes the usual round of work,
And this night will seem a dream flight to the moon."

By this time Su Tungpo was loved and honoured and admired by all scholardom. At a grand gathering at the end of September that year at the Yellow Tower, Su Tungpo, open-hearted and fun-loving and carefree, was warmly loved by them all. It was because of his popularity and prestige that his arrest and trial became a national sensation.

Chapter Fourteen

ARREST AND TRIAL

SU TUNGPO, to use the poet's own expression, had gone on "spitting out flies found in one's food", and had so far escaped scot-free. But the hundredth time he "spat", he was caught. In March 1079 he was transferred to Huchow in the lake district of Kiangsu. In his letter of thanks to the Emperor on assumption of the new office he said something that proved too much for the politicians at court. So long as he had sung about the poverty of the people, the tax, and the draft, it was quite possible for the petty men to ignore it. Now he made a direct reference to these men, among them Leeding and Sudan, who had risen to power as Wang Anshih's protégés. The government was in the hands of nondescript, third-rate men who merely temporised and stood for neither one thing nor the other. Su Tungpo had been sending letters to the Emperor, and every time the Emperor read them he had expressed his admiration to his courtiers. It will be recalled that these men had before prevented Su's entry into the capital. There was a real danger that he might be recalled to power, since all the leaders of the new economic policy had been dismissed or retired.

The letter of thanks was written according to the routine formula, briefly stating the official's past unworthy record and continuing with praise of the Emperor's great generosity in giving him such a splendid new post. However, Su Tungpo said: "Your Majesty knows that I am stupid and behind the times, unable to keep up with the young upstarts; seeing that in my middle age I am not likely to cause trouble, Your Majesty has entrusted me with the shepherding of the people." The phrase which I have translated as "young upstarts" did not sound so bad in Chinese; literally it referred to "those unqualified young men who have been suddenly promoted" by Wang Anshih. In the past fight over Wang's regime, this had become a fixed phrase with that definite meaning. Why, Leeding and Sudan thought, did he think he could get away with that? Moreover, he said that he was appointed to a local administration because at his age he was not likely to cause trouble. Did he imply that those remaining at the court were neces-sarily men who liked to cause trouble? Ancient scholars, in the absence of protection of civil rights, had developed an extreme subtlety in phrasing, saying more than was apparent, and scholar readers had developed the habit of hunting with delight for what was said between the lines. Court bulletins were regularly published, being the earliest form of Chinese printed newspapers. Whatever Su wrote attracted wide attention, and the letter of thanks made the "young upstarts" the laughing-stock of the reading public.

In June 1079, a censor took up the four sentences in Su Tungpo's letter of thanks and impeached him for casting a slur on the government. A few days later Sudan, who was still in the imperial censorate, took up some of the poems about the farmers' loans, the reference to farmers eating for three months without salt, and the parable about the argument between the swallow and the bat. To write such lines showed that Su Tungpo was not only impudent but disloyal to the Emperor. Sudan submitted with the impeachment four volumes of Su's published poems. Leeding, who was now promoted to a post in the premier's office, followed with another impeachment showing four reasons why Su Tungpo should pay with his life for such impertinence. Altogether, there were four impeachments. The case was handed over to the imperial censorate. Leeding, whom Szema Kuang had compared to a beast for neglecting his mother's mourning, was made court prosecutor of the case. He selected a very able man to go down to Huchow, relieve Su Tungpo of his office, and bring him to the capital for trial. The censors asked that on the way Su Tungpo be put in prison for the night at every stopping place, but the Emperor forbade this. Emperor Shentsung never meant to kill Su Tungpo, but since the case was officially put up, he was willing to have it fully examined.

One of Su Tungpo's best friends, Prince Wang Shien, who himself had published Su's poems, heard the news and hurriedly sent a messenger to the Southern Capital to Su's brother, who immediately dispatched a messenger to inform Su Tungpo. It was a race between the messengers. The official envoy travelled very fast with his son and two soldiers of the imperial censorate, but his son fell ill at Chinkiang and there was a delay of half a day, and the story goes that Tseyu's messenger arrived first.

It is important to understand Su Tungpo's state of mind when the news came. He had only recently arrived at Huchow and was very happy at his new post. He used to go wandering about the mountains with his eldest son, and Tseyu's son-in-law, and the latter's younger brother. In one of the poems recording their visit to the Temple of Flying Petals, he said: "Do not look upon me as an official. In my appearance I am one, but in my heart already I am not." His best friend, Wen Tung, the bamboo painter, had died in February, and he had wept over his death for three days. While the official messengers were on their way to make his arrest, he was, on July seventh, re-examining some of his collection of paintings, and taking them out to sun them in the courtyard. His eyes fell upon a wonderful painting of bamboos that Wen Tung had given to him, and he broke into tears again. He wrote on that day in his journal an entry typical of his whimsy, describing his friendship with Yuko, which is the courtesy name of Wen Tung.

"When Yuko started to paint bamboos, he did not think highly of it himself, but people from all places came with their silks and crowded his doorstep to beg for his paintings. Yuko was quite annoyed and, throwing the silks to the floor, said angrily: 'I am going to cut these up and have them made into stockings.' When Yuko returned from Yangchow [modern Yangshien in Shensi] and I was at Suchow, he wrote to me: 'Recently I have been telling scholars that my school of bamboo painting in ink has moved over to Suchow, and that collectors should all go there. I am sure all the material for stockings will come to you now.' He added two lines in postscript saying that he wished to paint a bamboo grove ten thousand feet high on a piece of Goose Valley silk. I said to him that for painting a bamboo grove ten thousand feet high one would require two hundred and fifty pieces of silk, and that I knew he was tired of painting but only wanted to get the silk. Yuko could not reply and only said that I was talking nonsense, and there were no bamboo groves ten thousand feet high anyway. I replied in a poem with the two lines: 'There are bamboos ten thousand feet high, when you look at their shadows cast by the moonlight.' Yuko laughed and said: 'Su always knows how to argue, but if I had two hundred and fifty pieces of silk I would buy a farm in the country and retire.' He gave me this painting of the Valley of Yuntang [tall bamboos], and said to me: 'This painting is only several feet high, but the bamboos appear to be ten thousand feet in height . . .'"

If we are to believe an eye-witness story recorded by Kung Ping-chung, a friend who had the story from the deputy magistrate at the time of the arrest, Su Tungpo was forewarned by his brother's messenger. He did not know, however, how serious the charge and punishment would be. When the messenger arrived, he was officially on leave of absence, and the deputy magistrate, Mr. Tsu, was acting for him.

The officer came, dressed formally in his gown and high boots, and stood with the ceremonial tablet in his hand in the middle of the court-yard. The two soldiers from the censorate stood by his side in white jackets and black turbans, glowering ominously. The people in the office were greatly disturbed, not knowing what was going to happen. Su Tungpo dared not come out, and consulted the deputy magistrate, who advised him that there was no use evading the messenger and that he might just as well receive him. They discussed how he should appear, because Su Tungpo believed that, being the accused, he should not appear in his official gown. Mr. Tsu was of the opinion, however, that before he was formally accused he should still appear according to his rank. Tungpo therefore also put on his gown and boots and stood with the ceremonial tablet in the middle of the courtyard, facing the official, while Mr. Tsu and the staff lined up behind him with small turbans on their heads. The two soldiers who held the message of the censorate in their hands hugged the package as if it contained a sword. The grim silence of the official messenger caused an unbearable suspense. It was Su who spoke first.

"I know I have done many things to anger the court. I am sure this is a sentence for my death. I don't mind dying, but please allow me to go home to say farewell to my family."

The official, Huangfu Chun, replied curtly: "It is not so bad as that."

Then the deputy magistrate advanced a step. "I am sure there is an official message."

"Who is he?" asked Huangfu Chun, and the deputy magistrate told him who he was. The soldiers then formally handed over the message to the deputy magistrate. On opening it, he found that it was only an ordinary message depriving Su Tungpo of his office as magistrate and summoning him to the capital. The official messenger asked him to start at once.

Su Tungpo was permitted to go home and see his family before he started. According to the record in his own journal, the whole family was weeping. Su Tungpo laughingly told them the following story to cheer them up:

In the reign of Chentsung, the Emperor was looking for great scholars living in retirement. Somebody recommended a scholar by the name of Yang Pu. Greatly against his own wish, Yang Pu was escorted to the court and presented to the Emperor.

"I hear you write poetry," said the Emperor.

"No, I don't," said Yang Pu, who was trying to conceal his talent and desperately trying to keep out of politics.

"Didn't some of your friends give you some poems when they were sending you off?" asked the Emperor again.

"No," replied Yang Pu. "Only my wife wrote one."

"What is that poem, may I ask?" said His Majesty.

So Yang Pu recited for the Emperor the poem that his wife had given him on his departure. The poem was:

"Don't be too greedy for the cup.
Please stop fussing over poetry.
Today you are arrested under guard,
This time you'll lose your upper storey."

When Mrs. Su heard this, she laughed through her tears, in spite of herself. This story comes from Su's own journal, but we do not know whether he had invented it on the spot or not.

It was decided that his eldest son, Mai, would accompany him to the capital. Wang Shih, who had been tutoring Tungpo's children, and his younger brother were to stay behind and later bring the whole family to the capital. The officials were all scared out of their wits and in hiding, but the common people went out to see the departure of the magistrate, and according to the official history of the district they "shed tears like rain". The manner and procedure of the official messenger and the soldiers were very high-handed, and later Su Tungpo, in a letter to the succeeding emperor, said that they arrested a chief magistrate and laid hands on him like a robber. Only the two Wang brothers and a secretary on the staff of the magistrate's office went out and gave him a little wine dinner to send him off.

There are several stories that Su Tungpo thought of committing suicide while on the way. According to his own letter to the Emperor, he thought of jumping into the Yangtse River while crossing at Yang-chow, but according to the record of Kung Pingchung, it was at the beginning of the voyage, when the boat was anchored on Taihu Lake for repair of the oars. That night the moon was very bright and there was a high wind over the lake. Su Tungpo had no idea how he was going to be punished, and his case might implicate many of his friends. He thought it would be a simple matter to close his eyes and jump into the lake, but on second thought he realised that if he did this it would be sure to bring his younger brother into trouble. In his letter to Wen Yenpo he described how his family had destroyed much of his correspondence and many of his manuscripts. When the family reached Sushien in Anhuei, the censorate again sent messengers to search their luggage for further poems, letters, and other possible documents. The womenfolk and children had a great scare when a number of soldiers surrounded the boat, ransacked their trunks, and threw their contents about, as all soldiers on such duties do. After the soldiers had gone, the women said angrily: "This all comes of writing books! What does he get by it? It scared us to death." Then they burned his manuscripts, and later the poet found that only about a third of them survived.

Su Tungpo was arrested on July 28 and was thrown into the imperial censorate prison on August 18. It was a long trial, lasting six or seven weeks. While in the prison he had a very kind warden who evidently knew who he was. This warden treated him with great respect, and every night prepared hot water for his foot-bath, which even today is the regular custom of people from Szechuen.

There was an amusing incident while Su Tungpo was in jail, which turned out a help to him at the trial. His son saw him in prison every day. It was his duty to send food to his father, and Su Tungpo had a secret agreement with him that he was only to send vegetables and meat, but that if he heard of any bad news, he should send fish. During a few days when Mai was forced to be away from the city to borrow money, he entrusted the sending of food to one of his friends, but forgot to tell him about the secret agreement. The friend sent in some smoked fish and Su Tungpo had a scare. He thought that affairs had taken a turn for the worse and perhaps he was doomed. He entered into a plot with the warden. He wrote two poems of farewell to his brother, couched in very sad language, saying that his family of ten mouths would have to be fed by his brother, while his spirit lying on an abandoned hillside would be listening to the moaning winds and dripping rains. He expressed the hope that for generations and generations they might be born brothers again. In the poems he also took care to express gratitude to His Majesty for his previous kindness, and took all the blame on himself. Tseyu, on reading the poems, was so overcome that he fell weeping on his desk, and the warden took them away. It was only upon Su Tungpo's release that the warden returned the poems, saying that his brother just would not receive them. It is my belief that Tseyu knew all along what the plot was and purposely returned the poems to the warden. For, meanwhile, the two poems in the hands of the warden served a very useful purpose. It was his duty to hand over any writings by the prisoners for examination by the prison authorities. The story goes that Su Tungpo had felt sure these poems would reach the Emperor himself. And so it fell out. The Emperor was greatly moved by them, and that was one reason why later Su was let off with a comparatively easy sentence in spite of the high pressure of the censors.

We are indebted to the poet Lu Yu for the history of a manuscript in Su Tungpo's own handwriting containing all the documents of the trial. Today we have a book called *The Case of Poetry at the Black Terrace,* the Black Terrace being the name of the censorate prison. The book contains the four impeachments, a complete record of the trial, Su Tungpo's affidavit, the summing up of the testimony, and the sentence. Lu Yu, who was industrious in keeping his diary and took a special interest in all the manuscripts and inscriptions left by Su Tungpo, which he saw about sixty or seventy years after Su's death, told the following story about this book. When the northern Sung dynasty fell in 1126, the whole government staff fled south in the direction of Hangchow, taking all the precious documents they could. While at Yangchow, an official by the name of Chang Chuanchen got hold of this manuscript and removed it from the government files. Later, when this Chang died, a premier, also by the name of Chang, was asked by the family to write the tomb inscription for him. As a price, the premier asked for this manuscript, but it was decided that the family would give the premier only half of it, keeping the other half in the family. Lu Yu recorded that he saw the manuscript all in Su Tungpo's own handwriting, and that in case of corrections they were always initialled by Su himself and marked with the stamp of the censorate. We cannot be sure today that the book which has survived to this day was based on the manuscript which Lu Yu saw, but it does give full details of the court report, including Su Tungpo's own interpretations of his verse.

Judgment of the trial seems to me to depend entirely on our interpretation of the justness of Su Tungpo's criticism of the administration. Chang Fangping, who along with Fan Chén was trying to save Su Tungpo, summed up the case best by drawing a distinction between honest criticism and malicious slander. While we today cannot but regard these poems as expressions of honest criticism, the censors interpreted them as malicious and wilful slander of the government and of the Emperor. Chang Fangping pointed out that the *Book of Songs*, edited by Confucius himself, was full of satire of the rulers of those days, and that in a good government frank criticism was perfectly legitimate. On the other hand, the censors, if we can believe them, were bursting with righteous indignation and deep distress at this impudence and insult to their most beloved Emperor.

As Sudan says in his impeachment: "I have read Su Shih's recent letter of thanks on his assumption of office at Huchow, containing satire on current affairs. While the common people pass it from mouth to mouth in admiration, all the loyal and righteous scholars are angered and distressed. Since Your Majesty instituted the new and beautiful laws, there have been many critics who disagreed with your policy. . . . But there is none like Su Shih, who with malicious intent and a disgruntled heart slanders Your Majesty beyond the rules of propriety of a subject." Sudan went on to mention Su's poems of satire. "These lines are aimed at the person of Your Majesty, and are the height of impudence. . . . Your Majesty walks in the path of virtue, guides the government, and raises scholars to benefit the world. Your heart is truly that of Yao and Shun. At such a time appears Su Shih, backed by a false, fortuitous reputation and useless abstruse learning. Yet he was given the post of a chief magistrate. I do not understand how Su Shih could have conducted himself with such 'ungrateful insolence. Besides," Sudan went on in his righteous anger, "the first principle in human relationships is a sense of duty, and among the various relationships none is more important than the duty of a subject towards his ruler. That Su Shih could have the heart to say such things against Your Majesty shows that he has forgotten the duty of a subject to his sovereign. Now," Sudan pointed the moral finger, "when a minister loses his sense of duty and follows his selfish interests, there is nothing that such a person will stop at. What may he not do next? ... Su Shih's crimes are more than unpardonable; even ten thousand deaths will not suffice to make amends for his insult to Your Majesty. I hope Your Majesty will hand him over to the court for criminal effrontery to the throne, as a warning to all Your Majesty's subjects. I am bursting with a spirit of loyal indignation."

There was a bit of curious casuistry in another censor's impeachment. When Su Tungpo was on his way to assume office at Huchow, he had written an inscription for a certain Chang's garden. In this inscription Su had said: "The gentlemen of ancient days did not insist on going into office, nor did they insist on keeping out of office. If a scholar insists on being an official, he is likely to forget his soul; *if he insists on not becoming an official he is likely to forget his Emperor.*" This was a summing up by Mencius of Confucius' attitude toward joining a government. The censor, however, in his great loyalty to the Emperor, tried to persuade the latter that Su Shih was preaching a dangerous doctrine. "A scholar," he said, "should never forget his Emperor whether he is in or out of office. Now Su Shih is preaching that one should not forget his Emperor only when he is out of office!"

It was left to Leeding to show four reasons why Su Tungpo should pay with his life. He prefaced his memorandum by the remark that "Su Tungpo is a shallow scholar and won a reputation only by chance; by an accident he passed the special examinations and was favoured with a government post." Leeding went on to say that Su was sour because he had hoped to get a higher post, and to give expression to his petty disgruntled heart slandered those in authority. One of the reasons why he should be killed was that the Emperor had tolerated him long enough, hoping for him to reform, but that Su could not take a warning. Another reason why he should be killed was that although Su's writings were nonsensical, they had an important influence on the country. "In my office as guardian of the law, I cannot allow such crimes to go unpunished. I hope Your Majesty will exercise your enlightened judgment and carry out the law, not only to put a stop to this demoralising influence but to give encouragement to those who are loyal and sincere in their service to the country. Thus good and evil men may be sharply distinguished and the moral atmosphere of society will be purified."

The trial began on August 20. The defendant deposed that he was forty-four years of age (forty-two in the Western reckoning), and gave an account of his ancestry, his place of nativity, the years in which he passed the imperial examinations, and the different official posts he had held. Then followed a long list of the persons he had recommended for office, for it was usually considered an important measure of an official's worthiness whether he had put forward good or bad men for public duty. It was stated that during his official career he had received two demerits. Once he was fined eight catties of copper for failing to attend the official autumn ceremony when he was deputy magistrate at Feng-shiang at the time when he had a quarrel with his superior. He was also fined eight catties of copper during his term at Hangchow for failing to report the embezzlement of public funds by a certain minor official. "Outside these two cases, he has a clear official record."

At first Su Tungpo acknowledged responsibility only for those poems he had written when he was visiting the villages near Hangchow, those in which he complained of the farmers eating without salt and the abuse of the farmers' loans, and certain others mentioned in the impeachment. He could not recall having written anything else that had any bearing on current politics. For some days he denied having written satirical poems to his friends, and continued to plead not guilty. It was a question of what should and what should not be considered "slander of the government", and what constituted "slanderous attacks". But on the thirtieth of August he decided to plead guilty; he then admitted that he had written satirical poems about the regime and had exchanged such poems with his friends. He said, however, that he "had not tried to conceal them", since it was a question of interpretation. In the course of the trial he was made to sign an affidavit admitting: "Since I joined the different ministries, I have not received rapid promotions. Besides, the people promoted during the new regime were mostly young men and differed in opinion from myself. Therefore I composed poems and other writings of protest and criticism, in the hope that many people would read these poems and be brought around to my point of view." There were altogether thirty-nine persons among the friends of Su Tungpo who were implicated in the case, and over a hundred poems were brought up in the trial for examination, each of which the author was required to explain. As Su Tungpo had in all his poetry used the choicest phrases and a great number of literary and historical allusions, we are indebted to this record of the trial for the author's own elucidations of many passages in his texts. Some of these poems were highly deceptive and had hidden points to be appreciated only when one understood the historical references. I have so far avoided these poems with learned allusions, because they would require a separate explanation for each literary metaphor or historical reference, and would make difficult reading, besides burdening the reader with pedantry. Such an exhibition of pedantry would not be at all difficult because for centuries Su's commentators have been busy unearthing the original passages in history and Tang poetry to which his lines referred.

Some of the accusations were far-fetched. One of the most interesting cases was a poem about two old cypress trees. It said that the winding roots of these trees reached the underground springs where only the "hidden dragon" would know what they were like. This was considered an insult to the Emperor because the dragon was the symbol of the ruler who was presently reigning over the empire, and therefore one should only refer to a "dragon in the skies", and not a dragon hidden in the underground springs. There was also a poem about peonies in which the poet admired the incredible ingenuity of nature in creating such a great variety of the same species. This was taken by the judges to be intended as a sly reference to the ingenuity of those in power in devising new forms of taxation. The preface to the descriptive poem "The Medlar and the Chrysanthemum", where he spoke of eating these bitter seeds, was considered a direct satire on the poverty of the district in general and on the poor pay of the government officials in particular. The parable of the blind man's idea of the sun was considered a reference to the ignorance of the scholar candidates, who knew nothing about Confucian philosophy except what was in Wang Anshih's commentaries.

However, in most of the cases the defendant frankly admitted criticism of the various new government measures in his poems, and certainly there was enough feeling of anger and disappointment in the tone of his poems to justify the verdict that he was voicing a sharp criticism of the regime.

Among the different poems that he had sent to his friend Prince Wang Shien, there was a line where he said that he had to sit and "listen to the screams of the prisoners being flogged". He did say that "in a famine year there was no way of sending the fugitives home", fugitives compelled to flee their villages because of debt. He did refer to the "difficulty of painting a tiger", which was a symbol of the rapacious government. In his poem to his friend Li Chang, he did say that he "had gone along the city wall" of Michow and "buried the exposed corpses with tears in my eyes", corpses of men, women, and children who had died of starvation and fallen on the wayside, and that "there was no joy in being a magistrate" at that time. Concerning his poem to his friend Sun Chueh, containing a line saying that they would not talk politics, he confessed that at a dinner together they had agreed that whoever mentioned politics was to be penalised with a cup of wine. In a poem to Tseng Kung, an obscure official but a major prose writer, he mentioned that he was annoyed by all the hubbub of the politicians who "sounded to him like the ever-crying cicadas". In his poem to Chang Fangping he had compared the court to "a deserted forest where cicadas are dinning the air", and "an abandoned pond where croaking frogs are making so much noise" that he wanted "to close both my ears

with my hands". In his poem to Fan Chen he made a direct reference
to the "petty politicians" and we already know that in the one to Chou
Pin he made an implied comparison of the ruling authorities to the owl.
In a poem on the Hangchow bore he had said that if the China Sea had
known of the good Emperor's intentions, it would "change the salt-
producing areas into mulberry fields".

It is interesting to take a closer look at two poems he wrote to one of
his best friends, Liu Shu, when the latter was dismissed from the capital.
We shall understand better the officials' resentment and also get an idea
of the hidden meanings in most of Su Tungpo's lines. Incidentally, it
will be seen that a literal translation of some of the poems would be
meaningless to an English reader unless properly supported with footnotes. One of the poems says:

"How dare I express discontent in a time of peace?
I only sigh that my teachings are following you east.
By your conversation, you can frighten the south of Huai River,
And after your departure stripped bare will be the north of Chi.
A lone stork does not have to sound alarm at midnight,
It is difficult to tell the sex of black crows . . ."

Su Tungpo confessed that he was a great admirer of this friend, and
that he had therefore compared him to Confucius by the phrase about
not expressing discontent. The second line refers to the great commentator of the eastern Han dynasty, who was sending his disciple to
the east. The third line refers to a great, courageous official who quelled
a plot for rebellion by the Prince of Huainan ("south of Huai River")
by his presence at the court. The fourth line refers to a passage in the
ancient classics saying that the best horses were produced in the north of
Chi district (modern Hopei), and furthermore, to a line by a Tang
poet, Han Yu, who on sending a friend off said that after his departure no good horses were left in the countryside of the north of Chi.
It therefore meant that the whole court was now empty of good men.
The fifth line about the "lone stork" refers to an ancient passage where
a distinguished man in a company of petty men was compared to a
stork standing alone in a poultry yard of ducks and chickens. The
implied meaning was that those at the court were just common fowl
and crying at midnight was supposed to be a function of the stork. The
last line was even more offensive, because there are two lines in the
Book of Poetry which assert: "Everybody is saying I am a saint, but
who can distinguish a male from a female crow?" The court consisted,
therefore, of no more than a pack of black crows in which there was no
way of telling which was good and which was bad.

In a second satirical poem to the same friend he had written:

"Benevolence and righteousness are the great avenues,
Poetry and history are the stepping-stones.
They show off their flowing belts to each other
And sing of the wheat's shining green.
Thanks for your exhibition of rotten mice,
But the high-flying crane dives into the clouds.
You don't have to wake me up from my madness;
I shall be sober when I wake up from the drink."

The first three lines refer to the scholar hypocrites who talk of benevolence and righteousness as avenues of official promotion and deride them for being proud of their official pomp. The reference to the "wheat's shining green" is, according to Su Tungpo, a reference to a poem in the *Book of Chuangtse* about officials who sought honour in their lifetime and were buried with pearls in their mouths, but in time their graveyards became wheat-fields. The fifth line contains another reference to Chuangtse. On being offered a high post by the king of his country, Chuangtse declined it and told the official messenger the following story: There were some carrion crows who had caught dead rotten mice and were making a feast on a tree. A crane (symbol of the pure and retired scholar) happened to fly by, and thinking that the crane was going to deprive them of the feast of mice, the crows screeched to frighten it away, but the noble bird flew on up to the clouds. The moral of this story was that Su had a haughty contempt for the petty squabbles for power among the politicians.

I have the feeling that Su Tungpo thought it rather wonderful to be arrested and tried for writing poetry. He must have enjoyed lecturing the court on the literary references.

It was, therefore, well established that Su Tungpo had been highly disrespectful to the government. He had compared those in power to croaking frogs, to chirping cicadas, to owls, to black crows feeding on rotten mice, and to common fowl in a poultry yard. More unbearable was his reference to "monkeys who were given baths and caps" to look like human beings. It all amounted to this: Su Tungpo did not think very much of people like Sudan and Leeding, so why should Sudan and Leeding think well of Su Tungpo?

The trial was concluded, probably, at the beginning of October, and the testimony submitted to the Emperor. A great many persons were involved, particularly Prince Wang Shien, who had, as was brought out in the course of the trial, exchanged various gifts and presents with the poet. The Emperor ordered that all those who had exchanged poems with Su Tungpo should submit poems in their possession for examination by the court.

Meanwhile, Emperor Jentsung's wife, who had always stood up for

Su Tungpo, fell ill and died. Before her death she had said to the Emperor: "I remember that when the Su brothers passed the examinations, our ancestor Jentsung told members of the family that he was greatly pleased, for he had that day discovered two future premiers for his royal descendants. I hear now that Su Shih is on trial for writing poems. It's the little fellows who want to destroy him. They couldn't find any fault with his official record, and now they try to convict him on his poetry. Is not the charge rather trivial? I do not think I can recover, but you must not condemn the innocent. It will anger the gods." This practically amounted to her dying wish.

On the thirtieth of October the judges made a summary of the case, which was submitted to the Emperor. On account of the funeral for the Empress Dowager, the case hung fire for a long time. While Su Tungpo was waiting in jail for the outcome of the trial and the determination of his fate, something mysterious happened.

"One night after the completion of the trial," Su Tungpo told his friends years later, "the night drum had been struck and just as I was going to bed I suddenly saw a man come into my room. Without saying a word, he threw a small box to the floor and, using it as his pillow, lay down to sleep on the ground. Taking him for another prisoner, I let him alone and fell asleep. About the time of the fourth watch [about 3 a.m.] I felt someone shaking me in my bed, and the man said to me: 'Congratulations!' I turned and asked him what this was all about. 'Sleep well and don't worry,' said the man, and mysteriously left the room with his little box.

"What happened was that when I was first impeached, Sudan and the others tried their best to persuade the Emperor to put me to death But His Majesty had never intended to kill me, so he secretly sent a small palace servant to the prison to watch me. Soon after this little fellow came, I fell asleep, snoring like thunder. He immediately rushed back to report to His Majesty that I was sleeping very soundly and peacefully, and His Majesty said to the courtiers: 'I know that Su Shih's conscience is clear!' That was how later I was forgiven and sent to Huangchow."

It was the usual custom to grant a general amnesty on the occasion of an imperial funeral, and by law and custom Su Tungpo should have been pardoned. To the censors, who had hoped to involve the whole opposition by this case, this would have meant that all the trouble they had taken had come to naught. Leeding and Sudan were greatly worried. At this point, Leeding submitted a strong protest against any possible pardon of the accused that might be under consideration. Sudan went further and demanded that Szema Kuang, Fan Chen, Chang Fangping, Li Chang, Sun Chueh, and five others of Su Tungpo's friends be killed.

One of the vice-premiers at the time, Wang Kuei, under pressure of the censors, suddenly said to the Emperor one day:

"Su Shih is at heart a rebel against Your Majesty."

"He may have committed some offence," replied the Emperor with an expression of surprise, "but he is not thinking of rebellion. What makes you say so?"

Wang Kuei then mentioned the poem on the two cypresses with a reference to the dragon hidden in the underground springs, which could mean that someone destined to become emperor in the future would arise from his present obscurity. But the Emperor only said:

"You cannot read poetry that way. He was singing about the cypress. What has that to do with me?"

Wang Kuei therefore kept quiet, and Chang Chun, who was still Su Tungpo's friend at this time, defended Su by explaining to the Emperor that the dragon was not only the symbol of the ruler but could refer to ministers as well, and quoted examples from literary history in support of his argument.

When the examination of further evidence handed in by Su Tungpo's friends was completed, the Emperor appointed his own man to review the case. According to the judge's summary a slander of this kind against the government was punishable by exile and hard labour for two years, and furthermore, in the case of Su Tungpo, whose offence was considered serious, the punishment should also deprive him of two of his official ranks. That was the legal view of the case. The power of decision, however, lay entirely with the Emperor himself in a case of such serious nature.

On December 29, to the great disappointment of Leeding and Sudan, a palace official handed out an order sending Su Tungpo to Huang-chow, near Hankow. He was given a low rank, with the nominal office of a lieutenant in an army training corps, but the terms of the order were that he was to be "kept" or "confined" there within that district; that is, he was not free to leave that district, and had no right to sign official documents.

Among those implicated in the case, three were dealt with severely. Prince Wang Shien was deprived of all his ranks on the ground that he had betrayed official secrets to Su Tungpo and had constantly exchanged gifts with him, and that, moreover, as a member of the royal household he had failed to report such slanderous poems as were in his possession. The second was Wang Kung, who had not received any particularly slanderous poems, but who was evidently being victimised in this case, perhaps because for private reasons the censors wanted to dispose of him. In the years after, Su kept referring to Wang Kung as one who suffered on his account. We know Wang Kung's luxurious habits, and his banishment to the remote south-west was hard for him.

G

The third was Tseyu, who had written to the Emperor begging for
his brother's pardon and offering to surrender all his own official ranks
and office to redeem him. In the testimony, Tseyu had not been charged
with receiving any seriously slanderous poems from his brother, but on
account of the family connection he was degraded and sent to Kao-an,
about a hundred and sixty miles from the detention place of his brother,
to sell wine at a government bureau.

Of the others, Chang Fangping and another high official were fined
thirty catties of copper, while Szema Kuang, Fan Chen, and eighteen
other friends of Su Tungpo were fined twenty catties of copper each.

Su Tungpo was let out of prison on New Year's Eve, after detention
for four months and twelve days. Coming out of the prison gate on the
north of the Tungcheng Street, he stopped for a while, sniffed the air,
and felt pleasure in the breeze blowing on his face, in the noise of
the magpies, and in watching the people passing by on horseback in
the streets.

Incorrigible as he was, that very day he wrote two poems again
wherein he said that "facing the wine cup" he "felt like coming out of
a dream", and trying his poetic pen, he "found it was already inspired".

"In all my life, writing has brought me into trouble.
From now on the lesser my fame, the better it is for me.
I feel like the old man's horse that has returned to the fort,
And will no longer have youth's cock-fights in the east city."

His lines began to flow again, and in these two poems there were
certainly at least two lines that under the scrutiny of the same prose-
cutors could equally convict him of disrespect for the Emperor. The
reference to an old man at the fort losing his horse was harmless
enough, since it referred to a parable that losing one's horse did not
mean bad luck and finding it again did not mean good luck; in other
words, one never knew what was good luck or bad. But the phrase
"youth's cock-fights" refers to a certain Chia Chang. In his old age
Chia told people that when he was a boy, he had obtained the Tang
emperor's favour with his fighting cocks and the emperor had treated
him as court jester and an actor. The point could be stretched that
once more he was referring to those at court as "jesters and actors"—a
term of abuse. In another line he said that he had "stolen an office",
that is, occupied a post without qualifications; but again, the phrase
used was taken from a letter written by a great scholar and addressed
to Tsao Tsao, a man popularly considered a great hypocrite and a
wicked ruler. On completing the poem, Su threw down his pen and
said: "I am really incorrigible."

BOOK THREE

MATURITY

(1080–1093)

Chapter Fifteen

FARMER OF THE EASTERN SLOPE

SU TUNGPO now was to become a farmer by necessity and a recluse by temperament and natural inclination. What society, culture, learning, reading of history, and external duties and responsibilities do to a man is to hide his real self. Strip him of all these trappings of time and convention, and you have the real man. A Su Tungpo back among the people is like a seal in water; somehow a seal dragging its fins and tail on land is only half a seal. Su is never more likeable than when he is an independent farmer trying to make his own living. The Chinese mind usually glamorises a poet wearing a "coolie hat", putting his hands to the plough and standing against an idyllic hillside, provided he can also compose good verse and beat time to it by striking the buffalo's horn, and provided further that he occasionally, or even frequently, gets drunk and climbs the city wall to prowl in the moonlight. Then he becomes Nature's great playboy—perhaps Nature never intended man to be otherwise.

On January 1, 1080, Su Tungpo had left the capital with his eldest son Mai, who was now twenty-one, for his place of confinement at Huangchow. He had hastened there by the most direct overland route, leaving his family to come after him in charge of his brother. Poor Tseyu had to bring his own large family (seven daughters, three sons, and two sons-in-law) to his new post at Kao-an some hundred miles south of Kiukiang, in addition to Tungpo's family. The post of supervisor of the wine monopoly was less attractive than we might suppose, for it amounted to no more than being the keeper of a government wine store. After a voyage of months, Tseyu arrived at Kiukiang, left his own family there waiting for him, and took Su Tungpo's wife and Chaoyun and the two younger children up the Yangtse to his brother. Tungpo arrived at Huangchow on February 1, the family not coming until May 29.

Huangchow was a poor, small town on the Yangtse some sixty miles below Hankow. While waiting for his family, Tungpo put up at a temple, the Tinghueiyuan, situated on a thickly wooded hill-side at some distance from the river. He shared the meals of the monks, and after lunch or supper would pace about under a crab-apple tree. concerning which he wrote one of his most admired poems. Very soon a group of friends formed around him. The chief magistrate, Shü, was cordial and often invited him to wine feasts. Across the river, the chief magistrate of the district of Wuchang (which is not the modern Wuchang) was one Chu, who kept sending him wine and eatables. On rainy days Su Tungpo slept late and then took a walk alone in the late afternoon,.wandering over the rolling foothills of the Eastern Knoll, and exploring the temples and private gardens and shady streams. On other days his friends came to visit him, and they went together on trips to the mountains on both banks of the Yangtse. This was a hilly woodland district and the country was very picturesque. On the south bank stood the tall Fanshan Mountain, high above a plain cut up by large lakes and connecting waterways.

Su Tungpo had had a narrow escape, a soul-shaking experience, to say the least. He began to consider what was life. In the poem of farewell to his brother written in June, he said his life was like a little ant crawling against a turning millstone, and again, like a feather carried about by a whirlwind. He began to ponder very deeply his own character and to consider how he could achieve true peace of mind. He became religious. In his sketch of the Ankuo Temple he said: "I, arrived in February at my residence in Huangchow. After getting settled and solving the problems of food and shelter, I shut the door, put the broomstick behind it, and began to collect my frightened spirits. I examined myself to see how I could start a new life. It seemed to me that so far I had always acted on impulse and at variance with true humanist principles. I do not mean only the things I did which have brought me into the present trouble. I might try to correct one fault, only to find another and yet another, so that I would not know where to begin. With a sigh I said to myself: 'I have not been able to control my impulses by tao [religion], nor overcome my habits by the light of reason. Without seeking a spiritual renovation at the roots, any corrections of habits would be temporary. Why don't I devote myself to the brotherhood of the Buddha in order to make a clean start?' I was able to find a quiet, beautiful place in the south of the city called the Ankuo Temple, with tall trees and bamboos and fish ponds and pavilions around. Every one or two days I would go there, burn incense, and sit in quiet meditation. There I learned to forget all distinctions between the self and the non-self, and my mind· was cleared of incumbrances. I arrived then at a state where it was impossible to have thoughts of the material world arise in my mind. Once the human mind reaches that purified stage, sense perceptions fall away, because there is nothing to which these thoughts can attach themselves. It is then that one's external and internal selves become one. I began to experience a great happiness. . . ."

Against this religious impulse, a trend of Confucianist teaching, which lay deep in Su Tungpo's soul, seemed to draw him in another direction. It was true that one could seek peace in religion, but if Buddhism was right and life was nothing but illusion, one should let human society alone entirely, and for that matter the human race might just as well go out of existence, and good riddance, too. There was, therefore, the continual struggle between the Buddhist goal to reach a spiritual void and arrive at a non-personal spiritual existence, free from all personal attachments, and a more realistic Confucian sense of duty towards one's fellow men. The question of salvation is, after all, only the achievement of spiritual harmony in which the baser instincts of man can be brought under control of his higher nature. If one could attain such a spiritual harmony through intelligent self-discipline, one did not have to leave human society entirely in order to achieve salvation.

For instance, there is the question of the fight against evil or evils in human society. The neo-Confucianist Chu Shi criticised Su Tungpo's two poems written on his coming out of prison as showing no intention to check himself and start a new life. Those two poems, as we have seen, seemed to show that it was the same old Su Tungpo writing. The question is, did he intend to reform or not? Did he mean to keep his mouth shut and stop criticising things that were wrong in the country? To his less intimate friends he gave one answer; to his best friends he gave another.

There are two interesting letters that he wrote to friends to whom he revealed his innermost convictions. One was to his close friend Li Chang. The latter had written poems to comfort him in his misfortune, but their tone was too sentimental for Su Tungpo, who wrote the following reply: "Why are you like this? I had expected you to be brave in trouble. It is true that we are growing old and are in distress, but down in our bones we are conscious of having done the right thing, and with all the philosophy that we have learned, we should be able to take life and death with a laugh. If you are pitying me because I have been overtaken by misfortune, then we are in no way different from the uneducated. . . . We are in present difficulties. *But, if an occasion comes up again when we can do something to benefit the people and show our loyalty to the ruler, we shall do it regardless of all consequences for ourselves and leave the rest to the Creator's will.* I wouldn't say this to anybody except yourself. Please burn this letter after reading it. Other people may misunderstand."

To Wang Kung, who got the worst of the deal in the prosecution of Su's case, and who was now exiled to the remote south-west, Su Tungpo wrote several letters. He first expressed his sorrow for causing him all this trouble, but then said that on receiving Wang Kung's letter, he saw that Wang was able to enjoy the consolation of philosophy. "Now I really know your truly amiable character and entertain the hope that in my old age when we meet again, I may still be counted among your friends. . . ." He went on to speak of the Taoist art of prolonging life, to which he was applying himself.

"Recently I have begun to understand something about the secret of prolonging life. Those who see me all say that my face looks different now. When we meet again after another few years, you will find me looking like an immortal. I have also been able to paint inspired pictures of winter forests and bamboos in ink. My running and cursive styles of calligraphy have especially improved, but my poetic pen is not as facile as before—I don't know why. . . . I have received your two letters discussing how we should face a misfortune of this kind, and I am both enlightened by, and greatly pleased with, what you say. *But remember this. If I had known that I was going to get into this trouble, I still would have done it without any hesitation.* During all his adversities, Tu Fu never for a moment forgot about his country. That is why he was the incomparable one among all poets."

To his old friend Chang Chun, however, he had something different to say. Chang Chun, now vice-premier, had written him a letter urging him to reform. To this friend he wrote a perfectly correct answer, full of a contrite spirit. It was so correctly written that the letter could very well have been shown to the Emperor. "You have always given me very frank and straightforward advice, but I was stubborn and did not listen to you. When I was in jail, I thought it was too late to repent and that I was certainly doomed. Luckily, His Majesty was generous and granted me my life. If I don't reform now, I am indeed less than a man. . . . In the early years of my life I received many kindnesses from the ruler, and if I had behaved dutifully and correctly I wouldn't be today where I am. Now that I think of what I did, I realise that I was wrong. I acted like a madman or one who walks into the sea. When the spell of madness came, I was unconscious of what I did, and felt as if something was urging me along. When the spell was over, I felt ashamed of myself. How can you ever doubt my determination to reform? . . ." He went on to describe his life. "Huang-chow is a poor district. If often rains and the sky is usually overcast. However, fish and rice and fuel are cheap here, and it is a suitable place for a poor fellow like me to live in. You know that I never tried to save money and spent all my salary as soon as I received it. Tseyu has seven daughters and has piled up a mountain of debts. He is bringing my family here and I don't know when he will arrive. I am living alone at a monastery, dressed simply and eating vegetarian food with the monks. It's a simple kind of life, and I am worried about what I shall do when the whole family arrives. I understand that success and failure are relative terms, but my salary is cut off and I am afraid in a year's time we may have to starve. I cannot help being a little worried. But as the proverb says: 'Where a current goes, it forms its own canal.' What's the use of troubling about it beforehand? I have seen the magistrate only once since my arrival. The rest of the time

I shut myself up and don't even read books, but spend my hours over
the Buddhist scriptures."

Things began to look settled with the family's safe arrival, although
Tungpo did not know yet how they were going to live after their
money was gone. His two younger sons, Tai and Kuo, were twelve
and ten. Through the courtesy of the chief magistrate, they were able
to put up at the Linkao House, later made famous by the poet. This
was an official station where government people stopped during their
voyages on the Yangtse. To a friend Su Tungpo wrote: "My house
is only about a dozen steps from the bank of the river. The beautiful
mountains on the south bank lie spread before my window, and with
the high winds and changing clouds and misty weather, the view
changes a hundred times a day. I have never had such luck before."
The place was beautiful enough, but the glamour that has been
attached to it was largely due to the poet's imagination. He saw more
in this poor little building facing the hot sun in summer than other
tourists, who were deeply disappointed when they actually saw it. Later,
when a studio was added for his benefit, he could boast that he would
wake up from an afternoon nap, forgetting where he was, and when
the window screen was up, he could watch from his couch a thousand
sailing boats going down the river, until the water merged with the
sky in the distance.

The Linkao House might not be much, but half of the beauty of
a landscape depends on the region and the other half on the man looking at it. Su Tungpo, being a poet, saw and felt what the others could
not see and could not feel, even if they were in Paradise. "After a
drink and a good meal," Su wrote in his journal, "the Recluse of the
Eastern Slope leans over his desk, with white clouds on his left and the
clear river on his right. Both the outer and the inner doors are wide
open, giving a direct view of the hills and the peaks. At such a time
I sit there as if I were thinking of something and again as if I were not
thinking at all. In such a state of mind I receive so freely the bounty
of nature spread before me that I feel almost ashamed of myself."
A second note he wrote on this house, addressed to Fan Chen's son,
has a twist of sly humour. "The great river lies only a few dozen steps
below me and half of its water comes from the Omei Mountains, so
that it is almost as good as seeing our home town. The hills and the
river, the wind and the moon, have no owner; they belong to anybody
who has the leisure to enjoy them. How would your new garden compare with mine? I suppose you have the advantage of paying the
summer and autumn taxes on it, and the draft exemption tax besides,
while I don't."

But Tungpo was really hard up. He had a peculiar system of budgeting his expenditure. This is how he told the story in a letter to Chin Kuan: "Li Chang has been here and we spent a few good days together, during which he never stopped mentioning your name. I have not received any letter from Sun Chueh. I suppose he is busy. . . . On my arrival at Huangchow, my salary was cut off, and I have such a big family to support. I am now compelled to practise the greatest economy. I allow myself to spend only 150 cash [roughly fifteen cents] a day. On the first of every month I take 4,500 cash and apportion them into even lots, and suspend these individual strings of cash on the ceiling. Every morning I take one string down by means of the hook used for hanging up paintings, and put away the hook for the day. Then I provide a large bamboo section, in which I save up what is left over for the day, with which I can entertain my friends. This is the method of Yunlao [Chia Shou]. In this way, I figure my money will last for a year. I shall think of some way to provide for the family when it's all used up. . . . I don't have to worry ahead. For this reason I haven't a single care in my breast."

From Linkao House he could see the beautiful mountains of Wuchang across the river. Sometimes he went out in sandals and hired a small boat to spend the day in the company of fishermen and wood-cutters. Often he was pushed around and abused by drunkards and "felt happy" that he was "beginning to be unknown". Sometimes he visited Wang Tsiyu, his friend from Szechuen, who lived across the river. Often, when he was held up by a storm, he stopped over at his place for several days. Sometimes he took a small boat and went straight to Pan Ping's wine shop at Fankow. The village wine, he found, was not so bad. The district grew oranges and persimmons and taros more than a foot long. A bushel of rice was only twenty cash because transportation on the river was cheap. Mutton here tasted just as good as pork and beef in the north. Venison was very cheap, and fish and crabs cost almost nothing. The director of the wine bureau of Chiting kept a very big library, and liked to lend people his books. The magistrates had good cooks and often invited him to their homes.

In 1081 Su Tungpo became a real farmer. He began to work a piece of land on the Eastern Slope (Tungpo), and to call himself "the Recluse of the Eastern Slope". He had wanted to retire to a farm, but he had not expected to be compelled to be a farmer in this way. In his preface to the *Eight Poems on the Eastern Slope* he said: "In the second year of my stay at Huangchow, my money was running out. My old friend Ma Mengteh was worried for me, and obtained from the district government a grant of land, about eight or ten acres, on the location of an abandoned barracks. This enabled me to live there as a farmer. The land had been abandoned and was full of brambles and

débris. It had not rained for a long time, and the work of clearing the
rubble and converting it into rice-fields was a back-breaking task.
After working until I was utterly exhausted, I took my hands from the
plough with a sigh, and wrote the following poems in commemoration of my own labour and my hope that my toil might be well
rewarded with next year's crops."

The *Tungpo* or Eastern Slope homestead occupied actually about
ten acres and lay only one-third of a mile east of the city, directly on
a hill-side. On top was the house with three rooms overlooking a
pavilion below, and below the pavilion was the famous Snow Hall.
This hall, with a five-room front, was completed in the snow in
February of the following year. The walls were painted by the poet
himself with snow scenes of forests and rivers and fishermen. Later,
this was where he entertained his friends, and where the great landscape painter of the Sung dynasty, Mi Fei, then a young man of twenty-
two, came to make his acquaintance and discuss painting with him.
The poet, Lu Yu, who visited the Eastern Slope in October 1170, some
seventy years after Su's death, recorded that there was a portrait of
Su Tungpo hanging in the middle of the hall. The portrait showed
him dressed in a purple gown and a black hat and reclining on a rock
with a bamboo cane in his hand.

Below the steps of the Snow Hall a little bridge spanned a small
ditch, usually dry except in the rainy season. On the east of the Snow
Hall there was a tall willow tree planted by the poet himself, and
farther to the east there was a small well containing delightfully cool
spring water, but having no other merit than that it was the poet's
well. On the east and below, there were rice-fields, wheat-fields, a long
stretch of mulberries, vegetables, and a great orchard of fruit trees.
Somewhere he also planted tea, which he obtained from a friend in a
neighbouring district.

Behind the homestead rose the Prospect Pavilion, situated on top
of a mound and commanding an unobstructed view of the countryside. His neighbour on the west was Mr. Ku, who owned the
forest of huge bamboos, seven inches in circumference, growing so
thick that in it one could not see the sky. There in its shade Su
Tungpo spent the hot summer days, and besides gathered the dry and
very smooth sheaths of the bamboo for lining his wife's shoes.

Su Tungpo was now a real farmer and not merely a landlord. In a
poem echoing one by his friend Kung Pingchung, he said:

"Last year I cleared the rubble on the Eastern Slope,
And planted myself mulberries a hundred yards long.
This year I cut the hay to thatch the Snow Hall.
Exposed to the sun and wind, my face becomes well tanned."

There had been no rain for a long time, and when it came he felt happy and gratified as only a true farmer can:

> "Suddenly rain came from heaven three inches deep.
> The Creator's mercy is beyond comprehension.
> After my work I enjoy such sweet sleep, listening
> To the clack of wooden shoes outside the eastern wall.
> With coarse meals a humble man can support himself for life,
> And tilling his fields, look proudly into people's eyes.
> I built myself a pond one thousand feet around,
> To dam the spring water coming from the north-west.
> My neighbours helped me stamp the embankment,
> Knowing that my pocket is empty and bare."

Building was an instinct with Su Tungpo. He had made up his mind to make himself a comfortable home. All his energy was used up in damming water, building a fish pond, getting saplings from neighbours, flowers from friends' gardens, and vegetable seeds from his home province. He jumped with joy when a boy came running with the good news that they had struck water in the well they were digging, or when he saw the needle-like green blades peeping above the earth. He watched with pride and satisfaction how his rice-stalks stood proudly erect and swaying with the wind, and how the bedewed stalks glistened at night like strings of pearls in the moonlight. He had been fed on official salary; now he began to "appreciate the full flavour of rice". On the upper lands he planted wheat. A good farmer came and gave him some advice, which was that he should not let the first sprouts grow up, and that if he expected a rich harvest, he should let cows and sheep graze over them for a time, for this made the crop grow better. When he did have a good harvest, he remembered gratefully the farmer's advice.

His friends and neighbours were Pan the wine-shop keeper, Kuo the pharmacist, Pang the physician, Ku the farmer; a loud-speaking, domineering peasant woman who often quarrelled with her husband and "screeched like a pig" at night; Shü Tashou, the magistrate of Huangchow, and Chu Shouchang, magistrate of Wuchang and a great admirer of the poet. Staying always with him was the faithful Ma Mengteh, who had followed him for twenty years, had always believed in him, and now had to share his poverty. Su remarked that for his friend to expect to become rich with him was like trying to make a carpet of wool from a turtle's back. "Poor crazy Ma, even now he thinks that I am a brilliant man!" A poor but good scholar from his native town, Tsao Ku, had come to tutor his boys. His wife's brother came to live with them for a period during their first year at Huangchow, and in the following years Tseyu's sons-in-law came by turns, from time to time, to visit them. Su Tungpo had secured another son-in-law for his brother, whom, according to Tseyu's poem, the latter accepted without ever seeing him. The poet also began to attract a collection of rather queer individuals, two of them Taoists, who believed in and practised the life of carefree vagabondage as preached by Taoism. One of these was supposed to be one hundred and twenty-seven years old when Tseyu sent him to see Su Tungpo, and as the poet was interested in the secret of prolonging life, this old Taoist practically became an established member of the family. In the third year the poet monk Tsanliao came to stay with him for about a year. But his best friend was Chen Tsao, with whose father Su had quarrelled in his young days. Chen was living some distance away at Chiting; but Su went to visit him several times, and Chen came to visit Su seven times in four years. By a literary accident Chen became immortalised as a henpecked husband. Today in the Chinese language, "Chichang's weakness" is synonymous with "being henpecked", Chichang being Chen's courtesy name. Chen was the kind of friend with whom Su could joke freely all the time. In a jesting verse, Su Tungo wrote: "Pity the poor Taoist of Lungchiu. He sits up chatting about ghosts and devils all night. Suddenly he hears a lion's roar, and in his dismay the cane drops from his hand." Henceforth his reputation as the classic henpecked husband was established. The interpretation of this verse is open to question. From all we know, Chen lived a very carefree, romantic, and happy life at home. The phrase "lion's roar" was also a Buddhist phrase signifying "the voice of Buddha". What seems to me probable is that his wife had a loud voice, and Su Tungpo was simply making fun of his friend as friends often do. But to this day, the phrase "the lion's roar" has become the standard reference to a nagging wife. If Su Tungpo had clearly referred to "a lioness's roar", the case could be better established.

Su Tungpo had a good home, and he said in one of his poems that he had a good wife. By that he meant that his wife did not boss him as many of his friends and noted scholars in past history had been bossed by their wives. His sons were not brilliant, although Mai could write verse by this time. A great poet, Tao Chien, had written a poem in a mood of sad resignation about his sons, saying that what they were was God's will, and he asked only for a cup of wine. Su Tungpo said: "My sons are like those of Yuanliang [Tao Chien], but my wife is better than the wife of Chingtung." This Chingtung was a scholar of the eastern Han dynasty. In his own footnote to this line, Su said: "My writing cannot compare with his, but my temperament and my life bear great resemblances to his. Under a good emperor, he was dismissed from the court and like me led a wandering life. But he had

a wife with a horrible temper. Here I am luckier than he, and that is
why I wrote this line."

It was about this time that the poet took Chaoyun as his concubine.
Chaoyun, as we remember, was a maid of twelve when Mrs. Su bought
her at Hangchow, and in the terminology of the Sung period, one
could speak of her as "Mrs. Su's concubine" (*chieh*), although this would
not make sense in English. It was quite usual in ancient China for
a wife's maid to be promoted to the position of "concubine". Such
a concubine was the wife's assistant in every sense of the word, and
for a wife who attended to her husband's personal comforts, such as
preparing him a bath, a concubine had certain advantages over a maid
in not having to avoid the husband's presence. Chaoyun had grown up
now. She was a remarkably intelligent girl, and admirers of the poet
are inclined to glamorise her. Some even write about her as if she had
been an accomplished courtesan in Hangchow when Su Tungpo
brought her into the family. Careful research proves that this was not
the case. On the poet's own testimony, Chaoyun learned to read and
write only after coming into his home. Her popularity with Chinese
admirers of the poet is deserved, because it was she who followed him
to his exile in his old age.

In 1083 Chaoyun gave birth to a boy, called Tun-erh (meaning "the
Little Hide-Away"), and at the ceremony of bathing the baby three
days after its birth, Su Tungpo wrote a poem which was a satire on
himself.

> "All people wish their children to be brilliant,
> But I have suffered from brilliance all my life.
> May you, my son, grow up dumb and stupid,
> And, free from calamities, end up as a premier."

His wife must have been pleased with the fact that her husband was
a good cook and loved to do his own cooking. It is on record that he
expressed regret that though pork was so cheap at this place, "the rich
men would not eat it and the poor did not know how to cook it." He
gave a formula for stewed pork which was simplicity itself—to cook
it in a very small amount of water and after bringing it to a boil, let
it simmer for hours and hours, with soya-bean sauce, of course. His
method of cooking fish seems to have been the one commonly known
in China today. He selected a carp, washed it in cold water, rubbed
some salt on it, and stuffed it with heart of Chinese cabbage. Then he
put it in the pan with a few strips of the white of small onions, and
pan-fried it without stirring. When it was half-cooked, he put in a few
slices of raw ginger, and poured over it a little pickled turnip sauce
with a dash of wine. Just as it was about cooked, he threw in a few
thin slices of orange-peel, and then had it served hot.

He also invented a vegetable soup which he named after himself. This was essentially a poor man's food, which he recommended to a monk. It was a simple method of cooking steamed rice over vegetable soup in a double boiler, so that both would be done at the same time. The soup in the lower pot consisted of a medley of cabbage, turnips, rape turnip, and shepherd's purse, which were carefully rinsed before they were put in the pot with a little ginger. As was usual in ancient days, some uncooked rice was thrown in the soup itself. The steamed rice was placed in a separate colander after the vegetables had been boiled sufficiently to get rid of their raw smell. Care was taken to prevent the boiling soup from touching the bottom of the rice, so that the steam could penetrate evenly.

In such a rustic atmosphere, he found his life resembled more and more that of the great bucolic poet Tao Chien, whom he greatly admired. Tao Chien, too, had laid down his office and retired to work a farm because he could not put on his official gown and adjust his belt in order to kowtow to a small bureaucrat from the provincial tax bureau. Su wrote a poem saying that Tao Chien must have been one of his previous incarnations, which would have been presumptuous coming from a poet of lesser stature, but was natural in the case of Su Tungpo. The more he read Tao's poems, the more he realised how they reflected his own sentiments and his present life.

There are certain pleasures that only a poet-farmer can enjoy. On quitting official life to go back to the farm, Tao Chien had written a classic poem called "Homeward I go!" which unfortunately could not be sung. Inspired by his daily labour at the farm, Su Tungpo rearranged the words and set them to the music of a folk-song. He taught the farm hands to sing it, while he, interrupting his work at the plough, joined in the singing and kept time by beating a stick on the water-buffalo's horn.

It was easy for Su Tungpo to accept the consolation of philosophy. On the walls and doors of the Snow Hall, he wrote thirty-two words for himself to look at day and night. They contained a four-fold warning:

"To go about by carriage is a good way to acquire infirm legs.
To live in great halls and deep chambers is an ideal method to catch cold.
To indulge oneself with pretty women is a sure way to destroy one's health.
To eat food with rich gravy is the proper way to develop stomach ulcers."

Blessed are those who are deprived of the good things of this earth! It was this type of humour that enabled Su Tungpo to be happy and contented wherever he was. Later, when he was exiled outside China where no medicine or doctor was available, he told his friends: "When I think how many people at the capital are annually killed by doctors I must congratulate myself."

Altogether, Su Tungpo felt that his labours were rewarded and he was happy. "I have now converted the Eastern Slope into rice fields, and in spite of the exacting toil I find many happy moments," he wrote. "I have a house with a fifty-foot frontage, a dozen vegetable patches and over a hundred mulberry trees. I shall till the field while my wife raises silkworms, and thus we shall pass happily the remainder of our days."

Su was now independent and contented. What brings him close to us today is his religion of kindness. The iniquitous custom of drowning babies at birth in the district where he lived stirred his soul to the depths. He wrote a letter to the chief magistrate of Wuchang which is worth a pot of gold, not because of its style, but because of its content. I have often wondered how Jonathan Swift could recommend babies' flesh as delicious food for the aristocrats and a profitable plan for wholesale slaughter of babies, even in a spirit of bitter satire. Swift intended this as a joke, but it was a bad joke that Su Tungpo would not understand. As soon as Su heard of the practise of infanticide in the district from a local scholar, he immediately took action by writing a letter to the magistrate and sent a friend with it to see him personally.

"Su Shih addresses you:

"Yesterday I was at Wuchang stopping over at Wang Tienlin's place. He told me a very touching story, and after hearing it I could not eat. I think I can bring this to your attention, if not to others, and am therefore dispatching this letter to you through Mr. Wang. Other people might be too busy with their own affairs to take the time and trouble to attend to something which is outside their official routine.

"Tienlin said to me that in the district of Yochow and Ochow [Wuchang], the poor farmers as a rule raise only two sons and one daughter, and kill babies at birth beyond this number. They especially dislike to raise daughters, with the result that there are more men than women and many bachelors in the country. A baby is often killed at birth by drowning in cold water, but in order to do this the baby's parents have to close their eyes and avert their faces while pressing the baby down in the water until it dies after crying a short moment. There is a man at the Shenshien village by the name of Shih Kuei who once killed twins. Last summer his wife gave birth of quadruplets. It was a horrible story—both the mother and the babies died. Such is God's retribution, and yet the people are too ignorant to change their ways. When Tienlin hears of cases of indigent expectant mothers in his neighbourhood, he usually runs over to the family, and by giving the parents food and clothing is able to save many babies' lives. After a baby is thus saved and is a few days old, the parents refuse to give it away, even if some family want to adopt it. This shows that parental love for one's child is always there, but is blinded by custom.

"I hear that there is one Chin Kuangheng in your district who has now passed the examinations and is a justice at Anchow. When his mother was expecting him, the mother's brother dreamed of a little infant tugging at his dress as if it wanted to say something to him. He had the same dream again the following night and the infant appeared importunate. Realising that his sister was going to have a baby and perhaps did not welcome any more children, he rushed to his sister's house just in time to find the water basin being held ready. In this way Chin was saved and grew up. This is a story well known to the people of your district.

"According to the law, a man who wilfully kills his descendant is punishable by two years' hard labour, and this is a law that the county officials can act upon. I hope you will instruct the officials of the different townships to call together the village elders and inform them about this law. They should be properly impressed with the idea of retribution, and be told that this law is going to be enforced; and they should go home and tell the other villagers. You can have official bulletins posted on the walls to this effect, and offer rewards to people who report such cases, the money to come from the parent who commits such a crime and his neighbours in the same *paochia* unit. If he is a tenant farmer, his landlord shall be made responsible for it also. When a woman is expecting a child, her neighbours and landlord are bound to know about it. Therefore, when an infant is killed, her neighbours are in a position to report such a case, and it is fair to punish them if they fail to stop it. If you will punish a few cases of offence as a warning to others, this horrible custom can be stopped.

"Furthermore, you should instruct your county officials to call together the richer families and plead with them earnestly for help. If the parents are really so poor that they cannot support their children, they can be aided with money and gifts. A human being is not devoid of feeling; he is not made of wood or rock, and will be all too glad to save his own child. If a parent can be prevented from killing the baby in the first few days, after that, even if you ask him to kill it, he can't do it. Do you realise how many lives you will have saved from now on, if you can have this done? Buddhism teaches against the taking of lives, and among these the killing of animals that suckle their young and that reproduce by hatching is considered a most grave offence. How much more serious is the killing of a human child! We often speak of a sick, suffering child as 'a poor innocent'; infanticide is truly the killing of the innocent. The law provides that only a man who commits murder in his senile dotage is exempt from the death sentence. How much more should we regard it as a heinous crime to kill an innocent baby! If you can save these babies' lives, your merit in heaven will be ten times greater than for pardoning adult offenders. . . .

"When I was serving in Michow, there was a famine year and many parents were forced to abandon their children. I was able to collect funds and obtain several thousand bushels of rice for the purpose of feeding orphans. Every family that took care of one child was given six bushels of rice per month. After a year, the parents who adopted these orphans loved them as their own children, and the orphans had found a home. I was thus able to save several dozen children. This is a very simple thing and easy to do. I have made bold to bring this matter to your attention because I know I am speaking to a true friend, and I crave your pardon for the intrusion.

To Chu Kangshu [Shouchang],
Chief Magistrate of Ochow."

For his own part, he established a Save-the-Child Association, and made his neighbour Ku, a very honest and philanthropic scholar, its president. The association collected money from the rich people, asking them to contribute ten dollars a year or more, with which they bought rice and cloth and cotton for quilts. Ku handled the money, and a monk at the Ankuo Temple was made treasurer in charge of records and accounts. These people went about the countryside to investigate cases of needy expectant mothers, and gave them presents of money and food and clothing if they promised to raise their children. Su Tungpo said that it would be a great pleasure if they could thus save a hundred children a year, and he himself contributed ten dollars per year. He was acting in the best tradition of Buddhism.

It has always seemed to me that wherever the spirit of man lives, religion comes to life again. Whenever the spirit of man dies, religion also decays.

Chapter Sixteen

POET OF THE RED CLIFF

SU TUNGPO now lived an enchanted life. Perhaps Huangchow was a sordid little town, but infinite leisure, the landscape, a poet's sensitive imagination, and devotion to the moonlight and to wine produced a powerful combination to make the poet's life what it was. After the farm was planted and he was free from financial worries, he began to enjoy each day for what it could give. He had a group of friends whose time was as free as his own, and who were, like him, poor in cash but rich in leisure. Among these was an incomparable Li Chiao, not known to posterity otherwise than by Su Tungpo's record of his great capacity for sleep. After lunch, when the friends were playing chess, Li would go to lie on a couch and fall asleep. After every few rounds of chess, Li would turn about and remark: "I have just slept one round. How many rounds have you played?" Su remarked in his journal that Li was playing alone on a chessboard supported by four legs (the bed) and with one black piece (the sleeper). "During the game, there's winning and losing, but at the end, neither the chess nor the player exists." It was a kind of unsubstantial dream life, which Su says was beautifully expressed by the following verse of Ouyang Shiu:

"A cool night, the sound of a flute, and the moon upon the mountains—
A darkening valley, a riot of flowers, and the wanderer lost his way.
After a game of chess, one is not aware that a whole generation of
time has passed.
The wine is finished, time hangs heavy, and the traveller thinks of
home."

Su Tungpo continued to live both at the farm Snow Hall and the Linkao House in the city, and he passed daily between them. That little stretch of less than a third of a mile became probably the most celebrated dirty mud path in history. After passing the small shops in the city, one came upon that stretch of road called the Yellow Mud Flat, leading to the rolling foothills. It seemed that everything around was yellow, except for the green trees and bamboos. He had built the *Yellow* Tower at Suchow. He was living at Huangchow, which meant "The *Yellow* District", and he daily crossed the *Yellow* Mud Flat to reach the Eastern Slope under the *Yellow* Knoll. He had changed his scholar's cap and gown for the jacket of an ordinary farmer so that the common people would not recognise him. Daily he covered this stretch.

In the intervals between his work at the farm he would come to the town, get a little tipsy, and lie down on the grass to sleep until some kind peasant waked him up at dusk. One day in a drunken fit he wrote a hobo rhapsody, entitled "The Song of the Yellow Mud Flat", ending as follows:

"I admire the white clouds over the Yellow Mud in the morning,
And stop under the blue smoke of the Snow Hall at night,
Pleased that the fowl of the forest are not disturbed,
And happy that woodsmen ignore me and pass me by.

"I had tramped singing after a jolly sip,
And it pleased me to lay down my cane and fall asleep drunk,
With the meadow for my bed, sod for my pillow.
Such happiness can compare with dinner in a gilded hall!
The falling dew began to wet my clothing,
And the rising moon appeared full and round.
A kind elder waked me up,
Lest I should be trampled upon by the sheep and cow.

"Then I got up,
And after I got up I sang:
'The moon is clear; the stars are dim.
They sent me off on my start,
And now accompany me home.
The year is drawing to an end;
The leaves are turning golden;
I want to go home,
I want to go home,
I have loitered round the mud flat for too long."

But his nocturnal visits with his drinking friends produced some amusing rumours, both locally and at the court. Thanks to his devotion to the moonlight and to drink, it was also this kind of life that produced some of the very best of Su Tungpo's writings, both in poetry and in prose. In the "Beef and Wine Script", a rather extraordinary one of these night ventures is recorded.

"Today I was drinking with several friends when Chunchen arrived. The late summer heat is still on, and the wine is white in colour. What a brew! The moment it enters your body you see the King of Hell. We were greatly exercised over what we could get for dinner to go along with the wine. It happens that our western neighbour has a buffalo suffering from a foot disease. We killed it and

had it broiled. After we got drunk, we went along eastward from
the Eastern Slope and went as far as the Spring Grass Pavilion. By
the time we returned, it was already midnight."

A contemporary remarked that, as the Spring Grass Pavilion was
situated outside the city wall, the script bore witness to the fact that
Su Tungpo drank bootleg liquor, killed a farmer's buffalo, and in a
drunken spell climbed back over the city wall after lock-out hour.
"Was Chunchen, too, perhaps a dubious character?"
 On another night trip, he scared the chief magistrate out of his wits.
He was drinking on a boat on the river. The night under the open sky
was beautiful, and he was inspired to sing:

> "After a drink at night, Tungpo wakes up and gets drunk again.
> By the time I come home it seems to be midnight.
> The boy servant is asleep snoring like thunder
> And does not answer the door.
> Resting on a cane I listen to the murmur of the river
> And feel with a pang that I am not master of my own life.
> When can I stop this hustling about?
> The night is late, the air is calm,
> And the water a sheen of unruffled light.
> Let me take a small boat down the river hence
> To spend beyond the seas the remainder of my days."

The next day a rumour spread that Su Tungpo had come to the river-
bank, written this poem as a farewell, and sailed down the river and
fled. When the rumour reached the chief magistrate's ears he was
greatly frightened, for it was his responsibility to see that Su did not
leave this district. Immediately he went out and found the poet was
still asleep and snoring like thunder. This rumour finally spread to
the capital and even reached the ears of the Emperor.
 The following year a more serious rumour arose. Su Tungpo had
been suffering from a kind of rheumatism in the arms. Later his right
eye was affected, and for months he shut himself up and was not seen
by anybody. At that time the great prose master Tseng Kung died in
another province, and a rumour spread that Su Tungpo and this other
writer were called back to heaven by God on the same day. The
Emperor heard about it and inquired of a high official, a relative of
Su Tungpo, who replied that he had also heard the same rumour but
that he did not know for certain what had happened. The Emperor
was about to have his lunch, but could not eat. "It is difficult to find
another such genius," he sighed and left the table. The rumour also
reached Fan Chen, who fell to weeping bitterly and told his family to

send funeral gifts to Su's family. On second thought, he felt he ought to send a friend to Huangchow to verify the news first. It was then that he found that the news was untrue and that it all arose from the fact that Su Tungpo had shut himself up and had not been seen for several months. In his reply to Fan Chen, Su said: "All my life, the rumours about me have been just like this one."

Out of the emancipated life he was leading now came a transformation of his spirit, reflected in his writings. The bitterness of his satire, the sharpness of his pen, the tension and the anger were gone, and in their place we find a glowing, warm, intimate, and tolerant humour, thoroughly mellow and mature. If philosophy has any value, it teaches man to laugh at himself. Among the animals, as I understand, only the apes are able to laugh, but even if we grant this, I am quite confident that only man can laugh at himself. I do not know whether we can call this the laughter of the gods or not. If it were the Olympian gods who were full of human mistakes and foibles, they would have frequent occasions to laugh at themselves; but a Christian God or angels could not possibly do this because they are so perfect. I think it would be a greater compliment to call this quality of self-laughter the unique saving virtue of degenerate Man.

Characteristic of this kind of mature humour when he was completely relaxed and his spirit was at ease are the little notes that Su Tungpo wrote. He began to write a great number of inconsequential little entries in his journal that have no moral purpose and no message, but are among the most loved of his writings. He wrote one concerning his poverty and that of his constant follower. "Ma Mengteh was born in the same year and month as myself, but is younger by eight days. No man born in this month and year ever became rich, but Mengteh and I top them all in poverty. Between the two of us, however, I think Mengteh should take first place." Another note was a story of two beggars. "There were two beggars who were talking about what they would like to do if they had money. One fellow said: 'What I have always wanted to do is to eat and sleep all I like. When I am rich, I am going to eat and then go to sleep and then wake up to eat again. That would be Heaven for me.' The other beggar said: 'I disagree with you. When I'm rich, I am going to eat and eat and eat. There will be no time to sleep.'"

Happiness under any circumstances is a secret. But it is not difficult to peer into the secret of Su Tungpo's happiness by studying the inner man through his writings.

It is characteristic of this prodigal genius that he gave more to the world than he received from it, and by capturing certain poetic moments and immortalising them wherever he went, he has enriched us all. It is difficult to think of the vagabond's life that he was leading now as a form of punishment or of official confinement. While he enjoyed that life, he gave to the world four of his best pieces: a short lyric, "The Great River Flows Eastward", two sketches of his moonlight voyage to "The Red Cliff", and "A Night Promenade at Chengtien". These alone more than justify sending the poet into imprisonment. The two sketches of the moonlight voyage are in the form of a *fu*, or impassioned descriptive poem in prose, with a definite cadence and occasional rhyme. Su Tungpo worked entirely by tone and atmosphere, and these two poems are deservedly famous because, more convincingly than writings by other men, they express in a few hundred words the sentiment of the smallness of man in the scheme of the universe, and at the same time the boundless feast of nature that man can enjoy in this earthly life. Here, even without rhyme and with only the dexterous use of language, the poet establishes a prevailing mood that casts a hypnotic effect on the reader, no matter how many times he has read them before. The smallness of the human being in the scheme of the universe is expressed here exactly as it is in all Chinese landscape paintings. One sees very little of the details of the landscape, which are submerged in the blank whiteness of the water and the sky, while two tiny human beings float down the glistening river on a little wisp of a boat under the moonlight. From that moment on, the reader himself is lost in the atmosphere.

Su Tungpo is enjoying the night with a Taoist from his home province, Yang Shihchang. It is a midsummer night in the seventh moon. A gentle breeze comes slowly up the river without disturbing the surface of the water. Su Tungpo and his friend are having a little wine and humming some favourite melodies. By and by the full moon comes up from the east and loiters between the Dipper and the Cowherd. A white mist blankets the river and the light of the water merges imperceptibly with the light of the moonlit mist. There they are in that little boat, floating over the wide expanse of the white river, and they feel as if they were sailing in the air, careless of their destination. They begin to sing a song, beating time by striking on the side of the boat.

> "Oars of cassia and sculls of the fragrant lan
> Strike at the gleaming surface;
> Follow the stream of light.
> My heart wanders in the gloaming,
> Thinking of the fair one far away."

His friend, who is a good flute player, begins to play on his flute while Su Tungpo hums the tune. It is a strange, sad melody, speaking of longing and fond regret, soft and plaintive with diminuendos that gradually disappear into the thin air. The melody is so sad that a widow sitting in another boat begins to weep, and even the fish in the water are moved.

Overcome by the music, Su asks his friend why the music is so sad. His friend tells him: "Don't you remember what happened on this river below the Red Cliff?" A thousand years before, a historic naval battle had taken place here, deciding the fate of the Three Kingdoms. Could Su Tungpo not imagine the great fleet of Tsao Tsao, its masts resembling a forest, sailing down the river from Kiangling? He, too, was a poet. Did Su not remember the song that Tsao Tsao wrote on this occasion about the magpie flying south under a moonlit sky? "But where are these great warriors of the past? Tonight you and I are sitting here in a tiny boat, just two carefree wandering vagabonds enjoying a short happy moment over a cup of wine. We are no bigger than a gnat in the universe or a grain of corn in the vast ocean. Our life is brief and evanescent, while I envy the eternity of time like the unending flow of this great river. I would like to fly up to heaven, my arms supported by two angels, and ascend to the moon, to live for ever there. But I realise that this can never be, and therefore have I confided my sorrow to the song of the flute."

Su Tungpo begins to comfort his friend and says to him: "Look at this water and this moon! The water passes continually by, and yet it is always here. The moon waxes and wanes but it always remains the same moon. If you look at the changes that take place in the universe, there is nothing in it that lasts more than a fraction of a second. But if you look at the unchanging aspect of things, then you realise that both the things and ourselves are immortal. Why should you envy this river? Besides, everything in this life has its proper owner; there is no use trying to take what does not properly belong to us. But this clean breeze over the river and this clear moon over the mountain-tops are for everybody to enjoy. This life and this sensuous existence are here; they strike our eyes and become colour, strike our ears and become sounds—truly a boundless treasure, the inexhaustible gift of the Creator, a feast for us to enjoy, free and costless."

Upon hearing this, his friend begins to smile. They wash the cups and dishes and begin to eat again. Without clearing the dishes from the table, they stretch themselves and fall asleep, unaware that dawn is breaking in the east.

Three months later, in the tenth moon, Su Tungpo wrote another sketch. It is a full moon again and Su Tungpo strolls out from the Snow Hall with two of his friends towards the Linkao House. They pass the Yellow Mud Flat on the way. The ground is already white with frost and the trees are bare. They can see their own shadows on the ground and when they lift up their heads to look at the moon, they feel thoroughly enchanted with the evening and begin to sing by turns, each singing one stanza. Then someone says: "How shall we do justice to such a night as this? It's so perfect and we are company to each other, but where shall we get food and wine?" One of them says: "I caught some fish this evening—they have fine scales and big mouths, like the perch of Sungkiang. Ah, but how shall we get wine?" Su Tungpo decides to turn back to cajole his wife into producing some wine for them, which is always a wifely accomplishment. To their delight, his wife tells them that there are a few gallons in the house which have been kept for a long time. The company then, carrying the wine and fish, take a boat to spend the night under the Red Cliff again. The water level has fallen greatly, showing many rocks above the water, while the Red Cliff appears very high on the bank. The scenery has changed so much in a few months that Su can hardly recognise it. Inspired by the night, Su Tungpo asks his friends to climb up the Red Cliff with him, but the friends decline and Su goes up alone. Tucking in his gown and picking his way among the underbrush and brambles, he climbs to the very top, where he knows two ravens make their nest. Standing on top of the rock, he holloas into the night so that his voice resounds from the surrounding mountains. Suddenly he has an unsubstantial feeling of not knowing where he is, and, seized with a sense of grief, he feels he must not remain there long. He comes down, steps into the boat again, and they set off and let it drift with the current.

It is about midnight, and all is silent around them. Two lone storks appear in the east, flying with their white wings spread like fairies in white garments. The birds cry out and pass westward directly over their boat, and Su wonders what that omen means. Soon they go home, and he goes to bed and has a dream. In the dream he sees two Taoist priests dressed in the feather dress of immortals. They recognise him, and ask him if he enjoyed the night voyage under the Red Cliff. Su asks them their names, but they do not reply. "Ah, I know," says Su Tungpo. "I saw you flying tonight over our heads! Wasn't it you who made a cry when you passed over our boat?" The Taoists smile, and Su wakes from his sleep. He goes to open the door and finds nothing there except the bare street and silence.

Su Tungpo's method of establishing an atmosphere, as seen in this sketch, was to suggest another world, a dream world of Taoist immortals (of which the stork was a conventional symbol), and so confuse the reader that he did not know what plane of existence Su was describing. According to Chinese belief, our present human life is merely a temporary form of existence upon this earth, and though we may not be aware of it, we may have been fairies ourselves in our previous existence and may become fairies again in our next. •

About this same time Su wrote another very brief sketch on a moon light walk. It is a record of a passing mood when he could not sleep one night and got up to walk in the moonlight at the Chengtien Temple, which was very close to the Linkao House. This little sketch has now become a classic, very much loved for its casual charm.

A Night Promenade at Chengtien (1083)

"On the twelfth night of the tenth moon of the sixth year of Yuanfeng, I had undressed and was going to bed, when the moon light entered my door, and I got up, happy of heart. There was no one to share this happiness with me, so I walked over to the Cheng tien Temple to look for Huaimin. He, too, had not yet gone to bed, and we paced about in the garden. It looked like a transparent pool with the shadows of watergrass in it, but they were really the shadows of bamboos and pine trees cast by the moonlight. Isn't there a moon every night? And aren't there bamboos and pine trees everywhere? But there are few carefree people like the two of us."

The sketch is brief, but it is the perfect sensitive record of a completely happy moment. If we believe in Su Tungpo's theory of inner form in writing, by which a man's personal style is merely the natural overflow of his spirit, we can see that to write in perfect peace and simple con tentment, he had first to have that spirit. How he cultivated that mental poise and self-possession we shall see in the next chapter.

Chapter Seventeen

YOGA AND ALCHEMY

SU TUNGPO had said: "No one who does not achieve control of his mind can ever understand God." Salvation, or the knowledge of buddhahood, begins with mental self-discipline. Before one can achieve peace of mind (which in Buddhist philosophy is salvation itself), one must conquer one's own emotions of fear, anger, worry, and the like. During his Huangchow period Tungpo began to study Buddhist and Taoist philosophy, and this coloured his thinking and writing afterwards. He delved into the mysteries of the soul. He asked himself, how does man achieve peace of mind? Here were Indian yoga and Taoist mysticism which afford a definite, specific technique for mental control, with promises of emotional stability and improved physical health, and, even though only a remote probability, the discovery of the elixir of immortality. Of spiritual immortality Su had no doubt, but what about physical immortality? He grew deeply interested in the quest for *chang sheng,* or immortal life. Physical and spiritual immortality could not be distinguished from one another because the body was a carcass anyway, however he looked at it. If the mind were properly cultivated, in time it would leave this temporary carcass behind and soar aloft into the spiritual spheres. Besides, the promise of bodily immortality included at least one practical and attainable objective, the delay of old age and the prolongation of the span of life.

The so-called art of prolonging one's life included a good many factors and aims, elements of yoga and of Buddhist, Taoist, and Chinese medical traditions. Its purpose was both physical and mental. Physically it aimed to achieve a glow of physical health, the strengthening of one's constitution and vitality and consequent disappearance of long-standing ailments; mentally it aimed at establishing stability of mind and emotions and release of psychic energies. Combined with a simple way of living and with the help of certain Chinese medicines, it aimed at rejuvenation and enjoyment of a long life, which imperceptibly merged, in Taoist conceptions, with the art of achieving immortality. Briefly, this art is called in Chinese the art of "conserving life" (*yang sheng*), and again, "manufacturing the pill" of immortality (*lien tan*). The "pill" sought was both external and internal; the "internal pill" was something to be developed somewhere below the navel by Taoist practice, while the "external pill" was some kind of elixir which the Chinese alchemists were searching for and which, once found and taken into the body, was to assure bodily ascent to heaven, probably

on the back of a stork. The most important element in this external
pill was a mercury compound. At this point the art of prolonging
life and the search for transmutation of gold were hopelessly mixed up
together, just as in European alchemy. Of course, to a philosopher,
if one could live to a grand old age in good health and have gold
to spend, going to heaven could become secondary. What more could
a man ask of God?

Su Tungpo's brother was ahead of him in following yoga practise,
having begun it, according to Tseyu's own testimony, as far back as
1069. He had learned it from the Taoist priest Li, who was once asked
to cure the ailments of Su Tungpo's second son by blowing "spirit"
into his belly. When Tseyu came to Huaiyang to see his brother off
to Huangchow, Su Tungpo observed a new glow of vitality in his
brother's appearance. Tseyu had suffered in his childhood from indi-
gestion in summer and cough in autumn, and medicine had proved of
no avail. He now claimed that by following yoga deep breathing and
concentration, he had been cured. When Su Tungpo arrived at Huangchow, besides occupying himself with Buddhist scriptures, he also shut
himself up in a Taoist temple for forty-nine days, beginning from the
winter solstice of 1080. As we have seen in his record on the Ankuo
Temple, he was occupied with Buddhist meditations. Shutting himself
up in a Taoist temple, Tienchingkuan, on the other hand, was definitely
for the practise of fasting and deep breathing exercises, which, curiously, were developed more by Taoist priests than by Buddhists,
although these practises undoubtedly came from India with the Buddhist priests. At the same time he wrote to the chief magistrate of
Wuchang to ask formulas for methods of treating cinnabar, and in one
of his poems he said that a room had been set aside in the Linkao
House with a furnace for experiments in search of the magic pill.

His letter to Wang Kung gives the best all-round view of the factors
involved in the practise.

"When I was at Huchow, I took several ounces of a soft mer-
curial ointment given me by Chang Fangping, and felt it did me a
lot of good and could be taken continuously. Tseyu came yesterday
to Chenchow to say good-bye, and I saw his healthy complexion and
the bright twinkle in his eyes. At night he regulates his abdominal
breathing and is able to hear a rumble in his belly. His method is
something which we all have often discussed together, but he has
the persistence to carry on. Indulgence in sex is a kind of fire that
burns up the body, and I hope you can see through illusions of sense
with your spiritual eyes. In addition to this, one should live a simple,
frugal life. . . .

"Someone has recently given me large crystals of cinnabar, which have a bright lustre. I did not dare take them, but for my own pleasure, I heated them over the fire to look at the changes from crystal to powder and liquid form. Pinchow [Pinyang in Kwangsi, where Wang was now living] is not far from Kweilin, where it is easy to buy mercury crystals. If convenient, will you obtain a few ounces and send them to me? If it is difficult, don't bother, for I don't need it immediately. While living far out in such remote mountains you should be on the look-out and may come upon something exciting. Generally speaking, a Taoist cannot go up to Heaven unless he has found the pill of immortality. The material for making such pills is to be found mostly in the mountains of the south. That was why Keh Hung asked to be sent as magistrate to Koulou, and he left this earth at Lienchow. So you might just keep this matter in mind. Chen Tsan went to Kao-an to see Tseyu a month ago and revealed some secrets to him. I hear that he is coming back very soon. He not only understands these things but is also a true and good friend. There are so many things to learn about the Taoist art, but it seems to me the important thing is to practise mental poise by concentration, for, you can believe me, after a period I seem to be able to feel definite benefits. If one achieves a perfect circulation of the vital spirit, how can pains and ailments attack the human body?"

It is easy to understand how the Hindu yoga practice and theories were easily absorbed by the Chinese Taoists, even more than by the Chinese followers of Buddhism. It is true that there was the Zen Buddhist sect, which specialised in meditation, and which was a product of the mixture of Hindu Buddhism and Chinese Taoist philosophy. However, it was the Taoists who provided the natural ground for the absorption of yoga doctrine. Taoism was characterised by its emphasis on meditation and contemplation of nature, on achieving mental calm by simplifying human wants, and particularly on attaining immortality. In the book of the Taoist Chuangtse, we find a few phrases of advice on concentration, meditation, and even on "introspection of the mind", which are strikingly Hindu in character. Even if we grant that such passages were interpolated, still the interpolations were as early as the third or fourth centuries at the latest.

In no other school do we find religion and physical training so uniquely and intimately combined. The teaching of yoga offers a channel to religious mystic perception through mind and body control. Its field extends from acquiring control over reflexes and usually involuntary muscles to tapping the deeper levels of psychic energies. Its benefit is both physical and spiritual. Through the adoption of certain postures of the body and control of breathing followed by

meditation, it enables the yogi to arrive at a state of mind where first
the perception of gross matter of the universe falls away, and finally
the mind loses all sense of subject-object relations and attains a complete thoughtless vacuum, characterised by a feeling of ecstatic bliss.
Yogis admit that such a state of blissful vacuum is only temporary and
cannot be permanently achieved except by death; nevertheless, the
blissful feeling of a trance is so pleasant that the yogi desires to repeat
that experience as often as possible. Modern Hindus and Chinese who
have followed the yoga exercises claim a great improvement in their
physical health and a new mental poise and emotional equilibrium
that they did not have before. Chinese practitioners sometimes are not
aware that this is yoga, but call it by the name of "sitting still", "introspection", "meditation", and other Buddhist-Taoist terms. Naturally
the violent contortions of the body in the adoption of fantastic postures,
such as the "peacock posture" and the "fish posture", are rejected as
too strenuous by Chinese scholars, and Su Tungpo contented himself
with adopting a *comfortable* position, which may be regarded as the
Chinese contribution to yoga.

We are not interested in yoga practice in general, but in the specific
practise of yoga as detailed by Su Tungpo, in the year 1083. He had
read and absorbed a vast amount of Buddhist and Taoist scripture, and
had constantly discussed these things with the priests. Following his
brother's example, he began to take more and more interest in controlled breathing and mind control. He rather played with the idea of
finding the elixir of immortality, but even without attaining that
supreme goal, the idea of achieving better health and mental poise was
appealing to him. It must be remembered that the Chinese idea of
hygiene differs in practise, if not in principles, from Western hygiene.
According to the Chinese, one should not squander one's physical
energies in batting a ball and chasing about the field to catch it. That
would be the antithesis of the Chinese principle of hygiene, *yang sheng,*
which really means "conservation of energy". Yoga presents a formula
for physical and mental hygiene most acceptable to the Chinese scholar,
for the very essence of yoga is rest, calculated and self-conscious rest.
It prescribes not only the holding of the breath in regulated periods and
the adoption of a bodily posture of rest, but even tries to eliminate the
mental activities which are natural when we are sitting restfully in an
arm-chair. The whole effort of the yoga practice may be described in
simple and untechnical terms as an effort to think less and less until
one thinks of nothing at all. The last is of course the most difficult of
all. First it aims at concentration on one point—which is difficult
enough, because the mind naturally keeps wandering from one thought
to another related thought. But even that is only the lower stage,
dharana; in the higher stage, one advances from *dharana* to *dhyana,*

i.e., from concentration on one point or object to pointless meditation, and finally to the blessed stage of trance known as *samadhi*.

The peculiarity of yoga is that it combines this complete physical and mental rest with the increased intake of oxygen through different forms of controlled breathing. Nothing can be more ideal, for it seems that with a light stomach, a posture of complete relaxation, and deep respiration, the body is put in the unusually favourable state of getting extra supplies of oxygen without corresponding expenditure of energy, which is not the case in sports. It seems therefore understandable that when this is practised at night in the complete silence of the household, the mind can be brought to a state of acute consciousness of the body's internal functions and of itself. For in the final stages, what the mind does is to detach itself from itself and becomes its own spectator. In the more subtle stages the mind as spectator tries to observe even its own blank interval between one thought and another. The final stage, when the mind is described as completely without thought and capable of perceiving the subtler forms of sub-atomic matter, and divested of the usual idea of personality or self or the ego, is given various religious interpretations. One interpretation is the complete union of the individual soul with the world soul, and this is the goal of all religious efforts in Hinduism. But however one interprets the religious significance, that yoga state of mind, although similar to sleep and a condition of auto-suggestion, is different from these other states in that the mind retains complete consciousness of itself and its control of reflexes, and the yogi remembers vividly everything that happens in this state.

In the description of his own practise, Su Tungpo revealed many definite features of yoga. He controlled his breathing, which seems to be one cycle of respiration in five pulse-beats, the ratio being 1:2:2, for inhalation, holding, and exhalation respectively; and the maximum period of holding his breath was "120 pulse-beats or over twenty cycles of respiration", which, according to Hindu standards, is about the lower limit of *dharana*, or 144 seconds. Like the yogis, he counted his respiration cycles, and like them again, he claimed a period when controlled breathing—regulation of the ratio of intake and expulsion—became automatic. In point of concentration, he also concentrated his thought on the tip of his nose (the "nasal gaze"), which is definitely yoga. He also described a known yoga sensation when in the period of complete mental rest plus heightened mental awareness he observed vibrations going up his spine to the cerebrum, and also the raising of his hairs in their follicles all over his body. And finally in the "Essay on Conservation of Life" in his *Journal* he described the state of happiness and the benefits of mental poise acquired from such exercise.

Concerning the mental part of the exercise his observations were also strictly yoga. In a note to his brother he described the final goal of meditation in the orthodox yoga manner. He did not think that the state of true perception of truth or God or the world soul, as a result of emancipation from sense perceptions, consisted in seeing anything, but rather in seeing nothing at all.

"If the mind is divested of all its sense perceptions, this is the goal. It seems to me that whenever the mind is so divested, it is already the perception of truth. But this perception of truth, or *samadhi,* is not something that exists or does not exist, and is not to be described by words. Therefore the Masters taught their disciples that they should stop there. It is like removing the cornea from the eye; the eye sees as soon as the cornea is removed. A doctor has a way of removing the cornea, but he has no specific way of conferring vision upon the eye. If vision is *something,* it is itself a cornea. . . . People who do not understand sometimes describe a state of animal unconsciousness as the state of buddhahood. If so, then when cats and dogs sleep after being well fed, their bellies moving rhythmically with their respiration, these animals, too, do not have a thought on their minds. It would obviously be incorrect to argue that therefore the cats and dogs in such a state have entered buddhahood. . . . Am I correct in thus interpreting what you taught me? March 25, 1083."

To this yoga practice Su Tungpo brought additional factors that were purely Chinese, so far as I am aware. He not only excluded the acrobatic bending and twisting of loin, leg, and neck, and other grotesque contortions of yoga, but introduced the periodic swallowing of saliva, which springs entirely from Taoist speculations on physiology. In a letter to Chang Fangping, to whom he was recommending his own practise, he describes it as follows:

"Sit up in bed any time between midnight and dawn. Wrap yourself with a bed quilt. Sit with crossed legs facing east or south. Move your lower jaw up and down thirty-six times. Clench your hands, either digging the thumbs against the inside of the middle fingers or enclose the thumbs by the fingers, and rest the two against the small of the waist. Hold your breath, for this is a most important point in the Taoist art. First, close your eyes and relax your mind, trying to clear it of all thoughts and maintaining as far as possible a mental void. In consequence you will find your respiration gradually slowed down. Then close your mouth and nose and hold your breath. Try to imagine and see your inside organs. Try to think that your heart is fire, but direct its light downwards to the pill region below. Wait until you can no longer hold the breath and then let it out gradually, taking care to make it absolutely noiseless. After an even respiration has been established, turn your tongue about inside the mouth to stimulate the circulation of saliva, but do not swallow it. Repeat the above three times. After the third expelling of the breath, swallow the saliva while bending your head, and send it down to the pill region with some force, so that the saliva goes down with a gurgle. Repeat this again three times so that you swallow the saliva three times in nine periods of holding the breath. Then rub with both hands the inside of the arch of your feet, the pill region, and the back and the waist until they feel hot. Massage slowly without quickening your breath, but you may perspire slightly. Then massage your eyes and ears and face and neck with both hands until they are very hot, and rub down the right and left of your nose five to seven times. Comb your hair over a hundred times and lie down with the hair untied, and sleep until dawn."

The swallowing of saliva is based upon the following physiological speculations, which are closely connected with Taoist cosmogony of Five Elements, and sound to us fantastic. But to a believer in this cosmogony it made sense. In his "Second Essay on Conservatism of Life", one of the most difficult essays to read intelligently, Su Tungpo interpreted satisfactorily an extremely difficult ancient passage about "making the dragon in the body come up through the fire" and "the tiger in the body go down through the water". Su Tungpo observed that we are burning up energy all the time, mainly in two forms: (1) *fire,* which includes all emotional disturbances, such as anger, chagrin, love, sorrow, etc., and (2) *water,* which includes perspiration, tears, and excreta. In Taoist cosmogony the element of fire is represented by the term "tiger", while the element of water is represented by the term "dragon". The organ representing or controlling fire is the heart, while the organ representing the water principle is the kidneys. According to Su Tungpo, fire represents the righteous spirit; therefore, when a man's heart is in control of the body, his actions tend to be good. On the other hand, a man tends to become immoral if his functions are controlled by the kidneys, which in Chinese usage of the word include the sexual organs.* When the kidneys take control of the body, then we are subject to all kinds of animal desires: then *"the dragon comes out in the water",* which means destruction of our vital spirit. In another direction, we are subject to other emotional dis-

* The Chinese Taoists cultivated, among other secret arts, the art of lovemaking and some claimed extraordinary sexual vigor. They believed in stimulation of sex hormones plus mental control. In Tungpo's circle, Chang Lei was the one who believed in it.

turbances from the heart fire. We fight when angry, stamp our feet
feet in sorrow or disappointment, and dance about in times of joy.
Whenever the emotions are so disturbed, bodily energy is burned up
through the heart fire; *"the tiger comes out through the fire"*. Both
these forms of destruction of energy are, according to Su, "the road
to death". We should reverse these normal functions of fire and water
through mental control. The swallowing of saliva comes in here as
an effort to turn the heart fire materially downwards in the direction
of the kidneys.

In addition to this, the Taoists were constantly occupied with a
search for an "external pill", or the elixir of immortality, or the
"philosopher's stone". Like European alchemists, the Chinese Taoists
sought the philosopher's stone for the double purpose of transmuting
base metal into gold and of rejuvenation of old age. Like the European
alchemists, again, they worked principally with some form of mercury
compound. Because of the very peculiar qualities of quicksilver—its
metallic lustre, its great weight, approximating that of gold (atomic
weights 200 and 197 respectively), its comparatively constant fluidity,
its easy amalgamation with gold, copper, and others metals by contact,
and its interesting transformation into various states of gas, powder,
and liquid—this element naturally attracted the attention of the
alchemists, east and west, as offering the best approach to making
artificial gold. It is possible that Chinese alchemy in the time of Su
Tungpo came largely from Arab influence, as did European alchemy.
But as far back as the Han dynasty there were records of Chinese who
succeeded in producing gold from what we must consider gold compounds. Back in the fourth century a Taoist, Keh Hung, spoke of the
importance of exploiting the possibilities of gold and mercury to discover a formula for delaying old age or death itself. "All plants become
ashes when they are burned," says Keh, "but when you burn cinnabar,
you get quicksilver. After going through certain processes, the quicksilver becomes cinnabar again. It is therefore quite different from
plants [and minerals] in its nature. Hence its power to prolong life."
This author claimed that there were nine grades of pills, differing in
their efficacy according to the number of processes through which they
had been treated. The best kind enabled one to "become a fairy" in
three days and the lowest kind in three years. The elements involved
the making of this pill were cinnabar, white alum, orpiment (arsenic
trisulphide), loadstone, and *tsengching*.

Ho Wei, the author of *Chunchu Chiwen*, whose father was once
recommended to a post by Su Tungpo, devoted an entire chapter in his
book to stories about the elixir of immortality, which were quite current
in those days. Some of the persons Ho tells of are already known to

the reader of this biography; some of them were relatives of Ho's, and a few of the stories were witnessed by him. This book, and the book on medical recipes bearing the names of Su Tungpo and Shen Kua as co-authors, gives some idea of the methods of treating cinnabar. Reading these stories and formulas, one gets the following impressions. There was always "a pill furnace". The alchemists worked with mercury, sulphur, copper, silver, arsenic compound, and nitrate, or saltpetre. It is possible that they also played with gold sulphide. Both mercuric sulphide (cinnabar) and gold sulphide form red pigments, and various mercury compounds were taken as medicine. In the inaccurate records of those days, popular tales credited various Taoists with the possession of a formula to transform copper into gold. It is certain that people had been able to produce a purple-red gold alloy, which was fashioned into various kinds of vessels, and made a profit for themselves. It is also possible that some Taoists rubbed mercury on copper and passed it on as silver to ignorant people. They made an amalgam of gold and mercury, which was an easy thing to do. They also combined sulphur with mercury, calling the product "yellow gold" and again, in the same sentence, "dead sulphur".

There is a story that a monk was actually able to produce pure gold which passed the tests of the gold merchants of the capital. From the description Ho gives I am quite sure that the Taoist worked from gold ore gravel and was able to extract pure gold from the alloy. The tricky part of it was that the priest described this gravel as a form of copper, so that the story of transmuting copper into gold was quite exciting. He was able to demonstrate to a relative of Ho the transformation of some of this gravel into gold. He said that the gravel was copper and that he carried it in this form rather than as pure copper because it might be stolen when he was travelling. The ore was heated over a fire but would not melt. Then the priest dropped a little white powder into the pan and the result was pure gold.

The monk's story was as follows: He and two friends had years ago decided to go each his own way and then meet again in a certain place after ten years. They were to go out and search for the "philosopher's stone", and when they met they were to share the secret. The man who discovered the formula and was now telling the story had become a monk instead of a rich merchant, and this was how it happened.

When the three friends met at the appointed time, they compared the results of their search. The priest showed his friends that he had found a good formula, but that the product still contained impurities. One of his friends told him that he had obtained a powder for removing impurities. By adding this powder, they were able to produce pure gold.

"Let us go to the capital," said the friends to one another. "The firm of Luan are the biggest gold dealer of the country. If we pass their tests, then we really have the right formula." They took ten ounces of this stuff to the firm and offered to sell it. The firm examined, weighed, and heated the stuff and paid them the price for real gold. The friends were very happy and congratulated one another on their success.

"Now we can become immortals," they said, "or if we are not willing to forsake the world, we can use this money to drink and eat and enjoy a good life. Let's make a hundred ounces and divide it among ourselves."

That night they had a big wine dinner and got a little drunk, and went to sleep leaving the "copper ore" in the furnace. During the night, the "liquid copper" splashed about and set fire to the house. The fire brigade arrived when the three friends were still asleep, drunk. "I was comparatively awake and ran through the flames and escaped from the house. Afraid of arrest, and being a good swimmer, I jumped into the Pien River and swam down the current. Only when I had passed the National Gate did I dare to come ashore. While in the water, I repented and promised God that I would become a monk and would never do it again. I would never again try to make gold for my own benefit, but when some temple wanted to raise funds, I would do it and ask God's permission first." That was why the priest said he could not possibly reveal the secret formula to others, but that he would gladly produce a hundred ounces if it were for some good cause. Of his two friends, one was burned to death and the other was arrested and died of wounds a few days afterwards.

Su Tungpo was interested particularly in various preparations from mercuric sulphide. He was extremely cautious at testing these because it was recognised that mercury was poisonous. As they were shrouded in the mystery of secret formulas, one was never quite sure what the contents of the mercury preparations were. A contemporary recorded a man's death from swallowing a mercury compound when he made good an offer to take it in the Emperor's presence; probably he took mercuric chloride instead of mercurous chloride. In addition, the Taoists also experimented with other chemicals such as saltpetre, sulphur, and even limestone taken from stalactites; they sometimes "grew ulcers in consequence". Su Tungpo himself took two other kinds of food that were supposed to be the food of the fairies: namely, Indian bread ("tukahoe") and sesame. That sesame is rich in oils and contains a certain amount of protein gives it some food value, but I am inclined to think that these were considered "food for the fairies" chiefly because the Taoist priests living on the top of mountains often could not find anything else to eat. The more a plant grew in remote places and the more it differed from grain, the more likely it was considered to be the food of the immortals.

Su wrote two notes in connection with the manufacture of the external pill, one called the "male pill" and the other the "female pill". The female pill was made from milk taken from a mother who had given birth to her firstborn boy. This milk was heated over a slow fire in a pan made of a silver amalgam of mercury and slowly stirred with a spoon of the same material until it clotted and could be made into a pill. The male pill was made of urea taken from the breakdown of the albumen in urine. This albumen deposit was carefully strained and purified through repeated processes until it became a white odourless powder and then was made into a pill with date meat and taken with wine on an empty stomach.

Su Tungpo searched for the philosopher's stone until the end of his days; however, he retained a certain amount of good sense with regard to this quest for immortality. All the Taoist immortals had passed away; at least they had always left a corpse behind, although the theory was that their bodies had been transformed, and that when nobody was by, they could have ascended to heaven either riding upon the back of a stork or having become storks themselves ("featherised"), leaving merely a carcass which had nothing to do with their immortal selves. This carcass was then regarded in the same light as the dry shell or skin shed by a cicada or a snake, and their miraculous death was called "cicada escape". But Su Tungpo wanted to see someone who really never died.

"Ever since I was a child, I have heard of Taoists who can prolong life. But people like Chao Paoyi, Shü Teng, and Chang Yuanmeng all lived to about a hundred, and then died just like any other people. After I came to Huangchow, I heard of Chu Yuanching at Foukuang, who enjoyed a high reputation and was regarded as master by many people. But he, too, died of an illness in a violent paroxysm. However, he really could transmute gold and left some gold and powder behind, now in the hands of the government. I am beginning to wonder whether such immortals ever existed, or whether they do exist but are not seen by people. Or are we all mistaken? Is it not possible that the stories in the ancient books about Taoists who never died are just like the cases mentioned above and exaggerated by the writers?"

Apart from this futile search for the philosopher's stone, I do not think the principles of hygiene inculcated by the Taoists very much differ from the advice of modern doctors. Forgetting the wild goose chase after immortality, one comes back always to the principles of moderation, simple living, enough work, enough rest, and above all no worries and avoiding emotional disturbances of all kinds. In othe words, one always comes back to common sense. Su Tungpo expressec his common-sense philosophy of simple living in the form of four rule: for living which he had culled from the ancient books. One Chang asked him for a recipe for long life, and he wrote the following:

"1. Having leisure equals having power.
2. Going to bed early equals having wealth.
3. A leisurely stroll is as enjoyable as a drive.
4. Eating late is as good as eating meat.
"This is a good recipe for a contented life. If a man eats when he is ravenously hungry, any vegetable tastes better than all the delicate foods. On the other hand, when one's belly is full, he thinks nothing of the best food laid out before him and wants only to have it removed. I consider, however, that this formulation is unfortunate. It is enough to say that it is good to take a slow stroll and that food tastes good when one is hungry. Why should we speak of such pleasures as compensations for the luxuries? That shows those who invented these phrases always had the idea of a carriage and of meat in their minds."

I like best Su Tungpo's common-sense counsel on moderation and simplicity in his letter to his friend Li Chang.

"I am approaching the age of fifty and am beginning to try to save up something. I suppose it is mostly plain stinginess and that I am rationalising it by the beautiful word 'thrift'. But when people like us try to provide against the rainy day, we don't do it like the others. The whole beauty and charm lie in aiming only at having enough to live on. There is no limit to our material desires for food and clothing and shelter. But if we can be thrifty and moderate, we shall be following the road to happiness and a long life. This may sound like parsimony, though it is a parsimony that is forced upon me, but I do believe it is a good satisfactory design for living, and I wish to share it with you. Have a good laugh!"

Li Chang had now returned to the capital, and even Wang Kung had been pardoned and come back north. The Emperor was repenting of the punishment he had dealt out to the opposition. It is an irony of fate that just when Su Tungpo was about to get settled and live a happy retired life, following his "satisfactory design of living", he was whisked away from his place of rest into political turmoil once more. The ant which had been running against a turning millstone thought that the stone was now definitely standing still. But it began to turn again.

Chapter Eighteen

YEARS OF WANDERINGS

IF Su Tungpo's fate in the next twenty months is indicative of an official's lack of freedom of personal movement, it should be a powerful argument against any scholar's joining politics who can make a living otherwise. He was now to follow a zigzag course of wanderings and changes of plan before he ended up, much against his wish, in a position very close to the Empress. The Emperor wanted to make him the court historian, but was blocked by those around him. Finally he handed out a personal note in his own handwriting, shifting Su Tungpo's place of confinement from Huangchow to Juchow (modern Linju), which was very much nearer the capital and was a good city in which to live. This news broke in on him at the beginning of March in 1084.

He dodged the appointment, in his own words, "like a schoolboy trying to play hookey". A man joins a government for money or fame or power or service to the country. Su Tungpo, we know well enough, was not the type to get rich by being an official, and as for power, he had no desire whatever to rule others. There is a curious instinct in some men who already have money and fame to enter politics just to push other people around. The first taste of power is fine, but, barring exceptional circumstances, an American president who runs for a second term either does not know what is for his own good or, more probably, is no longer his own master. He runs because his party wants him to run. The zeal for service to one's country is scarcely reasonable, for are there not many opponents crying for a chance to do just that? As for fame, Su had sense enough to know that even being a premier could not possibly add anything to his immortal fame as a writer and a poet. What could he want in politics, and what could he accomplish, anyway?

On March 3 he was still having an unsuspecting good time with his friends. They spent the day at Shang's garden on the mountain-side behind Tinghueiyuan, where Su Tungpo had a beautiful nap on top of a small tower after a wine dinner. After the nap he strolled outside the East Gate, where he saw in a shop a big wooden basin, which he bought, intending to use it for watering his melons. Then, following a small creek, he entered Ho's garden. Ho was just starting to build another wing to his house, and asked him to stay for a drink in the bamboo grove. A friend produced a kind of pastry which Tungpo aptly named "Why-So-Crisp?" They all drank, but the monk Tsanliao took only date soup. Suddenly, Su felt he wanted to go home. Seeing that there were orange trees in Ho's garden, he begged for some saplings to plant on the west of the Snow Hall.

Two or three days later, the news came that he was to be transferred. While technically he was still to be "confined", he would be living in freedom in a rich and beautiful town. For a few days he hesitated whether he should not ask for permission to stay at Huangchow. Then, considering that the new appointment was a sign of the Emperor's kindness, he decided to obey and quit his farm on the Eastern Slope. At a stroke, the rewards of his years of labour were wiped out, and probably he had to begin all over again to start another farm somewhere else.

Yet even after his transfer under such straitening circumstances, his enemies were restless. A contemporary tells the following story: Su sent a letter of thanks to the Emperor. His Majesty looked around and told his courtiers: "Su Shih is really a genius."

But his enemies still tried to pick fault even in Su's formal letter of thanks. "It seems to me," said one of them, "he is still grumbling in this letter."

"How do you mean?" the Emperor asked, surprised.

"Why, in this letter he says that he and his brother once passed the special examinations, and moreover he uses the words: 'My heart still flutters, and I still dream of being in chains.' He means that he and his brother passed the special examinations for frank criticism of the government, but now he is being punished for his criticism. He is trying to put the blame on others."

"I know Su Shih well," said the Emperor quietly. "Down in his heart he means well."

The petty courtier therefore kept quiet.

It took him several weeks to make preparations for leaving. He decided that he would go to see his brother first at Kao-an, and therefore left his good, dutiful eldest son, Mai, to bring the family after him and meet him at Kiukiang on his return from this visit.

Now came the official farewell parties and requests from his many friends for autographed scripts, of which he tossed off a great many. It was at this time that the courtesan Li Chi received the poem which immortalised her.* At one of the farewell parties given by his friends and neighbours, he wrote:

"Let me go home—
But where is my home? . . .
Human affairs shift and change like a shuttle.
Let me take time to gaze
At the clear ripples on the Lo stream in the autumn wind.

See page 12.

In kind remembrance of me,
Spare the gentle twigs of Snow Hall's willow.
And I pray my friends across the river
To come at times and sun my fishing raincoat."

A crowd gathered to see his departure. It was a motley company of gentry and poor folks that sent him off. We know by name nineteen of his neighbours and friends who were to go a certain distance with him on the boat. The roads were lined with friends and strangers, farmers and grateful poor parents with babies in their arms, babies whose lives had been saved by the departing scholar. The nineteen went with him as far as Tzehu Lake, where again they whiled away several days before Su Tungpo finally left.

There still remained three friends who accompanied him as far as Kiukiang. One was his closest friend Chen Tsao. Another was the monk Tsanliao, younger by five years, who had known him at Suchow and had popped up again to live with him at Huangchow for about a year. Among the people of ancient China, there were no greater travellers than Taoist and Buddhist monks, not only because they had complete leisure and freedom of movement, but also because they had probably the best chain of hotels to put up in wherever they went, namely, the temples. Tsanliao decided now to go and live on top of the famous Lushan at Kiukiang.

The third friend was the centenarian Taoist Chao Chi, who was now about one hundred and thirty years old, and who, according to legend, was later resurrected from his grave. After reaching Kiukiang, Su Tungpo went out of his way and made a land journey of over a hundred miles in order to entrust this old priest to one of his friends at Shingkuo. Chao Chi loved birds and animals and always travelled with one of his pets with him. Later, according to Tseyu's story, the old man died from a kick by a mule. Years after, a monk told Tseyu that he had recently met another monk at a certain place who claimed to be Chao Chi and to have known Su Tungpo at Huangchow. Tseyu asked about this monk's appearance, and the story-teller's description fitted exactly with that of the old Taoist. Among those who were listening to the story was a son of the magistrate at Shingkuo. He went home and told his father about it. In order to verify the story of Chao Chi's resurrection, the chief magistrate ordered his tomb reopened and found only a cane and two shin-bones. The corpse had disappeared.

Su Tungpo visited the famous Lushan for a few days in the company of Tsanliao. There was great excitement among the hundreds of monks, for the news had spread among them: "Tungpo has arrived!" Although he wrote only three verses on Lushan, one of them became the best-loved poem describing the essence of this mountain.

H*

On his visit to his brother, the poet was met by his three nephews, who had come some eight miles to receive him. The brothers had not seen each other for four years, and Tseyu had put on a little more flesh. He did not look in the best of health, for he was too busy to practice yoga at night. The office of the wine and salt monopoly was housed in a little shabby, rickety, leaky building overlooking a river. According to Tseyu's own story: "There used to be three persons in this bureau, but when I arrived two of them had been sent elsewhere, and I had to attend to everything myself. Every day I had to sit at the shop, selling wine and salt, and supervising the weighing of pigs and fish for tax assessment. In order to carry out my duty I had to wrangle with the farmers and merchants about weights and measures. At night when I came back, I was so tired that I stretched myself in bed and fell asleep and did not wake up till the morning. The next day I had to do the, same things again."

Su Tungpo stayed there six or seven days and then sailed down the river to Kiukiang in order to join his own family. With them he went down the Yangtse to Nanking in July. There, Chaoyun's son, then only ten months old, fell ill and died. It was a great blow to the parents, but especially to the young mother. In one of the poems on the death of the young child, Su said that the mother lay dazed all day in bed, and although he could wipe away his own tears, it was hard to listen to her weeping. Chaoyun never gave birth to another child.

While at Nanking, Su Tungpo went to visit Wang Anshih, who was now a tired, broken old man. They spent days discussing poetry and Buddhism; since both of them were major poets and believers in Buddhism, they had a lot to talk about. There was a story that once Su Tungpo outmatched Wang in writing verse on a given rhyme and subject, and Wang gave up half-way. In the course of their conversations, Su Tungpo frankly blamed Wang for launching wars and persecuting scholars.

"I have something to say to you," said Su Tungpo.

Wang's countenance changed, and he said: "Are you going to talk about the past?"

"What I want to talk about," said Su Tungpo, "is the affairs of the country."

Wang calmed down a little and said: "Go ahead."

Su proceeded. "Wars and party strife caused the fall of the Han and Tang dynasties. The present imperial house intended to avoid these dangers. But now the government has been engaged for years in wars with the north-west, and many scholars have been sent to the south-east. Why didn't you stop it?"

Wang raised two fingers and said to Tungpo: "These two things were started by Huiching. I am a retired man now. I don't think it is my business to interfere."

"True enough," said Su Tungpo. "To speak about politics only when in office is the normal rule. However, the Emperor treated you with rather more than normal courtesy, and therefore your loyalty should compel you to break the ordinary rules of courtesy also."

"Yes, yes," said Wang, getting annoyed. And then he continued: "This conversation comes out of my mouth and enters your ears." Wang meant that their conversation was not to go outside that room, for Wang had already been betrayed by Huiching once and was being careful.

The conversation rambled on, and Wang Anshih said rather disjointedly: "A man should refuse to do even one thing against his conscience. He should not kill one innocent man even if he is offered the entire world for his reward."

"Very true," said Su Tungpo, "except that nowadays some men are willing to commit murder if they can get a half a year's earlier promotion before their term is up."

Wang chuckled but did not reply.

According to many contemporary records, Wang was often seen during this period riding on a donkey alone in the countryside and "mumbling to himself like a madman". Sometimes, thinking of his old friends who had turned away from him, he would suddenly pick up his brush and with an eager face begin a letter. But after a while, he would lay it down again as if he were ashamed of himself, and the letters were never written. He continued his diary, which, some years after his death, was ordered returned to the government as containing important inside material on the regime. In his disappointed old age, Wang had become bitter and had made many disparaging remarks about the Emperor. Fortunately, at that time the government was in the hands of his own party; but the diary, running to over seventy volumes, was seen by many people. A few years earlier, when Wang had heard that Szema Kuang had come to power, he had ordered his nephew to burn the diary, but the manuscript survived because the nephew hid it away and burned something else instead.

Wang also began to see hallucinations. In one of his clairvoyant moods, he saw his only son, who was now dead, being punished in hell. The son, who he knew was a scoundrel, was pilloried and in chains. After a guard at his home reported also seeing the same thing in a dream, Wang was greatly frightened. To save his son's soul from torture in hell, he sold his property at Shangyuan county and donated it to a temple. Wang's report to the Emperor about this donation, in response to which the court granted the temple a special name, is still preserved. The day before his death, riding alone in the country, Wang saw a peasant woman coming towards him, and kneeling before him, she presented him with a paper containing a complaint. Then the ghost disappeared. He thought he had put the paper in his pocket, but after coming home he found that the paper was gone, too. He died of fright the next day.

When Su Tungpo had reached the fertile valley of Kiangsu, he was fascinated by the beauty and atmosphere of the region. While travelling between Nanking and Chinkiang, he was busy shaping his plans for buying a farm and a homestead somewhere in the lake district. His position was this: since the Emperor was willing to shift him from Huangchow to another place, he could be enticed into granting permission later for him to settle elsewhere. Everywhere he went, he was looking for a place for retirement in his old age. His many friends made different suggestions. His Buddhist friend, Foyin, wanted him to settle in Yangchow, where he himself had his farm. Fan Chen wished him to settle in Shüshia as his neighbour. He had an eye on a beautiful pine forest on Suanshan in Tantu. But all these plans fell through. The chief magistrate of Yichen, north of the Yangtse River near Nanking, urged him to come and stay with him, and although he had no idea of settling at Yichen, he was glad to find a place there for the temporary stay of his family. So while his family was put up at the district college of Yichen, Tungpo was free to go about visiting different places in search of a country home.

Finally one of his most intimate friends, Ten Yuanfa, persuaded him to settle in Changchow district, at Ishing, on the left bank of the Taihu Lake. Ten was now magistrate of Huchow on the south of the lake. Between the two of them, they hatched a plan for Su to buy a farm at Ishing and then petition the Emperor for permission to stay there on the ground that the farm was his only means of support. A relative of Ten's was able to find a farm some twenty miles from the city of Ishing, deep in the mountains. It was a fair-sized property that would yield eight hundred piculs of rice a year and should support the Su family comfortably. Su had only a few hundred dollars left, besides the house his father had bought at the capital, which he had asked Fan Chen to sell for him for about eight hundred dollars.

In September he went down alone to see the country farm. "The moment I go up the Ching River I feel completely at home, as if the wish of my life had been granted. Can it be that this was destined in my previous existence? I love to plant things, especially oranges, and I can graft my own fruit trees. Ishing is right on the lake and is just the place for an orange farm. I must buy a little orchard here and plant three hundred orange trees. October 2, 1084, written on a boat." Later he also bought another farm, from the government. There was some litigation involved later, but a writer in the following century recorded that one of Su Tungpo's great-grandchildren was still living on a farm at Ishing.

Su now made a deal, which was extremely foolish or very magnanimous, according to the way one looks at it. He wrote to Ten that he was going to find a house on the Ching River, and he did. With his friend Shao Minchan, he had found a good old homestead and had paid five hundred dollars for it. This took about all the cash that he had, but Su Tungpo was very happy and was planning to go back and bring his family to live in this new house. One night, however, he was walking in the moonlight in the village with Shao, when they passed a house and heard a woman sobbing inside. Su Tungpo and Shao knocked at the door and went in. An old woman was weeping in a corner. On being asked what was the matter, the old woman replied:

"I have a house which has belonged to our family for over a hundred years. I have a bad son who has sold it to somebody. Today I have had to move out of the old house where I have been living all my life—this is why I am crying."

"Where is your house?" asked Su Tungpo, greatly touched.

To his amazement, he found that it was the one that he had bought for five hundred dollars. Taking the deed of the sale from his pocket, he burned it before the old woman. The next day he sent for her son and told him to move his mother back to the old house, without asking for the return of the money. Whether the son had already used the money to pay debts or was otherwise unable to give back the money, we do not know. Su therefore returned to the city without a house, and minus five hundred dollars. But it was an impulse so fine and beautiful that the poet could not resist it, regardless of consequences for his own family. If that was a beautiful thing to do, it was a beautiful thing to do—that was all.

Returning from Changchow, he wrote a letter to the Emperor in October to ask permission to live there. Until the permission was granted, however, he had to proceed toward his designated post, which was far away west of the capital, a journey of about five hundred miles. He was travelling with his whole big family in the direction of the capital, taking plenty of time about it, in the hope that he would not have to incur the expenses of travelling back and forth in case his request was granted. Receiving no news from the court, he left reluctantly and approached the capital. His family was actually starving, if we can believe his own poems. When they came to the Huai River at Szechow, he wrote to his friends at least three poems in which he mentioned hunger. In one of these he compared himself to a hungry mouse gnawing at something all night. When the magistrate sent some food to the boat, a cry of joy went up from the children. It looked as if they could not proceed farther, and he decided to send another petition, and to stop at the Southern Capital at Chang Fangping's home until he heard the Emperor's reply.

The second pathetic letter to the Emperor, written in February at Szechow, read partly as follows:

"My salary has long been cut off and I am finding it difficult to make ends meet. Travelling with a whole family, I had to take a boat from Huangchow, and have had many troubles on the voyage. My family fell ill and I lost a son. Now though I have reached Szechow, my money is all used up and I am still far from my destination. It will be difficult for me to undertake a land journey. I have no house to live in and no farm to bring me any income. Travelling with a family of over twenty mouths, I know not where to go. Starvation is at my door. Rather than turn to my friends for help, I think I should appeal directly to Your Majesty. I have a little farm in Ishing county, district of Changchow, which will give me enough to live on. I pray that Your Majesty will allow me to live at Changchow."

While on this journey, two amusing, or sad, incidents happened. He wrote a poem at Szechow after taking a trip across the river to the Southern Mountain. There was a long bridge across the river, and as Szechow lay in a strategic place, nobody was allowed to cross the bridge after dark. The severest penalty was given to any violators of this law. In practice, however, the chief magistrate of Szechow ignored it and crossed the bridge after dark with Su Tungpo. In celebration of their trip, Su wrote innocently the following lines:

"On the long bridge, lamplights glaring,
The chief magistrate returns."

The chief magistrate was a simple, honest Shantung scholar by the name of Liu. When he read Su's poem the next day, he had his heart in his mouth. He came to the boat to see the poet and said: "I have just read your poem. But this is serious, very serious! With your national reputation, this poem is bound to reach the court. An ordinary citizen crossing the bridge at night is punishable by two years' hard labour. For a magistrate himself to violate this law would be still worse. I beg of you to keep this poem to yourself and not show it to others!"

Su Tungpo smiled ruefully and replied: "God help me! I have never opened my mouth without deserving at least two years of hard labour!"

While he was staying at Chang Fangping's home, there was another touching incident. At a wine dinner given by the host, he recognised the concubine of Chang's son, who once was a concubine of the chief magistrate of Huangchow. This girl, Shengchih, was the magistrate's favourite. The magistrate had been a very great and dear friend of Su Tungpo, but he had died and the girl had remarried. When Su Tungpo saw this beautiful girl appear gaily at the dinner, he was deeply touched, and thinking of his dear friend, his eyes moistened with tears and his throat choked. This amused Shengchih, who could not conceal her laughter and turned round to make remarks to others. Su left the table feeling very badly about it, and he told his friends that one should never marry a concubine, citing Shengchih as an example.

The Emperor fell ill, and on March 1 his mother, the Empress Dowager, wife of Ingtsung, began to act as regent. On March 5 the Emperor died, and on the following day an edict was issued granting Su's request to stay at the lake district. The news meant much to Su, for now his wish was fulfilled and his plan settled. The family then began to move back to Ishing, leaving the Southern Capital on April 3, and arriving at their new home in the lake district on May 22, 1085.

At long last, Su Tungpo believed he was going to settle there for life. "For ten years the search for a home has been in vain, but now I am really to be an old farmer." He was going to spend his old age in idyllically beautiful surroundings. He could come and go in a small boat while his "spirit travelled unfettered beyond the material universe".

As fate would have it, just as his plan for a place of retirement had been realised, the news came that he was recalled to office. There was hardly an interval of ten days between his arrival at Ishing and the news of his appointment as chief magistrate of Tengchow, near Chefoo. He was told of the rumour which had come from the capital, but refused to believe it, saying that the capital was always full of rumours, and that there was no mention of it in the latest court bulletin, of April 17.

Su Tungpo was confused, and at heart he hated the change. A few days later, the official appointment arrived. The family was overjoyed and the children cried that they could not believe it. But in a poem Su Tungpo compared himself to a poor thoroughbred who had passed his prime and "had no desire to graze on the top of the Tienshan Mountain". In another poem he said: "Coming down south, I was prepared to take up farming, and after my garden was completed, I should have been able to enjoy many happy days. Who would think that in my remaining years I would have to be in the city again? I feel like a tired horse who balks at climbing up a hill." In his letter to Foyin, he said: "I am going to enter the village of scoundrels again"; and he wrote to Mi Fei: "I feel unhappy and a little worried at the thought of re-entering the troublous life of politics in my old age."

Nevertheless he accepted the post. The Empress Dowager was setting things moving. Szema Kuang had been appointed chief of the imperial

secretariat, which was practically the vice-premier's office. The manner
of his appointment was rather curious, for the Empress had him
"escorted" by armed guards from his home right into his office. This
method was adopted for fear that, on receiving the appointment, he
might delay or decline to come.

Su Tungpo started out in June for his post on the sea-coast of Shantung. From the neighbourhood of Tsingtao they took a boat, going
around the Shantung peninsula. Exactly five days after their arrival
at Tengchow on October 15, he was again recalled to the capital. The
family started moving again and arrived at the capital towards the
middle of December 1085.

Chapter Nineteen

EMPRESS'S FAVOURITE

SU TUNGPO always had luck with empresses. The empress of Jentsung had saved his life during the trial. The empress of Ingtsung now promoted him to power. Even later in his life, if it had not been for another empress, wife of Shentsung, ruling as regent, he would have died outside China in exile.

The new emperor now was a boy of nine, and it was his grandmother who became the regent. The Sung dynasty was unusually fortunate in having a succession of good empresses. In the great Han and Tang dynasties, some wives of the emperors either usurped the throne and ruled through powerful eunuchs and relatives of their maiden families, or otherwise succeeded in bringing about the fall of the imperial house. In the time of Su Tungpo, however, the wives of the four emperors under whom he served were all good women, and some were remarkable. Perhaps it was because they were women that they were able to retain an elementary sense of right and wrong and a simple, clear-cut judgment of the good and bad men at the court. For while living in the palace, they did not hear enough about the scholars' involved and learned arguments over policies to be confused by them, and yet they heard enough to know the general trend of public opinion. Modern democracy with universal suffrage is based upon the judgment of the common man, who often cannot follow a *New York Times* editorial. The Empress's judgments were those of the common man. In his last days the previous emperor had already begun to retrench on his policies, but he could do nothing like what his mother now did. As soon as the Emperor died, the Empress Dowager recalled Szema Kuang to power and at once effected a complete reversal of policies. Practically all of Wang Anshih's measures were suspended or abolished. The reign of Yuanyu had begun.

Su Tungpo now had a quick, dramatic rise to power. Within eight months of his arrival at the capital he was promoted three times. According to the ancient system, official posts were graded according to a uniform system of ranks, from one to nine. In this short period he rose from the seventh rank, passing through the sixth, jumping to the fourth, and ending with a third rank as *hanlin* academician in charge of drafting imperial edicts, at the age of forty-nine.

Before he was promoted to *hanlin*, he was already serving, in March 1086, as a fourth-rank secretary of the premier's office. It was a very important post, for he had to take part in the selection and appointments of government officials for all the ministries. While serving in this capacity, he had the interesting duty of drafting several decrees in which he had a rather personal concern. One was a decree depriving Leeding of his office and compelling him to make up the three years' mourning for his mother which he had failed to observe. A second one was for the banishment of Huiching. The decisions were not his, but the wording of the decrees came from Su Tungpo's pen. In the case of Huiching, the double-crosser, Su said that "when he was intimate with his friends, they rubbed their knees together, but overnight they could bite one another", and that "he covered half the country with his own clique". The most interesting job, however, was when he had to draft an edict conferring imperial honour upon Wang Anshih when the latter died in April. The wording of this decree required a great subtlety in the art of damning a man by left-handed compliment. Officially, it was to be issued in the name of the Emperor, praising Wang's life and character and conferring upon him the posthumous title of Grand Imperial Tutor. What Su Tungpo did was to praise Wang's originality while making it clear that he was referring to his self-conceit. "He encompassed the entire literature of the six arts and subjected them to his own judgment. Looking down upon the heritage of the hundred philosophers, he founded a new school." Subtly the text went on until Su said: "Alas, why does not such a man live to a hundred?—the thought draws tears from our eyes." The reader does not know whether he is reading a fulsome panegyric or a diatribe in reverse.

The post of "Hanlin Academician in Charge of Imperial Edicts" was one reserved for scholars of the highest reputation. Very often it was the next step to becoming a premier. Su Tungpo was therefore near the top, for although this post was third rank, a premier's position was only second rank, the first rank being hardly ever conferred in the Sung dynasty upon anyone. Moreover, the work of drafting imperial edicts brought him into intimate association with the boy emperor and the Empress Dowager. The appointment was brought to Su Tungpo's home by a personal servant from the palace, together with the gift of an official jacket, a gold belt, and a white horse with a set of gold-plated silver bridle and saddle ornaments. While the premier's office directly adjoined the palace on the west side, the *hanlin's* office was close to the North Gate of the palace and was considered a part of the palace compound. The work of the imperial secretary was usually done at night, and when a *hanlin* was in his office, he was spoken of as being "locked up for the night". It was the custom for the secretary to be locked up on the odd days of the month to prepare the edicts to be issued on the even days. In the evening he would go along the eastern wall of the palace until he reached the Inner East Gate, where a room adjoining the Empress's quarters was reserved for him. Sometimes the night was long and he had nothing to do except stare at the red palace candles and listen to the dropping of the sand in the hour-glass. Sometimes, when the night was cold, the Empress would send him some hot wine. Any decision about orders to be given was transmitted by the Empress orally, and he had to put it in writing in the most classic, dignified style and have it ready for promulgation the next day. .

There are some eight hundred of these edicts drafted by him in this capacity, preserved in his *Complete Works*. They are sonorous, apt, precise in language. The phraseology of imperial edicts was usually studded with historic analogies and allusions, but Su Tungpo always wrote them with great facility. After his death, another man, Hung, was acting in the same capacity. Very proud of his own compositions, he asked an old servant who used to attend upon Tungpo what he thought of himself as compared with Su. The old servant replied: "Su Tungpo wrote no more beautifully than Your Excellency, but he never had to look up the references."

One night, Su Tungpo was sitting in the small hall. He was thoroughly sick of the politicians' jealousy and had begged to be relieved of this post. The Empress summoned him to go inside and take orders. The young emperor, Tsehtsung, was sitting beside his grandmother, and Su Tungpo stood respectfully to receive the orders. After telling Su to draft an edict for the appointment of Lu Tafang as premier, the Empress Dowager suddenly said: "There is one thing I want to ask you. What office did you hold a few years ago?"

"I was a lieutenant in an army training corps at Juchow."

"And what is your office now?"

"Your humble servant is a *hanlin* academician."

"Why do you suppose you have been promoted so quickly?"

"Because of the favour of Your Imperial Majesty," replied Su.

"It has nothing to do with my old self," said the Empress Dowager.

Su made a blind guess. "Then it must be the kindness of His Majesty, the Emperor."

"It has nothing to do with him."

Su Tungpo guessed again. "Is it perhaps because some old minister recommended me?"

"It has nothing to do with them, either," she replied.

Su stood dumb for a second. After a pause, he said: "However bad I am, I would not use any influence to beg for a post."

"That is what I have long been wanting to let you know," the Empress Dowager said finally. "This was the dying wish of Shentsung. Whenever he stopped his chopsticks in the middle of eating, the servants always knew he must be reading some writing of yours.

Shentsung constantly spoke of your rare genius, and wished to make use of your talent, but unfortunately he passed away before he could do so."

The reference to the deceased emperor brought all three of them to tears. The Empress then granted Su permission to sit down, and giving him a packet of tea, said to him: "You must serve the young Emperor loyally, to make return for the kindness of his father." As Su bowed himself out, the Empress took from the table a golden candle-stand carved in the form of a lotus and presented it to him as a gift.

Very soon after Su Tungpo's assumption of office as secretary to the Emperor, Szema Kuang died, on September 1, 1086. The day happened to coincide with the fasting ceremonies for the official installation of the spirit tablet of Emperor Shentsung in the ancestral temple of the Sung house. It was the custom for friends to pay their respects to the dead while the coffin was lying in state, and during such an official call the friends were supposed to mourn aloud for a definite period. Owing to the coincidence, however, when all the officials had to observe the fast, they were not able to pay their respects to the dead premier. On September 6 the spirit tablet was formally installed in its place in the ancestral temple with all the pomp and circumstance and classical orchestral music appropriate to the occasion. A general amnesty was granted, and the court suspended its daily audience with the Emperor for three days. All officialdom was gathered at the ceremony. Then an amusing but pregnant incident occurred.

It happened that Szema Kuang's funeral ceremony was in the charge of an ultra-puritanical neo-Confucianist, Cheng Yi, the younger of the two famous Cheng brothers. This puritan was far from being an amiable character, to say the least, and his holier-than-thou manners irritated Su Tungpo greatly. He was running the funeral ceremony according to "ancient rites". Although it had been for centuries a pre-vailing custom for some relative of the deceased to stand by the coffin and bow in turn to the guests, Cheng Yi insisted that this custom was not classical and therefore forbade Szema Kuang's son from standing beside the coffin to receive the guests. The idea was that the bereaved son should be, if he were truly "filial", so overwhelmed with grief that he was not in a condition to see people. When the ceremony at the imperial ancestral temple was over, Su Tungpo, at the head of the staffs of the imperial secretariat and the premier's office, was about to lead the entire court over to Szema Kuang's home to pay their respects. Cheng Yi, who was going there anyway, protested that this was against the rule set by the austere example of Confucius. There is a passage in the Confucian *Analects* recording the fact that "on the day when he had wept, Confucius did not sing." They had been singing that morn-ing, or at least had been listening to orchestral music. How could they

go and weep on the same day? The company went along and came to
the entrance. The little Cheng Yi still tried to stop them. There was a
hot argument.

"Don't you read the *Analects?*" said Cheng Yi. "On the day that he
had wept, Confucius did not sing."

To this Su Tungpo replied: "The *Analects* does not say that on the
day that he had sung, Confucius did not weep."

He was much annoyed, and he led the company indoors, over Cheng
Yi's protests. Each one by turn stood before the coffin and made his
bows, and in a seemly and correct way wiped his eyes with his sleeves
before he turned away. Su Tungpo noticed that the son of Szema
Kuang was not present to receive the guests, and upon inquiry was told
that Cheng Yi had forbidden it as a custom unsupported by the ancient
classics. In the presence of the entire court Su Tungpo remarked upon
this aloud, using a classical phrase of cultured abuse, which in simple
English means: "That is the ceremony of a dumpy, dowdy school-
master." Everybody roared with laughter and Cheng flushed all over.
The taunt stuck, for it fitted. It was a phrase that neither Cheng Yi
nor his deriders were likely to forget. Nobody liked to carry such a
label all his life. The seed of hatred between Su Tungpo and the
Honan party, of which Cheng Yi was the leader, was planted.

Very soon they saw the carriages of the Emperor and the Empress
Dowager coming, the former with carved dragons and the latter with
phoenixes, supported on crimson wheels. They came to pay their
personal respects to the dead, and also wept before the coffin in the
orthodox approved manner. Szema Kuang was buried with the highest
honours. His body in the coffin was covered with quicksilver and
"dragon's brains" (Borneo camphor), gifts of the imperial house. The
family was given three thousand taels of silver and four thousand pieces
of silk, and two palace officials were appointed to escort the coffin to its
burial-place in the native district of Szema Kuang. Ten of his relatives
were also given official jobs.

Besides his duties as imperial secretary, Su Tungpo was given also, by
an appointment in July of the next year, those of an imperial lecturer.
The Emperor was but a child, but even with middle-aged emperors
there was a regular series of lectures given on odd days of the month
for the emperor's special benefit. It consisted of two semesters, the
spring semester running from February to the dragon boat festival on
the fifth day of the fifth moon, and the winter semester from the mid-
autumn festival to winter solstice. Officials well known for their learning were selected to take turns giving discourses on the classics and the
art of government as exemplified by instances in history. After the early
morning audience, the selected officials went over from Wenteh Hall
and followed the western covered corridor to Erhying Hall. In Su

Tungpo's time, the lecturer stood up while the other officials were permitted to sit down during the lecture. When Wang Anshih was a lecturer, he wanted to have the lecturer sit down while the others stood up, but another official had objected and overruled him. During this period the pompous, self-important Cheng Yi also took part in the series because of his knowledge of the classics, but he was only a tutor of the lowest rank. He, too, demanded the privilege of sitting down while lecturing, as a sign of respect for the teacher that was an important Confucian tenet. It was Cheng Yi who constantly lectured the young Emperor Tsehtsung about the power of the devil and the seductiveness of women, until the boy, who felt no attraction towards women then, was firmly resolved that he was going to have a gay time by the time he was grown up. The young emperor later divorced his empress and died at the age of twenty-four.

As far as the Su family was concerned, there was decided advantage in living at the capital. Having sold their old house, Su Tungpo now established his residence on Paichia Alley. Even if they had not sold their house, it would have been too far from his office. The new residence was close to the Eastern Palace Gate (Tunghuamen) through which the officials entered at dawn to go into the imperial audience. It was, therefore, in the popular residential district of the officials, what we might call the mid-town section, where the most expensive shops and restaurants were located.

The family began now to enjoy the new life of the capital, a far cry from the farm at Huangchow. They had not lived in the capital for about fifteen years, with the exception of the three months when Tungpo was brought to the capital under detention and the time when he was denied entry and stopped in the suburb. We do not know whether the dutiful Mai, who had left for a small post in Kiangse, came back to join the family. But the two younger sons, Tai and Kuo, sixteen and fourteen years old respectively, were at home. Both Mrs. Su and Chaoyun were now able to enjoy a comfortable life, a little awed by the luxury of the capital. Jewellery shops, silk shops, medicine shops, imposing structures two or three storeys high, stood all around them. The best of everything China could produce was there near the Eastern Palace Gate, selling at prices that would frighten a woman from the countryside. No matter how expensive the goods were, like fruit and flowers out of season, there were always people willing to pay for them. One great convenience was the hiring of servants from employment bureaus. The place swarmed with wine restaurants and other eating-places. At night, when one entered a wine restaurant, prostitutes lined the main corridor ready for the customers to call them to serve at the tables, and young boys had to look straight ahead or pin their eyes to the ground while going in with their fathers. During dinner, peddlers and solicitors went from room to room selling sweet- meats, dried fruits, cold roasts, and pickles. At the rice restaurants where people went for their meals, it was said that there was a long list of forty or fifty kinds of dishes carried around by the waiters, who kept circulating through the room for the customers to choose what they liked. If there was one dish missing from the list, the restaurant would lose customers.

Su Tungpo preferred to give dinners at home, and restaurants com- peted in catering for home dinners. Silver was provided by these caterers, and even the poorer restaurants would send a cook and a complete dinner with silver wine pots, cups, saucers, spoons, and silver- tipped ivory chopsticks. The custom was such that, after a few calls, the restaurants thought nothing of leaving overnight the silver service, costing four or five hundred taels a set, and collecting it the next day. A contemporary who wrote in fond reminiscence after the city was captured by the northern invaders said that the people were proud of the capital and very hospitable to strangers. Whenever they saw a stranger being taken advantage of, they would come and defend him, even if it involved a scuffle with the police. Neighbours would call on newcomers, give them presents of wine and tea, and advise them about the shops. There were also people who had nothing to do and who carried teapots during the day from home to home merely to purvey gossip.

In the midst of all this, Su Tungpo still carried on his yoga and hygiene practice. Every other night he had usually to sleep in the palace. But whether in the palace or at his home, he used to get up at dawn, comb his hair over a hundred times, put on his official gown and boots, and then lie down again to take a nap. According to him, the sweetness of that nap was incomparable. When the time came to go into imperial audience, he was all dressed and ready, and he would go out and mount his white horse with the gold-plated saddle and proceed to the Tunghua Gate.

The audience was usually over by ten o'clock at the latest, and then, unless there was special business, his time was free. He would go shop- ping with his wife and children when he did not have other social engagements. The Shiangkuo Temple was near-by, its courtyards filled with vendors of fans, knives and scissors, curios, antiques, paintings and rubbings of calligraphy. Sometimes the family wandered in the forty or fifty bazaars in the eastern city, where one could get everything from a hair-cut to pot flowers and caged birds, and could spend an entire day without being aware of it. Sometimes they would go through the Red Sparrow Gate to the outer city where there was another large residential section. The Confucian Temple and the National College stood in the southern outer city, and farther out were various Taoist temples. Sometimes when they came back they had dinner at "the Terrace", which was the name of the best wine restaurant in town. Or they could follow the main South Gate Avenue and visit the famous Tang jewellery shop or choose lacquer ware from Wenchow or examine the finest herbs at the pharmacy on Paotse Temple Street.

As a matter of fact, there is not very much difference in actual happiness between living a luxurious life and a simple one. The honour of a high position appears enviable only to one who is unqualified for it. The usual rule is, one is wanted for a post when he does not want it, and one wants a post when the post does not want him. Once the "official craving" is satisfied, being a high official is not likely to be more fun than being a successful blacksmith. Su Tungpo in a note "On Happiness and Unhappiness" expressed this point:

"One desires pleasure and fears a hard life. These are sentiments one entertains before leading the so-called pleasurable or hard life. After one is in it, one tries to think of the envy and the fear and finds that they are gone. Then where are the pleasurable and unpleasurable moments after they are past? They seem to be like a sound, a shadow, a breeze, or a dream. Even these four things are somehow more tangible. Besides, how is one ever going to find happiness by countering one illusion with another illusion? I wish I could express this deep truth to you, but I cannot. August 5, 1088."

There were others who looked upon the life at the capital in a more earthly manner. His relative Pu Tsungmeng enjoyed its luxuries to the limit. Pu's daughter-in-law occupied herself with nothing else the whole day but directing the maidservants to drip "butter flowers" in different designs to be sweetened and solidified and served as desserts. The daughter-in-law insisted that she would never serve her guests with butter flowers of the same design a second time, and the maidservants were kept dripping these flowers night and day. Pu also had interesting personal habits, which included "the big wash face", "the small wash face", "the big foot-bath", "the small foot-bath", "the big bath", and "the small bath". Every day he would wash his face twice and have foot-baths twice, and every other day he would have a regular bath. At a "small wash face", during which he washed only his face, he changed the water in his basin once and was attended by two servants. At a "big wash face" he changed the water three times, was attended by five servants, and washed down to his neck and shoulders. At a "small foot-bath" he changed the water once, was attended by two servants, and washed up to his ankles. At a "big foot-bath" he changed the water three times, was attended by four servants, and washed up to his knees. At a "small bath" he used twenty-four gallons of water and was attended by five or six servants, while at a "big bath" he used also twenty-four gallons, but was served by eight or nine attendants. At this "big bath" he used medicated ointment, and had his clothes perfumed on a wire netting placed over slowly burning rare incense. He wrote to Su Tungpo saying that this system of regular baths did him a lot of good, and Su Tungpo replied: "I am pleased to hear this, but I also suggest two ingredients which can further increase your happiness, namely, thrift and compassion."

There are decided social and material advantages in being a high official. In those days, the simple choice for the educated class was between being an official and obscurity—the latter usually meant poverty. One could achieve lasting fame, of course, by devotion to scholarship; but to many, immortal fame, even if one could be sure of it, was poor consolation for a hungry stomach. In Su Tungpo's time there was a satire on scholars who, after passing the examinations and accepting an office, continually protested that they were doing so as a personal sacrifice for the country. The story was as follows:

Once upon a time there was a poor scholar who was so poor that he had no money to buy bread. He was famished, and thought of a way to get some bread to eat. He went to the outside of a bakery shop and started to run away in horror, but failed to attract any attention. Then he went on to another bakery where stood a big crowd in the street. Upon catching sight of the buns, he gave out a loud scream, ran away in fright and then fell upon the ground. The crowd gathered around him and asked him what he was frightened of. "Those buns!" the scholar replied. Everybody laughed; they had never heard of such a thing. Incredulous, the owner of the bakery shop wanted to test him. He induced the scholar to go into a room where he had placed a big pile of buns, and watched him from a keyhole. Happy at the success of his stratagem, the scholar dug into the pile with both hands and began to gorge himself. Greatly touched, the baker broke into the room and said kindly to him: "Is there anything else you are afraid of?"

"I am now afraid of a really good cup of hot tea," replied the scholar.

One day the two sons-in-law of Han Wei, belonging to the great, rich and powerful family which produced several premiers, came to see Su Tungpo, and he asked them how their father-in-law was doing.

"He is doing very well," replied one of the young men. "He tells us that he has now reached old age, and that he is going to enjoy his remaining years with music, wine, and women; otherwise, he wouldn't know how to pass his days."

"Indeed!" said Su Tungpo. "I'm afraid he is on the wrong track, exactly because he has only a few remaining years to live. I want to tell you a story which you can repeat to your father-in-law. Will you do that?"

"Why, of course," the young man replied.

"There was a certain old man," began Su Tungpo, "who had never taken up Buddhist meditations. But he lived in accordance with true Buddhist principles and took life and death very philosophically. One day he called all his children and relatives together and gave them a big wine dinner. After the dinner was over, he told his family: 'Now I am going to depart from this life.' Thereupon, he gathered up his gown and sat in an erect posture and looked as though he was ready to remain in this position until he gave up the ghost. His sons were frightened, and cried to him: 'Father! Are you going to say good-bye to us? Won't you leave some parting advice?' The old man replied: 'I did not intend to give you any advice, but since you ask for it, I will say only this: Get up at the fifth watch.' His sons could not understand and asked him for an explanation. 'Only at the fifth watch,' said the old man, 'can one attend to one's own business. As soon as the sun rises, it is not possible to do it.' His sons were still more puzzled, and said: 'Since our family is well-to-do, why should we get up so early? Besides, the family business is the same as one's own business. What is the difference?' 'No,' said the old man, 'what I mean by one's own business is that which you can take with you when you depart from this world. You see, I have built up this fortune and now I am about to depart. What can I take with me when I go?' His sons then understood.

"Now," continued Su Tungpo, "your father-in-law thinks he has only a few remaining years to live and wants to enjoy them. Will you two take a message for me to him? Only say that I ask him to attend to his own business. Rather than dissipate his waning strength with wine and women, he had better think of what he is going to take with him at the journey's end."

About his revered friend Fan Chen, Tungpo said after Fan's death: "Chingjen never liked Buddhism, but in his old age he lived a simple, quiet life with few material desires and not a care on his mind. He really was the kind to make a good Buddhist, yet he was against Buddhism to the end of his days. In my opinion, he was a Buddhist without knowing it. Such a man may smash the idols and abuse the monks and still go up to Western Heaven."

Su Tungpo was now at the height of his fame. He was honoured by all scholars and friends, and he had a high official position. He had, more than any of his friends, suffered for his opinions, and was greatly admired for it. After Szema Kuang's death he became the undisputed first scholar of his time, and while he did not seem exactly cut out for a premier, it was generally admitted that as a personality he towered head and shoulders above the entire officialdom. For a time, two of his friends were at the head of the government, namely, Lu Kungchu and Fan Chunjen. His brother, too, had come back to the capital, arriving in January 1086, to take the post of high censor in the premier's office, and was made vice-minister of the interior in the following year. All his friends who had been banished to the south were now occupying important positions at the court, including Prince Wang Shien, Wang Kung, Sun Chueh, and Fan Tsuyu. His old friend at Huangchow, Chen Tsao, too, had come to the capital, not to be an official, but to see Su Tungpo and enjoy his company. The great poet Huang Ting-chien, who had corresponded with him years ago, came to make his acquaintance and to be formally accepted as his disciple. For a number of years, in his correspondence, Su Tungpo had repeatedly praised four scholars of his time and this had greatly enhanced their reputations. It became established during this period that there were "four disciples of Su Tungpo," namely, Huang Tingchien, Chin Kuan, Chang Lei, and Chao Puchih. Later two more persons were accepted, Li Chih and Chen Shihtao, making a total of "six disciples" of Su.

Su Tungpo's popularity broke up a marriage. The scholar Chang Yuanpi was a great admirer of the poet. He was not much to look at, but had married a beautiful wife. Very soon after the marriage the wife found that the husband read Su Tungpo's poems all night and did not pay any attention to her. It got to the point where she could not bear it any more, and she said to her husband: "So you love Su Tungpo more than me! Well then, I want a divorce." She got it, and Chang told his friends that he was divorced by his wife all on account of Su Tungpo.

Such was Su's popularity at this time that many scholars began even to imitate his hat. He wore a particularly high hat with a narrow bend forward at the top, and this became known as the "Tsechan hat", Tsechan being Su's courtesy name. One day he accompanied the Emperor on a pleasure trip to Lichuan, where there was a theatrical performance by the court actors. One of the comic actors wore this hat on the stage and boasted: "I'm a far better writer than all of you!" "How do you prove it?" said the other actors. "Don't you see the hat I'm wearing?" replied the comedian. At this the Emperor smiled and looked significantly at Su Tungpo.

In the midst of all this, Su Tungpo indulged in a great deal of joking and fun-making with his friends. While he was minister of education and chief examiner, he was shut up with his friends the other judges for weeks. While they were busy looking over the papers during office

hours, Su went from room to room, chatting and cracking jokes and
generally making it impossible for them to attend to their duties. Then
at night he would do his own work, going through the papers with
great rapidity.

There were many tales of how he made up stories on the spot. Many
of these contain puns, particularly those in which he exchanged repartee with another great wit, Liu Pin. But there are some stories
which can be translated into English.

Once Su Tungpo went to call on Lu Tafang, who was then premier.
Lu was a very fat person, and was taking an afternoon nap when Su
Tungpo called. Su was kept waiting a long time and felt annoyed. At
last Lu appeared. Su Tungpo pointed to an earthen basin in the living-
room in which was kept a tortoise with moss on its back.

"That's nothing rare," said Su Tungpo to his host. "What is really
difficult to obtain is a tortoise with three pairs of eyes."

"Is that so?" said Lu, with wide open eyes. "Is there such a thing
as a six-eyed tortoise?" Lu had a feeling that he was being fooled; but
then, Su Tungpo was such a widely-read man and he might have read
about it somewhere.

"Certainly," replied Su Tungpo. "In the time of Emperor Tsung of
Tang, he once received a six-eyed tortoise as a present from a minister.
On being asked what was the virtue of a six-eyed tortoise, the minister
replied that a six-eyed tortoise had three pairs of eyes, while a common
tortoise had only one. Therefore, you see, when a six-eyed tortoise takes
a nap, it is equal to the nap of three tortoises put together."

Su Tungpo used to boast to his friend Chien Shieh how he loved
the simple life he used to lead in the country. He said that at dinner
they had only rice, turnips, and a plain soup; nevertheless, he was
thoroughly happy and contented. One day his friend Chien sent him
an invitation to dinner, which read: "I am going to give you something special. We shall have a 'whitewhytewhight' dinner." Su Tungpo
had never heard of such a thing and could not make out what it meant.
When he came to the dinner he found that Chien offered him a very
simple dinner with only three white things on the table, a bowl of
white rice, a dish of white turnips, and a bowl of colourless soup.
Reminded of his boast, Su realised that he had been fooled. Su Tungpo
allowed some time to elapse, and then sent Chien also an invitation
asking him to attend a "noughnoknow" dinner. When Chien appeared,
he found a bare table. Su Tungpo invited him to sit down and the two
sat down. After a long while, still no dishes appeared, and Chien complained that he was getting hungry. Very pompously Su Tungpo said
to his friend: "Let's start without waiting. I have invited you to a
bowl of 'no' rice, some 'nough' turnips, and 'know' soup." After Su

Tungpo had his revenge, the friend was forgiven and they had a hearty meal together.

While he was acting as secretary to the Emperor, Su Tungpo was often locked up during the night in the palace. There was a great admirer of his and an assiduous collector of his autographs who used to give ten catties of mutton for every short note of Su's brought to him by Su's secretary. The poet had learned of this. One day his secretary asked for a reply to a friend's message, which Su gave orally. The secretary came a second time, and Su said: "Haven't I told you already?"

"The man insists on a written reply," said his secretary.

"Tell your friend, no butchery today," was Su's answer.

In the Confucian *Analects,* there was a man by the name of Szema Ox, bearing the same surname as Szema Kuang. One day Tungpo had had a hot argument with Szema Kuang on state policy and the latter would not be convinced. Returning home, he threw his gown on the couch and groaned to Chaoyun: "Szema Ox! Szema Ox!"

During these years Su Tungpo constantly developed in his state papers the two ideas of "independent thinking" and "impartiality" as the prime requisites of a good minister. But independence of mind and impartiality of opinion were something that the party men heartily disliked. One night after a good supper Su paced about the room, feeling his belly with great satisfaction. He asked the women in the family what they thought his belly contained. In the Chinese language, one speaks of a "bellyful" of thoughts, feelings, scholarship, etc. One woman replied: "Your belly is full of ink." Another replied: "Your belly is full of beautiful writing." To these answers, Su Tungpo said: "No." Finally his clever concubine, Chaoyun, said: "Your belly is full of unpopular ideas." "That's right!" the poet exclaimed, and he had a good laugh.

Once an unknown scholar came to see Su Tungpo with a volume of his verse and asked Su's opinion of it. The poor scholar read his own composition aloud, intoning it very expressively, and was evidently well satisfied with himself. "Now, what is your opinion of my humble composition, Your Excellency?" he asked.

"One hundred marks," said Su.

The scholar's face beamed with pride. Then Su added: "Seventy marks for your beautiful recital and thirty for the verse."

Chapter Twenty

THE ART OF PAINTING

IT is not surprising that Su Tungpo's genius and high spirits should have given birth to a new form of Chinese art, essentially designed to express the joy of the brush. The most important of Su Tungpo's amusements was his "play with ink", for it was through this that his great creative artistic impulse was given free play and left a permanent influence on Chinese art. Su Tungpo not only originated his famous "ink bamboos", that is, paintings of bamboo in ink; he first created the name for a new style of Chinese painting, the style of "scholar painting" (*shihjen hua*). With the younger Mi Fei, he pioneered in what was to become the most characteristic and representative style of Chinese painting. The southern school of painting, emphasising rapid rhythmic strokes done in a unifying conception, had been founded, it is true, as early as the eighth century, by Wu Taotse and Wang Wei —in sharp distinction from the northern school of Li Szeshün, with their minute delineations, their golden tracings, their use of green and crimson. It was, however, in the Sung dynasty that the impressionistic "scholar painting" was firmly established. This school, with its emphasis on rhythmic vitality and a controlling subjective conception of the artist, still contains some secrets of artistic principles and techniqus that are of importance to modern artists.

We are therefore fortunate to be able to see, through the many art criticisms preserved for us by Su Tungpo, Mi Fei, and Huang Tingchien, the origin of "scholar painting" in the life of Su Tungpo. The scholars were poets, calligraphers, and painters at the same time. At the outset it must be made clear that in China calligraphy and painting are one and the same art, the same in technique, in medium and in spirit and principles of criticism. One cannot understand the origin of the southern school of Chinese painting without understanding the æsthetic principles involved in Chinese calligraphy.* For the founders of this school, of which Su Tungpo was one, were men nurtured in the spirit of Chinese poetry, and trained in the mastery of the brush and in all the principles of rhythm and composition in Chinese calligraphy itself. Calligraphy provides the technique and æsthetic principles

* As a connoisseur, Su Tungpo wrote one hundred and thirty-six notes or comments on calligraphy, thirty-three on painting, thirty-six on ink, and eighteen on the brush. Huang Tingchien, the poet, wrote over a hundred notes on calligraphy that he had seen, an even greater number than the notes he wrote on painting.

for Chinese painting, while poetry provides the spirit, the emphasis on tone and atmosphere, and the pantheistic delight in all the smells and colours and sounds of nature.

Before Su Tungpo was born, China was already rich in artistic tradition, both in calligraphy and painting. Su Tungpo had from his youth been a strong admirer of Wu Taotse, and all through his years at Huangchow he had spent his time improving himself as a painter. Now all his poet and painter friends were gathered at the capital, and the atmosphere was stimulating to his poetic and artistic creativity. As life is transformed when one good chess player finds another good chess player in the same city, so Su Tungpo's life was now changed. After all, he was a scholar and not a politician, and as a scholar his primary occupation was with ink, brush, and paper. His disciples, great scholars themselves, were continually calling at his house. Mi Fei, who later became the most outstanding painter of the Sung dynasty, once was so enamoured with the massive rhythms of the silent rocks that he prostrated himself before a mountain cliff and called it his "father-in-law". He styled himself, or was called by others: "Crazy Mi." Mi, Su, and Li Kunglin, the three great Sung masters, were now constantly in each other's company.

This group of scholars gathered together in one another's homes, had wine dinners, joked, versified, and were more usually in the intoxicated state than not. At such times Su or Mi or Li would approach the desk, with ink, brush, and paper spread before him. As one started to paint, to write, or to versify, the others looked on and joined in, adding poems for postscripts. The circumstances and atmosphere were ideal. The most essential materials for the practise of poetry, painting, or calligraphy are two liquids, ink and liquor; they had the best of wine and the best of ink, besides the best of brushes and the most expensive and rarest quality of paper. When a good calligraphist or painter found an especially rare paper, he was like a good violin player finding a Stradivarius before him—he just could not resist it. Su Tungpo's favourites were Chengshintang paper, Chuko brushes from Shüancheng, or brushes made from a mouse's whiskers, and ink made by Li Tingkuei. After one scholar had completed a painting, it was customary for the others to write in turn a few lines or a couple of poems in comment on the painting, or perhaps merely to record a joke that had passed around at the time. Sometimes Su Tungpo and Li Kunglin (better known to Western art collectors as Li Lungmien) co-operated in working out a picture, Su painting the rocks and Li painting the cypress trees, and Tseyu and Huang Tingchien making verse comments on it.

There was once a great occasion, celebrated in the history of Chinese art, at which sixteen of these scholars were gathered together in the

garden home of Prince Wang Shien. This is the great "Gathering of
Scholars at the Western Garden",* celebrated in painting by Li and
fully described by Mi Fei. Present were the three great painters of
Sung dynasty, Su Tungpo, Mi Fei and Li Lungmien, and Su's brother
and his four disciples. Stone tablets are spread beneath the tall cypresses
and bamboos in the garden. At the top, a cascade flows into a great
river, covered on both banks with flowers and bamboos. Two concubines of the host, wearing high coiffures with many hair ornaments,
are standing behind the table. Su Tungpo, in his black cap and yellow
gown, is leaning over the table writing, while Prince Wang Shien sits
near-by looking on. At another table, Li Lungmien is writing a poem
by Tao Chien, while Tseyu, Huang Tingchien, Chang Lei, Chao
Puchih are all grouped around the table. Mi Lei, standing, head up-
turned, is inscribing something on a rock near-by. Chin Kuan seats
himself among the gnarled roots of a tree listening to someone playing
on a stringed instrument, while others are scattered about, kneeling or
standing in different postures. Monks and other scholars make up the
rest of the crowd.

It is generally recognised that Su's writing was at its best when he
was intoxicated or inspired, and considering the rapid rhythm required
in the execution of Chinese calligraphy or paintings, one can well
believe it. When he was chief examiner of the imperial examinations
in 1088, he and his artist friends Li Kunglin, Huang Tingchien, and
Chang Lei were locked up for a period of at least seven or eight weeks
as fellow judges of the examinations, forbidden to communicate with
the outside world until the final grading of the papers had been completed. In their spare time, Li Kunglin painted horses to amuse himself, Huang wrote lugubrious or macabre verse on ghosts, and they
told one another tall tales of Taoists and fairies. As for Su Tungpo,
Huang wrote: "Tungpo loved to write, but one must not beg for his
autographs. Those who do so are sometimes bluntly refused. When
we were locked up in the ministry of education during the examinations, every time he saw paper lying on the desk, he would start to
cover it up with his writing, regardless of the quality of the paper.
He loved to drink, but after four or five cups was already dead drunk.
Without ceremony he went and stretched himself out and began to
snore like thunder. After a while he woke up, approached the table
and began to write or paint as fast as the wind. Even his jocular verses
had a great charm. Indeed, he was one of the fairies."

Su Tungpo says of his own practice of the art: "I realise that full
mastery is not just license, but arises from perfection of details. But

* The painting reproduced in the book is a late copy, probably Ming, and some
of the details have been changed. Three of the original figures are missing. In
the copy at the Peking Palace Museum, of which I have seen only a reproduction,
all sixteen figures are preserved.

when my brush touches the paper, it goes as fast as the wind. My spirit sweeps all before it, before my brush has reached a point."

In his lifetime Su had several portraits made of himself, the most famous ones being those by Cheng Huaili and by the renowned Li Kunglin. In Li's portrait, Su is painted as sitting on a rock with a cane resting in his lap. Huang remarked that this portrait* caught Su Tungpo's expression when he was a little drunk. In this posture one can see him sitting relaxed, pondering over the laws of growth and decay of the material world, while he enjoys the infinite rhythms of nature spread before him. At any moment he may get up, take a brush, dip it in ink, and write out what is there in his breast, either in the beautiful words of a song or in the beautiful rhythms of a painting or a script.

Once Tu Chishien came with a good piece of paper and asked Su Tungpo to write something on it, but he suggested the measurements of the script. Tungpo jokingly asked: "Now, am I selling vegetables?" Kang Shihmeng had already, in March 1087, published facsimiles of nine scripts by the two Su brothers. His own friends were among the zealous collectors of his autograph scripts. One evening when his friends were at his home, they were turning over the contents of some of his old trunks. Someone spotted a scrap of paper containing some barely legible script in Su's handwriting. Upon examination it was found to be the manuscript of his hobo rhapsody, called "The Yellow Mud Flat", written "when drunk", while he was in confinement in Huangchow. There were places so blurred that Su could hardly read his own writing. Chang Lei made a copy and gave it to Su and kept the original himself. A few days later Su Tungpo received a letter from Prince Wang Shien as follows: "I have been trying ceaselessly day and night to collect your writings. Recently I have obtained two pieces of paper by exchanging three pieces of silk for them. If you have recent manuscripts, you should give them to me and not let me keep on wasting my silks."

A collection of facsimiles of some of the most intimate letters of Su Tungpo, *Western Tower Scripts,* engraved on stone and published as rubbings soon after his death, has survived to this day. These facsimiles are like glimpses of a friend next door. In a postscript to one of the letters he gave his wife's thanks to a friend who had sent her a comb, and in another postscript he said he was sending a pot of pickled pork.

It is perhaps easiest to explain Chinese calligraphy by saying that it is really a form of abstract painting. The problems of Chinese calligraphy and of abstract painting are similar. In judging Chinese calli-

* See the reproduction following page 18.

graphy, the critics completely ignore the meaning of the words, and treat it essentially as an abstract composition. It is abstract painting in the sense that, unlike painting in general, it does not try to portray any recognisable object. Chinese characters are composed of lines and combinations of lines put together in an infinite variety of ways, and art requires that these characters be put together beautifully in themselves, and in relation to other characters on the same line or page. As the Chinese characters are composed of the most complex elements, they present all the problems of composition, including axis, contour, organisation, contrast, balance, proportion, and above all, a central unifying conception of the whole.

All problems of art are problems of rhythm, whether in painting, sculpture, or music. As long as beauty is movement, every art form has an implied rhythm. Even in architecture, a Gothic cathedral aspires, a bridge spans, and a prison broods. Æsthetically, it is possible even to speak of the "dash" and "sweep" and "ruggedness" of a man's moral character, which are all concepts of rhythm. The basic concept of rhythm in Chinese art is established by calligraphy. When a Chinese critic admires calligraphy, he does not admire it for its static proportions or symmetry, but rather follows the artist mentally in his movement from the beginning of a character to the end and so on to the end of the page, as if he were watching a dance on paper. The approach to this type of abstract painting is therefore different from that of Western abstract painting. Its fundamental thesis is that *beauty is movement;* and it is this basic concept of rhythm which develops into a guiding principle of Chinese painting.

This conception of rhythmic beauty in movement changes all the artist's concepts of line, mass, surface, composition, and material. For if beauty is dynamic and not static, all even, straight lines and surfaces, resembling engineers' blue-prints, are ruled out, and instead one must seek, for instance, the twisted and uneven lines of a tree branch, for only bending and twisting can suggest life and movement. One can easily see the life and movement of such uneven lines where the sensitive pressures, pauses and sweeps, and accidental splashes of the brush are carefully and purposefully preserved. It may be stated as a fundamental principle of Chinese painting and calligraphy that straight, even lines are abhorred and strictly taboo, except in case of necessity, as when one is sketching the outline of a desk or table. The very concept of composition is changed, too. A Chinese artist cannot be satisfied with merely the static arrangement and contrasting of lines and surfaces, so long as those lines and surfaces are dead in themselves. From here on begins the emphasis on vital lines, which accounts for the difference between Chinese painting technique and other forms of the same art.

For the basis of these vital lines, the calligraphist goes back to nature. Nature's lines always suggest movement, and their variety is rich and infinite. There is one type of beauty in the smooth body of a greyhound, built for fast running, and another type of beauty in the hairy, squatty lines of an Irish terrier. One can admire the light agility of a young deer, and at the same time the massive muscular strength of a lion's paw. A deer's body is beautiful not only as a harmonious contour but because it suggests leaping motion, and a lion's paw is beautiful because it suggests pouncing, and it is these functions of pouncing and leaping that give organic unity to the lines. When it comes to beauty of rhythm as such, one can admire the unwieldy form of an elephant, or the wriggling tension of a snake, or even the lanky and awkward movement of a giraffe. Nature's rhythms are, therefore, always functional, because the lines and contours are results of a process of growth and serve a definite purpose. Through the rich rhythms of nature, the utmost sophistication in appreciation becomes possible. It is exactly these rhythms of nature that the Chinese calligraphist tries to imitate in his brush movements, and obviously they can be copied only by the sensitive brush. Some strokes, firm and well rounded, suggest the massive power of a lion's paw, some the sinewy strength of a horse's leg, where the bones and joints are clear. Some try to suggest a clean-cut neatness and the characters have well-shaped shoulders and waists and supports, like a woman perfectly formed, or as the Chinese critics say: "Like a beauty wearing a fresh flower in her hair." Some copy the inimitable grace of a dried vine ending in a gentle, restful curl, with a few delicate leaves for balance. It should not be forgotten that the balance of a withered hanging vine is naturally perfect because the shape and angle of inclination of the tip depends upon the total weight of the vine, the support of the stalk, and the weight of the remaining leaves on one side or the other.

Su Tungpo said that his friend Wen Tung practised the art of calligraphy a long time without success until one day, walking alone on a mountain path, he came across two fighting snakes. Getting his inspiration from the rhythm of the fighting snakes, he incorporated their sinuous movement into his style of calligraphy. Another calligrapher once learned the secret of rhythm when he watched a woodcutter and a country girl meeting each other on a narrow path. Both of them hesitated and both of them tried to give way to the other and both of them were confused, not knowing who was to stop still and let the other pass. This momentary back and forward movement of the two persons produced a certain tension and play and counterplay and was said to have enabled the calligrapher to understand for the first time the principles of his art.

Carried over to painting, this riotous yet harmonious rhythm of lines produces what may be broadly considered the impressionistic school of Chinese art, in which the artist is concerned with recording an impression in his mind expressed in a controlling rhythm, rather than with making a copy of the objects before him. It is natural that the fewer details there are in a composition, the easier it is to express or convey this rhythm. Hence Su Tungpo's concentration on a few sprays of bamboo or a few rugged rocks as adequate paintings in themselves. The rhythm alone compels the elimination of all material and all objects irrelevant to the unifying conception. It is perhaps easier to see extreme examples of impressionistic art in a chicken or a fish by Pata Shanjen or in an orchid by Shih Tao of the sixteenth century. Whether it is a picture of a fish or of a chicken or of a bird, Pata Shanjen's art may be considered as the art of expressing the most by the fewest lines and the smallest amount of ink. The artist completes his picture of a fish or a horse or a portrait in a matter of a few minutes by a few rapid splashes of ink; he either succeeds or fails, and if he fails, he crumples up the paper, rolls it into a ball, throws it into the waste-basket, and starts all over again.

This economy of brush work accounts for the spontaneity of Chinese painting. But the economy of brush work and extreme concentration on the main subject also bring other results. Su Tungpo's painting of a few sprays of bamboo leaves with a barely visible moon shining from behind creates two effects. First, because of the absence of irrelevant matter, it stimulates the imagination of the spectator; and secondly, it implies that these few bamboo leaves, whether resting peacefully in a moonlight night or violently tossing about in a storm, are worth looking at for ever and ever in the delight of the simple rhythms they express. The purpose and motivation in painting a few bamboo stalks, a curling line, or a few rugged rocks, are exactly the same as the artist's purpose and motivation in writing a certain group of characters. Once the mood is expressed and the impression put down on paper, the artist is satisfied and pleased. He is therefore able to convey that same pleasure and satisfaction to people who look at the picture.

Hence, this school of scholars'. paintings is also called the school of "writing out a conception" (*shieh yi*), which is impressionism. This word *yi* is extremely difficult to translate; it means something the artist wishes to express; for substitutes we have to render is as "intention", "conception", "impression", or "mood". It would not be at all inappropriate to designate this school of painting by a new term "conceptivism", the idea being emphasis on a unified concept which it is the sole object of the artist to portray.

The central problem of art is the same, east and west, ancient and modern. Impressionism may be briefly summed up as a revolt against photographic accuracy, and the setting forth of a new aim in art by expressing the subjective impression of the artist. Su Tungpo fully expressed this revolt in two lines. "To judge a painting by its veri-similitude is to judge it at the mental level of a child." In a comment on one of the younger impressionistic painters, Sung Tsefang, Su says: "Judging scholars' paintings is like judging horses. What you want to look at is the spirit of a horse. The professional artists often see only the skin and hair, the whips, the trough and the hay. That is why the paintings of professional artists are lacking in spirit, and after seeing a few such paintings, one is bored."

Here the Sung painters advanced one step further; in a painting, they tried not only to express the writer's impression or conception, but also the *li* or "inner spirit". A simple way of stating it would be to say that the Sung painters tried to paint the spirit rather than the form of things. The Sung school of philosophy was called the study of *li*. Under the influence of Buddhist metaphysics, the Confucianists turned their attention from rules and forms of government and society, and began to delve into problems of the mind and the universe. With the help of Hindu mysticism and metaphysics they began to speak of this *li*, which broadly means "reason" in nature and human nature, or "the laws of nature", or the "inner spirit of things". Hampered by Chinese incapacity or distaste for abstract metaphysics, the Sung philosophers did not get very far with this *li* as laws of nature, but did completely believe in a pervading force or spirit or "reason" behind the shape of things; nature is spirit and alive, and a painter should catch that indefinable inner spirit of things in his painting. It should not be the artist's object in painting an autumn forest to copy the lavish colours of leaves, but to copy that invisible "spirit of autumn", or "mood of autumn", or, in other words, to make one feel like putting on a light overcoat and going out to breathe the crisp, chilly air, to feel almost visibly the *yin* overcoming the *yang* in nature's metamorphosis at this season. Su Tungpo taught his son in writing poems to bring out the individuality of a flower, so that a line about the peony could not possibly be mistaken for a line about the lilac or the plum blossom. The essence of a peony is festive gorgeousness, that of a plum blossom is seclusion and refinement. This "essence" has to be seized by the painter's eye and the poet's imagination. In order to paint a fish, the artist must understand the "nature" of fish, but in order to do so he must, through the exercise of his intuitive imagination, mentally swim with it in the water and share its reactions to current and storms and light and food. Only an artist who understands the joys of the salmon in leaping the rapids and realises how exciting it is to him should try to paint the salmon. Otherwise he should leave the salmon alone, for no matter how accurate the painting is of its scales and fins and eyelids, the painting will be dead.

One must of course observe details. Su Tungpo once recorded an amusing incident. There was a Szechuen collector of paintings, and among the hundred odd paintings in his possession he valued most highly the one of a fight between bulls, by Tai Sung. One day the collector was sunning this painting in a courtyard. A young cowherd happened to pass by; he looked at the painting for a second and shook his head and laughed. On being asked what he was laughing at, the boy replied: "When bulls are locked in combat, their tails are tautly drawn between their hind legs. This painting makes the bulls' tails stand up straight behind!"

Su Tungpo also condemned Huang Chuan, a famous painter of birds, for his inaccurate observation of the habits of birds. But mere observation and accuracy cannot give us true art. One must exercise intuitive insight, amounting to a pantheistic delight in the birds and animals of nature. Perhaps the best insight into what Su Tungpo was trying to do in portraying the inner spirit of things is afforded by a poem he wrote on a picture of a crane painted by himself. He remarked that when a crane standing in the marshes sees a human being approach, he has set his mind to fly even before moving a feather. But when no human beings are around, the bird has an air of complete relaxation. This is the inner spirit of the crane that Su Tungpo tried to reproduce in his painting.

In speaking further about painting the inner spirit rather than the external forms of objects, Su Tungpo says:

"It has been my opinion concerning painting that men and animals and buildings and structures have a constant material form. On the other hand, mountains and rocks, bamboos and trees, ripples of water, smoke and clouds do not have a constant form (*shing*) but do have a constant inner spirit (*li*). Anybody can detect inaccuracy in the constant forms, but even specialists often fail to note mistakes in painting the constant inner spirit of things. Some artists find it much easier to deceive the public and make a name for themselves by painting objects without constant forms. When one makes a mistake in the form or contour of an object, however, the mistake is confined to that particular part and does not spoil the whole, whereas if one misses the inner spirit, the whole painting falls flat. Because such objects do not have a constant form, one must pay special attention to their inner laws. There are plenty of craftsmen who can copy the minute details of objects, but the inner law of things can be comprehended only by the highest human spirits. Yuko's [Wen Tung's] paintings of bamboos, rocks, and dried up trees may be said to have truly seized the inner spirit of the objects. He understands how these things grow and decay, how they twist and turn and are sometimes blocked and compressed, and how they prosper and thrive in freedom. The roots, stalks, joints, and leaves go through infinite variations, following different rhythms independent of one another. And yet they are all true to nature and completely satisfying to the human spirit. These are records of the inspirations of a great soul. . . . Those who understand the inner spirit of things and examine these paintings carefully will see that I am right."

All painting is unconscious reflection of a philosophy. Chinese paintings unconsciously express the oneness of man with nature and the essential unity of the great mystic procession of life in which the human being occupies but a small and transitory part. In this sense, the so-called impressionistic Chinese painting, whether of a twig of bamboo, a group of gnarled roots, or rain in the mountains, or snow over the river, is a pantheistic revelry. The complete *identification* of the painter with the painted object cannot be more clearly expressed than in the poem Su Tungpo wrote about a picture of bamboos and rocks which he painted on the wall of a friend's house.

> "Receiving the moisture of wine,
> My intestines sprout and fork out,
> And from out my liver and lungs
> Shoot rocks and bamboos,
> Surging through my breast, irresistible,
> They find expression on your snow-white wall."

Chapter Twenty-one

THE ART OF GETTING OUT OF POWER

THERE is an art of rising to power and an art of getting out of it, and it is of the second that Su was a master. Today the spectacle of Su Tungpo, not chasing after politics but chased by it, is rather amusing. It was not so surprising that he failed politically when Wang Anshih was in power; it was much more surprising that he "failed" when his own party was in. Su Tungpo never made a good party man, for he had too high a stature as a man. With his own party in power, himself enjoying prestige and popularity, and with the Empress herself among his personal admirers, he nevertheless managed to lose a much-envied and coveted political position. He did not succeed at once, but anyone who knew Su Tungpo's temperament could tell that he would not stay in politics for long. The first law of the art of delaying old age and prolonging youth was the avoidance of all emotional disturbances, and Su Tungpo was now having plenty of emotional disturbances in the "village of scoundrels", as he called the official world. The game of politics is fine for those who love it; to others not interested in ruling other men, the loss in human dignity is hardly worth the gain in power and tinsel glamour. Su Tungpo's heart was never in the game of politics. What he deplorably lacked was determination to get on and rise to premiership, as he easily could have done if he had been differently inclined. As secretary to the Emperor—that is, really to the Empress—he enjoyed the intimacy of the imperial household, and if he had cared to play the game, there was no question that he had enough intelligence to play it well. But to do so would have been to do violence to his own nature.

The governmental system of the Sung dynasty was particularly adapted to the struggle for power by politicians. Power was purposely concentrated in the hand of the Emperor. Even after the complete re-organisation and simplification of the governmental system in 1078, there was still no post for a premier with undivided responsibility. There was no well-defined principle of joint responsibility for a cabinet, so that the premier and his cabinet could act as a unit. Neither were there, as I have pointed out previously, well-defined responsibilities and privileges for the ruling party and the opposition. The mechanics of a government by the majority party were not there. So, even more than in the West, the game of politics was essentially a fight of personalities. But the rules of politics are similar enough in the East and West. It is a system designed to ensure the rise of mediocrity to the top. There are certain rules of the game, played chiefly behind the scenes. The first rule is, a good politician is one who has mastered the art of saying nothing with a great number of words. A good official never states, but only denies. With a sufficient schooling in the art of saying perpetually: "No comment", and "You are right", a good official can go a long way. A second rule is that he should oblige his friends. A third rule is that he should take care not to offend. With a tight mouth, a cultivated, low, pleasant whisper, and a great desire to oblige, such a man can never be thrown out of power even if he does not rise to the top. He will die at his desk.

Unfortunately, Su Tungpo was not this type. In the next few years he broke all these rules of success in politics. On the birth of his boy by Chaoyun, he had written the following wish:

"May you, my son, grow up dumb and stupid,
And, free from calamities, end up as a premier."

The infant died and so had no chance of carrying out his father's wish. So we must ask whether a poet-painter can become a successful official. Conceivably, yes, in time of peace, but peace is a relative word, and there is not a decade in politics in which there are not hot issues to fight about. A poet-painter, with his detached philosophic point of view, can scarcely become so involved in the political issues that he is willing to play the game and accept the penalties. More often than not, after a few trials, he laughs at himself for trying to play it at all.

But if Su Tungpo was running away from politics, politics was running after him. He and Szema Kuang had disagreed on policies, as independent minds always disagree, but half a year after his arrival at the capital, Szema Kuang died. Su was left alone in a very prominent and all too enviable position. It did not take long for the first storm to break over him, and soon the court fight centred around him. By January of the following year several dozens of memorials to the throne had been sent against him. With the death of Szema Kuang, political cliques were shaping up—the "Hopei clique", the "Honan clique", led by the neo-Confucianists, and the "Szechuen clique", of which Su Tungpo was considered the head. Judging by the records and Su Tungpo's insistent desire to get out, he certainly did not know what that word "Szechuen clique" meant. However, there were enough provocations for his political opponents to put up a bitter fight against him. This fight, it must be said in fairness, was started by his brother, Tseyu. When Tseyu arrived at the capital as a high censor in the premier's office at the beginning of the new regime, he thought it was his duty to clean up the government and get rid of all the fence-riders and remnant politicians who had played ball with Wang Anshih. He succeeded in banishing the notorious Huiching, and in temporarily

I*

degrading Tsai Chueh, Tsai Ching, and Chang Chun, who were, however, to stage a powerful come-back later. But Tseyu had also impeached one of the leaders of the Hopei party by as many as seven memorials, until the leader fell, and he had characterised other people. of the Hopei party as "rice bags".

The fight was on. Dirty squabbles of politicians are never interesting to anybody else, for unlike the fight over Wang Anshih's state capitalism, for instance, they involve no question of policy or principle. Su Tungpo had fought against the restoration of the military draft, but this was not the issue that the partisans took up. It was a matter of mere quibbling. As an examiner giving out a subject for examinations of scholars for ministry posts, he had asked the candidates to write on the following question: The Emperor Jentsung inclined towards *laissez* faire and the Emperor Shentsung inclined towards rigid governmenta control. A *laissez faire* type of government leads to lazy and la administration, while a strict governmental system tends to become too severe. Now, in the Han dynasty, Emperor Wen ruled by an easy-going administration without causing inefficiency, and Emperor Shüan ruled by strict control without over-severity. The candidates were asked to explain the secrets of the happy medium. The politicians objected to this subject for the examination papers, and Su Tungpo was brought to task in repeated letters to the Empress asking for his trial. The charge was disrespect to Emperors Jentsung and Shentsung.

As usual when the Empress put a protest on the shelf, the officials followed up with successive memorials. From the middle of December 1086, to January 11, 1087, four or five impeachments of Su Tungpo were delivered. On January 12 the Empress ordered the officials to stop. On January 13 the officials received the edict at the premier's office. Defying the edict, the same officials sent up another memorial the following day. Meanwhile, Su Tungpo had not bothered to reply, but had submitted four letters of resignation begging to be sent away from the capital. By about the sixteenth it was clear that the Empress was going to stand up for Su Tungpo, because she had said to the courtiers that what Su Tungpo had meant was the laxity or severity of the governmental personnel, and that he had not meant disrespect to the emperors themselves. There was even talk of the punishment of the officials who impeached Su Tungpo.

It was then that Su Tungpo decided not to beg for release but to fight the case. He sent a letter of two thousand words to the Empress on January 17, outlining his position and condemning petty politics. He was fighting for the principle to disagree. He pointed out in the letter that it was not to the interest of the State that officials should all express the same opinions or should avoid expressions of opinion for fear of giving offence to others. The ministers and the ruler should help one another with ideas, for if the ministers said yes to everything that the ruler approved, they would be the kind of yes-men that Confucius condemned as capable of ruining a country. Then he outlined his disagreement with Szema Kuang on the military draft. They had disagreed, yet had respected each other's opinion. But now Szema Kuang had died, and the herd, presuming that the government was going on with his policies, wanted only to agree with the ruler. As a matter of fact, it was his opinion that Szema Kuang had not wanted people always to agree with him, nor did he think the Empress wanted only servile unanimity of opinion. Another point of disagreement was his proposal that out of the thirty million dollars collected from the surtax on draft exemption, of which half still remained after defraying the expenses for the wars in the north-west, the government should buy land in the suburbs of cities upon which to settle the retired soldiers and thus reduce by half the number of drafted men. "This money comes from the people," he wrote: "it should be returned to the people." Over such points he had steadily fought for his opinion and had offended many people.

In a letter to his friend Yang Kwei, written around the twentieth, Su Tungpo again condemned those that followed the herd and was justifiably proud of his own independent thinking.

"I have sent several letters to the Empress asking for a post outside the capital, but my request has not yet been granted. In the last few days I have shut myself up waiting for the imperial order, and still hope that I may have my wish. You must have heard of all this trouble. The fact is, these censors don't like me. The gentlemen in other days all followed Wang Anshih, and today these gentlemen all followed Szema Kuang. The persons they follow may vary, but in the fact of following, the herd remains the same. I am an old intimate friend of Szema Kuang and our friendship never altered, although I never completely agreed with him. That was the beginning of all this trouble. But I have long regarded power as of no importance, and these things don't matter."

Finally, on the twenty-third, Su Tungpo was ordered to resume his post, and on the twenty-seventh it was decided that the officials who had requested his trial should be pardoned.

Su Tungpo was trapped. The Empress had stood for him; his opponents had clearly failed in their objective and lost face. There was nothing for him to do but to resume his office. His idea of showing gratitude to the Empress was a firm resolve from now on to be even more frank and straightforward, and to tell her things about the government that others would not dare to tell. Today there exist in Su Tungpo's works a great many state papers and letters to the throne that he wrote during the following two years. These letters to the throne are clearly dated, and give us some idea of what he was fighting for.

The first thing he fought for was "to keep open the channels of speech". In modern days he would be fighting for free speech, or a strong, healthy public opinion. This was the theme he returned to again and again. He pointed out that in a good government an emperor always took care to make himself accessible to everybody. For instance, in the reign of the Emperor Taitsung of the Tang dynasty, probably the best emperor in China's four thousand years, he allowed anybody, even people without rank, to come up to the palace and speak to him. The palace guards were forbidden to stop people at the palace gate if they requested an interview with the Emperor. Su reminded the Empress that it was the practice at the beginning of the dynasty to grant interviews even to low-ranking officials and scholars without rank. Now the number of those people who could have an interview with her was limited to a bare dozen. How could these dozen people know all that was happening in the country? If it should happen that these few people consisted of incompetent men who were afraid to tell her of the true conditions, Her Imperial Majesty might be led to think that nothing was ever wrong with her people. Would that not be an unhealthy state of affairs? It is true that the other officials were per-mitted to send memorandums, but once these papers reached the sacred precincts of the palace, they were as good as lost. Without personal interviews, how was the Empress to get a clear view of the subjects discussed? Besides, there were many things that could not be put down in writing. Affairs are sometimes too complicated to be clarified even by a personal discussion. Much less could a letter serve such a purpose! In another letter he said that when horses suffer, they cannot talk, and "when people suffer and cannot make their voice heard by the ruler, they are no more than horses".

But free speech was useless unless the scholars themselves had acquired the spirit of independent thinking and courageous criticism. On this score alone he extolled Ouyang Shiu and deprecated Wang Anshih, for Ouyang encouraged free criticism, and Wang suppressed it. Su Tungpo was deeply concerned with the deadening atmosphere of the time when scholars had forgotten to think for themselves. In his letter to one of his disciples, Chang Lei, written in this period, he said: "Literature has never sunk so low as it has today. The origin of this may be traced back to Wang Anshih. Wang himself was not a bad writer; his fault lay in the fact that he wanted others to think like him. Even Confucius could not make all persons alike. He could not change the individual character of his own disciples, like the quiet, kind Yen

Yuan, or the pugnacious Tselu. But Wang attempted to make the whole world agree with him. A rich soil grows all kinds and varieties of plants. But on a bad piece of land you see not the same richness and variety of growth but only a wearisomely uniform stretch of rushes and weeds. This is the kind of uniformity desired by Wang."

In August 1086, Su Tungpo succeeded in putting a complete stop to the farmers' loans. Earlier that year, in April, an edict had been issued for a half-hearted reform in the administration of these loans. The price stabilisation granaries had been restored, but the farmers' loans, while restricted to the amount of half of the value of the stocks of these granaries, were still to be issued to the people. The court did this with good intentions. It forbade the officials to go to a village, as had been done, call a meeting, and allocate the loans to the villagers, and it forbade the clerks to visit the people's homes from house to house and force their subscription. To Su Tungpo, however, this half-hearted measure was not enough, and could lend itself to abuse as had been proved before. On August 4 he wrote to the Empress, first asking for putting a complete stop to the farmers' loans and second asking for the forgiveness to the very poor of all debts, including principal and interest. He again compared the act of April to that of a chicken thief who said that he was going to reform and would confine his stealing to one chicken a month, an analogy taken from Mencius. "These loans have been in force for about twenty years. During this period the people have become steadily poorer, lawsuits have multiplied, and banditry has increased. . . . The officials established amusement places and gambling-houses at the time of giving out these loans. Very often the farmers returned to the city empty-handed. One can see this from the fact that at the time of giving out the loans, the receipts of the wine monopoly always increased. I have personally witnessed these things with tears in my eyes. In the last twenty years numberless people have sold their houses and farms, sent away their wives and daughters to work as servants, jumped into the river, or hanged themselves because of inability to repay the loans." Why should an emperor, Su Tungpo asked, demean himself to the point of lending money to the people for interest? He suggested that an order be issued for the people who owed debts to the government to pay them back in ten semi-annual instalments, and made bold to express the hope that, considering the fact that the debtors had already paid a lot of interest alone on these loans, the Empress might be kind enough to forgive at one stroke all debts owed by the poorer people below the fourth class. The next month, the farmers' loans were completely stopped. But the proposal for the forgiveness of debts was not accepted until six years later, after further tireless efforts by Su Tungpo.

Alone, he went ahead in a one-man crusade against corruption and incompetence in the government. He wanted to reform the civil service from the bottom. The imperial examinations were the basis of the selection of government personnel, but the system had become lax. He was, on three or four occasions, made chief examiner and, while acting in this capacity, did his best to select talent by his personal attention, sometimes saving a candidate's paper already rejected by the other judges. Once, when the candidates were taking their examinations under routine supervision and inspection by imperial guards, the insolence of the guards shocked Su Tungpo. The sergeants shouted at the candidates as if herding a company of raw privates. Some scholars were caught cribbing and were thrown out of the hall with much fuss and noise. There was a great commotion, and the sergeants then restored order as if they had been quelling a riot. The haughty behaviour of the sergeants was an insult to the scholars. Su Tungpo immediately sent two letters to the Empress and had the two sergeants dismissed.

What troubled the government at this time, as at all times in China's history, might be called over-population of mandarins. There were too many scholars and too few posts to give to everybody, a perennial disease in China, where it is hardly thinkable that a good scholar should not try to join the governing class. Unless this idea is changed today, universal education alone can ruin the country. How are we going to, provide posts for 450,0000,000 educated men? If the civil service system had been strictly adhered to and selection had been based upon talent, the number of successful candidates could have been limited and the quality of men selected improved. But nepotism flourished, even in the times of Su Tungpo. There were many candidates from the provinces who, upon the recommendation of their friends and relatives, were given posts without submitting to the imperial examinations at the capital. For every examination which selected three or four hundred talented scholars, there were eight or nine hundred people who were exempt. The ministry of education could recommend as many as two or three hundred exempted candidates, and there were others recommended by the military officers and relatives of the imperial household. At the spring sacrifice to Heaven, numbers of scholars were exempted by "special grace" of the Emperor. The result was, as Su said, that "every time a vacancy is available, there are six or seven people waiting and fighting shamelessly for it. Many of these are men past their prime of manhood and are merely seeking for employment. It is certain that when they are given posts in the country, they will become a menace to the people." He went on: "The people who receive this special favour are now spread all over the country. Most of them are old and without any ambition except to make money quick, and feather their own nests. Eighty to ninety per cent of these people are corrupt and incompetent. Of the thousands of officials who have received this special favour, do we ever see one who is energetic or has established a good record for himself? On the other hand, those who prey upon the people are numberless. Everywhere they go, the people are victimised. How this can be referred to as a 'special grace', I do not understand." Su suggested cutting out these special exemptions and putting a strict limitation upon the sons and relatives of high officials and upon persons recommended by the imperial household.

Su Tungpo considered it his duty to inform the Empress of the sloth and incompetence and downright deceit of government officials in cases which had been carefully concealed from the court. And here began a number of letters which he sent confidentially to the Empress. In many cases he added one or several postscripts, begging her to keep the memorandum to herself for his own protection and not have it passed to the premier's office.

There was, for example, the case of a raid by the north-western tribes, during which probably ten thousand Chinese peasants were slaughtered. The military commander had tried to conceal this from the court. Even when the news seeped through to the capital and a commissioner had been sent out to investigate, the latter, following the ancient practice of "officials protecting officials", reported that only "a dozen people" had been killed. The commissioner, thus minimising the disaster, had asked that the commander first be pardoned and the case slowly investigated. Two years had elapsed, and nothing was done about it. The villagers to whom compensation was due were thus deprived of their benefit. In his private letter to the Empress, Su Tungpo pointed out that such neglect of the people was not calculated to win their good will towards the government.

The practice of "officials protecting officials" naturally resulted in "officials versus the people". Again, there was the case of Tung Cheng, a commander in Kwangtung who massacred several thousand citizens of a recaptured city in his futile effort to fight certain bandits. But the report to the government by fellow officials made out that he was in fact a hero, defending the city successfully against the bandits. There was the case, too, of Wen Kao, who killed nineteen civilians and escaped with a small demerit. A certain minor army officer, in his desire to claim credit for killing bandits, went into a family's home and murdered five or six women in broad daylight. With their severed heads, he reported that he had beheaded a number of bandits. The case was too outrageous to be covered up, and when the court ordered an investigation, the officer's defence was that at the time of the action he could not tell whether the victims were men or women. Such were the cases of misrule which existed, and about which Su Tungpo found it impossible to keep silent.

The most important case, which stirred up a hornet's nest, was that of Chou Chung. In this case Su Tungpo lost all restraint. Temporarily out of power and occupying posts in the outlying provinces, the remnants of Wang Anshih's party were fighting for a come-back. The leaders, Huiching, Leeding, Tsai Chueh, etc., had been ousted, but many of their friends were still holding posts in the capital. In order to test the attitude of the court, they asked an obscure and unknown college teacher, Chou Chung, to submit a memorandum recommending that Wang Anshih's spirit tablet be placed in the imperial ancestral temple below that of Emperor Shentsung, and that it receive sacrifices with those offered the Emperor. If the Empress had granted this, it would have been a clear signal to the plotters to come out and work in the open. Sensing their meaning, Su Tungpo lashed out at these fortune-hunting opportunists. He named sixteen men of this group and stigmatised them as "lice", "bugs", "rogues and scoundrels", and "enemies of society". For once he did not mince words about Wang Anshih, whom he all but called a great humbug and charlatan. He told the Empress that if Fu Pi, Han Chi, or Szema Kuang were living, "these rats" would not dare to show their faces. He warned that if the schemers were not stopped now, "the future would see men like Huiching and Tsai Chueh return to power and the farmers' loans and trade bureaus restored." From his own observation he was sure this was going to happen. In fact, his decision to leave the court was already made. He said that upright men, like unicorns and phœnixes, were difficult to keep, but petty politicians were like "market flies which swarm wherever there is a refuse-heap". The logic is clear: If a man doesn't like to associate with flies, he should keep away from the garbage himself.

In the course of two years, Su Tungpo, by his strong individualism and outspoken, fearless criticism, had succeeded in offending a great number of people, including the Hopei and Honan cliques. And Tungpo had made himself a menace and a nuisance to Wang Anshih's party men! Unless Su Tungpo was removed, these men could not come back to power.

It is interesting to read some of the impeachments. Probably the most interesting case was an imperial edict drafted by Su Tungpo for an appointment of Lu Tafang, an opponent of Wang Anshih, to a high office. Praising this official's courageous stand, the edict said that during Wang's administration, "the people were weary and hard pressed". This phrase was a classical one that anybody might use. But it was taken from a satirical verse in the *Book of Poetry* written in the ninth century B.C. against a notorious emperor. The censors' eyes brightened. They said Su was slandering Emperor Shentsung by comparing him to Emperor Li of the Chou dynasty. The censors' hearts were distressed and their "legs shook" with anger to hear their beloved deceased emperor so defamed.

There was another interesting case concerning one of Su Tungpo's poems, written years before when Su Tungpo was returning from the Southern Capital, happy with the news that he had been granted permission to settle at Changchow. While passing through Yangchow, he had scribbled three poems on the wall of a temple. Read as a whole, the theme of these poems was unmistakable: after searching in vain for a home, he was glad now to be permitted to retire and enjoy his old age on a farm. In the third poem he wrote:

> "Now I am free of all cares in this life,
> And this year the farmers are promised good crops.
> Coming down the hill, I hear the good news;
> Even the flowers and birds wear a face of joy."

It happened, however, that this poem was written on May 1, and the Emperor Shentsung had died on March 5, fifty-six days before. Here was this poet singing about his joy during the period of imperial mourning! What was he joyful about, and what did he mean by the "good news"? Evidently it could not mean anything except the news of the Emperor's death. What a coward—what an ungrateful heart! This was probably the most serious impeachment of Su Tungpo in this period and it was a very grave charge. I am sure the "good news", in the light of the context, was no other than that of promising harvests. But Tseyu invented, I think, a better defence of his brother. During the testimony in 1091, Tseyu explained that Su Tungpo was at the Southern Capital in March, where of course he had already heard the news of the Emperor's death, and certainly he could not have first heard it fifty-six days later at Yangchow. He told the Empress that the "good news" referred to the fact that, coming down from the hill, Su Tungpo had heard the farmers speak with joy about the ascension to the throne of the bright young boy emperor. It made a better direct appeal. Having given his own testimony, Tseyu withdrew from the imperial presence and let the other officials fight it out.

Su Tungpo had the impression that the Empress had received a good many more impeachments against him than he knew. She had consistently put these impeachments on the shelf. He had demanded the publication of all memorials against him so as to give him an opportunity to clear himself, but the Empress never complied with his request. He knew that his enemies were determined to overthrow him. Even his drafting of the imperial edict decreeing the punishment of the notorious double-crosser Huiching was snatched at by his enemies as containing defamation of the preceding Emperor. He was rather tired of constantly brushing off the market flies. Not only Su himself but his friends Chin Kuan, Huang Tingchien, Wang Kung and Sun Chueh were constantly made targets of criticism, either in formal protests or by the more subtle method of a smear campaign. The method of working by underhand grape-vine rumours, leaving a man no chance to defend himself, is by no means a modern invention; only in modern days has it been elevated into a part of Communist revolutionary tactics. Su Tungpo felt as if he were walking upon a snake-infested slime pit. He decided to get out.

He had tried to resign during the first attack, in December 1086, and in the following year kept begging for release from his post. Two of these letters contain autobiographical material outlining his long official career and the many troubles he had got into through his headstrong individualism. In the letter dated October 17, 1088, he said: "When a ruler is not careful, he loses his minister, and when a minister is not careful, he loses his life. In serving a ruler, one should serve the country first, but in order to be able to serve the country, one should first preserve his own life." In two years' time he had "four times received smears" from his enemies, and people recommended by him were also under attack by groundless slanders. He reminded the Empress that in the previous regime he already had been impeached by Leeding. He had written satirical poetry in the hope that the Emperor might hear of the people's sufferings and change his policy. The censors had called his honest criticism "slander", and there was some "semblance of truth" in the accusation. Now there was not even a semblance, such as in the criticism of his use of the phrase, "the people were weary and hard pressed." "This only shows that these people are even more determined than Leeding to overthrow me by all methods at their command. . . . As the ancient saying has it: 'It is difficult to be a king, but it is not easy to be a minister, either.' If I were to follow the herd and try to please everybody, I would be acting against my conscience and be disloyal to Your Majesty. But if I should try to maintain my integrity and continue to speak the truth, I would be making more and more enemies and eventually be punished by death or dismissal. I hope Your Majesty will appreciate my difficult position and protect me by sending me to a less enviable post." In this letter he wrote four postscripts, marked P.S., P.P.S., P.P.P.S., and P.P.P.P.S. In the last of them he said that if she considered that the things he said were not true, she could turn this letter over to the premier's office and have a public investigation. But if she believed that he was telling the truth, would she please keep this letter to herself? He would send another formal letter of resignation, asking for a post in the country, which could be published.

The best letter expressing his determination to get out was written later on May 19, 1091, when after his term of office at Hangchow he was again asked to resume his old post. This was Su Tungpo's longest autobiographical letter, outlining all the past mishaps that he had run into, including the episode of his arrest and trial. The party men were even "more jealous" of him than of his brother. After outlining his long political career, he said: "Thus you see a long record of how, by always taking a fearless stand, I have succeeded in making enemies all around me." His letter against Chou Chung had greatly angered his enemies and had increased their hatred. They bristled with attacks. The ancient proverb says: "Enough humming mosquitoes put together can produce a thunder, and a load of enough feathers can sink a boat."

He went on:

"How can I in my remaining years submit myself to be their target? I know I have done nothing wrong, but nowadays right and wrong have nothing to do with anything. It is natural that, after a long life of trials and tribulations, I should want to enjoy a life of peace in my remaining years. My request for resignation is entirely sincere. . . . If I were to change my nature, and hold on to a coveted post by swimming with the tide, of what real use could I be to Your Majesty? But if I try to keep my own soul and continue as I have been doing, I shall incur the hostility of the petty politicians, and sooner or later must come to the end of my career. . . . Therefore, after careful consideration, I have decided to quit. It is not that I am not grateful to your kindness, but that in my old age I am ashamed to fight and wrangle with these little wretches, and be laughed at by the high-minded recluse scholars. . . . Please give me a post in the province, and do not publish this letter, for my own protection. You may give me a troublesome district on the border if you wish . . . but I am strongly determined not to occupy an important post by your side, so as not to increase the jealousy of the party men and be subjected to further under-handed attacks."

Following his repeated entreaties the request was granted, on March 11, 1089. He was appointed military governor of the province of West Chekiang and commander of the military district of Hangchow, with a very high official rank. The post of governor of West Chekiang gave him jurisdiction over six districts, which included the lake district of modern Kiangsu. He was sent away with imperial gifts of tea and silver boxes and another white horse with gold-plated saddle and a gold belt for his official gown. This was one horse too many for Su, and he gave it away to his poor disciple Li Chih to sell for money.

On his departure, the old minister Wen Yenpo, then eighty-three years old and still active, came to send him off and cautioned him against writing poems again. Su Tungpo was already mounted on his horse. "If I do," he said with a laugh, "I know there will be plenty of people ready to write commentaries on them!"

Chapter Twenty-two

ENGINEERING AND FAMINE RELIEF

IT really seems that a man can do much more for his country when he is serving on the land than at the capital. At the age of fifty-two, Su Tungpo arrived in July 1089 in Hangchow to be the governor of West Chekiang province and commander of the military district. His brother had been promoted from vice-minister of the interior to minister of the civil service, with the rank of a *hanlin* scholar; that winter Tseyu was sent as the emperor's emissary to the Kitan tribes in Mongolia on a trip that lasted four months.

Su Tungpo plunged into his work. For a year and a half, Chin Kuan's brother, who came to stay with them, never saw Su open a book. Instead he took advantage of the favour of the Empress to ask for special grants of money to carry through important measures of reform. In the short space of one and a half years he put through measures of public health and sanitation for the city, including a clean water system and a hospital, dredged the salt canals, reconstructed West Lake, successfully stabilised the price of grain, and single-handedly and passionately worked for famine relief against the colossal indifference of officials at the court and in the neighbouring provinces.

The office of the governor was in the centre of Hangchow. But Su Tungpo preferred to execute his official duties in more poetic surroundings. Often he worked in a picturesque house with thirteen rooms in the Stone Buddha Court below the Kehling Hill. He would go through the official documents either in the Cold Emerald Hall or the Rain-Lent-Excitement Hall, which we remember was named from his celebrated verse on West Lake, containing the line:

"Misty mountains lend excitement to the rain."

There, surrounded by tall bamboos and looking out on a clear stream, he performed his duties.

Sometimes, however, he preferred to execute business still farther away in the high mountains ten or fifteen miles from the city. Sending his official retinue with flags and umbrellas to go on foot by the Chientang Gate, he himself, accompanied by one or two old body-guards, would take a boat from the Yungchin Gate and cross the lake westwards, stopping for lunch at Pu-an Temple. Taking a few secretaries with him, he would go and sit at the Cold Spring Pavilion. There amidst chatter and laughter he would go through the business of the day, writing his official decisions "as fast as the wind". After business was over, he would have a good drink with his colleagues, and then towards sunset come home on horseback, the people of the city lining the streets to look at this strange famous scholar.

On hot summer days he would retreat to Shiangfu Temple and take a nap in the room of his friend Abbot Weishien. Throwing down his hat and his official dignity, he would take off his gown and stretch himself on the couch and have his legs massaged by attendants. The servants then saw that he had tied his hair on top of his head with the cheapest kind of packing string.

A a judge, Su Tungpo did many strange things.

There was a merchant who was on trial for debt. The accused was a young man, and Su Tungpo asked him to explain his predicament.

"My family runs a fan shop," said the defendant. "Last year my father died, leaving me some debts. It has rained so much this spring that people do not want to buy fans. It is not that I do not want to pay the debts."

Su Tungpo paused. His eyes brightened with a good idea. He looked at the brush and ink on the table and felt fit for good exercise that morning.

"Bring me a pile of your fans and I will sell them for you," he said to the man.

The man went home and soon brought back twenty round silk fans. Using the judge's brush on the table, Su began to write running scripts, and painted bare winter trees, bamboos, and rocks on these fans. In an hour or so he had finished painting all twenty of them. Giving these to the man, he said: "Go out and pay your debts."

Surprised by his luck and thanking the governor profusely, the man hugged his fans and hustled out of the court. Reports were already going around that the governor was painting fans for sale. The moment the man stepped outside the gate, he was surrounded with people who offered to pay a thousand cash for a fan, and in a few minutes all the fans were sold, to the regret of the late-comers.

Once a scholar from the country, who was going to the capital for the imperial examinations, was arrested and brought to him on suspicion of fraud. The scholar had brought along two large packages, marked as addressed to Vice-Minister Su (Tseyu) at Bamboo Pole Alley in the capital, and as sent by Su Tungpo himself. Clearly this was fraudulent.

"What is in those packages?" asked Su Tungpo.

"I am sincerely sorry," replied the scholar. "The people of my home town have presented me with two hundred pieces of silk as a contribution towards my travel expenses. I know that these goods will be taxed all the way by the custom officers, and by the time I arrive at the capital, probably I shall have only half of them left. I thought that there were no better-known and more generous scholars than you two Su brothers, and I decided to make use of your names. In case I was caught you would understand and let me off easily. I crave your pardon —I will not do it again."

Su Tungpo smiled and asked the clerk to tear off the old label and write a new one bearing the same address and sender's name. In addition, he wrote a note to Tseyu and, handing it to the trembling scholar, he said: "Uncle, this time you are safe, even if you are brought up before the Emperor himself. When you pass the examinations next year, don't forget me."

The poor old scholar was overwhelmed and thanked him heartily. He passed the examinations successfully, and when he returned, he wrote a letter expressing his profound gratitude to the poet. Su Tungpo was so delighted with this episode that he entertained him at his house for several days.

Su also did something for the support of the college students. Such acts endeared Su Tungpo to the populace. There were many things wrong with the city of Hangchow. The government buildings were very old. The soldiers were living in leaky barracks. The arms depot was in a dilapidated condition. The roofs of the gate towers revealed glimpses of the sky. These were all buildings over a hundred years old, built by the great kings of the family of Chien, who had maintained peace and governed the country justly in the first half of the tenth century, when all the rest of China was in turmoil. They were popular kings and they had earned the undying gratitude of the people of the south-east because, when the founder of the present dynasty had conquered all parts of China except the south-east, the king had voluntarily surrendered his power to the emperor for peace and unity and thus had saved the people much unnecessary bloodshed. The preceding governors had built new residences for themselves, such as the Chungho Hall and the Yumei Hall, and left the old buildings alone. In Su Tungpo's time two men were killed when a building collapsed, and a family of four persons was buried when another tower fell in.. Still making use of his special connections with the Empress, Su Tungpo asked for a grant of $40,000 to repair the official buildings, the city gates, the towers, and the granaries, twenty-seven in all.

Hangchow was a city with half a million population and without a single public hospital. Situated at the mouth of the Chientang River, where travellers by sea and land converged, it was subject to frequent epidemics. There were certain medical recipes that were of proved value. While he was serving at Michow, Su Tungpo had ordered the more useful prescriptions copied out by hand in large characters and posted as magistrate's bulletins in the squares of the town to make them better known to the common people. There was one particular recipe in which he greatly believed and which, according to him, cost only a penny a dose. The prescriptions are usually made up of a large number of herbs, some for lowering temperature, some for stopping perspiration, others for increase of appetite, or for purgative or tonic effects. It is the belief of Chinese doctors that, when one organ of the body is sick, the whole body is sick. The prescriptions are therefore directed toward the strengthening of the body as a whole rather than toward the cure of any particular organ. One prescription in particular, the "Divine Powder", contains twenty herbs, including thorny limebrush, sickle-leaved hare's ear, water plantain, liquorice, wild cardamon, "pig's head" (*carpesium abrotanoides*), autumn root, magnolia officinalis, and acorus calamus. It includes also *mahuang*, or *ephedra sinica*, which has been proved to be a powerful stimulant to the production of gastric juice.

Dissatisfied with such piecemeal unorganised aid to sufferers, Su Tungpo set apart two thousand dollars from government funds and contributed, himself, fifty ounces of gold (about a thousand U.S. dollars) to found a public hospital at Chungan Bridge in the heart of the city. So far as I know, this Anlofang was the first public hospital in China. In three years' time it took care of a thousand patients, and the priest in charge of the hospital was rewarded with a purple gown and a gift of money from the government. Later the hospital was moved to the lake shore, was renamed Antsifang, and continued to function after Su Tungpo's days.

But Su Tungpo was most troubled about the water supply for the residents of Hangchow and the dirt along the canals which ran through the city. In the time of the Chien kings, a sea wall had been built along the shore to prevent the tide from coming into the canal and polluting the city water with salt. This sea wall had fallen into disrepair. There were two canals running north and south through the city directly connected with the Chientang Bay at Zakou. As the water of the bay, mixed with the river water, was full of silt, the canal beds required dredging every three to five years. There was no modern machinery, and the mud taken from the bed of the canal was dumped on the banks in front of the people's homes. These canals were about four or five miles long and the dredging was always a costly operation, besides being a great nuisance to the residents. What was even worse, the condition of the traffic was such that it took a boat several days to get out of the city. Boats were pulled by men and oxen, and the canal scene was usually one of indescribable confusion.

Su Tungpo consulted experts, made a survey of the levels of the canals, and worked out a plan to prevent the silting and thus clean up the whole canal region. This was the first of his engineering works in

Hangchow, started in October, three months after his arrival, and finished in April of the following year.

The problem was that these canals needed the sea water to carry the traffic, while the water itself brought in the silt. After careful study Su Tungpo established the fact that it was important to keep the Salt Canal, which ran through the busy sections of the city, free of muddy water, while ways could be devised for the sea water to come in through the other canal, Maoshan, which ran through the less populated district on the eastern suburb. By building locks on the Chientang River in the south, he could shut off the flow during high tide and release it again at low tide. The two canals were connected in the north of the city, and by the time the bay water had come through the canal in the suburb, it would have travelled three or four miles and the sediment already would have had a chance to settle. The Salt Canal, which had to be kept clear, was four feet below the level of the other, so that while the water from the suburban canal would partly supply the canal in the city, it would give it water almost clear of silt. In order to maintain the proper water level in the city canal, he also constructed a canal outside the Yuhang Gate in the north of the city to join it up with the lake. Thus a continual supply of water was assured, and the cost and nuisance of dredging the Salt Canal inside the city was avoided.

The system worked, and he succeeded in giving the canals a depth of eight feet, which, according to the elders of the town, had never been achieved before.

Equally as important as the canal traffic itself was the problem of water supply. Various attempts had been made to guide the fresh water of West Lake, which came from the mountain springs, to the city. Distributed in various sections of the city were six reservoirs, but the fresh-water mains had frequently broken down. Eighteen years earlier, when Su was deputy magistrate at this place, he had assisted in the repair of the mains, but now West Lake had become shallow through the ever-spreading growth of a kind of water plant whose abundant roots, tangled in the mud, continually raised the lake bed. The mains had broken down and the city people were drinking slightly salty water, or had to buy water from the lake, costing a penny a gallon. Su Tungpo consulted the surviving monk, now over seventy years old, who had supervised the repair of the mains before. The mains, made of sections of large bamboo pipes, could not last long. Su Tungpo had the entire system replaced with strong clay pipes, protected on the top and bottom by flag-stones. It was an expensive project, requiring the building of new sections sometimes three hundred yards long, leading from one reservoir to another. Furthermore, he guided the lake water to two new reservoirs in the northern suburb

to furnish drinking water for the army barracks. As military governor
he put a thousand soldiers to work, and the job was done well and
efficiently. It was said that by the time he had finished these reservoirs,
almost every section of the town could have fresh water from the lake.

From his work on the six small reservoirs for the water supply to
the city, Su Tungpo naturally proceeded to tackle the problem of the
main reservoir, which was West Lake. In popular imagination, Su
Tungpo still is connected with the development of West Lake into
what it has become today. West Lake gives Hangchow the name of
"Paradise on Earth", and it is as nearly perfect as anything ever
designed by man. While man developed it and built round it, man
knew where to stop and not intrude upon nature. It is nature
trimmed, but never nature disfigured. No elaborate structures pro-
claim man's ingenuity. A magic island, throwing images of weeping
willows into the mirror of the lake surface, seems to belong there by
nature and to have grown out of the water. The arched bridges of
the long enbankments fit in with the clouded peaks above and the
fishermen's boats below. The greenish-yellow twigs of willows sweep
the half-hidden low stone embankments, while centuries-old pagodas
breaking the skyline remind one of the monks and poets of the past.
Su Tungpo said West Lake was to Hangchow as the eyes to a beauty's
face, and I have often wondered what West Lake would be like if it
were a bare stretch of water—an eye without the graceful long eyebrows of Su's embankment or the magic island like the light in an iris
to give it point and emphasis. For centuries, Chinese tourists have
flocked to Hangchow in spring, and honeymooners spend their days
boating on the lakes or fishing or walking on the willow-covered
promenades around the lake bank. The ten famous views of Hangchow include one on the east bank, called "Listening to the Oriole
among Willow Waves". Another place situated on an islet in the
middle of the lake, started by Su Tungpo, is called "Three Pools
Reflecting the Same Moon". Truly, there is not a nook around the
lake which does not thrill the tourist anew with a breath-taking surprise, in rain or shine. Two long embankments cut across the surface
of the lake, known as the Po Embankment and the Su Embankment,
built by its two famous poets, Po Chuyi of the Tang dynasty, and Su
Tungpo of the Sung. The Po Embankment runs east and west near
the northern shore, while the Su Embankment, one and two-thirds
miles in length, runs north and south near the west shore. Each embankment marks an inner lake on the shore side, while the arched
bridges on the embankment permit the boats to pass through from
the inner lakes to the main lake. These embankments, which were fifty
feet wide in Su Tungpo's time and planted with willows and sur-

rounded by lotus flowers, became grand promenades for the pleasure-seekers of Hangchow.

The prosperity of Hangchow has always been connected with its water supply. The growth of Hangchow as a city dated from the Tang dynasty, when a minister opened up the lake and gave fresh water to the residents of the city. Previous to that, it had been only a small town. Before Su Tungpo began work on West Lake, it was steadily narrowing, covered with rapidly multiplying weeds. Eighteen years earlier these weeds had covered twenty or thirty per cent of the lake surface. On his return, he was surprised and saddened to see that they had rapidly spread to cover half of the lake. In Po Chuyi's time the water supply of the lake irrigated large areas of rice-fields; the falling of an inch of the water level was enough to irrigate 250 acres, and every twenty-four hours the lake could supply water for 800 acres. All the work of Po Chuyi of the eighth century was now destroyed.

No sooner had Su Tungpo completed the work on the canal system of Hangchow and the six small reservoirs in the city than he began work on West Lake itself. From the engineering point of view it was a simple job, involving merely the clearing out of the weeds. It was an improvement that could easily be done, only none of his predecessors had thought of doing it. Before the work on the small reservoirs was completed, Su Tungpo sent a letter to the Empress, in April 1090, outlining the reasons for his plan to open up and dredge West Lake. In May he sent another letter, addressed to the premier's office, the executive board, and the imperial secretariat. If nothing was done about it, he said, in twenty more years the whole lake would be covered up, and the people of Hangchow would be deprived of their fresh-water supply. Su pointed out five important reasons why this must not be allowed. Curiously, the first reason he advanced was a Buddhist one, namely, that the fish would suffer. The other reasons were usefulness in providing fresh-water supply, in irrigating rice-fields, in supplying water for the canals, and lastly, in supplying good water for making wine, which had something to do with the government revenue. He proceeded to clear off the weed-covered area of twenty-five thousand square *chang* (a *chang* is ten Chinese feet), or eleven Chinese square *li*, or approximately one square mile. For this work he needed 200,000 man-days, on the supposition that one man-day would clear about one square *chang*. Each worker would be paid 55 cash per day (100 cash equals one dime) plus three-tenths of a bushel of rice. The whole project required $34,000, of which he had already one half, and he asked the Empress to give another $17,000.

The request was granted, and Su Tungpo started work with thousands of workers and boatmen. In four months' time he had the work completed. The problem arose as to how to dispose of the mountains of weeds and mud that had been thrown up from the dredged area. Su struck upon the idea of making use of them to build the long embankment. The lake shore had been closely built up, and was covered with rich men's villas. People who wanted to cross over from the south to the north lake shore on foot had to follow the winding bank of about two miles. The straight embankment consider-ably shortened the distance, besides creating a beautiful promenade. It was provided with six arched bridges and nine pavilions. In Su Tungpo's own lifetime one of the pavilions served as a "living temple" to him (*shengtse*) in which the people placed a portrait of the poet in order to worship him and commemorate his great work. When the double-crosser Huiching came into power again, he succeeded in getting an order for the memorial to be destroyed.

There was also the problem of how to keep the lake for ever free of the growing weeds. Su Tungpo conceived the idea of farming out sections of the lake surface along the shore to farmers to grow water caltrop, a kind of water chestnut. The farmers would see to it that their areas were periodically cleared of weeds. He petitioned the premier's office to ensure that this revenue would be strictly set aside and devoted to the upkeep of the embankment and of the lake itself.

Consciously or unconsciously, Su Tungpo had beautified West Lake, besides increasing its practical advantages. But even this work was later to come under severe attack by his political enemies as "wasting government money solely for serving the pleasure of tourists".

Su tried other, more ambitious projects—the development of the canal systems of Kiangsu; a tow-barge project outside the city of Soochow—and later he did for the West Lake of Fouyang what he did for the West Lake of Hangchow. Some of these projects failed of realisation, but the detailed plans with maps bore witness to his engineering imagination.

We must mention a great engineering project which he had no chance to complete because of his recall to the capital again. The detailed plan is still preserved. There was an island at the entrance of the Chientang River to the Hangchow Bay which claimed a heavy toll of shipwrecks and drowned passengers every year. The swift, broad current of the Chientang ran into the incoming current of sea-water at the bay and, blocked by this island, turned into a dangerous whirling cross-tide. This "Floating Island" took its name from the fact that around it bars appeared and disappeared in a matter of weeks, and navigators had no way of knowing the proper channel for sailing. Some of these sand bars were one or two miles long; it was said they sometimes disappeared completely overnight. It was the most feared section of the traveller's voyage to Hangchow. People who came along the eastern coast of Chekiang preferred to cross the bay at Lungshan, but those who came down the Chientang from the south-west districts had to take the risks. Drowning men and children were seen crying for help, and were swallowed up by the current before anybody could do anything about it. The Hangchow river traffic, however, was important. The people in the poor south-western districts depended upon rice grown in the lake district north of Hangchow, while the people of Hangchow themselves depended on the south-west for fuel. Salt also was produced in the Hangchow Bay and transported to the south-western region. A heavy traffic went on, in spite of the danger, and the cost of transportation was greatly increased because the agencies had to give their employees large gifts in compensation for the risks. The invisible loss to the country amounted to "millions of dollars".

This problem Su Tungpo tried to solve, with the aid of someone who was familiar with the whole valley of Chientang. The new plan was designed to take the boat traffic to Hangchow by a route passing above the dangerous point. Su Tungpo had a project worked out which would cost $150,000, employ 3,000 labourers, and take two years to finish. It involved channelling the Chientang into a new course for eight miles, deep enough for navigation; building a stone embankment two and three-quarter miles long, and tunnelling a hill 615 feet through. Unfortunately, he had to leave Hangchow when the plan was just being completed.

Meanwhile he was overwhelmingly busy with another and more pressing problem, the threat of a coming famine. There had been a failure of crops in the year he arrived. The price of rice had risen from 60 cash a bushel in July to 95 cash in November. Luckily, there were grain reserves in the price stabilisation granaries, and he had succeeded in getting a grant of 200,000 piculs (1 picul equals 10 bushels). By selling 180,000 piculs of government rice, he had been able to stabilise the price and bring it down to 75 cash per bushel in January 1090. The spring of that year was rainy but looked very promising. The farmers borrowed money to improve their land in full expectation of a good harvest in summer. Then in May and June a heavy storm with a steady downpour broke over Hangchow and most of the lake district. Flood broke into the city of Huchow, and there was one foot of water in the people's homes. All the farmers' hopes were destroyed and, as any man with common sense could see, they were threatened with starvation when their grain reserves should run out. Su Tungpo sent out inspectors to investigate the conditions at Soochow and Changchow, and received reports that the whole region had been inundated. Dams had been broken, and some of the rice-fields were buried under water. Farmers were going about in boats to save what they could. The wet rice which they salvaged could still be fried, and the stalks were given to feed the buffaloes. Something had to be done, and done quickly.

Su Tungpo planned far ahead, although it required no great talent. to know what was coming. He had always believed in price stabilisation rather than in relief after famine came, and he worked steadily to get more rice for the government granaries in order to fight off the coming famine. As the rains continued without let-up, he became more and more desperate. In the course of half a year, beginning from July, he sent seven reports to the Empress and to the government, outlining the actual conditions and urging the need for prompt action. The first two papers were called "Reports on Natural Calamity, I and II", and the last five were called "Reports on Famine Relief", but the seven letters formed one passionate and impatient clamour for help. He kept up this clamour until everybody at court was annoyed. His impatience was highly un-Chinese. A number of commissioners were on the spot. They had said not a word. What was Su Tungpo shouting about? What was so surprising about a little more rain than unsual? He was digging his own political grave.

But he believed an ounce of prevention was worth a pound of cure. By building up grain reserves, either locally or by importation from other regions, in anticipation of a grain shortage, and selling it to force prices down, famine could be prevented. Famine relief by doling out food to starving and sick people was always wasteful, futile, and never touched more than the surface of human misery; the thing was to prevent it. Clear-minded men who think ahead of their times are always impatient. He pointed out that in the year 1075 nobody did anything about it until the great famine arrived. Then Emperor Shentsung had to give a million and a quarter piculs of rice in order to set up soup kitchens and distribute food to the poor, and even then half a million people died. Apart from the human misery involved, the government lost a total of $3,200,000 in actual relief cost, in remission of taxes, and in loss of revenue. Compared with that, Su Tungpo pointed out that in the previous year, with one-sixth of the amount of rice, he had been able to stabilise prices and stave off a famine. Now, the second famine promised to be worse than the first, for it was like a patient suffering from relapse of a disease. The people's little reserve of grain was dwindling. Something must be done immediately.

The curious thing was, nobody was concerned except Su Tungpo. He read the court bulletins in a rage. Many local commissioners in Chekiang and neighbouring provinces had reported only the good promise of crops in the spring—but none had reported about the recent rainstorms and the floods. Su asked permission to divert the money for repairs of government buildings to purchase of rice, for famine came first. Six months earlier he had petitioned for about $50,000 to buy rice, of which the Hangchow district was entitled to one third. The government gave the money, but Su Tungpo was deprived of the proper share by a commissioner in the neighbouring district, a man who bore the poetic name of Yeh Wensou, or "Yeh Gentle-Old-Man". Everybody had been interested in a share of the allocation when the money was granted, but nobody would take steps now to report on the true condition. In a confidential postscript to the Empress, Su said: "It is the habit of officials to report only favourable information. They have reported fully on the good weather conditions of March and April, but no government official will do anything until a famine has actually arrived and people are actually dying." He then demanded that the court order a full investigation of all the affected areas. If his fear was ungrounded, and if the other commissioners disagreed with him, they should be compelled to sign a report guaranteeing that in their opinion a famine was not forthcoming and that people were not going to starve next winter. There was one commissioner by the name of Ma Chen. Su Tungpo had written again and again for a conference with him because the work on the project required co-ordination of all districts. But Ma had replied that he was busy with other things, and his tour would keep him away from Hangchow until winter. In a letter to another official in East Chekiang, his good friend Chien Shieh, Su said: "Can't you induce him [Ma] to come by telling him how marvellous the Hangchow bore is to look at, and that he should pay us a visit in August? Put this as your own idea, and don't let him know that it comes from me." In his July report Su Tungpo asked only for a grant of 200,000 piculs of rice. The plan was very simple. As a rich rice-producing district, Hangchow was required to send 1,250,000 to 1,500,000 piculs of rice annually to the capital. Hangchow was still rich and could afford to pay the price of that amount. If it was only permitted to keep part of this rice, Hangchow could send its equivalent in silver and silks. A permit from the court to keep some of the rice due to the imperial government and transfer it to the local granaries was all that was needed.

Meanwhile, on July 21, 22, and 23, another big rainstorm broke out. The rain stopped for a while on the twenty-fourth, but that night it poured again. Su Tungpo could not sleep, and the next morning he wrote the "Report on Natural Calamity II". The flood in the lake district was getting worse. Would the Empress please give his previous report immediate attention? The courier system for official mail was fair. It only took twenty days from Hangchow to the capital. On August 4, the Empress received Su's first report and immediately acted upon it. As usual, it was passed from the premier's office to the ministry of the interior with the request that a report be made on it within a fortnight. Twenty days later, on August 25, the communication reached Su Tungpo. As far as he could see from the official communication, the most important parts of his first report urging immediate action had been deleted. Immediately he wrote back to the ministry of the interior asking for joint investigation, and again demanded that those who disagreed on the prospect of a famine should be made to sign a statement of their belief.

From the middle of August another downpour had steadily continued. The situation became more threatening than ever, and on September 7, Su Tungpo raised his demand for rice from 200,000 to 500,000 piculs. This rice was intended for stabilisation to force the price down. Even if the government lost ten cash or one penny per bushel, or one dime per picul, the total loss to the government would be no more than $50,000. He was afraid that when the famine actually arrived the government might have to spend ten or twenty times that amount and yet not be able to save all the starving people. This request was granted by the Empress but, as we shall see, there were always ways for bureaucrats to frustrate an imperial edict. Su still had some cash in the government treasury, but the question was not where to get the cash, but where to get the rice. The merchants were hoarding the grain in anticipation of rising prices. At Soochow, prices had already soared to 95 cash per bushel. Su Tungpo offered to buy rice, but could not obtain much. He secured thirty thousand bushels here and forty thousand bushels there. That was all. The officials in the neighbouring districts were not willing to buy in the grain on account of the high prices. Su Tungpo believed that the government should go into the market and pay what the merchants offered and be prepared to sell at a loss.

Time was running short, for rice from the harvest would be bought up within a few weeks. It looked pretty bad all round, even in the neighbouring districts. In despair Su Tungpo wrote again in the latter part of September asking that the government order the officials to buy rice from Honan and Anhuei and have it stored at Yangchow to be held ready for distribution to the lake district when the famine arrived. His plan was that the rice was to be kept there midway, and if it was not needed, it could always be sent on to the capital. Hangchow could pay for it by the equivalent of what they sent for the annual contribution in rice. Again his request was granted, and the Empress allocated the sum of $1,000,000 for this purpose. In the postscript to this third report he said: "This year's calamity is in reality worse than that of last year, but officials high and low prefer to conceal the actual conditions. Recently over forty people were trampled to death in a riot because the magistrate of Kiashing refused to accept the people's demand for relief. Most of the officials are like that. The case of

Kiashing merely happened to become known because so many were trampled to death." If the Empress were to rely on official reports, she would never know the actual conditions. He reminded her of the death of half a million people in a previous regime when the people had cash, but no rice. But he knew now that the people had neither cash nor rice. "If all my worries are ungrounded and there is no famine next year, I am willing to take the punishment. I will take a chance on that, which is better than taking no steps to prevent a calamity and watching the people die without moving a finger."

What happened to the million-dollar grant was this. The money was there, but no rice was being bought. He was also deprived of the grant of 500,000 piculs. Su Tungpo reckoned accounts with the government. The officials insisted that 360,000 piculs had already been given. Su insisted that, of this amount, the 200,000 piculs he obtained in 1089 should not be credited to the 1090 grant, and 160,000 piculs were already in the granary at the time he petitioned for the grant. Receiving an edict granting a sum was one thing, getting it past the obstruction of bureaucracy was another. Writing to his good friend Kung Pingchung in his lone fight against bureaucracy, he cried: "Alas, who will help me?"

Su Tungpo's plan was to begin to sell government grain that winter. As he had anticipated, the prices of grain soared. When winter came, he started to sell the reserve in the government granaries. But in February 1091 he was removed from his office in Hangchow and recalled to the capital to serve again as *hanlin*. Leaving Hangchow with this work uncompleted, he wrote to his successor Lin, telling him to get in touch with all the imperial commissioners and to arrive at some decision. He told Lin that in the previous month he had asked for the holding up of half a million piculs from the amount due to the imperial government, and that Lin should continue to hold it up for the present. On the excuse that he was waiting for a reply to Su's last petition, he could safely delay the sending of the rice. It would not be too late, if the rice proved to be not needed, to send it in June.

On the way to the capital he took the opportunity to visit the flooded areas of Soochow and the neighbouring districts and to arrange conferences with high officials in the fellow provinces. He saw whole areas still buried under water, for the flood had not yet receded. This was in spring, and the farmers still hoped that the water would recede in time for the spring planting. It looked hopeless for the farms on lower levels, while on the higher levels he saw women and old men working day and night to drain water from their fields in a hopeless struggle against the weather. The rain continued, and no sooner was water drained from the fields than they began to fill up again. Famine had arrived. People were beginning to eat chaff and bran, usually considered hog feed,

K

mixed with celery and other vegetables. Because of lack of dry firewood, people had cold meals and many of them had bloated stomachs.
"I have seen this with my own eyes; it is not hearsay. I expect an
epidemic and corpses on roadsides between spring and summer."

Su Tungpo left. Then the famine came, and people died. It is hard
to believe that when Su returned to the capital, he was actually
impeached for "exaggerating famine conditions". But saving the
people from hunger and starvation became an issue for politicians to
throw someone they feared out of power. As far as the imperial government was concerned, there was no famine in the capital. Half the
population of the lake district had not died yet. That year, back near
the capital at Yingchow, Su Tungpo was to watch the effect of the
famine from north of the Yangtse river when famine refugees, after
abandoning their homes and trudging five hundred miles driven by
hunger, reached his district. But the failure of crops in 1091 was to
have worse consequences yet. The next year it became a disaster.

Chapter Twenty-three

FRIEND OF THE PEOPLE

SU TUNGPO had failed in his one-man fight for reform of the civil service system. He had failed in making the government take preventive measures for relief of a famine that he saw was coming. He succeeded, however, through his persistent battle against shadows for the next two years, in saving the people of China from the terrible aftermath of Wang Anshih's state capitalism. According to Su, millions of people had been ruined, or were in jail for debt, or had fled their homes to escape payment of capital and interest. While the government of China was well provided, the nation was bankrupt. The people of China were in a state of perpetual receivership as debtors to the government. The government had foreclosed so many mortgages that it did not know how to collect on a bankrupt people who had run away in default. Wang Anshih was dead and had been buried with the highest imperial honours. It was left to Su Tungpo to salvage the people from bankruptcy by making the government declare a universal moratorium of the people's debts. The people who died are now long dead, so that we can watch with some detachment and even wide-eyed curiosity the unfathomable mind of bureaucracy, cold-hearted and stolid and ruthless, as it played the game of stalking the people for prey in the limitless jungle of old debts started by Wang Anshih.

When Su Tungpo arrived at the capital, he was greeted with a volley of attacks and criticisms. The situation was actually dangerous for the politicians of the Hopei party. It looked as if the Empress had called him back to the capital to make him premier. His brother had been steadily promoted until he was now chancellor of the executive board, which, along with the imperial secretariat and the premier's office, was one of the three chief departments of the Sung government. In June 1092, Tseyu was again promoted, this time to be chancellor of the imperial secretariat. In the loose terminology of the period, he was spoken of as one of the "premiers". The fear of his political opponents was justified. Now the Empress called his brilliant brother back to the court. For self-preservation alone, the political enemies of Su had to make a determined and bitter fight.

The two brothers were now in a highly enviable position, and there was a long argument as to which one should get out in order to save the other from political jealousy. Su Tungpo was determined to get out, but Tseyu argued that a younger brother should give way to his elder brother. After being greeted with a storm of censors' criticism, upon his arrival, Tungpo was even more determined to withdraw, and sent his fifth and sixth letters begging for release.

The more Su Tungpo pleaded to be sent away from the capital, the worse it looked for his political opponents. Chia Yi, the disciple of Cheng Yi, said in his memorial of fifteen hundred words that by these letters of resignation Su Tungpo was using his pressure on the court to fish for the premiership. Anything that Chia Yi could dig up to discredit him was fully exploited. That curious little poem that he had written on the wall of a temple at Yangchow two months after the previous emperor's death was now completely aired in a court audience. The long embankment on West Lake was characterised as "of no benefit to the government or to anybody". He was accused of constantly misleading the government about the famine conditions at Hangchow. Su sent a letter to the court curiously entitled "Memorandum Begging to Run Away from Chia Yi". "Chia Yi is only concerned with private vengeance. He will do anything to get me out, even if it involves leaving people of an entire district to die in the gutter." Here was, then, a serious open quarrel at court. Among the enemies of Su Tungpo were this Chia Yi, who had deserted his own Honan party after it was overthrown, and another man, Yang Wei, who was nicknamed "Three-faced Yang" because he had played the turncoat with Wang Anshih, with Szema Kuang, with Lu Tafang, Fan Chunjen, and others, in a bewildering succession of changes of convictions. On Su Tungpo's side, however, there were many friends in power. The fight was an even one, but it could not end otherwise than it did, because both parties agreed on the one objective. His enemies wanted to drive him away, and this was exactly what Su Tungpo wanted. Famine or no famine, the political fight was carried to its logical conclusion when Su was given a post at Yingchow (Fouyang) three months later.

But his job was not done. Famine conditions grew worse and worse as the crops of 1091 again failed. He served at Yingchow for eight months, and then at Yangchow for seven months, and thus had an opportunity to see the condition of the country north of the Yangtse. In the winter of 1091, while at Yingchow, he once went outside the city and saw hordes of refugees coming towards the Huai bank from the south-east. He reported that the farmers were beginning to tear off elm bark and cook it with purslane and bran to make a mealy paste. Roving bandits were multiplying, and Su reported many cases of looting and robbery. He predicted that the worst was yet to come, and that when it came, greater hordes of refugees would flee from south of the Yangtse. The weak and the old would fall by the roadside, while the young and strong ones would join the bandits.

It was New Year's Eve. Su Tungpo went up the city tower with his colleague, Chao Lingshih of the royal family,* to look at refugees trudging through the deep snow. Chao tells how he was waked up next morning before dawn by Su.

"I have not been able to sleep all night," Su told him. "I must do something about the refugees. Perhaps we can take grain from the government granary and make wheat cakes to feed them. My wife says that when we were passing through Chenchow, Fu Chinchih told us about his success in giving famine relief. We forgot to ask him exactly what he did. That's why I'm calling you. Do you have any suggestions?"

"I have thought about it," replied Chao. "These people need only food and fuel. There are several thousand piculs of grain in the government granary which we can distribute at once. There are also several thousand tons of firewood at the wine bureau—we can give it to the poor people."

"Good," replied Su Tungpo. "Let's do it immediately."

Thus some temporary relief was given to the immediate neighbourhood. But the officials in the neighbouring district south of the Huai River were still imposing a tax on the traffic in grains and firewood, and Su Tungpo wrote to the government to stop this nonsense, now when the greatest freedom of movement of food and fuel supplies was necessary.

In February 1092, Su Tungpo was transferred to Yangchow. His eldest son had been appointed to serve as a magistrate elsewhere. But he took his two younger sons with him on his way to Yangchow to visit the different districts of Anhuei. He dismissed the attendants and went to the villages to talk with the people. There he saw an incredible spectacle. The land was covered with green wheat-fields, but many farmhouses were deserted. A year of good crops was what the farmers most feared, because the clerks and soldiers of the district governments would come and press them for the return of capital loans and interest and throw them in jail. When he reached Yangchow, Su Tungpo said in his letter of thanks for the new post that "both good years and bad years have become calamities for the people". The farmers and the business-men of China were trapped. They had to choose between the alternatives of hunger and starvation during a famine year and court proceedings and jail sentences in a good year.

This then was the aftermath of Wang Anshih's social reforms. While at Hangchow, besides pestering the government with requests for money and grain to forestall a coming famine, Su Tungpo had sent also a long memorandum on the forgiveness of debts owed by the people to the government. Trade was paralysed and even rich families

* Taking warning from the rebellion of princes of royal blood which ended the Tang dynasty, the Sung house gave its princes hardly any power at all.

were wiped out. Currency had disappeared, following the government's demand for taxes in cash instead of in kind. All the wealth of the country was now concentrated in the imperial treasury, and the government was spending it for wars with the north-west. Compared with twenty years earlier, the population of the Hangchow district had dwindled to forty or fifty per cent. The government itself was suffering too, for, as Su Tungpo pointed out, the receipts from the wine monopoly had decreased from over $300,000 per year to under $200,000. The state capitalists' trade bureaus had driven small business-men out of existence. The system of making the rich stand guarantor for their poor neighbours had involved many of the well-to-do in ruin. Unimaginable lawsuits and complications arose from the farmers' loans. Some people had, perhaps with the connivance of officials, borrowed in other people's names. These other people either repudiated the loans or were just non-existent. The government's files were a skein of tangled, unsettled confusion. It found on its hands thousands of mortgaged properties, some of which had been confiscated. Did the confiscated properties cover the capital, or did they cover capital and interest? How was interest to be compounded? More people were put in jail for buying property of which, in the confusion of lawsuits, nobody knew who was the lawful owner. Everybody owed money to everybody else. The courts were too much occupied with cases of debts owed to the government to take care of litigation over private debts. Trade, which was always founded upon credit, was at a standstill because nobody's credit was good. At the same time, the corruption of bureaucracy was unbelievable. Hangchow had to send an annual tribute of silks to the Emperor. Some of the bad silks were rejected by the commissioners, who were interested only in collecting the tribute to the full amount. The money from the rejected silks had to be recovered somehow; it was up to the district magistrates to produce money from the rejected silks, and these were forced upon the people at the price of good silks. The district magistrates were hard pressed by their superiors above and by the clerks below who thrived on the pasture ground of uncollected debts as sheep thrive on the meadows.

The story of the indifference and procrastination of the central government is amazing. Back in May 1090, Su Tungpo had drafted a proposal which he had submitted to the court for cancelling all debts owed to the government. With the coming of the new regime, the government under Szema Kuang had started to return confiscated properties. But the original intention of the court was always thwarted by the bureaucrats. It is not possible to go through all the quibbling over technicalities which enraged Su Tungpo. Some bureaucrats maintained that the court had ordered the return of confiscated properties only of those who had submitted to a "forced" confiscation after the third evaluation, but that such forgiveness should not cover cases of people who had accepted the government's evaluation at once. There was a subtle distinction between the two, for these bureaucrats thought that people who had at once accepted the government's evaluation had recognised its justice, and therefore their property should not be returned. Su Tungpo was indignant over such fine distinctions, and contended that this was not the original intention of the edict.

But this was only one example of the way in which the people were cheated of their rights and benefits. Su Tungpo pointed out instance after instance where the edict had been misinterpreted and misapplied, all to the disadvantage of the people. His great argument was that the last drop of the people's blood had already been squeezed, and he did not see what purpose it served for the government to keep on trying to collect twenty-year-old bad debts from people who could not pay anyway. For instance, out of 1,433 cases of people involved in indebtedness to the government in the wine business, after twenty years of government efforts to collect the debts, still 404 cases remained of people who had fled and who were afraid to return home. The sum involved was only $13,400. What good did it do the government to keep these people from their homes just to collect $13,400? Besides, if this state of things continued, the government was never going to get that $13,400. Should not the government rather earn the gratitude of the people by cancelling such debts at once?

After waiting 108 days in vain for a reply, in September of that year he followed up with another memorandum, asking what had happened to the first one. This was a confidential letter to the Empress, and on December 8 the Empress passed the letter on to the premier's office with the order that action be taken. On December 19 the ministry of the interior sent Su Tungpo a letter saying that *the memorandum had been mislaid* and he was to send a duplicate. On January 9, 1091, Su Tungpo sent the duplicate with the additional comment that for the last twenty years trade had been paralysed and that the government could increase its revenue only by taking measures to restore the general credit and cash reserves of the people. That was the end of that petition. Almost two years elapsed, and still nothing was done about it.

Meanwhile, one failure of crops followed another in the lake district and in Hangchow, and the famine reached catastrophic proportions in 1092. Now, according to Su Tungpo's report, over half the population of the districts of Soochow, Huchow (Wushing), and Shiuchow (Kiashing) died. Great hordes of roaming refugees were coming across the Yangtse. Although the water was beginning to subside, all markings and boundaries of the fields had been wiped out. "There are farms without owners, and owners without food. Those who have food are without seeds, and those who have seeds have no buffaloes. Those who

are not dead look like ghosts." In Su's opinion, with the best help from
the government, it would take ten years for the districts to recover from
the disaster. He pointed out that if the government had taken the
measures he had recommended, the expenses incurred would not have
been half as much as what was now required for relief. "These officials
were concerned only with saving money for the government and not
with saving the people for their Emperor." What about the sea of
toiling humanity?

On May 16, 1092, therefore, Su Tungpo took up this matter of forgiveness of debts again. In his own district, unlike the other officials, he
interpreted the imperial orders in his own light and forgave all cases
that could be covered by the edicts, while in doubtful cases where the
statutes were conflicting or unclear, he suspended the prosecution for a
year, pending the government's action. It was his belief that there was
no way to alleviate conditions and restore trade to normal unless the
people's credit recovered. The outstanding debts with their multiplying
interest hung like a stone around the people's neck. By destroying the
people's credit, trade and commerce were paralysed. This was the root
of all the evils. He sent a five-thousand-word memorandum with
detailed proposals on what to do with the outstanding debts. There
were debts owed on account of sales of government properties, of
farmers' loans, of public granaries, of regular autumn and spring taxes,
debts owed to the trade bureaus which had already been abolished,
and debts owed on failure to pay according to a decree ordering repayment in ten semi-annual instalments. These, together with four other
kinds of debts covered in his Hangchow memorandum, made a total
of ten kinds of indebtedness about which the government had already
issued various orders from time to time for partial forgiveness. Su
Tungpo reviewed the whole situation and worked out detailed suggestions. Finally he said:

"I served at Hangchow, and then at Yingchow, and now I am
serving at Yangchow. I have had therefore the opportunity to
observe personally the conditions of the people in three provinces.
They are all being crushed under the heavy burden of the old debts
and steadily impoverished. Half of the population have died or fled,
and the records of their debts are still on government files. Farmers
and small business-men are all suffering, which in turn decreases the
government revenue. From my experience in the three provinces
covered, I can safely assume that the same is true of the entire
country.

"When travelling from Yingchow to Yangchow, I passed the
various districts on the Huai River. Everywhere I went I saw a sea
of green wheat-fields. Leaving my official attendants, I went into the

villages. The elders all said with a sad face: 'It is better nowadays to have bad crops than to have good crops. In case of floods and drought, we can skimp and save and somehow live in freedom. But when a good year comes, the tax-collectors come to the door and the people are led away in chains. It is worse than death itself.' After saying this, the elders wiped their eyes, and I shed tears too. Furthermore, in all the towns that I visited, there are hordes of refugees. . . .

"Confucius said: 'An oppressive government is more to be feared than tigers.' I used to doubt this statement. After seeing the present conditions, I think what Confucius said was an understatement. Famines and floods kill hundreds of times more people than tigers, but today the people of the country fear the tax-collectors even more than they fear famines and floods. I have made a private calculation of the number of these tax-collectors. Taking the average of 500 tax-collectors per district, I estimate there are over 200,000 tigers and wolves let loose in the whole country to prey upon the people. I ask Your Majesty, how are the people going to live, and how do you expect to succeed in establishing a benevolent administration?"

Exactly one month after he sent the first memorandum, he followed it with a second private letter to the Empress, in which he suggested the following wording of an edict to be issued by her: "It has come to óur knowledge that in the provinces along the Huai and the Cheh rivers [Chekiang], there is the greatest amount of outstanding debts owed by the people to the government. These districts have suffered from natural calamities for the past years and corpses lie on the roadside. Although the first wheat harvest is good this year south of the Huai River, it is yet uncertain what kind of a harvest there will be in West Chekiang. We therefore wish that all debts owed to the government in the districts south, east, and west of the Huai River, and in West Chekiang, be suspended for one year, regardless of the age of these debts and without taking into account whether the capital has been recovered or not. It is our wish that through this measure our long-suffering people may have the pleasure of a full belly." Then he advised the Empress to draw up separate statutes regarding the disposal of all debts according to his previous detailed recommendations.

In July 1092, the recommendation of Su Tungpo was formally issued as an edict. His wish was fulfilled and the people's debts to the government covered by his memorandum were entirely forgiven.

BOOK FOUR

YEARS OF EXILE

(1094–1101)

Chapter Twenty-four

SECOND PERSECUTION

IN the autumn of 1093 two women died. They were Su Tungpo's wife and the Empress Dowager, both of whom we might almost believe had mystically acted as the guardian angels of the poet. Their deaths were coincident with a complete reversal of fortune in Su Tungpo's life. Mrs. Su died on August 1, the Empress Dowager on September 3. At the time of his wife's death, Su was at the height of his fortune, and she left him exactly at the right moment to be spared the saddest period of his life. After recall from his office at Yangchow, Su had served first for two months as minister of war and then ten months as minister of education; his brother was then serving as chancellor of the imperial secretariat. Su's wife had participated in the visit of the Empress to the ancestral tombs and had enjoyed all the honours of a lady of her rank. Her children were now all married and by her side. Mai was thirty-four, Tai twenty-three, and Kuo twenty-one. The second son had been married to a granddaughter of Ouyang Shiu. Mrs. Su's funeral ceremony therefore took place with all the pomp and circumstance appropriate to her station. Her coffin lay in a Buddhist temple in the western suburb of the capital until ten years later, when Tseyu buried her remains in a common tomb with her husband. Su Tungpo's sacrificial prayer to her was written with the usual felicitous expressions, but also with classical restraint. It spoke of how good a wife she had been, and how good a mother; how, too, she had treated the son by the first wife as her own. He said that she had shared the ups and downs of his fortune with perfect content, and he pledged that he would be buried in the same grave with her. On the hundredth day after his wife's death, Su Tungpo had a portrait of the ten disciples of Buddha painted by the famous painter Li Kunglin, and dedicated it in her honour at a ceremony when Buddhist monks were asked to say mass for her soul and bless her on her journey by land and water into the spiritual world.

In a true sense, the Empress Dowager, mother of Shentsung and grandmother of the present emperor, had been Su Tungpo's guardian angel, too. Her death marked Su Tungpo's downfall, and the downfall of all the officials in office during her regency. The wise old woman had felt a political change coming, for her grandson had grown up by her side and she knew him well. He was a boy artistically inclined, but otherwise rash, given to explosions of temper, and easily twisted around an experienced politician's finger. He had grown a sense of resentment against his grandmother which was played upon and probably first suggested by Wang Anshih's party men.

were underpaid, underclothed, and underfed, and the barracks were in a shabby condition. Corruption was rampant and discipline lax. Officers and soldiers were given to gambling and drinking. It was the kind of army that would run away and evaporate before any battle. Su Tungpo started to have the barracks repaired, enforced sharp discipline, dismissed and punished the corrupt officers, and made it possible for the soldiers to be well-clad and well-fed.

When some of the non-commissioned officers saw that Su Tungpo was punishing the corrupt officers, they came to inform against their superior officers. "This is none of your business," Su Tungpo told them. "It is all right for me to deal with it. If soldiers were allowed to inform against their superiors, what would happen to army discipline?" And he had these informers also punished. He had a sharp sense of the respect due to him as a military superior. He put on military uniform and held dress parades with his majors and adjutants standing according to rank. The military chief, Wang Kuangtsu, was an old, arrogant, jaundiced general who had been in command of the army at this place for a long time, and he now felt that he was being shorn of his power. On the occasion of a dress parade, the general refused to take part. Su Tungpo commanded him to appear, however, and the old general had no choice but to obey.

The tragedy of a monarchy arises from the fact that, for the maintenance of a royal house in power, it is necessary that the queens produce, in unbroken succession, good, wise, and able sons, grandsons, and great-grandsons—a biologically unwarranted assumption unknown to human experience. As geniuses do not produce geniuses, so sooner or later wise kings produce wicked or feeble-minded progeny. The peace and good government of a country and sometimes the course of history are made dependent upon the entirely fortuitous and uncontrollable transmission of the genes of one line. Nature provides that no single family shall have a monopoly of talent, and so Louis XVI just was not Louis XIV, and George III was not a replica of George II. Both the French Revolution and the birth of the American republic owed their success largely to the neurotic kings.

The boy of eighteen who now ascended the throne was known to be very fond of women and had frequently cancelled his classes. The seed of the young man's hatred against the Yuanyu officials was already planted when these scholars wrote both to the boy Emperor and to his grandmother against his indulgence with women and neglect of his studies. The Emperor was always surrounded by twenty grown-up girls, who were supposed to attend to his personal comfort, which was quite in accordance with the tradition. As he told Chang Chun later, the Emperor suddenly found one day that ten of the girls had been dismissed and ten new ones had come in their place. After a few days, again ten girls were dismissed, and when they came to say farewell, he saw that the girls had been crying, as if they had been severely questioned by the grandmother.

It must be explained why the boy Emperor now showed such a bitter hatred against two of his ministers. Liu Anshih was almost murdered and survived only by a lucky chance, while Fan Tsuyu died in exile. Something had happened four or five years earlier. One day Liu wanted to hire a wet nurse for his sister-in-law and found it very difficult to obtain one. After waiting a month in vain, Liu got very angry and asked the old woman of the employment agency why she had not obtained one.

"Your Honour," said the old woman, "I'm doing my best. The chamberlain's office has been asking for ten wet nurses, and I was able to send them in only today."

"What nonsense!" said Liu, shocked. "The Emperor is not yet married. Why should he want a wet nurse?"

The old woman then explained that she had received sharp orders from the officials of the East Gate to keep this a strict secret. Liu still refused to believe the story. He wrote a short note to a friend in the chamberlain's office and the friend confirmed it. Upon this, Liu Anshih sent a memorial to the throne which said among other things: "There is a rumour going around that the chamberlain has been looking for wet nurses. His Majesty is still young, and is not yet married. I do not think that he should be attracted yet by the opposite sex. At first I refused to believe the rumour, but the gossip is increasing and appears to be supported by some evidence." He warned that if this gossip were allowed to be spread, the people of the country were not going to like it.

The other official, Fan, wrote to the Emperor himself. "There is a rumour abroad to the effect that Your Majesty has intimate relations with the maids of the palace. In my stupidity, I cannot dismiss all doubts. Is this the age for you to have contact with women? Don't you value your sacred body?"

According to the story, the rumour arose out of a misunderstanding. One day after the audience, the Empress Dowager asked Lu Tafang to remain behind, and said to him: "Anshih has sent a letter regarding the procuring of wet nurses for the palace. His intentions are good, but he does not know the truth. The wet nurses are not wanted by the Emperor, but for some of the young princesses who still need breast feeding. He is always with me and sleeps in the inside chamber. I do not think there is any ground for the rumour. I have questioned the maids, and did not find anything. Please tell Anshih to stop memorialising the throne on this subject."

"Liu is a censor," replied Lu, "and according to custom, as the premier I am not permitted to see a censor in private."

"Then how are we going to convey my wish to Anshih?" said the Empress Dowager.

"I often see Fan Tsuyu at the office of the court diaries. I am bound to see him, and will tell him to tell Anshih of your wish. They come from the same province."

"Fan himself has memorialised the throne on the same subject," said the Empress Dowager. "You should tell him to stop, too."

When this message was conveyed to Liu Anshih, he said to Fan: "How can I keep quiet on such a thing which reflects on the Emperor's personal character? You yourself should speak up, too, as one of the close associates of His Majesty."

"I have," replied Fan.

The two agreed that although the story of the wet nurses might be due to a misunderstanding, they should continue with their official advice. But Liu Anshih had not only offended the Emperor. He had also opposed the pardon of Chang Chun during the regency and had incured the undying hatred of this sinister figure.

On the other hand, Chang Chun, Su's former friend, played upon the young Emperor's love of women. Later he was impeached with the following sentence: "He corrupted the Emperor's character with women and actresses and led him astray with immoral thoughts and suggestions." He knew that the Emperor's favourite was one "Glamor Liu" and not the queen. We cannot go into the amazing life history of the queen who survived the fall of the northern Sung dynasty and whose story would make a fine novel. Suffice it to say that by a frame-up, the queen was accused of practicing the black art. Papers containing Taoist charms were thrown into her room through the window and appropriately discovered by the investigators. Palace maids under torture were forced to testify that they had seen pins stuck through the heart of Glamor Liu's portrait, a method of causing heart burns to the rival by Taoist magic. About thirty palace maids were almost flogged to death; the case was handled not through the usual courts of iustice but entirely inside the palace. The queen was degraded to be officially a nun. Glamor Liu then alleged that the sharp pains in her chest stopped. She was installed and the young emperor was delighted. Later, however, Miss Liu had occasion to commit suicide.

Such was the character of the scion of the Sung house upon whom the destiny of an empire and the peace of a nation now depended. It took only a few wily ministers to manipulate a boy of eighteen and produce irremediable national chaos.

The great slogan of the Emperor's new regime was two words, *Shao Shu*, which meant "return to the way of one's ancestors", and this carried with it an automatic justification in Chinese eyes. The Emperor was ready to embark upon a policy of return to the economic policies of Shentsung. It was clear that under such a slogan all the officials during the Empress Dowager's regency could be charged with the mortal crime of destroying the works of his father. It meant disloyalty to the dead emperor. In the previous accusations of Su Tungpo, this charge had been brought up repeatedly. It did not matter that Shentsung's own mother had confirmed the fact—in the young Emperor's presence and in the presence of the high officials—that in the last years of his reign Shentsung had begun to regret his mistakes. It did not matter that the officials could remind the young Emperor of the Empress Dowager's words addressed directly to him. It was a useful label by which all the parties opposed to the new regime could be exiled and dismissed.

It was the beginning of summer, 1094. Upon the recommendation of "Three-faced Yang," Chang Chun had become the premier. In order to convince the young Emperor that all the Yuanyu officials were his enemies, it was not enough for Chang Chun to charge them with upsetting the policies of his father. This group of men were superb politicians. They had to make the young Emperor hate the Yuanyu people personally. Clearly, the most personal thing that could hurt the Emperor was the idea that someone had been plotting with his grandmother against his throne. Out of unverifiable reports of dead men's conversations and confessions of palace officials extracted under torture, the plotters were able to create rumours of a conspiracy which never existed.

When the Empress Dowager was acting as regent, Chang Chun and the Tsais had been thrown out of power. Embittered, Tsai Chueh had been circulating the rumour that the Empress Dowager had plotted to put her own son on the throne. Tsai was exposed, degraded and died. Now the Empress Dowager was dead, and the rumour was revived and raised into an important political issue.

The charge was now that Szema Kuang and Wang Kuei had been accomplices in this plot. No evidence could be produced except two alleged conversations. The dead men could neither confirm nor deny it. Szema Kuang was said to have discussed the idea with Fan Tsuyu, who was in exile anyway and who was expected to deny it if he was ever cross-examined. The impression was created that the Empress Dowager had always thought of ousting her own grandson. One of her two personal secretaries, Chen Yen, had been already exiled to the south. He was tried in his absence and condemned to death. The other secretary was brought to the capital. Chang Chun entered into a deal with him. After subjecting him to torture, Chang asked him to make a choice between death and turning witness for the prosecution by making statements as the Empress Dowager's private secretary that she had plotted against the young Emperor. "Heavens, I cannot accuse the Empress Dowager of something she did not do!" the secretary exclaimed. He refused to submit, and the investigation could go no further. But Chang Chun and the Tsai brothers succeeded in casting a cloud of doubt in the young Emperor's mind about Szema Kuang and the Yuanyu men.

"Were all the leaders of Yuanyu like that?" the Emperor asked.

"It was what they intended to do," replied Chang Chun," but they had no opportunity to carry it out."

A great "plot" to dethrone the Emperor had been unearthed. The young man was in a rage. There was even talk of removing the spirit tablet of the Empress Dowager from the royal ancestral temple, but the young man had enough sense to stop it. He said to Chang Chun: "Do you want me never to enter again the ancestral temple of Ingtung?" Edicts for dismissals, banishments, and confinements flew thick and fast. Along with Su Tungpo, over thirty of the highest officials of the Yuanyu regime were variously degraded and exiled. The punishment assumed unusual proportions and went beyond all historical precedents. Chang Chun's chance for vengeance had come. He went into it with demoniacal fury for during the regency he himself had suffered imprisonment. The man who Su Tungpo had predicted could commit murder was now in power. Just as he had been fearlesss in crossing a narrow wooden plank over a hundred-foot chasm, so he had always dared anything. He had committed adultery with the mistress of his "clan uncle" at the capital. In danger, he had jumped out of a window and injured a passenger on the street, but the case had not been formally prosecuted. During Wang Anshih's regime, while all the good scholars had lost their jobs in protest, Chang Chun had gone on from one office to another.

Now as soon as Chang Chun was appointed premier in April, he called back to power the old gang. This was quite a group of men, all distinguished for fiendish energy and capacity for intrigue. "Three-faced Yang" was his great friend. Tsai Chueh was dead, but the others were living. The double-crosser Huiching returned to power, but still, with his past reputation, he did not go very far. The other henchman of Wang Anshih, Tseng Pu, was called back. The evil geniuses of the northern Sung, the Tsai brothers, stepped into the centre of the political arena and completed the work of the destruction of the country by misrule. If there was a period in China's history that could be characterised as one of callous tyranny and unqualified chaos, it was the regime under Tsai Ching. The building of an elaborate pleasure garden for the Emperor probably constituted one of the most gruesome stories in China's history, gruesome and fantastic because so much

human misery on a national scale was unnecessary in the building of
even an imperial pleasure garden. Every piece of rock and every rare
flower in that garden cost some human lives. A reading of the descriptive poem by Emperor Huitsung and other poems written by high
ministers in praise of this fabulously beautiful palace garden, with
artificial hills and streams and rockeries, gives one a thrill down the
spine and a sense of high tragedy unequalled in the annals of Chinese
literature. The high tragedy consists in the fact that the authors were
entirely unaware of it.

Compared with this second persecution of scholars, Wang Anshih's
dismissal of his political opponents was mere child's play. Szema
Kuang and Lu Kungchu were dead, but they were not to be allowed
to lie in their graves in peace. Twice these deceased premiers were
degraded and deprived of their ranks and honour. But still it was not
enough. It was formally proposed by Chang Chun that an order be
issued to dig open Szema Kuang's grave, smash his coffin, and whip
his corpse, as a warning to all disloyal subjects of the Emperor. In
the young Emperor's mind, Szema Kuang was the symbol of dishonesty, disloyalty, and iniquity of the Yuangyu regime. During the
discussion in the imperial audience, all the others approved. But there
was one man, Shü Chiang who kept silent. The young Emperor
studied him, and when the audience was over, he asked Shü to remain.

"Why didn't you say anything?" asked the Emperor.

"Because I believe it will serve no useful purpose and will remain
a blot upon the regime," was Shü's reply.

The order was not passed and Chang Chun did not have his wish,
but he did succeed in dealing out other punishments. The properties
of Szema Kuang's family were confiscated, all official honours and
emoluments were taken away from his children, the tomb structures
built by the government in his honour were demolished, and the stone
inscription erected by the Empress Dowager was ground off. One
official even petitioned that the monumental masterpiece of history
written by Szema Kuang should be destroyed. Someone objected by
pointing out that the Emperor's father had himself contributed a preface
to this work. This unanswerable argument seemed to go home to the
idiot's head, and the standard history of China up to the Sung dynasty,
the *Tsechih Tungchien,* was spared. Defeated in his dream of "exposing" and "whipping" the corpse of Szema Kuang, Chang Chun insisted that everything that could be done to injure his family should
be done. Tseng Pu was the restraining influence upon Chang Chun
and the Tsai brothers. He said:

"I do not think we should set up the precedent of depriving an
official's children of official ranks and benefits. Don't forget that the
same thing may happen to our own children one day. Besides, the

families of Szema Kuang and Han Wei have been enjoying government benefits for about ten years. It seems inhuman to take them away suddenly."

"No," said Chang Chun. "Han Wei laid down his office only a few years ago."

"Still, it is already six or seven years," Tseng Pu rejoined. "Besides, he was in power only a short time. If you insist on punishing the children, then only take action against the families of Szema Kuang and Lu Kungchu. But I do not think we should punish the families at all. It should be enough to deprive men of their ranks in death."

"What's the use of all this?" replied Chang Chun. "Even whipping their corpses wouldn't do them any real harm. What can they suffer from being degraded of ranks in death? The only substantial thing we can do is to make their children pay for it."

"That may satisfy you," said Tseng Pu, "but we should really consider it carefully. I have no other thought in mind except that we should not set up such a precedent."

Tseng Pu spoke with the voice of experience. Chang Chun later was hanged by his own gallows. Ruthless in his persecutions of the Su brothers, he did not want them to have comfortable shelter while in exile. When Tseyu was in exile in Luichow, he was driven out of an official building and forced to rent a house from the people. Chang Chun took this up, and accused the Su brothers of illegally occupying people's homes by force or official pressure. The case was investigated and Tseyu was able to produce a deed to show that he had rented the house by contract. It happened that, later, Chang Chun himself was exiled to the same town, and it was his turn to look for a house for rent. The people of the town hated him, and said: "How dare we rent a house to you? We once rented a house to the Su brothers and nearly got into trouble."

Chang Chun was not insane—he was merely consumed with a passion for revenge, plus a fear of letting the opposition survive and have a chance to come back. With the exception of Han Wei, all the officials were sent far out to the south and south-west in different forms of confinement, some in army confinement, some to keep wine bureaus, and the less hated ones to serve as magistrates. Even old Wen Yenpo, who hated and was hated by nobody, and who had served the court under four emperors, was degraded and humiliated at the age of ninety-one and died about a month later. Lu Tafang, Fan Tsuyu, Liu Chih, and Liang Tao all died in exile. The fact that the last two died within seven days of each other at a time when Chang Chun had sent out two commissioners to suggest suicide to various officials made people think that they were probably murdered. The hatred was so fiendish that an order was even given that Liang Tao's remains could not be carried back and buried in his ancestral place—one of the cruellest things a Chinese mind could conceive.

The man that Chang Chun hated most was of course Liu Anshih, who had obstructed his pardon. A commissioner was sent far down south to execute Chen Yen, the personal secretary of the Empress Dowager, and Chang Chun asked him to go and see Liu Anshih, who was then exiled in the south, and suggest to him that he commit suicide. Liu was known to be a good man, and the official refused to do it. Defeated in his purpose, Chang Chun made a deal with a local merchant, giving him an official post as tax collector and asking in return that he go and murder Liu. This merchant was already on his way, dashing in a hurry to carry out his murderous mission and make sure that his victim had no time to escape. The family of Liu had heard the news and were weeping, but Liu himself remained unperturbed and ate and drank as usual. About midnight the merchant arrived, coughed up blood, and fell dead on the floor. Liu died later a natural death.

In the dark picture of the persecution, the character of Fan Chunjen stands out as a bright light. Su Tungpo had met Fan Chunjen, son of the great premier, Fan Chungyen, very early in his life, when he and his brother and father were stopping at Kiangling on their way to the capital. They had always remained friends and respected each other. But it was not the kind of intimate friendship that Su enjoyed with the other Fan family, the family of Fan Chen and Fan Tsuyu. Fan had an unsullied official record, and as the great son of a great father, was one of the two to receive the dying wishes of the Empress Dowager. The young Emperor knew of his reputation, and so far he had been spared. In April, when Su Tungpo was exiled together with thirty others, Fan Chunjen begged to resign. Upon his insistence he was allowed to retire to his home in a town near the capital. Chang Chun wanted to have him exiled along with the rest.

"He is one of the group," Chang Chun said.

"Chunjen stands for the country only," said the Emperor. "He is not one of the Yuanyu party; he only wants to resign."

"But the fact of his resigning in protest shows that he is one of the party men," replied Chang Chun.

Fan did not remain at his home long. The old premier Lu Tafang, who had maintained a good administration even if he was not a great leader, and who was now seventy years old and ill, had been living in exile over a year. It was an inhuman thing to permit, by all Confucian standards. Nobody dared to speak up for the old man, but Fan did. His friends and relatives tried to dissuade him, but he said: "Do I desire to go on a thousand-mile journey in exile when I am nearing seventy and both my eyes are almost blind? But it is a thing that has got to be done. I know what is awaiting me, but I must do it." He sent a letter to the court asking for the pardon of the old premier, and naturally was himself exiled to the south.

The old man went cheerily on his way, accompanied by a devoted family. Whenever his children spoke bitterly about Chang Chun, he stopped them. Once their boat capsized and he was pulled out of the water with his clothing all wet. He turned round to his children and said jokingly: "Do you think that Chang Chun is responsible for this, too?" He almost lost his eyesight, but lived happily with his family. Later, when the young Emperor died he was showered with attention and favours from the succeeding emperor. The court sent its own physicians to attend to him and wanted to call him back to premiership, but he refused. At the time of his pardon he had lost over a dozen members of his family from disease and poverty, and he himself died on his journey back to the north.

Naturally, the persecution included all four of Su Tungpo's disciples. The exiled persons were not left at peace, for all of them were successively degraded and sent from place to place. In time, a special bureau was established to round up all supporters of the Yuanyu regime so that no one could escape. The bureau was to file and screen all official communications during the regency, beween May 1085 and April 1094. Any scholar who had said anything for reversal of the economic policies of Wang Anshih would be considered guilty of libelling Emperor Shentsung. By such close scrutiny they were able to round up and punish eight hundred and thirty officials, and the carefully classified ran to a hundred and forty-two volumes. Eventually the persecution culminated in the Yuanyu Partisans Tablet, referred to in Chapter I.

Tseyu had been dismissed in March. He had continued to oppose the policy of "return to one's ancestors ways", but the way in which he was dismissed showed something of the character of the boy Emperor. Tseyu had quoted historic examples to show how succeeding emperors had often modified the policies of their predecessors. Among the examples he quoted was the great Emperor Wu of Han, under whose regime the Chinese Empire was extended to Turkistan and beyond. Chang Chun had not yet become premier then, and there was another man, Li, who had hoped to replace Tseyu. Li told the young Emperor that his comparison with Emperor Wu was a great insult to his father; and, ignorant of history, the young boy believed him, and had Tseyu deprived of his ranks and sent as a magistrate to Juchow. Only a few months later, Tseyu was banished to Kao-an.

Chapter Twenty-five

HOME IN EXILE

WHEN Chang Chun became premier in April 1094, his axe fell first upon Su Tungpo. Su was the first to be exiled across the high mountain ridge in Kwangtung, a region known generally as "beyond Tayuling" (mountain pass). He was dismissed from his office, deprived of his official ranks and appointed magistrate at Ingchow (modern Kukong). He was not unaware of what was impending, but he did not realise yet how severe the second persecution was going to be. He had felt danger near when he could not get permission to see the Emperor in his formal leave-taking to go to his new office at Tingchow upon the Empress Dowager's death. He had lectured the boy off and on for eight years and knew him well. A year earlier he had said in a letter to the Emperor rather bluntly that if he would not listen to the minister's advice Su would "prefer to be a medicine-man or a fortune-teller" rather than remain at the court as the Emperor's tutor.

Nevertheless, he had no real inkling of what was coming. The degrading to the office of a magistrate at Kukong did not imply any special hardship. Chang Chun was one of his old friends. In their trip to the mountains of Shensi in their young days, Su Tungpo had jokingly said that Chang was capable of murder; but still, they were, friends. He was not at all surprised at his dismissal from office. The charges against him were the old ones that had been repeated again and again. They were the charges of "slandering the deceased emperor". The evidences were the various imperial edicts that he had drafted during the regency for the dismissal of Wang Anshih's party men. This "slander of the deceased emperor" was now the stock phrase used against all the Yuanyu officials. It did not matter that in drafting the edicts Su Tungpo had been taking orders from the Empress Dowager. The edict of dismissal said:

."I would not mind if Su Shih's criticism were directed against myself. But in my name, he slandered my imperial father. He tried to break the relationship between father and son and violated the rules of propriety between ruler and subject. A common citizen would regard any slanderer of his parent as a mortal enemy. How am I as Emperor to face my people if I allow such insults to go by? You, Su Shih, are clever with your pen and your tongue. But you have cut yourself off from your sovereign lord and should blame no one but yourself."

Su was now to begin a march of fifteen hundred miles from the north of China to the south, and it seemed to him that he had been journeying all his life from station to station and this was but another step in the course which had been plotted for him by the gods and predetermined at the time of his birth, but only now fully revealed to him. At the age of fifty-seven, he had known enough vicissitudes of fortune not to be much surprised by the new turn of events. Fate decreed that he was to be finally relieved of all politics and he was to live as a common man, as he had always wanted to do. He was marching on, unafraid, and with complete peace of mind. He had in his past life courageously faced every problem and every situation with truth and sincerity; he was willing to leave everything to Heaven's will.

Suffering from a strange sense of distinction as the first victim to be sent across the high mountain ridges of the south, Su set out with his family. His brother was already at his post in Juchow, quite near the capital, and he went first to get some financial assistance from him. Su Tungpo had no money sense. Though he had had a run of good luck in the nine years of the Empress Dowager's regency, he had constantly moved about and had always spent his salary. On the other hand, his brother had risen steadily to a "premiership". When Tungpo went to see him, Tseyu was able to give him seven thousand dollars for the settlement and support of his family at Ishing. Coming back from Tseyu's place, he found that he had been degraded in rank once more, though his appointment to Kukong remained unchanged. He sent a pathetic letter to the Emperor asking permission to travel by boat, as a favour that might be granted an old teacher. He was afraid that, marching on land over fifteen hundred miles, he might fall ill and die by the wayside. The permission was granted, and he sent his entire family, including the three daughters-in-law, to the Su home in the lake district at Ishing. Tears were shed, but Su decided to take only Chaoyun and his two younger sons with him.

June had arrived when they stopped at Yichen, across the river from Nanking. Persecution of the Yuanyu officials was at its height; over thirty of the highest officials were now exiled. Su Tungpo was degraded a third time. He was no longer to be a magistrate, but was to be confined with a nominal military rank in the district of Huichow, about seventy miles east of Canton. The situation had completely altered, and he decided to send his second son also to the Ishing farm and continue his voyage only with Kuo, then twenty-two, and Chaoyun and two old maid-servants. His disciple Chang Lei, who at the time was magistrate at Chinkiang, sent two old soldiers to serve him on the way.

But it was a pleasant journey through beautiful country, over hills and dales, exciting rapids, and tall mountain ridges, and he enjoyed them to the full. One exciting incident happened on the way. He had been travelling in a government boat. When he was stopping at Poyang Lake, south of Kiukiang, to his surprise a fourth order was issued, further degrading him in rank. The commissioner of transportation had learned of this order and had sent a troop of soldiers to take the boat away from him. It was midnight when the soldiers arrived. Su Tungpo stipulated that he be permitted to keep the boat till noon the next day, to which the officer agreed. He was still a dozen miles away from the lake port leading to Nanchang. If he had luck in reaching Nanchang, he would be safe, but if the wind were against him, he would be thrown out of the boat with his family and luggage. He went to pray at the temple of the Dragon King, who was in charge of the safety of sailors. He explained to the god the difficulty he was in, and said that if he did not reach his destination by the next morning he would have to sleep in the open. As soon as his prayer was finished a stiff wind arose and filled the sails, and the boat sped forward and arrived at the destination before breakfast-time. Later, on his return journey, he offered a prayer of thanks to the Dragon King.

In September he crossed the famous Tayuling (General Yu's Notch), through which travellers to Canton in ancient China had to go. The pass was a symbol of a long and hazardous journey into a region from which many travellers never returned. A paved road had been built three to four hundred yards on either side of the pass, planted with shady trees to give shelter and rest to the travellers. It was a sentimental place where many travellers scribbled poems on the rocks. Standing there on the peak of the mountain, so close to the sky and the clouds, Su Tungpo felt that he was living in a dream-world and he forgot the existence of his material body. From that height he could see the pettiness of men and their ways, and the clean mountain wind brushed away all mortal thoughts from his breast. After crossing the Notch, he took the occasion to visit modern Kukong and the Nanhua Temple, sacred to the memory of the Chinese Zen Buddhists.

Somewhere between Kukong and Canton he ran into an old Taoist friend, Wu Fuku, who was now to be closely associated with him during his exile days. Wu Fuku was a strange man. He had popped up at different places in the past years of Su Tungpo's life. Su had met him first at Tsinan, then again saw him at the captial. What was this man doing? Had he no profession? What did he live upon? Was he trying to befriend Su Tungpo in order to ask for something, particularly when Su was in power at the court? But Wu never asked favours from Su, nor from the other high officials he knew. He had disappeared, and now here, of all places, Su ran across him again. Wu was a real Taoist. Bodily and spiritual freedom, and a care-free heart, were what the Taoist cared for most, and by having a strong body and few simple wants, many of them were able to live a much-envied life of freedom. The price for such freedom was the willingness to forsake fame and wealth, the ability to endure simple food, dress, and shelter, to travel a thousand miles on foot, and to sleep in the open if necessary. Wu Fuku wanted nothing from the world. He appeared and disappeared, a reminder to the poet of what he might have been had he not got involved in politics.

On October 2, 1094, two years before the First Crusade in Europe, Tungpo arrived at the city of Huichow. Many things were new to him and yet familiar. It was a sub-tropical country and he saw orange-groves, sugar-cane, lichi trees, banana orchards, and *pinlang* palms. It was far from a bad place in which to live. Two rivers came from the north and joined at a point east of the city. For the first fortnight, Su Tungpo put up at a government building by courtesy of the local magistrate. Standing on top of the Hochiang Tower at the junction of the rivers, he saw the big broad stream flowing beneath past the city, and on the opposite bank the hilly town of Kueishan county was built on a sharp slope. Rocks and boulders lined the banks where idle citizens were fishing. Directly north of the city lay the tall mountains of Lofu and Elephant's Trunk, which he knew he was going to explore.

Here was the south of China, not as he had imagined it to be, but full of dark-green vegetation and sub-tropical fruits. "South of the high mountain teeming families enjoy an eternal spring." The people were surprised to see the poet and did not know for what crime he was banished to their district. Su thought of Su Wu, who was exiled to the Mongolian desert and never suspected that in his old age he was to return to China; and he thought of Kuan Ning, who was exiled to northern Manchuria and chose to remain there for life. Huichow was beautiful and the people were good to him. After he moved across the bank to Chiayu Temple, he said that very soon even the dogs and the chickens knew him.

His attitude towards life is well expressed in a little note he wrote on the Pinewood Pavilion across the bank. After moving to the Chiayu Temple, he often stayed at this pavilion on top of the hill. He was returning home one day and saw it appear high up above the tree-tops, and his old legs felt tired. Suddenly he thought: "Why can't I stop below? Where in the world cannot one rest? Once you perceive that, you feel like a fish that has escaped the fisherman's hook."

He was his natural self once more. While at Canton, he had bought
some good sandalwood incense, and now he enjoyed sitting indoors
with the door closed, quietly enjoying the perfume and thinking of
the mistakes of his past life. Sometimes he enjoyed an afternoon nap
with the cool river breeze coming in through the windows; and when
he was waked up by a cawing raven on the roof, he suddenly realised
that he was now free from all responsibilities. He saw the reflected
light of the broad river enter his own studio. It was good, his heart
declared, as good as a moon shining in a clear sky. He did not
understand why some people thought clouds in the sky made the
moon more beautiful. To him the clear sky was a symbol of a bright
conscience.

Writing to a friend, he said that after staying there half a year and
getting used to the climate he had not a care on his mind, for he had
made peace with his destiny and now accepted it without a doubt.
Another old friend at Huangchow, Chen Tsao, sent him a letter saying he was coming to visit him. It would be a journey of a thousand
miles from the neighbourhood of Hankow to Huichow, and Su wrote
the following reply:

"I have been here for about half a year and find the life around
here and the food and customs very agreeable. The officials and the
neighbours have been very kind to me. Confucius did not deceive me
when he said that one could get along very well even in a country
of barbarians. You had better stay at home and not hazard such a
long journey. Don't worry on account of my stupid old self. . . .
Nor do I think you should send someone to visit me. Don't be foolish.
We are both so old that our whiskers can prick each other. . . .
My eldest son conducts himself as an official like his father, and my
second son can write excellent poems and *fu*. It seems almost as if
he would outshine me. I believe you will be greatly delighted when
you hear this. Today I went to the Mountain of Buddha's Footprints. There was a waterfall thirty fathoms high. Its thunderous
roar and the awe-inspiring leaps of water are hard to describe. It
suggests the stampede of the Tsin army during the defeat by Shiang
Yu. I've just got your letter on my return and am writing this
reply under lamplight. This is the end of the paper and so I will
stop. March 4 [1095]."

Externally, he was living a far from solitary life. As was to be expected, all the officials of the neighbouring districts availed themselves
of this unique opportunity to make friends with the distinguished poet.
The chief magistrates of five principal districts east, west, and north
of Huichow kept making him presents of wine and food. The chief

magistrate of Huichow, Chan Fan, and the county magistrate of Poklo, Lin Pien, became his close friends. Other devoted friends of his, like the priest Tsanliao of Hangchow and Chien Shihshiung of Chang-chow, continually sent messengers with presents, medicines, and letters. There was a Buddhist convert at Soochow by the name of Cho who undertook a seven-hundred-mile journey on foot to bring messages from Su's children and his friends in the lake district. Su's two sons at Ishing were worried because they had not heard from their father, and when Cho heard this he said to them: "Why, that's easy! Huichow is not in heaven, is it? If you go on walking, you are bound to reach it." Cho undertook the long journey on foot, crossing the high mountain ridge, and arrived with a tanned face and calloused feet.

Through such means Su Tungpo kept in contact with his family in the north. The curious Taoist Wu Fuku stayed for months with him, and in the following two years travelled back and forth between Hui-chow and Tseyu's place at Kao-an. Another extraordinary Taoist from Su's home town, Lu Weichien, undertook a journey of two thousand miles to come and see him. Su Tungpo had discovered an extra-ordinary wine, the cinnamon wine, which he said was the nectar of the gods. He had written jokingly to Lu that the taste of this cinnamon wine alone would be worth the hardships of the long journey, and Lu arrived.

Some days the magistrate Chan Fan would send a dinner with his cook to Su Tungpo's own home. Some days Su would go and have a pint with his friend on the great lake west of the city, which lay at a foothill with a great pagoda and two temples by its side. Some days he would go and fish, sitting on a giant boulder on the bank of the river. One day when he had caught a big eel, he brought wine and the eel to the magistrate's home and had his dinner there. Some-times with his son, and sometimes with the local magistrates or with new visitors to the city, Su made repeated trips to the White Water Mountain.

Some of his letters to his brother were delightful. In one, he talked about the barbecued lamb spine that he had invented by necessity.

"Huichow is a small town, but they do kill one lamb a day. As this is intended for the rich, I dare not buy it in competition with the official families. So I ask the butcher only for the spine. There are little morsels of meat around the bones. I boil it in water and take it out and drain it while it is very hot; otherwise, the moisture will remain. Then I soak it in wine and sprinkle a little salt over it before broiling. I chew the thing all day, trying to get at the little

morsels around the joints, and am delighted with it. It is like picking the meat from crabs' claws. I order one every few days and
feel that it has great nutritive value. You have eaten food prepared
by official cooks for the last three years, and I don't think you ever
touched a bone. Do you suppose you can still discover this kind
of flavour, I merely write this down for your amusement, but you
may really try it. I am afraid when barbecued lamb spine becomes
popular, the dogs will be highly displeased."

Su Tungpo's greatest discovery upon arrival at this district was that
there was no wine monopoly and that every family brewed its own
wine. From the time he had his first sip of the cinnamon wine he felt
as if he had found a true friend in this remote region. In many letters
to his friends he praised this wine with its distinctive bouquet. It was
slightly sweet and did not cause a hang-over. It strengthened the vital
spirits and gave one a healthy complexion. In his exorbitant praise in a
poem about this wine, Su Tungpo said that if one drank enough of
it, one felt so light that he could sail the sky and walk upon water.
He learned the formula for making this wine and had it inscribed on
stone and hidden below the Iron Bridge of Lofu so that only seekers
after God could find it.

Su Tungpo wrote at least five or six rhapsodies on the virtues of
liquor. The most interesting one was the "Postscript to the Life of
Tungkaotse." The magistrate of a district on the east had sent him
some wine. He had been reading the life of Tungkaotse, a great
drinker of the Han dynasty. In his letter of thanks to the magistrate,
Su wrote the "Postscript", explaining his drinking habits, and incidentally laying down Two Freedoms which any bad writer can increase
to four, five, or any number he wishes.

"I can consume only one pint a day. There is no one in the world
with less capacity for wine than myself. But I like to see people
drink. When I see my friends lift the cup and slowly slip the liquor
down their throats, I feel exaltation and exhilaration in my breast,
and my joy is greater than even that of my friends. I never pass a day
without visitors, and never have visitors without wine. Consequently
there is also no greater lover of drink in the world than myself.

"It has seemed to me that there is no greater human happiness than
two things, freedom from sickness in the body, and freedom from
worries in the mind. I have neither sickness nor worries, but there
are others who suffer from them. How can I make them happy when
I see them? That is the reason why everywhere I go, I keep some
good medicines and give them to those in need. And I especially love
to brew wine for my friends. Someone might ask: 'You keep

medicine without being sick yourself and brew wine without drinking it. Why do you trouble yourself for others?' I would smile and
reply: 'No, this is all for my own benefit. When patients obtain
medicine, I feel better in my own body, and when drinkers get tipsy,
I feel happier in my own spirit.'

"Tungkaotse served at the palace and received three quarts of wine
per day. His brother once asked him: 'Are you happy serving the
court?' 'What happiness,' replied Tungkaotse, 'is there in serving the
court? But there is considerable attraction in the daily gifts of three
quarts of liquor from the imperial cellar!' There is no government
ban on wine here, and I can brew it at home, obtaining thirteen
gallons from ten bushels of rice. The five magistrates of Kukong,
Canton, Huichow, Shünchow, and Meichow give me presents of
wine from time to time, so that I'm having more than Tungkaotse.
Tungkaotse called himself 'Mr. Ten Gallons', but received only three
quarts a day. He did not have enough for himself, and certainly
could not spare it for his friends. As for me, if I were in his place
and received that amount, two quarts and a half would go into the
stomachs of my rustic friends. Tungkaotse was a friend of Chung-
chang Kuang. He practiced the art of prolonging life and foretold
the day of his death and wrote his own epitaph. I am his friend,
living a thousand years after him. January 13, 1095."

Su Tungpo wrote a dithyrambic verse in praise of liquor. Even to
ne who does not know the pleasure of wine, his description of the
lessed state of half stupefaction sounds convincing.

Praise of Strong Wine

"In men, one should prefer a mild temperament, but in wine, one
need not avoid strong potency. For through such wine, one forgets
one's sorrow as yesternight's dream, and arrives at an understanding
of the truth of the universe. . . . For wine is like a second life to
man. It is often in that state of blissful comfort and luxurious ease
after a drink that one finds one's own soul. True enough, rice and
yeast are ordinary insensate things, and one would not expect that
they would be instrumental in tapping the divine afflatus. But the
mysterious power of this magic potion seems to rival the mysteries of
the universe. It increases one's joy in times of success and keeps one
from harm in times of sorrow. It is cool like the autumn dew and
caressing like the spring wind. One's spirit flushes and flutters like
the glow of the morning sun after the night's clouds have melted
away. One's pores open and one's eyes become bright. . . . He sits
there oblivious of the material world, his spirit becoming expansive

and co-extensive with the universe. Completely at ease, he revels in
the material well-being; fully aware of what is going around him,
yet his mind is idle and free. When the room is full of guests, his
only worry is that the barrels may run out; careless of all posthumous
fame, the only weighty object seems to be that precious cup. You
cannot make nightshirts out of pearls, nor subsist upon jades that
glow in the night. The best food fills your belly, but cannot stimulate
your spirit; the best dress gives you warmth, but cannot delight your
soul. Of all things in the universe, only This One enables you to
transcend the material world. Truly, it is something that one cannot
go without for a day. What is this intoxicating potion which intoxi-
cates you and yet clarifies your mind, which sets you at ease with
yourself and enables you to perceive the ultimate truths of life?"

Su was not only a connoisseur of liquor and a good sampler, he made
his own wines. In his brief period at Tingchow he had experimented
with a kind of wine made with tangerines, and with a pine wine, which
was sweet and slightly bitter. In his dithyramb about this, he mentioned
the boiling of pine resin, but it is not clear how he made the wine. At
Huichow he made cinnamon wine and for the first time tasted a
particular product of south China, *chiutse*. This was rice wine taken
before it was fully fermented and contained very little alcohol; in effect,
it was like souring ale. Once in the introductory note to a poem he
mentioned that while he was straining the wine, he kept on drinking
it until he got dead drunk. In a letter to a friend he gave the formula
for making the "Wine of Divine Unity". This divine wine consisted
of the holy trinity of white flour, glutinous rice, and pure spring water
and it was the colour of jade. The very best quality of wheat flour was
mixed with yeast and was made into yeast cakes which were hung up
to dry for two months. Then he boiled one bushel of rice and after
taking it out and rinsing it under running water, let it stand to dry.
Then he took three ounces of the yeast cake, ground it into a fine
powder, and mixed it thoroughly with the rice. This was then put in
a jar and packed very tightly, leaving a conical depression in the centre.
Some of the yeast powder was reserved to sprinkle on the surface of the
fermenting liquid in the hole at the centre. When sufficient liquid was
formed, the packed rice was cut open and new boiled rice was added to
it at the rate of three pecks for every bushel of the original content,
together with two bowls of boiled water. After three to five days, about
six quarts of good wine were formed, but the length of the period
varied with the weather. In a hot season one should decrease the
amount of yeast by half an ounce.

It is fair to assume that Su Tungpo was a competent dabbler in wine-
making rather than a real expert. Wine-making was merely his hobby.

After his death, Kuo and Mai were frequently asked about their father's formulas for making different kinds of wine, particularly the cinnamon wine constantly mentioned in Su's letters and poems. The sons laughed. "My father loved to experiment with things," said Kuo. "He tried it only once or twice. That cinnamon brew tasted like Tusu wine." Su was perhaps too impatient to be a stubborn experimenter. It is alleged that people who drank his "honey wine" made while at Huangchow used to suffer from temporary diarrhoea.

On April 19, 1095, his female cousin died. Unfortunately her name has not been preserved; Tungpo always referred to her as "cousin-sister" or as "Miss Number Two" (of the Su family). It took three months for the news to reach him in a letter from her husband. That his affection for his cousin had not decreased was shown in a letter to a relative, written a few years earlier, when he said that he regretted not being able to see her at Changchow on a trip. In the last year she and her husband had apparently moved up north to Tingchow where he was governor. Her husband, Liu Chungyuan, was a poor but honest scholar who had not passed his examinations but was deeply interested in the collection of paintings and calligraphy. While Su Tungpo was at the capital, he had visited him, and Su had written and painted several pieces for him. In a letter to Cheng Chihtsai mentioning the news of his cousin's death, Su now told his relative that he "felt torn to pieces", and he wrote to the cousin's son that he felt as if a "knife had been thrust into his heart". Such phrases expressing sorrow were not uncommon in Chinese writing; still, they were expressions of a deeply felt sorrow.

The sacrificial prayer to her, apparently written after receiving the news, showed a deeply personal sentiment. It said that of all the grandchildren of his grandfather, only four had remained. These four were Tungpo, Tseyu, Tse-an (son of his uncle who had stayed at home and looked after the ancestral tomb for the brothers), and the last one, his cousin. She was "a filial daughter and was kind-hearted and refined, good to her mother-in-law and to her husband". Then came a more personal note. He had hoped that her two sons would grow up to glorify the family. "But alas, what have we done to offend the gods? One of them did not live. I was hoping that you would live a hundred years to see the younger generation grow up and carry life on. How was it that in a short moment you were lying groaning in bed? All medicine was of no avail and you passed away like a cloud. Living ten thousand *li* away in a remote region, I heard the news a hundred days after your death. Where is your coffin that I may fall on it and weep? My tears wet the grass on the meadows. Crying aloud in the north wind, I lift and offer this cup to you."

L

A year later her husband died, and their coffins were transported south to their home in the neighbourhood of Chinkiang.

Shortly after his arrival at Huichow, Su Tungpo received a piece of news which rather worried him. In all the forty-two years' time since his elder sister died and his father denounced his brother-in-law's family, he and his brother had neither spoken nor written to their brother-in-law Cheng Chihtsai, although they had kept up correspondence with the other sons of the Cheng family. Learning of this family feud, Chang Chun sent Cheng down south as an inspector of justice to handle outstanding lawsuits and cases of higher appeal. Cheng arrived in Canton in January 1095, only three or four months after Su's arrival. Su could not tell whether Cheng was in a mood to forget the past or what was awaiting him. Through a friend he sent him a letter in the most formal and respectful tone, and learned that Cheng was coming to Huichow in March. To be sure that he was doing the right thing, he sent Kuo to meet him upon his arrival with a letter of welcome, stating that he "had shut himself up to repent of the past". Cheng was an old man by this time, around sixty. It turned out that Cheng himself was most desirous of patching up the quarrel and winning the friendship of his distinguished relative. One of the favours that Cheng asked of him was to write a brief biographical sketch of his ancestor, who was Su Tungpo's great-grandfather on his mother's side. Perhaps blood was thicker than water; perhaps the whole town of Meishan was proud of its great poet, and Cheng shared that sentiment. Thereafter their relationship became really cordial, as evidenced by the many exchanges of letters and poems, and by Su's requests of his brother-in-law. After spending ten days at Huichow, Cheng left on his tour of inspection, but remained mostly around Canton for that year.

Cheng's presence and friendship now turned out to be the means by which Su Tungpo did quite a number of things for the people in this district. Although he was deprived of all rights to attach his name to official communications, he made full use of his influence over Cheng. He had said good-bye to high politics, but the welfare of his neighbours and of the common people of the town was still his business. If there was something wrong and he had some influence to correct it, Su Tungpo could not stand by and do nothing.

A great fire on New Year's Day in 1096 at Poklo greatly excited him. The whole town was burned down. There were relief to be given to the homeless, temporary shelters to be built, looting to be prevented. The government offices were entirely destroyed and had to be rebuilt. Su Tungpo feared the usual would happen. He was afraid that when the government tried to rebuild the city, there would be a chance to exploit the people, and that the local government would levy material and commandeer labour. He asked Cheng to order the local government to obtain material in the open market and forbid levies of labour and material. Otherwise, he pointed out, "the harm done to the people would be greater than the fire itself."

Standing in the streets of Huichow, he saw something that hurt him deeply. He saw the farmers sending cart-loads of grain and corn to the city to pay taxes to the government. Because of good crops, the price of grain had fallen, and the government bureau refused to receive them. This was characteristically Su's business. He made inquiries and found that the government wanted cash, since the price of grain was low. The farmers had to sell the grain at low market price to obtain the cash, but the cash that the farmers had to pay as tax was based on the prices of grain when they were high. The result was that the farmers had to sell two bushels of rice to obtain the cash for what they owed the government on one bushel. He wrote a long letter to Cheng, like those argumentative, impetuous letters he used to write to the Empress Dowager, exposing this practice for what it was—one-hundred-per-cent extortion from the peasants. He requested that Cheng arrange a conference with the tax commissioner and the transportation commissioner in the district, and propose to the government that the people should be taxed according to the current price of grain. Months later, he was happy to learn that the three commissioners had decided to sign a joint petition to the government.

He began now to be interested in the reform and improvement of the city. Following his instinct for construction, through a conference with Cheng and the district and county magistrates he had two bridges built, one across the river and one across the lake at Huichow. To the building of these bridges Tseyu's wife contributed a number of golden coins that she had received from the court. While engaged in this work, he did one thing that was specially appreciated by the populace, namely, the building of a great mound to rebury the skeletons found in owner-less graves. After the skeletons were reinterred, he wrote a sacrificial prayer to these unknown dead. He was sure they were either common people or soldiers. He regretted the fact that some of the skeletons were incomplete and that he had to put them all together in a common grave, but hoped that the spirits would live together in peace like members of a family. He also had a fish preserve built near the lake west of the city. This was a strictly Buddhist institution based on the theory of reincarnation and the belief that many of the fish may have been human beings before. Once let into this preserve, the fish were safe for their lives. This lake became known as "Su Tungpo's Let-Live Lake", and down to the nineteenth century the scholars and people of the district still kept up this custom of buying a few fish to loose them into the lake on festival days.

He was always interested in little things. One novelty that had fascinated him years before, when he was in confinement at Huang-chow, was a farmers' device, called a "floating horse", used at the time of planting seedlings in rice-fields. Planting rice was always a back-breaking task, the farmers having to wade in the flooded fields and bend over their work all day. The floating horse was a device like a small float upon which the farmers could sit while planting, and move about by using their legs as paddles, while the horse's head served as a receptacle for holding the seedlings. It speeded up the work and lessened the labour. He wanted to introduce it to the south. He was so enthusiastic about it that he recommended it in many of the letters he wrote to his friends. Sending a magistrate to his new post, he told him to introduce the floating horse and advised him that the secret of success as a magistrate lay in behaving so that "the people would not be afraid of the officials".

Shorn of his power and *persona non grata* with the ruling regime, Su Tungpo had outgrown his young ambition to make his "emperor the best", or to change the destiny of an empire. He was just a plain citizen of Huichow, and his problems were the problems of his neighbours, Mr. Chai and Mrs. Lin, an old woman wine-brewer who let him have wine on credit. His friends were the Taoists Wu Fuku and Lu Weichien and the Buddhist priests of Lofu. He had many friends among the scholars and magistrates.

He could not be a public servant, but he could still be a public-minded citizen. Canton, the capital of the province, was near-by, and the magistrate Wang Ku was his friend. Aware of the frequent epidemics at Canton, Su wrote to Wang Ku to have a fund provided for the founding of a public hospital, as he had done at Hangchow. The people of Canton, too, like the people of Hangchow, were suffer-ing from bad drinking water, which was one of the causes of disease in the city. A Taoist monk he knew had a complete plan for guiding mountain water to the city of Canton. There was one good well in the city, available only to the officials. However, seven miles out, there was good spring water on a very much higher level than the city itself. Su recommended the Buddhist priest's plan to Wang Ku and suggested the construction of water mains to guide this spring water into Canton. These mains could be made of large sections of bamboo, which grew abundantly in eastern Kwangtung. A great stone reservoir was to be built at the mountain spring and five bamboo pipe-lines were to carry the water from the mountain to another big stone reservoir in the city. Su Tungpo went into considerable detail about the pipe-lines, which he had known in his own province. Hemp cords were used to join the sections and these were then coated with a heavy layer of lacquer to make them leakproof. At every section a small hole was made and then stopped with a bamboo peg, for the purpose of inspection of the different sections when any part should be clogged up. He estimated that something over ten thousand large bamboos would be sufficient for the purpose. But these bamboo sections had to be inspected constantly and periodically replaced, like modern railroad ties. Officers should be appointed for the constant supervision of the pipe lines and requisitions should be made for an annual supply of bamboo from the eastern districts for the replacements. Afraid of causing trouble for his friend, he asked Wang Ku to let no one know that the idea came from him, for he was out of favour with the ruling regime. But Wang Ku was later cashiered for "giving famine relief without justification".

Chapter Twenty-six

ROMANCE WITH CHAOYUN

THE story of Su Tungpo at Huichow is popularly associated with his romance with Chaoyun. After the poet's death, his residence on White Stork Hill was preserved as Chaoyun Memorial. Wang Chaoyun was the girl of Hangchow whose infant son's death had saddened the journey back from his first exile, who had been living with him since and now had followed him to exile again. Chin Kuan's poem to her said that her beauty was like that of a garden in spring and her eyes were like the light of the dawn. She was yet young, being only thirty-one when she arrived at Huichow. Su himself was then fifty-seven, but their great disparity of age did not seem to make any difference. She was intelligent, gay, vivacious, spirited. Of all the women in Su's life, she seemed to understand him best. She adored the poet and tried to grow to her husband's spiritual level. Su Tungpo not only recorded his gratitude to the woman who shared his exile in his old age, but he honoured her with poems that elevated their passion into a high companionship in the quest for immortal life.

Su Tungpo always referred to Chaoyun as the celestial maiden of *Vimalakirti* ("Name Undefiled"), a classic bearing the name of an early Buddhist. In the classic, there was a story that when Buddha was living at a certain town in the form of a forest sage, he had a discussion one day with his disciples. From up in the sky appeared a celestial maiden who dropped flower petals down on the company below. The petals that fell on the boddhisattvas all slipped off to the ground, except those that fell on one person. The petals clung to his dress and could not be brushed off no matter how hard the others tried. "Why do you try to brush off the petals from this person?" asked the celestial maiden, and some of them said: "These petals are not in accordance with dharma, the law of the Buddha. That's why they cling to his dress." "No," said the celestial spirit, "these petals are not at fault, but rather the person to whom they cling. If believers who join the church still retain the sense of discrimination between individual beings, they act or think contrary to the dharma. If they abolish all the discriminations, then they live in accordance with the dharma. These boddhisattvas to whom the flower petals cannot cling have already achieved the aboli-tion of all sense discriminations. It is like fear; fear does not invade a man's heart unless he is already afraid. If the disciples love this life and are afraid of death, then the senses of sight, hearing, smell, taste, and touch have a chance to deceive them. One who has conquered fear stands above all the senses."

Su wrote two poems to Chaoyun in the year of their arrival. The poems were remarkable in that the sentiment of love was blended with the sentiment of religion. In the first poem, written within two weeks of his arrival, he paid tribute to her by saying that she was not like Hsiao Man, the concubine of Po Chuyi, who left him in his old age, but was like Tungteh, who remained with Ling Yuan all his life. He regretted the fact that the child she had borne did not grow up, but praised her as a celestial maiden of Vimalakirti in the service of God. Throwing aside the long-sleeved dancing dress of the past, she was now occupied with Buddhist sutras and the pill furnace. When the pill should be formed, she was going to say good-bye to him and enter the fairy mountains. No longer would she be like the fairy maiden of the Wu Gorges, tied to a mortal union.

The sublimation of the love passion to a religious level was even more apparent in the second poem, which contains a curious mixture of sensuous love and religious elevation.

> "When time's due course doth age with white hair crown,
> And Vimalakirti so well doth one become,
> Fear not the flower petals that do no harm,
> Though the heavenly maiden scatters them around.
> Thy cherry lips woo, and thy hair glorifies,
> So this eternal cycle of life goes on,
> Because this sentient heart of love is fond,
> Engenders human gestures and mortal ties.
> I see thee sit with a sweetly pensive smile,
> Setting thy curls, or letting them archly fall.
> Tomorrow is Tuanwu Day! Come, I shall
> Pick thee a corsage of orchids, with a poet's wile
>   Discover the best poem that can be found,
>   And write it on the flowing lines of thy gown."

Chaoyun also was interested in the Taoist art of prolonging life. In Huichow, Su felt that now was the time to take up again seriously the quest for the elixir of immortality. During his Huichow period he called his studio the "Studio of Clean Thinking", whether he was living on the right or the left bank. The choice of the name for a studio by a scholar is usually intended to express or sum up in one or two words a philosophy of life. Su Tungpo had arrived at a point where he believed not only in simple living and clean thinking, but that clean thinking was the basis for simple living. The idea of achieving control of the mind as the basis for long life and the road to immortality was his way of uniting the truths taught by Confucianism, Taoism, and Buddhism. The inscription he wrote on this "Studio of Clean Think-

ing", however, suggested more than that. It indicated a serious attempt
to form the "internal pill" of immortality in the lower part of his
abdomen. This was one of the inscriptions in rhyme of which the poet
himself was very proud; but couched in the mystic language of the
secret Taoist art, it would be unintelligible in an English translation
without lengthy footnotes. Briefly, he spoke of absorbing the vital
spirits of food and drink and the essence of herbs and plants which,.
helped by lead and quicksilver, were to nourish the vital principle. It
was to be aided by exposure to the morning sun and bathing in the
moonlight. The pill that he expected to form was the "pill of clean
thinking". He believed the time was just right. In a separate note in
his journal, he remarked that the poet Po Chuyi had also tried to carry
on experiments on the elixir but had failed. Po had built a country
house with a furnace on top of the Lushan, but the furnace and the
boiler broke down on the day before he received his appointment to
an office. This shows that the quest for the eternal life and for temporal
honours could not be carried on at the same time. One had to make up
one's mind either to live an active life in this world or to escape from
it and become an immortal. Now, Su was convinced he had said good-
bye to temporal honours and he was hopeful of success in the quest for
the eternal life.

Just how seriously he believed in the possibility of forming the pill
of immortality in his abdomen it is not possible to say. He was a keen
observer, and although he always played with such mysteries of the art
as the taking of mercury compounds, he began to see that the basis of
good health consisted in following a few simple rules of common sense.
In a note which he presented to the tubercular Taoist Lu, he said: "The
basis of this art lies in strengthening one's bodily vitality, in achieving
mental stability, and in cultivating peace of mind", plus such advantages
and exercises as the Taoists living on mountain-tops were able to enjoy,
and modern patients are able to enjoy in a sanatorium, namely, the
drinking of spring water and exposure to the morning sun.

In yet another curious way Chaoyun was to co-operate in Su's quest
for immortality. From about the beginning of 1095 Su Tungpo began
to sleep alone. "There is no secret to the art of prolonging life," he
wrote to a friend. "If one sleeps alone and controls one's passions, one's
vitality is naturally restored." In another letter to Chang Lei, he said
that he had slept alone for a year and a half, and had felt its good
benefits. He said continence was as difficult as the refusing of meat by
a beginning vegetarian, and recommended the following method: For
instance, when one decided to eat no more meat, one should not make
a resolution never to eat it. He should first try for a three-month period,
which was easier to carry out. At the end of the three months one
could extend it another three months, and so on.

Chaoyun was confronted with a religious dilemma. She had become a Buddhist, under the tutorship of Bikkuni (Sister) Ichung. On this question of sex, Buddhism is specific. Buddhist metaphysics assumes quite correctly that the world we perceive by the senses is all illusion, and that the ultimate reality is God, or the world soul. Our consciousness is encrusted with habits of perception, and salvation comes from an effort of understanding to break away from these perceptual habits and to escape the illusions of the sensory world. Su Tungpo and Chaoyun, who may be properly regarded as his wife now, were both Buddhist believers, in spite of what Confucian critics may say. Together they had built the fish sanctuary in the lake, and according to Su Tungpo's testimony she liked to practise charity, which was taught by Buddhism.

But Su Tungpo was called on to practise even greater severity. In the latter part of 1095 he suffered acutely from piles and lost a great deal of blood. He was his own doctor. He had not only read all the authorities on Chinese medicine, but frequently wrote notes on distinguishing varieties of plants often confused by others. His theory about piles was that there was a worm inside which had been gnawing away at his body, and his natural remedy was to "starve out the guest by starving the host himself". He denied himself all ordinary foods, including rice, and ate only unsalted wheat cakes and Indian bread. After doing this for several months, he recovered temporarily.

Meanwhile he was getting more sceptical of his success in forming the pill of immortality. He found that he was too easily involved emotionally to become an immortal. He wrote his brother about the proper way for preserving cinnabar, and remarked that Tseyu had a more tranquil disposition and was therefore more likely to succeed. In a poem about the *Shanhaiching,* an ancient work telling of fabulous creatures in remote countries, he said: "The quest for the elixir has failed. How can I hope to live in those remote regions?" Even if the pill was formed, of what use would it be? It was enough to control the vital liquids by practising deep breathing, and this he was already doing.

He was still uncertain of his future. Upon his first arrival he had mentioned that he was ready to make Huichow his home. On the other hand, he could never tell where he might be sent next. If he were to settle permanently at Huichow, he would build a house there and send for his children's families from Ishing. In September of 1095 there was a sacrifice to the ancestors of the emperor, and according to custom a general amnesty was granted on such an occasion. Quite late that year he learned that all the Yuanyu officials had been excluded from this benefit. The news had at least the value of a sedative because it enabled him to feel more settled. "From the development of recent events," he wrote to Cheng, "it seems there is no hope of my returning north. But I feel quite at peace. It is not necessary to philosophise about the vicissitudes of human life. From a very matter-of-fact point of view, I can just imagine myself to be a scholar candidate from Hui-chow who has failed in the examinations and decides to live in his home town for life. What's wrong with that?" In his letter to his good friend Sun Shieh he said: "Since all hope of return to the north was cut off, I have begun to regard myself as a native of Huichow." To Tsao Fu he wrote: "I have read the recent news that the Yuanyu officials will for ever be excluded from reappointment to office. It gives me a feeling of security at this place and I am willing to take what comes. Now I am exactly like a mendicant friar, except that I eat meat and drink wine."

Now that all was final, he decided to build his house. Late that year he wrote a long letter to Wang Kung. "I have been here for eight months, accompanied by my youngest son and some maidservants, and am feeling quite comfortable. Since I have been relieved of all official duties, I feel at peace in mind and body. My son also takes a poetic view of life. Indeed he is a chip from the old block. Ha ha! I hear from Tseyu quite constantly and learn that he is well satisfied there. Whether one lives north or south has all been predetermined. Nor do I have the desire to return north. Next year I shall buy a farm and build a house and then settle down as a citizen of Huichow."

In March of the following year, therefore, Su Tungpo began to build his house on top of a hill standing forty feet above the east bank of the river, quite close to the Kweishan city wall. Through periodic wars and devastations this house has been preserved down to this day and is known as the Chaoyun Memorial. Known in Su's works as "the house on the White Stork Hill", it commanded a wonderful view of the river on the north side where the water turned north-eastward. Situated on a small plot of land about half an acre wide, and strictly confined by the hill at its back and by sharp descent below, the plan of the house had to suit the limited flat area available, wider at one end than at the other. Two small houses already stood there on the city wall side, owned by Mr. Chai and the old woman wine-brewer known as Mrs. Lin, who were neighbours and close friends. He dug a well forty feet deep which also greatly benefited Chai and Mrs. Lin. On the other hand, Su Tungpo could obtain wine on credit. Later, when he was sent away from this place, he still kept on sending presents to this old woman.

The house was quite elaborate, containing a total of twenty "rooms", a room being a unit of space in the Chinese language. On the small vacant space on the south side he planted oranges, pumelos, lichi,

Chinese strawberries, loquat, and a few cypresses and gardenias. He told a local magistrate who was helping him to procure these fruit and flower trees to get medium-sized ones, for he was already old and could not wait for young trees to grow up, and really big trees would be difficult to transplant. In the case of the bigger trees Su Tungpo told his friend to mark the points of the compass before removing them from their original site. The Chinese way of removing a big tree was to cut one of its main roots and the centre root first, and cover the roots again with earth, thus giving the tree time to readjust itself. In the second year the main root on the opposite side would be cut and again covered up. In the third year, after marking the directions on the four sides of the trunk, the tree was removed, and at the time of transplanting care was taken that the tree faced the same way as it did in the original site. Su's "Studio of Clean Thinking" was there on White Stork Hill, and he named another hall the "Hall of Having Neighbours by Virtue". This comes from a saying by Confucius that a moral man is never without good neighbours wherever he goes. It happened that both these studio names consisted of four words, whereas studio names usually consisted of three. Su Tungpo's use of four-word names for his studio started this fashion in his time. The neighbours' houses were on the north-east behind his house and were completely shut out by Su Tungpo's residence. His front door on the north looked out on the river and commanded a superb view of the whole country for miles, including the great range of the White Water Mountain and the more distant Lofu Mountain.

His poem written on the ceremony of raising the main beam described well the views in all directions from this house. The raising of the beam, equivalent to the laying of the foundation-stone, was quite an occasion for the community. All his neighbours gathered and brought chickens and pork to the celebration. The song, written for popular singing, was in six verses all beginning with a phrase like "Anchors Aweigh", or like the "heigh ho" in Shakespeare's poems.

> "Erlang Weigh! Haul the beam to the east," etc.
> "Erlang Weigh! Haul the beam to the west," etc.

The six verses dealt with the views from the four points of the compass, plus the view above and the view below. Uphill on the east, a Buddhist temple nestled beneath a tall forest, from which came the sound of temple bells while he enjoyed his sweet sleep in spring. Looking down towards the west, he could see the arched bridge spanning the emerald stream, and when the magistrate in the city came to visit him at night, he could see the lights shining along the long embankment. On the south, ancient trees cast their shade on the deep, clear river, and there were two orange trees in his orchard that he had planted himself. His best view was towards the north where the river hugged the foot of the mountain as it wound its way towards the city. Near-by on the bank, there was a favourite place for fishing where he could play by the water all morning without being aware of the passing of time.

He called for the blessing of the gods and prayed that the farmers' granaries might always be full and there might be no storms upon the sea. With the clean air of the country, the people would be always in good health, and with good crops, the wine of Mrs. Lin could always be obtained on credit. The song ended with a prayer of blessing on all his friends, that they might enjoy good luck and long life.

But deep personal sorrow now befell Su Tungpo. On July 5, 1095, before their new house was completed, Chaoyun died of a kind of epidemic disease. This was a malarial region, and she could have died of malaria. Su's son Kuo was away from home getting lumber for the new house, and she was not buried till August 3. A devout Buddhist, she said a Buddhist *gatha* (verse) from the *Diamond Sutra* before she drew her last breath.

"This earthly life may be likened to a dream,
It may be likened to a bubble;
It may be likened to the dew and lightning,
For all sentient life must be so regarded."

In accordance with her wish, she was buried at the foothill around the Feng Lake, west of the city, near a pagoda and several Buddhist temples. Behind the grave, mountain streams fell in cataracts and flowed into the lake. The grave was in a secluded recess where the hill slope fell in different ridges, like the folds of a garment. Immediately at the back was a great pine forest, and while standing at the grave, one could see the top of the pagoda beyond the ridge on the west. To the right and left, within a distance of two-thirds of a mile, lay the big temples, and visitors could hear the temple bells at dusk and the song of the pine winds. The monks of the neighbouring temples put up the money to build a pavilion in her honour on top of the grave.

Three days after her burial, on August 6, there was a heavy rain-storm at night, and on the following day the farmers saw giant footprints in the neighbourhood of the grave. The belief was that some Buddhist saint had come to accompany Chaoyun's spirit on her voyage to Western Heaven. On August 9, there was to be a mass in the night, and before the ceremony, Su Tungpo and his son personally went to inspect the saint's footprints.

Su Tungpo's love for Chaoyun was recorded not only in the epitaph but also in two poems that he wrote shortly after her death. The poem

"In Memoriam" expressed his deep regret that her child had died young and that, unfortunately, there was no magic to stay the march of time. For his funeral gift, he could only extend the comfort of a Hinayana prayer. She had come to this world perhaps to pay a debt she had owed in a previous life, and now, in the twinkling of an eye, she had departed, perhaps for a better life hereafter. The saint's pagoda was near-by, and every night at dusk she could go and seek solace in the holy companionship.

Previously Su Tungpo had written three exquisite poems that displayed his full poetic powers on two plum trees near the Pine Wind Pavilion. In October of that year the plum flower blossomed again. Once more he wrote a poem on the flower, using it clearly as a symbol of Chaoyun, now lying in the grave. The symbol was appropriate because the white flower in the glamour of the moonlight had always been spoken of as a white-gowned fairy, dim and hazy in appearance and hardly to be associated with the life of the common world. He clothed the poem in such language that it could be read both as a poem to the flower and as a poem in honour of the woman he loved.

> "Bones of jade, flesh of snow,
> May thy ethereal spirit stand unafraid,
> Though the dark mist and the swamp wind blow.
> May the sea sprites attend thee,
> The paroquets and cockatoos befriend thee.
> Thy white face doth powder spurn;
> Vermilion must yet from thy lips learn.
> Flesh of snow, bones of jade,
> Dream thy dreams, peerless one.
> Not for this world thou art made."

Feng Lake had been Su Tungpo's favourite picnic ground. After her burial, he could not bear to visit it again. He had buried her in holy ground, and the fish sanctuary they had built together below would be a comforting sight for her spirit to look upon.

From now on, Su Tungpo lived as a widower. His house was completed in February of the following year, his orchard was planted, the well was dug, and Mai had brought Kuo's family and his own to Huichow. The second son, Tai, had remained with his family at Ishing because Su Tungpo had placed high hopes on him and wanted him to prepare for the imperial examinations. Along with two sons and daughters-in-law came three grandchildren, two children belonging to Mai, and one belonging to Kuo. The eldest grandson was already twenty and married, while the second grandson, Fu, was of marriageable age and Su Tungpo arranged to have him married to one of

Tseyu's grand-daughters, daughter of the deceased Wang Shih, Tseyu's son-in-law.

The building of the house had used up almost all the money he had, and he was counting on the small salary of Mai, who, by some arrangement, had been appointed magistrate near Kukong.

Then suddenly, just as Tungpo felt he could settle down in his old age as a native of Huichow, he was exiled outside the mainland of China. The order for his farther removal to the island of Hainan came about two months after the completion of his new house. According to one story, he had written two lines describing his beautiful nap in the spring wind, listening to the temple bells at the back of the house. When Chang Chun read the verse, he remarked: "So! Tungpo is having a good time!" Thereupon the order for the new exile was issued.

Chapter Twenty-seven

OUTSIDE CHINA

HAINAN was an island then under the Chinese empire, but inhabited chiefly by the Loi aborigines, with a sprinkling of Chinese settlers on the northern coast. Su Tungpo was there exiled beyond the pale of the Chinese civilised world. Of all the hundreds of victims of the regime, he was the only one to be sent to this place. Determined to prevent a come-back of the Yuanyu officials, the government ordered, in this and the following years, sweeping banishments and punishments for all those connected with the previous regime. The order for the banishment of Su Tungpo shortly preceded the depriving of all offices and ranks of the children of Szema Kuang and the transfer of a large number of the highest officials, including Tseyu and Fan Chunien, to other places in southern and south-western China. Even the old Wen Yenpo, who was now ninety-one, was not spared, but was deprived of several of his ranks. What hit Su Tungpo most closely was the order that the relatives of such exiled officials might not hold offices in neighbouring districts. As Mai was to be a county magistrate near Kukong, he also lost his job.

The house was about all that Su Tungpo had now. He had a total of $200 provincial money or $150 in the currency of the capital, owed him by the government for three years' service at his nominal rank. The salary had not been paid and Su wrote to his good friend the chief magistrate of Canton to use his good offices to have payment made by the tax commissioner. This friend, Wang Ku, who had followed Su Tungpo's suggestion in building a hospital and giving relief to the poor, was, however, shortly dismissed for "giving relief without justification", as mentioned before, and there is no record whether Su's claim was ever paid or not.

He was now sixty years old, according to Western reckoning. There was no telling how long his exile was going to be, and the chances were against his returning to China alive. The two sons accompanied him as far as Canton and Mai said farewell to him on the bank of the river, while Kuo, leaving his own family behind at Huichow, went with him to Hainan. In order to reach his destination, Su had to go up the Western River, journeying hundreds of miles, to Wuchow, in what is modern Kwangsi, and then turn south to cross the sea from the Luichow Peninsula. When he reached Wuchow, he learned that his brother had just passed the town on his way to his new place of confinement on that peninsula. One story based on conjecture says that the two Su brothers were banished to these two districts because

Chang Chun thought it was fun to send them to districts whose names bore component parts contained in the respective personal names of the Su brothers. Tseyu, too, had brought along his wife and his third son and daughter-in-law, who had been living with him in the preceding years at Kao-an.

At Tenchow, a short distance from Wuchow, Su Tungpo caught up with his brother. They met now under sad circumstances. It was a poor district and the two brothers went into a small eating-place for lunch. Tseyu had been used to good food, and could not touch the very bad wheat cakes sold at the shop. Tungpo finished his cake in a few bites and said laughingly to his brother: "Are you going to take time to chew this delicacy slowly?" They rose and left the shop and went along slowly together with their families on the way to their destinations, taking as much time as they dared, because Su Tungpo knew that as soon as they arrived at Luichow, he would have to depart at once to go beyond the sea.

The magistrate of Luichow was a great admirer of the Su brothers. He gave them a grand reception and sent food and wine to them—and was consequently impeached the following year and removed from his office. The house where Tseyu stopped at Luichow eventually became the temple, or memorial, to the Su brothers, after their death.

Tungpo had to leave, and Tseyu accompanied him to the coast. On the evening of departure the two brothers and their sons spent the night in the boat. Su Tungpo was again suffering from piles and was in pain, and Tseyu tried to persuade him to give up liquor. Part of the time they spent versifying, and Su tried out the skill of Tseyu's young son in verse-making. It was a sad parting, a farewell for life, and they sat up all night. Before his departure Su had written to Wang Ku as follows: "I am now proceeding to my place of exile in a barbarian country in my old age. There is no hope of my returning alive. I have said good-bye to my eldest son, Mai, and have given him instructions about my burial. As soon as I arrive at Hainan, the first thing to do will be to make a coffin, and the second to make a grave. I left a note to my children that when I die I am to be buried where I shall be, beyond the China Sea. It will become the family tradition of Tungpo that in life he does not bring his family along in his travels, and in death he does not require his children to transport the coffin home."

That day he had prayed to a human god. There was a temple to two old Chinese generals who had conquered the south of China. Travellers who wanted to cross the treacherous sea at this point always consulted the oracle at this temple on the propitious day for sailing. It was found that the oracle had always been a good weather prophet, and Su Tungpo followed the usual custom.

On June 11, 1097, at dawn, the brothers said good-bye and Su Tungpo embarked with his young son and some soldiers that the Luichow magistrate had sent along to attend him on the journey. It was only a short voyage, and on that clear day Tungpo could see the dim outlines of the mountains of the island appearing on the horizon. He was profoundly moved. The sea held no fascination for him as it has for many Western poets. In fact, he was "frightened out of his wits". But they had a safe crossing. After landing, Su and his son travelled to their destination at Tanchow on the north-western corner of the island, arriving on July 2.

Soon after his arrival a very good county official, Chang Chung, arrived. He was not only an admirer of the poet but also a great chess player, and a strong friendship developed between Chang Chung and Kuo. They used to play chess all day together while Su Tungpo watched. Through Chang's kindness Su was put up at an official building next to Chang's living-quarters. It was, however, a shabby little place, and when the autumn rains came, the roof leaked, so that Su had to change his bed from one place to another during the night. As this was a government building, Chang had the rooms repaired at government expense, which later got him into trouble.

The island was all but uninhabitable from the Chinese point of view. The climate was very damp, oppressive in summer and foggy in winter. During the autumn rains everything grew mouldy, and Su Tungpo once saw a great number of white ants dead on his bedposts. The unhealthy climate provoked reflections on prolonging life. This was what he wrote:

"The climate in south China is damp and in summer the humid swampy atmosphere rises from the ground. This is especially true of Hainan. Between the end of summer and the beginning of autumn, everything rots. How can a human being, who is not made of rocks or metals, stand this for long? But I see many old people here over a hundred years old, not to speak of those who are eighty or ninety. It occurs to me that a long life depends merely on adjustment to the surroundings. A salamander can live in the fire and silkworms' eggs can be preserved on ice. Sometimes by mental control I keep my mind a blank and make my consciousness transcend the material existence, whether it be in freezing cold or under a scorching sun. In this way, it shouldn't be difficult to live to over a hundred years. The illiterate old peasants here know nothing of this secret; they calmly get adjusted to the climate like the salamanders and the silkworms. Why shouldn't they live a long life if they just keep on breathing in the cold air and breathing out the warm air in continuous succession? Indeed, what Chuangtse said

is right: 'The days and nights are continuously causing our destruction by using up our energy. The great thing is to prevent this
waste.' "

Behind the coastal towns the island was inhabited by the Loi tribes,
whose relations with the Chinese settlers were far from cordial. The
tribes lived in the tropical mountains which, in a later day, served the
Japanese army for training in jungle warfare for some years before
the Pearl Harbour attack. The natives did not know any writing, but
were simple, honest souls, often cheated by the more cunning and
civilised Chinese. They were lazy at farming and depended on hunting for food. As in some parts of Szechuen and Fukien, it was the
women who did the work while the men stayed indoors to look after
the babies. The Loi women chopped firewood from the jungle and
carried it to town for sale. All metal utensils such as axes and knives,
all grains and cloth, salt and pickles were imported from China, and
they traded for these things by offering turtle-shells and aloes wood,
which was a costly incense extensively used in China. Even rice had
to be imported from the mainland, for the native inhabitants ate taro
and drank water for their meals, the food that Su Tungpo also had
to take in winter when the ships carrying rice from China did not
arrive.

The people were highly superstitious, and a medicine-man looked
after the diseases instead of a doctor. The only way the islanders knew
to cure a disease was to pray at the temples and offer cows in sacrifice.
As a result a great number of cows were imported annually from the
mainland to be slaughtered for this purpose. As a Buddhist, Su Tungpo
tried to change this custom, but of course customs could not be changed
easily. He wrote:

"The people of south China think nothing of killing cows, and
this is especially true of Hainan. Merchants transport these cows, a
hundred in a ship, to the island. Sometimes they die of thirst and
hunger on the voyage, or perish in a storm. When the cows embark
on a ship, they moo pitifully and shed tears. After they arrive, half
of them are used for tilling the fields and half of them for slaughter.
When the people fall sick, they do not take medicine but slaughter
cows as sacrifices to the gods, and sometimes a rich family will kill
several dozen cows in the hope of curing a disease. Whenever a
patient gets well, they give credit to the priests, but forget about all
those who fail to recover and die. The priests, therefore, are their
doctors and the cows are their medicines. Sometimes when a patient
takes medicine, and is found out by the priest, the priest will tell
him that the gods are angry at him. So they allow the patient to

die. The relatives of the sick reject medicines and ban doctors from their houses until both the patient and the cows are dead. The island produces aloes wood, but this is paid for by the Chinese merchants by offering cows in barter. As soon as the Loi tribes get hold of a cow, they sacrifice it to the spirits and none can escape. How can the Chinese people possibly get blessing from the gods by burning this incense in their prayer, when they are actually roasting beef?"

The Chinese had never been able to subjugate the jungle dwellers. When an army approached, the tribesmen merely retired to the jungles, and the Chinese did not push farther because no one cared to live or settle in the mountains. The tribesmen staged occasional raids into the towns when there was a quarrel. Sometimes they were cheated by a Chinese trader, and, unable to obtain justice by appearing in a Chinese court, their only resort was to capture him and hold him for ransom in order to recover the money. Kuo later wrote a long essay of two thousand words on this situation and showed that there was no way of subjugating or pacifying the natives except by fair play and a strict administration of justice. The natives, Kuo contended, were good, honest people, and they were driven to taking the law into their own hands only because the Chinese courts could not render them justice.

This was real exile, imposing bodily hardships on the old man. According to him, there was just nothing obtainable on the island. "We eat here without meat, get sick without medicine, seek shelter without houses, go out without friends, go through winter without charcoal, and through summer without cold springs. I cannot enumerate all the things that we have to do without. In short, we lack almost everything. There is only one consolation, and that is, we also lack malaria here."

But his indomitable spirit and his philosophy of life hardly permitted him to lose his joy of living. "I have still this material body left, which I have confided to the care of the Creator. I let it go through the eternal cycle, going and stopping wherever the fates decree. So I am at ease whatever happens. Don't worry on account of me," he wrote to a friend.

What exasperated Chang Chun and other enemies of Su Tungpo was that they could do nothing to him. On September 12, 1098, he wrote an item in his diary commenting on his predicament as follows:

"When I first arrived at the South Sea and saw a complete circle of water on the horizon, I felt disheartened and sighed: 'When shall I be able to get off this island?' But then I thought: the universe itself is surrounded by water. The Nine Continents are situated in the Great Ing Ocean, and China is situated in the Lesser Ocean.

There is not a time in our life when we are not living upon an island. Imagine that you pour some water on the ground. A little blade of grass floats on top of it, and upon this blade an ant is clinging for his life. The ant does not know what to do. In a little while the water dries up and the ant crawls away safely. Meeting other ants, it says with tears in its eyes: 'Alas I never thought I would see you again!' How could the ant know that in the twinkling of an eye it would be able to go wherever it wants? It amuses me to think of this idea. I am writing this after a little sip with some friends."

Su Tungpo was either stubborn, or else he was truly in possession of himself. At least he never lost his sense of humour. The monk Tsanliao sent an acolyte to Hainan to see him, with a letter and presents, and proposed to come himself and visit this poet. In reply Su Tungpo wrote: "I have been in this place over half a year and can somehow get along. I need not go into the details. Think of me as a monk who has been driven out of the Lingying Temple and is now living in a small cottage, eating simple peasant meals! I can live my life this way to the end of my days. As to malaria and other diseases, are there not diseases also in the north? One can die of all kinds of diseases and not of malaria only. It is true, there are no doctors around this place, but think how many people are annually killed by doctors at the capital! I know you will laugh when you read this, and cease to worry about me. When friends ask about me, just tell them what I have said."

Perhaps his attitude towards life in the island was best illustrated by a note in his journal written in the last year of his exile.

"This is January 15, 1099, the Festival of Shangyuan. I am living at Tanchow. Several old scholars have come to visit me. Kuo said: 'Father, can you come out for a stroll? There is such a beautiful moon and the night is so calm.' Happily I accepted the suggestion and we all went out to the western part of the town and entered a temple. We passed through small alleys filled with the Chinese and the tribesmen. There was quite a crowd at the wine shops. By the time we returned, it was already midnight, and the servants were snoring in their sleep. Thinking that fortune and adversity were all the same, I laid my cane behind the door and laughed. 'What are you laughing at, Father?' Kuo asked. 'I was laughing at myself and at Han Yu,' I replied. 'Han Yu was once fishing. He could not catch any fish, and thought he could catch them by going to another place. He did not know that by going to the sea, one does not necessarily catch big fish!' "

Su Tungpo had once said to his brother: "Up above I can associate with the Supreme Ruler of Heaven, and down on earth, I can associate with poor folks. In my mind, there is not a single bad man in this world." Now he was associated with humble, unknown scholars and peasant men and women. He did not have to be guarded in his speech with these simple people, and he was completely free and at his best. He could not pass a day without having visitors in his home, and if he did not, he had to go out and call on his neighbours. As during his period at Huangchow, he mixed with high and low, scholars and peasants. During conversations he usually took the floor; he simply loved to talk. But he also wanted others to talk. Followed by his big dog "Black Snout", a Hainan breed, he wandered where he liked. Sitting under the *pinlang* palms with the good villagers, he wanted a good chat. What could the poor ignorant peasants say to him? "We don't know what to talk about," said the peasants, awed by this learned scholar. "Then talk about ghosts. Come, tell me some ghost stories," said Su Tungpo. His interlocutors would say that they didn't know any good ghost stories, and he said: "Never mind, just tell me anything you've heard." Later Kuo told his friends that if his father failed to receive visitors for a day, he would feel as if something ailed him.

But he was not yet to be left quite in peace even in this remote region. The year 1098 was one when the persecution of the Yuanyu scholars was raging at its height. Towards New Year's Eve, 1097, two of the highest Yuanyu officials died within a week of one another under suspicious circumstances. In spring the children of the two officials who had died were also imprisoned, and the private secretary of the Empress Dowager was condemned to death. Again there was a whole-sale transfer of the banished officials to different places. Among those who were transferred in the summer of the year were Tseyu, Chin Kuan, and Cheng Shia, the palace gatekeeper who, we remember, had succeeded in ousting Wang Anshih from the premiership.

In March the curious Taoist Wu Fuku turned up in Hainan again, to remain with Su Tungpo for several months. He brought with him the message that the court had sent Tung Pi to make a report upon, and if necessary prosecute, the exiled officials. Tanchow belonged at that time in Kwangsi province, and at first Lu Shengching, brother of the notorious Huiching and bitter enemy of the Yuanyu officials, was to be sent to this province. It meant sure disaster, if not death, for the Su brothers. Tseng Pu and another official intervened and warned the Emperor that to send Shengching would only be to encourage private vengeance, since he could not be expected to make an impartial report. It would mean that the government was willing to do the extreme. On account of this intercession, Shengching was sent down to Kwang-tung, while Tung Pi was sent to Kwangsi. Sure enough, Tung Pi found that something was quite wrong; he reported that Tseyu had occupied people's homes by force and that the magistrate of Luichow had generously entertained and looked after an exiled person. The magistrate was cashiered and Tseyu was transferred to a district east of Huichow, where Su Tungpo had once been confined.

Tung Pi was descending like a plague from the Luichow Peninsula to Hainan. But his assistant, Peng Tsemin, said to him: "Don't forget that you yourself have children, too." Tung Pi stopped and merely sent one of his officials across the sea to find out how Su Tungpo was doing. The official found that he was living in a government building and that he had been well treated and befriended by Chang Chung, who was subsequently dismissed.

Su Tungpo was driven out of the house where he had stayed and immediately had to build a kind of shanty for himself with whatever money he had left. This was in a palm grove south of the city. The people of the district, particularly the young sons of a few poor scholars, came and helped him build the house with their own hands. It was a simple house, the size of five "rooms", but probably consisting of three rooms. The house was christened Kuanglangan, or the "Palm Lodge". Behind it was the forest, and in his bed at night Su Tungpo could hear the tribesmen hunting deer, abundant in this region. Sometimes in the morning a hunter would knock at his door and present him with some deer-meat. He wrote in May to a friend: "I have been driven out of a government house and have built myself a little hut which barely serves the purpose of giving shelter. I have used up all the money I have. When one finds oneself in such straits, anything may happen. You just expect it to happen and laugh over it."

He seldom hated anybody, but he certainly did not like Tung Pi. He had to have his fun about this official who had driven him out of his house. This official's name, "Pi", has the same sound as the word for turtle in Chinese, and he wrote an allegory which ended up with a remark about Commissioner Turtle. Once he, Su, got drunk, so the story begins, and by order of the Dragon King was dragged by fish-headed devils into the sea. He went along in Taoist dress and a yellow hat and sandals, and soon found himself walking under water. Suddenly a great thunderbolt crashed, the sea turned, and in a blinding flash he found himself standing in the crystal palace of the Dragon King. As usual, the palace was decorated with pearls, coral, amber, and other precious stones in great abundance. The Dragon King appeared fully dressed, accompanied by two maid-servants, and Su asked what was wanted of him. Very soon the Queen came out from behind the screen and gave him a piece of precious gauze over ten feet long, upon which he was asked to write a poem. The writing of the poem was the easiest part of it for Su Tungpo. He painted a marvellous picture

of the life of the watery kingdom and the strange lights shooting forth
from the crystal palace. When he had finished the poem, the different
spirits stood round to look at it. Captain Bass and Sergeant Lobster
and the others all expressed their deep admiration. Commissioner
Turtle was also there. He stepped forth and pointed out to the
Dragon King that in this poem Su Tungpo had used one word which
was the personal name of the King and was therefore taboo. When
the Dragon King heard this, he became very angry with Su Tungpo.
"When I retired, I sighed and said to myself: 'It's my bad luck to run
into Commissioner Turtle.'"

Su Tungpo wrote three or four allegories, but imaginative writing
by Chinese scholars did not really develop until the thirteenth century,
and, like the allegories written by other writers in Tang and Sung
times, Su's stories were hardly more than thinly covered inventions for
an all too obvious moral.

For the next two and a half years after he had built his little hut, Su
led a carefree but bare existence. He had two wonderful friends, one
Ho Tehshun, a Taoist at Canton who forwarded all mail for him, and
the other a humble scholar who went about and sent him foodstuffs,
medicines, rice, pickles, and books that he needed. The summer months
in the tropical island were very trying on account of the dampness,
and Su would sit in the palm grove counting each day until autumn
was come. The rains fell in autumn and the big ships from Canton
and Fukien stopped coming on account of the stormy weather. The
food supplies ran short and even rice was not obtainable in this island.
Su Tungpo was really stranded. He wrote to a friend in the winter of
1098 to say that he and his son "sat facing each other in the bare hut
like two hermits". All that winter, supplies did not come, and they
were in danger of starvation. He resorted to his old recipe for vegetable
soup and began to cook cockle-burrs for his food.

One does not know how serious he was when he wrote in his journal
an entry about stopping hunger by eating the rays of the morning
sun. It is well known that Taoists usually starved themselves to death
when they decided to quit this world, and there was a period when
they stopped eating grain altogether. In this note about "dispensing
with grain" Su told the story of a man at Loyang who once fell into
a pit. There were frogs and snakes in the pit, and the man observed
that at dawn the animals turned their heads towards the morning sun
that came through the crevice, and made a motion of gulping down
the rays. Hungry and curious, he imitated the animals, and found that
his hunger was gone. Later the man was rescued and was said to have
not known hunger thereafter. "It's such a simple thing. Why does
nobody know about it, or practise it? The reason must be that it takes
a man with great self-discipline to put it into practice. Rice is expen-

sive at Tanchow and my supplies are running out. My son and I are
thinking of practising this art of eating sunshine. April 19, 1099."

Actually, Su Tungpo never had to starve. His good friends and
neighbours would not have permitted it. The impression is that he had
rather a carefree life. One day he was carrying a huge water-melon
on his head and singing on his way through the fields. An old peasant
woman over seventy said to him: "*Hanlin,* you were once a great
official at the court. Doesn't it seem to you now all like a spring
dream?" Thereafter Su Tungpo called this peasant woman "Mrs.
Spring Dreamer." Sometimes when he was caught in the rain while
stopping at a friend's home, he would borrow the peasant's hat and
waterproof and wooden shoes and come home splashing on the muddy
road. The dogs barked and the neighbours screamed with laughter.
Always when he had the opportunity he continued his habit of prowl-
ing about on a moonlight night, as he did everywhere he went. Sometimes he went with Kuo six miles out to the north-western point of
the coast, where stood a great rock resembling a monk looking out
towards the sea. Many ships were wrecked here, and the local population associated that rock with mystic powers. Lichis and oranges grew
in abundance at the foot of the cliff. It was all right to pick the fruit
and eat it there, but if anyone attempted to pick more than he could
eat and carry some away, immediately there would be a storm.

Su Tungpo had always been very kind to the monks, but he didn't
like the priests around Tanchow, who had wives or affairs with
women. While here, he wrote a pointed satire against them. The
entry was called: "The Story of a Girl Who Came Back to Life." It is
supposed to be a true story.

"November, 1098. I am living at Tanchow. I hear that there is
an unmarried girl in the west of the city who died of an illness
and came back to life again after two days. I went along with Ho
Min to see her father and was told the following story. At first, she
felt giddy and fell unconscious. She saw a man who came to lead
her to a magistrates's office in the under-world. Before she entered
the gate someone said that this was a mistake, and another official
said: 'Her time of death hasn't come yet. We should send her back.'
The girl then saw that there was a tunnel underground, and sixty or
seventy per cent of those who were led out and in through this
tunnel of hell were priests. There was a peasant woman sitting on
the ground in shackles, whose body had grown hair like a donkey's.
The girl recognised her as the mistress of one of the priests. The
woman told her: 'I am being punished for making use of money
and food given by donors to the temple. I have grown three kinds
of hair already.' There was also a monk who lived in the neigh-

bourhood of the girl's home and who had died two years earlier. During an anniversary of the monk's death, many friends and Buddhist followers came to make gifts of food for the benefit of the deceased monk. The monk's spirit received these gifts and distributed the money to the fellow ghosts. Keeping only a little rice for himself, the monk's ghost entered his house and then was robbed by the doorkeeper and the other devils. In the end he got very little. Then another monk arrived. He appeared to be an important personage and all the devils prostrated themselves before him. The monk then said to the others: 'This girl has been sent here by mistake. I will send her home.' With wave of his hand he pointed at a wall, and the girl walked through it. Then she came to a river and saw a boat on the bank. She went up to the boat and when someone pushed the boat from the bank, the jerk waked her up and she returned to life. I am writing this story down as a warning to people."

During these years Kuo was his father's constant companion. According to Su, Kuo was everything that a father could expect. He not only did all the chores but also acted as secretary. Under the guidance of the illustrious father, Kuo rapidly developed into a poet and painter. Of all the three sons of Su Tungpo, it was Kuo who became a writer of some importance and whose literary works are preserved today. He was made to go through the training that Su Tungpo himself underwent in his young days. He once copied the entire Tang history as a help to memory, and after that was finished, he started to copy the Han history. With his prodigious memory, Su Tungpo still remembered every line that he had read in those histories, and now and then, while he lay on his couch listening to his son reciting these passages, he would point out certain parallels and make comments on small details of the lives of the ancient scholars.

They suffered from having no good paper or brush, but with what they had Kuo learned to paint bamboos and rocks and winter scenes. About twenty years later, when Kuo was visiting the capital and stopping at a monastery, some soldiers from the palace suddenly arrived with a small sedan chair, ordering him to appear before His Majesty, Emperor Huitsung. Kuo didn't know what it was all about, but he had to obey. As soon as he got into the sedan chair, a screen was put all around him, so that he could not see where he was going. The sedan chair had no cover on top and someone held a large parasol over him. He seemed to be carried along very fast, and after four or five miles they arrived at a certain place. When he came out he found himself standing in a covered corridor and somebody led him to a beautiful hall. When he went in, he saw the Emperor sitting there, wearing a yellow vest and a hat with pieces of green jade on it. The Emperor was surrounded by a great number of palace maids, all gorgeously dressed. Kuo had an idea that there were a great many of them, but he dared not look up. Although it was June, the room was freezing cold. Large chunks of ice were piled up in the room and perfume from the incense filled the air. He realised that he was somewhere in one of the great palaces. After the proper greetings, the Emperor said to him: "I hear that you are the son of Su Shih, and are good at painting rocks. Here is a new hall and I want you to paint the walls. That is why I have sent for you." Kuo drew a deep breath. Emperor Huitsung was himself a great painter and even today many of his paintings are preserved. Kuo bowed twice and then started to paint the walls, while the Emperor left his seat and stood around to look at him while he was at work. When the painting was finished, the Emperor repeatedly expressed his admiration, and told a palace maid to hand Kuo a cup of wine, and gave him many valuable gifts. After he had withdrawn from the imperial presence, Kuo again took the sedan chair in the corridor and was again screened in on his way home. After arriving home, he felt as if he had lived through a dream.

The difficulty of obtaining ink in that island place led Su Tungpo to an experiment. Kuo later told the story of how his father nearly set their house on fire. This tale concerned a famous maker of ink in Hangchow whose products sold for two or three times the price of other makes because he said he had learned the secret formula from Su Tungpo himself at Hainan. Some of the scholars asked Kuo about his father's formula for making ink. Kuo laughed and said: "My father didn't have any secret formula. He just played with it when we had nothing to do in Hainan. One day, Pan Heng [the famous ink maker] arrived and my father started to make ink with him in a small room, by burning resin to form soot. At midnight the room caught fire and the house just escaped being burned down. Next day we collected several ounces of soot from the charred ruins. But we had no glue and my father took ox-hide glue and mixed it anyhow with the soot. It would not solidify properly and we obtained only several dozens of pieces the size of a finger. My father had a great laugh. Soon Heng departed." The people of those times did find that the ink made by this merchant was of a very fine quality. Evidently he had learned his secret from some other person than Su Tungpo, but sold his product on Su's reputation.

Now that his time was idle, Su contracted the habit of going about the countryside picking medicinal herbs and identifying the different varieties. He identified with great satisfaction a certain herb which was referred to in the ancient histories by another name, and which nobody else had been able to find. Among the various notes on medicine may be mentioned one he wrote on the cure of rheumatism by the use of nettle, which contains urticin and lutein. It was like poison ivy, and contact with human flesh caused painful swellings. According to him, by applying nettle to the inflamed joints where rheumatism first started, such pains could be stopped at all points of the body. He was also a great believer in cockle-burr, a common plant which grew everywhere, was harmless, and could be taken for any length of time in any form. (The plant contains fat, a small amount of resin, vitamin C_1, and xanthostrumarin.) He gave a formula for making a white powder out of this plant by heating the ashes of the leaves over a slow fire for twenty-four hours. This white powder, when taken internally, was said to beautify one's skin, making it soft and smooth "like jade". Other notes deal with hemlock parsley, asparagus lucidus, and shepherd's purse, which Su called "God's gift to the poor man", rich in food value and delicate in taste.

Besides such occupations, with the help of his son, he collected his miscellaneous notes, which became known as *Chihlin,* or his book of journals. Of the five Confucian classics, which were divided among the two brothers, Su Tungpo undertook two. He had completed his interpretations of the *Book of Changes and the Analects** while in confinement at Huangchow. Now in Hainan he completed his interpretation of the *Book of History*. The most imposing single task was a volume of one hundred and twenty-four poems using the same rhyme words as the poems written by Tao Chien of the fourth century. He had started "echoing" some of the poems while at Yingchow, but when he came to Huichow, forced to a life of retirement in a rustic atmosphere, he found that his life was almost a complete duplication of that of Tao Chien, whom he greatly admired. By the time he left Huichow, he had already written a hundred and nine of these poems, and the last fifteen poems, which were all of Tao's poems that yet remained unechoed, were completed during his stay on the island. He asked Tseyu to write a preface for this collection of poems, and said in the letter: "I love Yuanming [Tao] not only as a poet, but even more as a human character." This may be said by many admirers of Su Tungpo himself.

---

* The *Analects* is not one of the "Five Classics."

Chapter Twenty-eight

THE END

IN January 1100 the young Emperor Tsehtsung died at the age of
twenty-four, leaving behind him a generation of dead, broken, and
tired scholars. Whereas his father, Shentsung, had fourteen sons, he
had only one child by "Glamor Liu", and it had died in infancy. His
brother Huitsung succeeded to the throne. Huitsung in turn produced
thirty-one sons, a few good paintings, and a national chaos. What his
brother had started, Huitsung completed. He used the same men and
followed the same policies. Wang Anshih's state capitalism was now
associated with the regime of Shentsung and honoured with the name
of "the Ancestor's Way". Both in methods of enriching the imperial
treasury and in the war policy towards the northern tribes, Huitsung
followed in the footsteps of Wang Anshih. Perhaps it was hard for an
emperor to resist a policy which centred the wealth of the country in
the government and in the imperial household. But every emperor
who did this had to pay the price for it. In Huitsung's case the price
was the loss of his throne, the capture of the capital, and his death in
captivity by northern tribes. Perhaps Huitsung did paint beautiful
birds, including romantic mandarin ducks, but any ruler who could
stand heart-rending oppression of the people to build a pleasure garden
for himself deserved to lose his throne.

The national fibre was sapped and weakened by the time Huitsung
ascended the throne. Men of character and ability and moral rectitude
are rare products of a civilised society and thus take a long time to
grow up and mature. The generation of Szema Kuang, Ouyang Shiu,
Fan Chunjen, and Lu Kungchu was now gone. This generation of
men had variously been punished, exiled, died of illness or old age,
or had been murdered. The atmosphere of independent criticism and
fearless thinking and writing was stifled, and all political life was
tainted. Su Tungpo and his disciples had suffered too much for their
opinions to wish to go into politics again, particularly when the political
wind was against them. It is difficult to expect that a new generation
of upright, learned, and fearless scholars could just turn up at court,
by a fiat of the Emperor. It is also too much to expect that a large
clique of men who had tasted power for eight years should not attempt
to remain in power.

There was, however, a temporary spell of good luck for Su Tungpo.
For the first six months of 1100 the new empress dowager, wife of
Shentsung, ruled as regent. In April of that year all the Yuanyu
officials were pardoned, and although she returned the throne to her

son in July, she remained a powerful influence in favour of the men of
Yuanyu until she died in January of the following year. As long as she
was living, the exiled scholars were pardoned and either promoted or at
least granted complete freedom of movement. Apparently the wife of
Shentsung, like her mother-in-law, had a surer instinct for what was
good for the country than her sons, and in simple feminine wisdom
was a better judge of men. Critics and historians, lost in their fine
phrases and abstract distinctions and deep in the research of problems
and policies of a period, sometimes forget that in the ultimate judgment
of men we cannot escape the simple adjectives of "good" and "bad".
After all, the phrase "a good man" is one of the highest tributes a man
can aspire to have when the time comes for summing up his career
and character. The empresses whom Su Tungpo served never seemed
to be very much involved in the problems and policies of the government leaders. Certainly Chang Chun was a man of great strength and
determination. Huiching was an eloquent speaker. Tsai Ching had
great energy and ability. But the Empress Dowager now simply
summed them up as bad men.

In May, the one carefree soul of his time, Wu Fuku, turned up again
to bring Su Tungpo the first news of his pardon and transfer to a
district west of the Luichow Peninsula just across the sea. The news
was soon confirmed by a letter from Chin Kuan, who had been confined at Luichow and had just received a pardon himself.

From now on, Su Tungpo was again to follow a wandering course.
After his voyage to Lienchow across the sea, and just one month after
his arrival there, he received orders to go and live at Yungchow, which
is modern Lingling in Hunan. After four months of futile changes of
route on his journey in order to reach Yungchow, and while still half-
way to his second appointed place, he finally received permission to live
wherever he chose. If he had been granted freedom of residence in the
first instance, the two Su brothers could have met very easily at Canton
and gone on north together. Tseyu had received his transfer to a
district on Tungting Lake in Hunan. Since at that time Su Tungpo
was only transferred to the coast opposite Hainan, quite far away from
Canton, Tseyu had left immediately for the north with his family, who
had been staying at Tungpo's house in Huichow. After he had arrived
in the neighbourhood of Hankow, on the way to his destination he
was promoted in rank and given freedom of movement; he returned to
Yingchang, where he had a farm and where his other children were
living.

Unlike Tseyu, Tungpo took a long time to leave Hainan. He was
waiting for one of those big Fukien ships to cross the sea, but after waiting in vain, he left with Wu Fuku, Kuo, and his dog, Black Snout.
The party went up to Luichow to see Chin Kuan, and then Wu Fuku

left and disappeared. While both Su Tungpo and Wu Fuku travelled all over China in their lifetime, the difference between the two was that Su was sent about by someone else's orders, whereas Wu was sent about by nobody but himself. In retrospect it would seem that Su Tungpo would gladly have changed his lot with that of his friend. He would have been a happier man, and certainly would have been a freer man.

We need not follow his journey in detail on his return north. He was entertained and greeted at every town and it might be called a triumphal return. Everywhere friends and admirers gathered around him, took him to see mountains and temples, and asked for his autograph. After receiving the order to proceed to his appointment in Hunan, he went north from the coastal town Lienchow with his son and constant companion to Wuchow, where he had asked his other children to meet him. When he arrived at this place, he found that his children's families had not yet arrived. Furthermore, the water in the Ho River was very low and it would have been very difficult to go up straight north to Hunan. He decided to take a long and circuitous route, returning to Canton, where he would proceed to cross the mountain ridge on the north and then strike westward from Kiangse towards Hunan. The journey would have taken about half a year, but luckily he did not have to complete it.

In October he arrived at Canton and was reunited with his children and their families. The second son, Tai, had now arrived from the north to see his father. Su Tungpo wrote that he felt as if he had been living through a dream.

He was lavishly entertained at Canton. In the second year of his stay at Hainan, there was a rumour that he had died. At one of the dinners, a friend said jokingly to him: "I thought you were dead."

"Indeed, I died and went to hell," said Su Tungpo. "But I met Chang Chun on the way there and decided to come back."

It was a big family with many babies and young women, and the whole company left by boat for Kukong. Before they had gone very far, Wu Fuku and a number of monks overtook them and spent several pleasant days together with the poet. Then, suddenly, Wu Fuku fell ill and just died, very simply. Tungpo asked him on his deathbed what he could do for him. Wu merely smiled and closed his eyes.

Before leaving Kwangtung, he had received news of his freedom of residence. In January 1101, Su Tungpo crossed General Yu's Notch and then was held up for seventy days at Kanshien, just north of the mountain. He was waiting for boat accommodations for his large family, but many of the children fell ill and six of their servants died of some kind of plague. During his stay here, he spent his time, when he was not busily occupied writing autographs, treating the sick and dispensing herbs to people of the city. A number of friends were usually with him, and they planned their trips or outings together. His movements would become known, and when they arrived at their chosen destination, he would be confronted with a pile of silks and paper with requests for him to write poems on them. Su Tungpo responded cheerfully, for he loved writing. Only when the day was getting late and he had to hurry home would he ask to write a few big characters, and all those who came with such requests returned well rewarded and satisfied.

By May 1 he arrived at Nanking. He had written his faithful friend Chien Shihshiung to look for a house for him in the city of Changchow. But the letters he wrote during that half year show that his mind was really undecided. Tseyu had by this time returned to his old farm at Yingchang and had sent a letter urging him to come and live with him. Su Tungpo did not know what to think. He knew he would enjoy the landscape of Changchow in the lake district, where besides he had a farm in the country, which would be a means of support. He equally desired to live with his brother, but he had a big family now and Tseyu was living in reduced circumstances. He was not quite sure that he should bring along "three hundred fingers"—that is, about thirty persons of his family and children's families and servants—and impose them on his brother. But after receiving the letter, he decided to go and live as his brother's neighbour. He crossed the river at Nanking and told Mai and Tai to go down to Changchow to clear up family affairs and meet him at Yichen. He actually wrote to ask for four boats to take his large family up north in the direction of the capital.

However, the Empress Dowager had died in January of that year, and this was May. All evidences pointed to another reversal of policy. Su Tungpo judged that there might be trouble again, and he did not want to live too near the capital. He wrote a long, sad letter to Tseyu blaming their inability to meet now on God's will. "What can I do against God's will?" That being the case, he would do the natural thing, which was to settle at Changchow. After his family was settled, he would ask Mai to go on to a new post, but he and his two younger sons would live at the farm in the lake district.

Meanwhile, waiting at Yichen for his children to meet him, Su Tungpo lived in a boat on the river. The summer had come suddenly and it was an unusually hot year. He was surprised that upon returning from the tropics he should have felt the heat so much in middle China. The sun beating down upon the water near the bank caused the humid air to rise from the river and made it very miserable for him. On June 3, he developed what could have been amoebic dysentery. He

thought he had "drunk too much cold water"; the probability is that
he had been drinking water from the river. The next morning he felt
extremely weak and tired and stopped taking food. Being a doctor himself, he ordered a Chinese medicine, yellow vetch soup, and felt much
better. The yellow vetch, *huangchi,* is believed by Chinese doctors to be
a great body-builder, enriching the blood and strengthening the constitution generally. It is a general tonic, good for cases of debility, rather'
than a medicine for specific diseases. Modern study still has to be made
of this herb, for many contemporary Chinese have profited from drinking bowlfuls of this soup day after day.

However, his digestive system was out of order and he could not
sleep at night. The great painter Mi Fei came to see him many times,
and when he was well enough, they even made trips together to visit
the Eastern Garden. The nine notes he wrote to Mi Fei at Yichen show
quite plainly the course of the illness. Once he wrote: "I could not sleep
all night, and sat up providing food for the mosquitoes swarming
around me. I don't know how I am going to get through tonight."
Mi Fei sent him a medicine, black leek soup. Su Tungpo had always
regarded Mi Fei as a junior and the latter had always looked up to him.
Now, after reading a descriptive poem by Mi, he predicted that the
younger painter's reputation was secure, and expressed the regret that
he had not come to know him better in their twenty years of friendship.
Some days Su felt better and on others he felt weak and exhausted. His
life was being destroyed, not by the Emperor or Chang Chun, but
possibly by amoebas. The place was so oppressive with the tepid
atmosphere of the river-bank and he ordered his boat moved to a
cooler place.

On June 11 he said good-bye to Mi Fei, and on the twelfth he crossed
the Yangtse River and went down to Chinkiang. He was particularly
popular in this region. Coming back to this district was like coming
home. News had gone abroad that the great poet had returned from
overseas and was arriving. Thousands of people stood on the bank at
Chinkiang to take a look at the famous man. There was general talk
that he might be recalled to assume the reins of the government.

His cousin's grave lay at Chinkiang, and her son, Hung, was in the
city. On June 12, even in his weak health, he went with his three sons
and the nephew to say prayers at the grave of his cousin and her
husband. A second time, he wrote sacrificial prayers to the dead. It is
possible that one was addressed to the husband and the other to the
wife, but this is not quite clear from the text. In the first one, entitled
"The Prayer to Liu Chungyuan", he started by mentioning the wife
first, and then continued: "*Besides,* my dear Chungyuan, you were a
kind and gentle person and a filial son." The second prayer was more
emotional.

"I was punished for my crimes and was living in hardship in the south. Compared with the ancients, I should have deserved more than death. But God did not take away my life—he took away my relatives. My sister was married to the Liu family in a happy, worthy marriage. Why did you both die? Why did not one of you remain? Now I have returned from the south and the grass over your graves has seen its second spring. I weep my eyes out while you lie underground a few feet away. Hung has a good character and can take care of himself. I am old and poor, of what use is such an uncle to him? . . ."

The next day some visitors found him lying on his side facing the wall and shaking with sobs, so that he could not get up to receive them. The visitors were the sons of a retired premier, Su Sung, and they thought that Su Tungpo was weeping on account of the death of their father. Su Sung had died at the age of eighty-two. Although bearing the same surname he was not from the same province as the poet. Su Tungpo had known him for thirty or forty years, but it is difficult to believe that he was so much shaken even upon learning of such an old friend's death. Besides, on the previous day, when Su heard the news, he did not go personally to say prayers at the grave but had sent his eldest son Mai in his stead. The source of this grief, I believe, must be read in the poem just quoted.

Among the scholars of the town who were unable to see Su Tungpo there was Chang Yuan, the eldest son of Chang Chun. As Su Tungpo was very ill, he had refused to see many visitors. Chang Chun had a year ago been banished to the Luichow Peninsula and his son was on his way to visit him. When Su Tungpo was chief examiner, he had picked Chang Yuan as first among the candidates, and so Chang, according to the old custom, was considered his disciple. That was about nine years before. Chang Yuan knew what his father had done to the Su brothers, and he had heard that they might be recalled to power any time. Therefore he wrote a letter of seven hundred words to Su Tungpo. It was a very difficult letter to write. He gave the many reasons why he had not dared to call, and frankly said that he had hesitated a great deal because of his father. Very gently he suggested that when Su should again be serving by the Emperor's side, a word from him might decide the fate of others. Chang Yuan was afraid that Su Tungpo might do to his father what his father had done to him. He hoped perhaps for an interview with the poet, or to get a reply indicating his attitude.

If Chang Yuan thought that Su Tungpo entertained ideas of revenge, he was greatly mistaken. Su Tungpo had heard of Chang Chun's banishment while on his return journey. There was one Huang Shih who was related to both the Su and the Chang families. Huang was Chang Chun's son-in-law and at the same time the father-in-law of Tseyu's third son. When Su first heard of Chang's banishment, he had written to Huang: "When I heard the news, I was shocked for a whole day. Although the place Luichow is very far away, it is free from malaria. My brother lived there for a year and was quite comfortable. Please tell your mother-in-law about this and tell her not to worry." Now in reply to Chang Yuan he wrote:

"I have been a friend of your father for over forty years, and although we have had political differences, our friendship never altered. You can imagine what I feel when I hear that in his old age he is sent to remote places by the sea. But what is the use of talking about the past? It is better to think of the future. The Emperor is very kind. . . . You can judge by the title of the new reign [which suggests compromise of party strife] . . . So you should not worry. As to what you say about my being able to decide the fate of others, I am sure you're mistaken. I've seen enough troubles in my days, and my only wish now is to be left alone to complete my journey to my new home. Judging by my present condition, I cannot yet say whether I shall get well. For the last fortnight I have not taken more than a cup of rice per day, and have a distaste for food generally. I am starting for Changchow today, and I hope that I may have a good rest there and that I shall not die immediately. I'm very tired now, and must lay down my pen. June fourteenth [1101]."

St. Francis of Assisi, born later in that century, would have approved. Together with Su's letter to Chu Shouchang against infanticide and his letter of 1092 to the Empress begging for forgiveness of debts to the poor, this letter must rank among the three greatest human documents written by the poet.

On June 15 he continued his voyage up the canal from Chinkiang towards his home in Changchow. The news of his coming had caused a sensation, and all through his trip on the canal, people gathered on both banks to stage a spontaneous welcome. He was well enough to sit up in his boat, wearing a small cap and a vest, leaving his arms quite bare on the hot summer day. Turning around to the people in the boat, he said: "They will kill me with their welcome!"

It was a short voyage, and he soon arrived at Changchow and put up at a house near the east gate of the city, which his good friend Chien Shihshiung had rented for him. The first thing he did was to write a letter to the Emperor asking for complete retirement from politics. It was the custom in the Sung dynasty for officials to be appointed on semi-retirement as directors of temples, and Su had received the rank of director of certain temple properties back in his own province. There was a superstition that when an official was seriously ill, resignation from politics could help cure his illness and prolong his life. This is based on the very sensible assumption that politics and robbery of the people are almost synonymous in God's eyes. Retirement from politics was like a promise to reform. Su Tungpo mentioned that he had heard of such cures and said he would like to try it.

His illness dragged on after his arrival at Changchow. He never recovered his appetite and for about a month remained most of the time in bed. He had a feeling that his end was coming. Besides his own immediate family, his good friend Chien Shihshiung saw him almost every other day. Chien was a friend who had kept on sending him letters and medicine while he was in the south. Whenever Su Tungpo felt better, he would ask his son Kuo to write a note to ask Chien to come over for a chat. One day when Chien came, he found him lying in his bed unable to sit up.

"I'm so happy that I have returned alive all the way from the south," said Su. "What is difficult for me to bear is the fact that I have not been able to see Tseyu on my return. I haven't seen him since we parted on the coast of Luichow."

After a while he said again: "I completed the three books on the *Analects*, the *Book of History*, and the *Book of Changes* while I was overseas. I want to confide them to your care. Keep the manuscripts safe without showing them to other people. Thirty years from now, they will be greatly appreciated."

Then he was going to open his trunks but could not find the keys. Chien comforted him by saying that he was going to get well and that there was no hurry. During those four weeks Chien came constantly to see him. Su's first and last joys were in his writing. When he showed Chien the different poems and prose that he had written while in the south, his eyes brightened and he seemed to forget everything else. On certain days he was still able to write short notes and postscripts, including a postscript in praise of cinnamon wine, which he gave to Chien, knowing that his friend would treasure it carefully.

On July 15 his illness took a decided turn for the worse. That night he had high fever, and the next morning his gums were bleeding and he felt extremely weak. He analysed his own symptoms and believed that the illness came from *jehtu*, a general term describing infection. He believed there was no cure for it except letting the sickness run its course; there was no use meddling with different kinds of medicine. He refused food, and took only soup of ginseng, Indian bread, and black leek. The latter was made into a thick soup, and whenever he felt thirsty, he drank a little of it. In a letter to Chien he said: "According to Chuangtse, there is no such thing as governing a country; one should merely let the country alone. These three articles are designed to let the body cure itself. If I don't get well by the help of these three herbs, then it is God's will and not my fault." Chien offered him some very rare medicine said to have a magical power, but Su Tungpo refused to take it.

On July 18 Su Tungpo gathered his three sons together by his side and said to them: "I have done nothing wrong in my life, and I am sure I shall not go to hell." He told them not to worry and gave instructions that Tseyu was the person to write his tomb inscription and that he was to be buried with his wife at the foot of the Sungshan Mountain near Tseyu's home. After a few days he seemed to improve and asked his two younger sons to help him get up from bed and assist him to walk a few steps. But then he found he could not even sit up for long in bed.

On July 25 all hopes of his recovery were given up. One of the old friends in his Hangchow days, Abbot Weilin, had now arrived, and was constantly in his company. Although Su could not sit up, he liked to have the abbot in the room so that he could talk with him. On the twenty-sixth, he wrote his last poem. The abbot had been talking with him about the life here and hereafter, and had suggested saying certain Buddhist incantations. Su laughed. He had read the histories of the Buddhist monks and he knew all of them died.

"What about Kumaradiva? He died, didn't he?" Kumaradiva was a Hindu priest who came to China in the fourth century. Single-handed, he translated some three hundred volumes of Buddhist classics into Chinese, and he was generally acknowledged as the first Buddhist missionary to lay the foundation for the Mahayana sect, which is the prevalent sect in China and Japan. When Kumaradiva was about to die, he asked his Hindu brothers who were with him to say certain Sanskrit incantations for him. But in spite of the incantations Kumaradiva grew worse and soon died. Su had read his life in the Chin history and still remembered it.

On July 28 he began to sink rapidly and his breath grew short. According to custom, the family put a tuft of cotton at the tip of his nose to indicate his breathing. His entire family was in the room. The abbot went very close to him and spoke into his ear. "At this moment, think of the life hereafter!"

Su Tungpo whispered slowly: "The Western Heaven may exist, but trying to get there won't help." Chien, who was standing by, said to him: "At this moment especially, you must try." Su Tungpo's last words were: "It's a mistake to try." That was his Taoism. Salvation consists in being natural and *unconsciously* good.

Mai stepped forward and asked for his last instructions, but without saying a word, Su Tungpo passed away. He was sixty-four years of age.

A fortnight ago he had written to the abbot: "Is it not God's will that I should not have died during the exile in the south, but only now, after I have returned to my home? But life and death are mere accidents and not worth talking about."

By all earthly standards, Su Tungpo had a hard and unfortunate life. Once the disciples of Confucius asked him about two ancient sages who had suffered for their convictions and died of actual starvation. The disciples asked Confucius if the two recluses, Poyi and Shuchi, regretted it at the time of their death. Confucius replied: "These two men were trying to save their souls, and they succeeded. Why should they regret it?"

The "vital spirit" that was the incarnation of Su Tungpo had now spent itself. Human life is no more than the life of a spirit, a force that governs one's career and personality, given at birth and taking form in action only by the accidents and circumstances of one's life. As Su Tungpo describes it, this "vital spirit has an existence independent of the body, and moves without dependence upon material force. It was there before one was born, and does not vanish after one's death. Therefore this vital spirit appears as heavenly bodies above, and as mountains and rivers below. In the occult world, it appears as spirits and ghosts, and in our conscious life, as men and women. This is a common truth and we need not wonder at it."

In reading the life of Su Tungpo, we have been following and observing the life of a great human mind and spirit, as they took temporary shape on this earth. Su Tungpo died and his name is only a memory, but he has left behind for all of us the joys of his spirit and the pleasures of his mind, and these are imperishable.

Appendix A

CHRONOLOGICAL SUMMARY

JENTSUNG, emperor of northern Sung dynasty (1023–63):

1036	Su Tungpo born	Dec. 19
1054	Married Miss Wang Fu ·	
1057	Passed *chinshih* examinations at top; mother died; mourning for mother	Apr. 1057–July 1059
1059	Family moved to capital	Feb. 1060
1061	*Fengshiang* assistant magistrate	Nov. 1061–Dec. 1064

INGTSUNG (1064–7):

1064	Secretary, department of history	Feb. 1065–Apr. 1066
1065	Wife died	May 8
1066	Father died; mourning for father	Apr. 1066–July 1068

SHENTSUNG (1068–85):

1068	Married Miss Wang Junchi	Oct. (?)
1069	Returned to capital	Feb. 1069
	Secretary, department of history	Feb. 1069–Dec. 1070
1071	Magistrate of metropolis	Jan.–June 1071
	Journey to Hangchow	July–Nov. 1071
	Hangchow deputy magistrate	Nov. 1071–Aug. 1074
1074	Journey to Michow	Sept.–Nov. 1074
	Michow magistrate	Nov. 1074–Nov. 1076
1076	Journey to Suchow	Dec. 1076–Mar. 1077
1077	*Suchow* magistrate	Apr. 1077–Mar. 1079
1079	*Huchow* magistrate	Apr.–July 1079
	In prison	Aug.–Dec. 1079
1080	*Huangchow* banishment	Feb. 1080–Apr. 1084
1084	Journey to Changchow, etc.	Apr. 1084–Mar. 1085
1085	Journey to Tengchow	June–Oct. 1085
	Tengchow magistrate	Oct. 1085
	Journey to capital	Oct.–Dec. 1085
	Secretary at premier's office	Dec. 1085–July 1086

* The dates here given are for the official "reigns," used in Chinese chronicles. Usually an emperor began his rule after his predecessor's death, and then changed the "reign" the following year.

345

346   THE GAY GENIUS

Tsehtsung (1086–1100); Yuanyu regency under Empress Dowager (Mar. 1085–Aug. 1093):

1086	Secretary to Emperor; *hanlin*	Aug. 1086–Feb. 1089
1089	Journey to Hangchow	Apr.–July 1089
	Hangchow commander and governor of Chekiang	July 1089–Feb. 1091
1091	Minister of civil service	Jan.–Aug. 1091
	Journey to capital	Mar.–May 1091
	Yingchow magistrate	Aug. 1091–Mar. 1092
1092	*Yangchow* magistrate	Mar.–Aug. 1092
	Minister of war	Sept.–Oct. 1092
	Minister of education	Nov. 1092–Aug. 1093
1093	Wife died; Empress Dowager died	Aug.–Sept. 1093
	Tingchow commander and governor of Hopei	Oct. 1093–Apr. 1094
1094	Journey to exile at Huichow	Mar.–Oct. 1094
	Huichow banishment	Oct. 1094–Apr. 1097
1097	Journey to Hainan	Apr.–July 1097
	Tanchow (Hainan) banishment	July 1097–June 1100

Huitsung (1101–26); Empress Dowager's regency (Jan.–June 1100):

1101	Return to China; journey to Changchow	July 1100–June 1101
	Died	July 28, 1101
1126	End of northern Sung dynasty	

Appendix B

BIBLIOGRAPHY AND SOURCES

The following bibliography is prepared, first, for the intelligent Western reader who, without being able to read Chinese, feels the need for knowing something of the sources of the material he is reading, and second, for scholars who have access to Chinese books. For convenience, book references are not given by their long (and ineffectively romanised) titles, but by their numbers on the list, and sometimes by their authors.

A. EARLY EDITIONS OF SU TUNGPO (Nos. 1–8):

Of the volumes of Su's poems published in his lifetime, grouped by period, we know at least seven by name: *Southern Travels, Chientang* (Hangchow), *Chaojan* (Michow), *The Yellow Tower* (Suchow), *Piling* (Changchow), *Lantai* (his *hanlin* period), and *Haiwai* ("overseas"). The earliest known publisher of Su's poems was Prince Wang Shien, No. 1, who published a number of them before 1079. At Su's trial that year, four printed volumes of his verse were presented as evidence. About 1082, Chen Shihchung, No. 2, published *Chaojan* and *The Yellow Tower*. In 1085, after release from Huangchow, Su wrote to his friend Ten Yuanfa suggesting that the wood-blocks for his poems be destroyed. Between 1097 and 1100, Liu Mien, No. 3, wrote him about publishing a collected works, and Su praised the collection as containing entirely genuine material.

Soon after Su's death, editions with various commentaries on his poems appeared, the comments being elucidations of the sources of his lines, and notes on names and places and stories in connection with the writing of the individual poems. About 1111, ten years after his death, the *Four Commentators* edition had become the *Five Commentators*, arranged chronologically, the first commentator being Chao Tsekung, No. 4. About 1130 the *Eight Commentators* and *Ten Commentators* appeared, first arranged according to subjects by Chao Kuei, No. 5. About 1170, when Su's reputation as a great writer was firmly established, appeared the famous edition by Wang Shihpeng. This was known as *Wang's Commentary*, No. 6, or the *Hundred Commentators* edition, the editor's job here being a judicious selection of the best comments or notes by his predecessors. Naturally, among those most valued were elucidations by friends and disciples of the poet, namely, Huang Tingchien, Chen Shihtao, and Pan Talin, who knew the personal references contained in the poems. Of the list of actually ninety-seven commentators, forty-seven in the northern Sung and thirty-one in the southern Sung are known to history.

Towards the end of the twelfth century, Shih Yuanchih was compiling his famous chronological edition known as *Shih's Commentary,* No. 7, published with a preface by the poet Lu Yu, dated 1209. A revised edition of this *Shih's Commentary* was published by Cheng Yu, No. 8, with a preface dated 1262.

B. Modern Critical Editions (Nos. 9–14):

Shih's Commentary seems to have gone out of circulation in the Ming period, while popular editions of the poet's collected poems, arranged according to thirty or seventy-eight subjects, continued to be known as *Wang's Commentary.* Chinese philological research was at its height in the Manchu dynasty; and many old editions came to light, particularly in the nation-wide scouring for ancient scripts and rare books in connection with the great *Szeku Chuanshu* imperial library under Emperor Chienlung. Under Emperor Kangshi appeared the first modern critical edition, by Sung Lo, who had discovered an incomplete edition of the *Shih's Commentary.* The work of editing and rearranging the poems chronologically was entrusted to Shao Changheng and two other scholars, and the *Table of Chronological Events,* No. 43, was also revised. Published with a preface dated 1699, this claimed to be *Shih's Commentary* revised, but became known as the *Shao's Commentary,* No. 9. Certain poems not included in previous collections were added. Another great scholar, Cha Shenshing, published his edition, No. 10, in 1702, and amended Shao's errors.

Under Emperor Chienlung, the learned editor-in-chief of the imperial library *Szeku Chuangshu,* Chi Yun, a great admirer of Su, issued an edition of Su's poems in 1771, No. 11, appreciating or evaluating each from a literary point of view, and making the best text by a wise comparison of different versions. At this time a great scholar, writer, and collector, Weng Fangkang, had obtained the ancient copy of *Shih's Commentary* formerly belonging to Sung Lo, and this was such a great event in his life that he named his studio henceforth "the Su Studio". The portrait of Su reproduced in this book bears Weng's autograph on top. In 1782 he published his *Supplementary Comments,* No. 12. In 1793 followed the more important edition by Feng Yingliu, No. 13, who had obtained a copy of the ancient *Five Commentators* and a Yuan edition of the *Wang's Commentary.* In these successive editions the editors often disagreed; No. 10 tried to correct No. 9, No. 12 tried to correct Nos. 9 and 10, and No. 13 tried to correct all predecessors. In general, the chronological arrangement in the *Shih's Commentary* was corroborated.

The time was now ready for the definitive edition of Su's poems by Wang Takao, who combined conscientious scholarship with tireless devotion of thirty years of his life to research on Su Tungpo. As far as possible, he visited all places of interest connected with the poet. All the available material of the previous editions was before him, and he made literally hundreds of corrections in place and chronology, so that the edition superseded even the *Table of Chronological Events*, either in No. 43, or in No. 44, or in No. 9. I am greatly indebted to Wang, not only for his chronological arrangement of poems, but also for his voluminous parallel study of the different periods of Su's life. This is the work he published in 1822, reprinted in 1888, No. 14.

C. MODERN REPRINTS (Nos. 15-19):

Useful and easily available photographed reprints of Sung editions of Su's works are in the *Szepu Tsungkan collection*, published by Commercial Press, 1929: No. 15 is a reprint of Su's prose, and No. 18 is a reprint of his poems with *Wang's Commentary*. No. 16, Su's *Collected Works*, is the same as what is called the *Seven Collections* edition, containing his poems, letters and state papers in 110 volumes; of these, the state papers almost always bear clear dates. No. 17 is a convenient edition of the same in Western binding in two volumes, based on a Ming edition of 1468. No. 19 is a reprint of *Wang's Commentary*.

D. SPECIAL WORKS BY SU (Nos. 20-24):

Besides his poems and prose papers, Su Tungpo wrote five books. He and his brother had divided work on the Five Classics between themselves, Tungpo taking the *Book of History* and the *Book of Changes* besides the *Analects*. No. 20, his interpretation of the extremely difficult *Book of Changes*, a philosophy of the mutation of human events, is worth translating because it emphasises deep human truths rather than the cosmological-mathematical interpretation of the neo-Confucianists; Su said of himself that he was handicapped in mathematics. No. 21, his interpretation of the *Book of History* was thought highly of even by the neo-Confucianists, his political opponents. No. 22, his interpretation of the *Analects*, easily overshadowed by Chu Shi's commentary, has not survived; on the other hand, his brother's supplements have (together with the latter's interpretation of Mencius and Laotse). No. 23, *The Journal*, was edited by himself with his son's help while they were in Hainan, but was not completed; containing the fugitive pieces of the poet, it ranks among the most important of his works that are left to us. No. 24 is his "echo" of the complete poems

of Tao Chien, with a preface by his brother. Both Nos. 23 and 24 have
been mentioned frequently in the text, and in some editions they are
included in Su's collected works.

E. SPECIAL SELECTIONS (Nos. 25–32):

No. 25, a collection of Su's postscripts and comments on painting,
calligraphy, books and travel, is not included in Su's *Collected Works*
but is highly important, though it was not put together by the author
and not intended as a separate volume. No. 26, a medical work on
Good Recipes, bears the names of Su and a contemporary, Shen Kua,
as co-authors, but Su's pieces are found in the supplementary volume.
I can see that four or five of these tried recipes are worth testing by
Western doctors. No. 27 contains his casual pieces of Taoist subjects,
resembling somewhat the *Journal*, but of less genuine value. No. 28
is a collection of Su's literary opinions, and No. 29 a similar collection
of opinions on poetry. No. 30 is a collection of his *tse* poems, and No.
31 of his poems containing Buddhist ideas; however, for the study of
Su Tungpo's opinions on Buddhism, his prose collection is much more
important. A very good selection of Su's "light pieces", for which he
was greatly admired, is No. 32, published in 1694.

F. WORKS ASCRIBED TO SU TUNGPO (Nos. 33–39):

The following works are in all probability spurious, since there is
no evidence from Su's own writings or the testimony of his friends
that he ever wrote them. Nevertheless, No. 33 is a worthy collection
of salty jokes and humorous anecdotes built around an ancient figure.
No. 34 is an interpretation of a dubious Taoist treatise. Nos. 35 and 36
are much more interesting, being in fact two books of home formulas
(how to dye hair black, how to remove stains, how to paint colours on
candles, how to prevent freezing of water on the ink slab by adding
alcohol, how to eat garlic without getting a bad breath, how to boil eggs
so that the egg white hardens in different layers, how to boil tough pork
easily, etc., etc.). No. 37 consists of jokes between Su and his friend
the monk Foyin, and of verse games indulged in by "Su Tungpo's
younger sister" who never existed (this point has been covered in
Chapter III). Since this is, as far as I can find out, the earliest mention
of Su's sister, published in 1601 (five hundred years after Su's death,
in the *Paoyentang Collection*, the fable may well be dismissed. Of the
same questionable character is No. 38, *Conversations with the Fisherman and Woodcutter*, which bears a preface by the same man who

wrote a preface to No. 37, but dated one year later. No. 39 is short and valueless.

G. Sources on Su Tungpo's Life (Nos. 40–50):

No. 40 is the genealogy of the Su clan prepared by Tungpo's father. The most important two direct sources are No. 41, the official biography of the poet in *Sung History*, in eight thousand words, and No. 42, the long tomb inscription, in six thousand words, written by his brother. No. 43, *Table of Chronological Events,* is usually found incorporated in his *Collected Works;* such "tables" of a person's life are confined to a dry tabulation of data, but require painstaking research and can be highly controversial. No. 44 is another table by a different author, contained in No. 18. Because of the closeness of Su Tungpo to his brother Tseyu throughout their personal and political lives, the table of Tseyu's life, No. 45, is important. No. 46, *Genealogical Table of the Su Clan of Meishan,* published in 1929, contains imagined portraits of the three Su's and of Tungpo's three children, and of Tseyu's three children, and other relevant material on the family; but the more important data for Tungpo's immediate family are well provided in the compilation made by Su's father. Reference has been made in Chapter XIV to No. 47, the work on Su's trial. Nos. 48, 49 and 50 are able compilations of anecdotes and records concerning Su Tungpo, classified according to subjects. Although No. 48 was compiled by the great poet Wang Shihcheng (1526–1590), I find No. 49 both more complete and better arranged, and the sources more clearly indicated.

H. Collected Works of Su's Contemporaries (Nos. 51–62):

The works of Su's contemporaries and close associates are now all readily available in good reprints of early editions both in *Szepu Tsungkan* (photographed) and in the *Szepu Peiyao* (reset). As such collected works usually contain the more formal writings of the authors, they are not so revealing as the journals and memoirs (see Section I below). However, No. 51 is the *Collected Works* of Su Tungpo's father; No. 52, of his brother, and No. 53, of his third son, Kuo. Mention must be made also of No. 94, the reminiscences of Tseyu's grandson. Nos. 54 to 59 are the collected works of Tungpo's six "disciples", Huang Tingchien, Chin Kuan *et al.* No. 60 is the *Collected Poems* of the monk Tsanliao, who is mentioned frequently in this biography; No. 61 is the important collected works of Wang Anshih. No. 62 contains the works of the great painter Mi Fei.

Besides the above, works of important characters in this biography are available, though not listed here. These are, for instance, the works

of Ouyang Shiu, Szema Kuang, Chang Fangping, Fan Chunjen, Fan
Tsuyu, Wang Anli, Han Chi, Han Wei, Wen Yenpo, Liu Chih, Chen
Shiang, Cheng Shia, and the learned poet monk Teh-hung.

I. Sung Memoirs (Nos. 63–100):

Richest in material casting sidelights on Su Tungpo's life and times
are the memoirs of Su's contemporaries and those coming a little after
him. Memoirs or notebooks are the laziest form of literature, requiring
no organisation of material, and are therefore the most popular literary
occupation of Chinese scholars. Such notebooks vary from serious and
sometimes highly important records of historical events and documents,
written to supplement official histories, to the most disorderly jumble
of tales of ghosts, fox spirits, and reincarnations, all these sometimes
co-existing in the same volume. In general, the notebooks come well
under the general classification of "scholars' gossip". I have made full
use of the literary gossip in the categories shown below, but have
excluded from the list the many *shih-hua*, or "talks on poetry", very
popular with the Sung scholars, which usually tell why certain famous
lines were written and under what circumstances.

Many duplicate editions of the following memoirs are available in
the different *tsungshu*, or "collections" or libraries". In general, the
text of the *Tsintai* Library is better than that of *Paoyentang*, and the
Shüehtsin is still better than the *Tsintai*. Since the appearance in 1935
of the *Tsungshu Chicheng* or "Collection of Collections", bringing
them all together in a uniform, inexpensive, and wisely selected edition,
scholars would do well henceforth to refer to this collection, because
now reference by a simple page number is possible.

(a) *Memoirs by two elder contemporaries:* No. 63 is by Szema
Kuang, and No 6. is by Fan Chen. For the source of important diaries
of the elder statesmen of the period, see No. 101.

(b) *Two highly important memoir writers:* These two authors'
works are considered of great value to historians; they also differ from
other memoirs in that they often consist of very long sections on special
events. No. 65, in two series, is by the son and grandson of the neo-
Confucianist Shao Yung; the son lived for a time in close association
with Szema Kuang during his retirement at Loyang. Because of a split
within the neo-Confucianist camp, the grandsons' record upheld Su
Tungpo against the Cheng brothers, who were rivals of his grandfather's school. Nos 66 to 68, written between 1166 and 1200, are by
Wang Mingching, an indefatigable writer of memoirs; they were submitted to the emperor by decree on account of their importance. As
the writer's mother was a granddaughter of Tseng Pu, Wang Anshih's
henchman, he was inclined to be partial towards Tseng Pu and Wang

and harsh on Mi Fei. Particularly No. 66 contains important studies of Sung customs and institutions and preserves certain historic documents.

(c) *Memoirs by Su Tungpo's disciples and close associates:* Nos. 69 to 76 contain important material. No. 69, by Li Chih, is short, but interesting throughout. No. 70, by Chen Shihtao, includes some jokes of Su Tungpo's. No. 71 is a collection of postscripts by Huang Tingchien, principally on manuscripts and paintings. No. 73, by Chang Lei, contains some intimate details of sex practices in connection with the art of prolonging life. No. 75 is by Li Chihyi, Su's associate at Tingchow, and No. 76 by Chao Lingshih, Su's associate at Yingchow.

(d) *Memoirs by other friends:* Less intimate than the above, but having access to first-hand sources, are the following. Nos. 77 and 78 are by Kung Pingchun, brother of Kung Wenchung, both on intimate terms with Su; No. 77, known to be not always accurate, contains stories of Su's arrest and trial. Nos. 79 and 80 are by the monk Huihung, alias Teh-hung, a close friend of Huang Tingchien, and contain many items on Su. No. 81, by Ho Wei, son of Ho Chufei, who was recommended to high office by Su, contains along with No. 84 probably the richest records on Su. The *Paoyentang* edition is incomplete, but the *Shüehtsin* edition has an entire chapter devoted to Su, including the story of his death. No. 82 is by Chao Yuehchih, brother of Chao Puchih, disciple of Su. Being in the inner circle, the author gives many conversations of the whole Yuanyu group, particularly Fan Tsuyu. No. 83, author unknown, appears clearly to have been written by a friend of the same circle; it disparages both Wang Anshih and the Cheng brothers.

(e) *Memoirs by neutrals:* No. 84 is extremely valuable and rich in material, written by Chu Pien, a contemporary. No. 85 is a small but much quoted volume containing humorous anecdotes.. No. 86 is independent in attitude. No. 87 is by Fang Shuo, who lived at Huchow.

(f) *Memoirs by the opposition:* The usual defence of Wang Anshih —that Sung historians and memoirs writers are all biased against Wang—is not factually correct; see also Nos. 66 and 101. The interesting thing about this group is that their records are quite favourable to Su, and records of Su's faults, such as Yeh Mengteh's story of how Su was never an expert wine-maker and how he nearly burned a house down in trying to make ink, only make him more human. Yeh Mengteh, author of Nos. 88 and 89, was related by marriage to Chang Chun and was an intimate friend of Tsai Ching. Wei Tai, author of No. 90, was the brother of Tseng Pu's wife (a famous poetess); he tried to whitewash Wang Anshih. The author of No. 91 was one of the two notorious sons of the notorious Tsai Ching; between the father and sons, who fought for power against each other, they brought the northern Sung to an end. No. 92, like Nos. 88 and 89, records Su Tungpo's personal faults, which were no more than his carelessness with his tongue. Chu Yu, author of No. 93, was the son of Chu Fu, who was a friend of Su, but who later served under Sudan and Lu Huiching.

(g) *Later memoirs:* On the whole, the above memoirs may be said to have been written in the northern Sung period, which ended in 1126, twenty-five years after Su's death, though there is no reason to draw a line between northern and southern Sung, since many of these memoir writers lived in both dynasties. Of great interest is No. 94, written by Tseyu's grandson, with a slight tendency to give more credit to his grandfather than to Tungpo. No. 95, written by a "hundred-year-old-man" around the year 1200, gives reminiscences about the northern Sung capital. No. 96 was written in 1241, interesting because the author's wife had burned his previous scripts.

(h) *Memoirs by prominent scholars and collectors:* Of the many records and postscripts of scholars in the twelfth century who took special interest in examining manuscripts by Su Tungpo, four are listed here. No. 97 is by Lu Yu the poet (1125–1210), who also wrote No. 118. No. 98 is by the great neo-Confucianist Chu Shi (1130–1200). Chou Pita (1126–1206), author of No. 99, was a zealous collector of Su's manuscripts. No. 100 is by another great neo-Confucianist scholar, Wei Liaoweng (1178–1237), who lived very near the end of the southern Sung dynasty.

J. HISTORY (Nos. 101–106):

The basic source of material for northern Sung times is not the official *Sung History,* No. 105, but No. 101, the monumental work by Li Tao (1114–1183), in 520 volumes. Defenders of Wang Anshih, such as Liang Chichao and Tsai Shangshiang, often use the argument that the *Sung History,* which is anti-Wang and pro-Yuanyu, was a sloppy job, compiled under a Mongol editor-in-chief, Toketok. It is true that *Sung History* is both sloppy and pro-Yuanyu, but the private work of Wang Cheng, No. 104, is pro-Yuanyu and not sloppy, and Li Tao's work utilised all sources, erring rather on the side of comprehensiveness, and giving all that could be asked of any great historical work. This work is richest for the period covered by Su Tungpo's entire life. It gives extensive quotations from the diaries of Wang Anshih, Szema Kuang, Lu Tafang, Lu Kungchu, Tseng Pu, Lin Shi, etc., and the famous *Court Records of Shentsung,* with dialogues in the imperial audience. It thus preserves parts of all these works now lost to posterity, and of other works, such as Nos 63. to 66, in an ancient version. Li's work occupied the author for forty years and was presented to the emperor in parts, in 1163, 1168, and 1174.

It may be noted here that the Sung scholars were history-minded. Szema Kuang compiled the monumental *Mirror of History,* and Ouyang Shiu compiled the *New Tang History* and the *New History of the Five Dynasties.* Li Shinchuan (not listed here) did for the southern Sung what Li Tao had done for the northern Sung; Wang Cheng undertook No. 104, and Peng Pochuan undertook No. 106, which all represent labours of private scholars.

Li Tao's comprehensive but unwieldy work almost went out of existence because of its size—like the dinosaurs—and two copies survived, one in the inaccessible great Yunglo library inside the Ming palace, almost perfect, but unknown even to the court scholars until it was discovered under Emperor Chienlung in the eighteenth century. This work, chronologically arranged, was put into a more digestible form by Yang Chungliang under a topical arrangement, so that one could follow the development of a particular military campaign or political phase conveniently. But Yang's work, No. 102, published in 1253 and 1257, was even less known to collectors and librarians, and came to light about 1800.

Yang's work is probably the most comprehensive yet handy history for basic research on northern Sung, preserving the original source material of Li Tao's work in sufficient quantity. It also preserves the material for the period 1101–1126, for which the volumes in Li Tao's work are missing. An even handier topical digest, No. 103, is that by Feng Chi, revised by Chen Pangchan, under the supervision of Chang Po (1602–41).

Most valuable for the study of Su Tungpo's life and times is No. 104, which, though the work of a private scholar, could well take the place of the official *Sung History* for the northern period. It is favourable to the Yuanyu group and anti-Wang, but is recognised by all as competent, discriminating, and judicious. Especially valuable are its 105 volumes of biographical sketches of the scholars and officials of the northern Sung.

K. SPECIAL STUDIES, INCLUDING WANG ANSHIH (Nos. 107–111):

No. 107, by Chu Shi, gives briefly the outstanding sayings and conduct of the famous ministers. No. 108 is a study of the different scholars' contributions to thought. The chapters on Wang Anshih and the Sus (Ch. 98 and 99) are by Chuan Tsuwang.

Three works are devoted to rescuing Wang Anshih from historical infamy. Basis research was done by Tsai Shangshiang, an obscure scholar; I have access only to the digest in four volumes by Yang

Shimin, No. 109; Volume 4 has some very good material. Both Liang Chichao, No. 110, and Ko Changyi, No. 111, made themselves special pleaders for Wang, which vitiates the quality of their arguments and evidence. This is not the place to enter into the controversial subject. Briefly, Liang and Ko pleaded (1) that Wang was a great poet and scholar, which nobody denies; (2) that Wang was a socialist and "therefore in line with modern thinking", (without distinguishing the particular variety of socialism that Wang put into practice); (3) that Wang was inspired for patriotic motives to make China a strong military state, and that it was justified by the times (forgetting that the wars of aggression were not so popular with the people who had to fight them); (4) that all history writing of Wang's period was based on biased sources by the generation that saw the fall of the northern Sung and therefore was prejudiced against him (without quite accounting for how that generation of men who tasted the fruits of his regime were so unanimous in their condemnation); and (5) that Wang was not responsible for the persecution of the Yuanyu scholars and for the party strife that grew out of his regime.

L. GEOGRAPHY (Nos. 112–119):

Nos. 112 and 113 are geographical works of the northern Sung period, with details of population and products, etc. A fascinating book is No. 114, a detailed description of the northern Sung capital, its palaces, streets, shops, customs, and festivals. Similar in content but twice its size is No. 115, a description of Hangchow when it was the capital of the southern Sung. No. 116 contains stories connected with Hangchow in the latter part of the twelfth century. No. 117 gives the artistic and literary history and miscellaneous anecdotes connected with West Lake and the Hangchow environs. No. 118 is the diary of Lu Yu's voyage up the Yangtse to Szechuen in 1170, including his visit to Tungpo's house at Huangchow. No. 119 is the record of Fan Chengta's voyage down the Yangtse from Chengtu in 1177.

M. FACSIMILES (Nos. 120–124):

Rubbings from inscriptions in Su Tungpo's handwriting are too numerous to mention. Particular note is taken here of No. 120, referred to on page 243 in Chapter XX. No. 121 contains the portrait owned by Weng Fangkang, reproduced in this book; its contents are told on pages 39-40 in Chapter XI. No. 122 contains facsimiles of Su Tungpo's writing and his brother's. No. 123 is a particularly good facsimile of Su's poem to his female cousin's father-in-law. Letters in the handwriting of at least a dozen characters in this biography are reproduced in the publications of the Palace Museum, Peking, No. 124.

書 目

（凡書收入數種叢書者，舉其佳者一種，列入叢書集成者加*號）

A. 最初刻本
1. 王詵刻詩集（1079以前）
2. 陳師仲編超然集黃樓集（1082前後）
3. 劉沔編文集（約1097-1100）
· 4. 趙次公等蘇詩五註（崇寧大觀間，約1110-1126）
5. 趙夔等蘇詩十註（紹興初，約1130）
6. 王十朋編蘇詩百家註（約1170）
7. 施元之蘇詩編年註（1208）
8. 鄭羽重刻施註（1262）

B. 清代刻本
9. 宋犖編施註蘇詩（邵長蘅李必恆補註）（1699）
10. 查慎行東坡編年詩補註（1702）
11. 紀曉嵐蘇詩點論本（1771）
12. 翁方綱蘇詩補註（1782）
13. 馮應榴蘇詩合註（1793）
14. 王大誥蘇詩編註集成（1822初刻，1888重刻）

C. 現代刻本
15. 經進東坡文集事略（四部叢刊）
16. 東坡七集（四部備要）
17. 蘇文忠公全集（世界）
18. 王狀元集註東坡先生詩（四部叢刊）
19. 蘇詩補註　翁方綱（國學基本）

D. 蘇東坡著作
20. 易傳（學津）*
21. 書傳（學津）*
22. 論語說（佚）
23. 志林（學津）*
24. 和陶合箋（順德鄧氏藏版）

E. 選集
25. 東坡題跋（津逮）*
26. 蘇沈良方（知不足）*
27. 仇池筆記（龍威）*
28. 東坡文談錄（學海）
29. 東坡詩話錄（學海）
30. 東坡樂府箋　龍沐勛編（商務）
31. 東坡禪喜集　劉仁肪編（商務）
32. 蘇長公小品　王納諫（康熙刻本）

F. 僞託書
33. 艾子雜說 （顧氏）*
34. 廣成子解 （說郛）
35. 格物粗談 （學海）*
36. 物類相感志 （寶顏）*
37. 問答錄 （寶顏）
38. 漁樵問答 （寶顏）
39. 雜纂二續 （說郛）

G. 年譜事類等
40. 蘇氏族譜 蘇洵 （說郛）
41. 宋史本傳
42. 墓誌銘 蘇轍 （見全集, 16, 17）
43. 年譜 王宗稷 （見全集, 16, 17）
44. 紀年錄 傅藻 （見 18）
45. 蘇穎濱年表 孫汝听 （藕香零拾）
46. 眉山蘇氏族譜 （1929刻本）
47. 烏台詩案 （學海）*
48. 蘇長公外紀 王世貞 （明刻）
49. 東坡事類 梁廷楠 （光緒五年刻本）
50. 東坡逸事 沈宗元 （商務）

H. 嘉祐至元祐諸賢文集
51. 嘉祐集 蘇洵 （四部叢刊本, 下同）
52. 欒城集 蘇轍
53. 斜川集 蘇過
54. 山谷集 黃庭堅
55. 淮海集 秦觀
56. 宛邱集 張耒
57. 雞肋集 晁補之
58. 后山集 陳師道
59. 濟南集 李廌
60. 參寥子集 道潛
61. 臨川集 王安石
62. 寶晉英光集 米芾

I. 宋人筆記 （詩話不錄）
(a)63. 涑水紀聞 司馬光 （學津）*
64. 東齋紀事 范鎮 （守山）*
(b)65. 聞見前錄, 後錄 邵伯溫, 邵博 （學津）*
66. 揮麈前錄, 後錄, 三錄 王明清 （學津）*
67. 揮麈餘話 王明清 （學津）*
68. 玉照新志 王明清 （學津）*

K. 特種參攷
107. 名臣言行錄　朱熹（道光壬寅刻本）
108. 宋元學案　黃宗羲（長沙河氏）
109. 王文公年譜　蔡上翔著，楊希閔節略（豫章先賢九家年譜）
110. 王荆公　梁啓超（廣智）
111. 王安石評傳　柯昌頤（商務）

L. 地理
112. 元豐九域志（聚珍）*
113. 太平寰宇記　樂史（乾隆刻本）
114. 東京夢華錄　孟元老（學津）*
115. 夢梁錄　吳自牧（學海）*
116. 武林舊事（知不足）
117. 西湖游覽志餘　田汝成（西湖集覽，嘉惠堂重刊）
118. 入蜀記　陸游（寶顏）*
119. 吳船錄　范成大（寶顏）*

M. 眞跡墨帖
120. 西樓蘇帖　汪應辰刻（文明書局）
121. 天際烏雲帖（嵩陽帖）
122. 剔耳圖二蘇題跋（文明書局）
123. 贈柳子玉詩帖（文明書局）
124. 故宮博物院週刊月刊

Appendix C

BIOGRAPHICAL REFERENCE LIST

The romanisations of Chinese names in this book are given without aspirate and tone marks. For the convenience of scholars, Chinese names are given here to help in their identification. I have abandoned the use of the atrocious "hs" and always spelled "sh" instead. The umlaut mark above *u* is dispensed with except in *shü*.

Brief terms of relationship indicate the person's relationship to Su Tungpo. Where exact dates are not available, *"d."* stands for "died", and *"c."* stands for *circa* or "about". Ages are given according to Western reckoning.

Chang Chun (*d.* after 1100, age 70), chief persecutor of Yuanyu officials	章 惇 － 子厚
Chang Chung, magistrate at Hainan, friend	張 中
Chang Fangping (1007–1091), friend of Su family, high minister	張方平 － 安道
Chang Lei (1052–1112), disciple, poet	張 耒 － 文潛
Chang Yuan, son of Chang Chun and disciple of Su	章 援 － 致平
Chao Lingshih, friend and memoir writer	趙令畤 － 德麟
Chao Ku, friend at Huangchow	巢 穀 － 元修
Chao Pien (1008–1084), old minister, fence rider	趙 抃 － 閱道
Chao Puchih (1053–1110), disciple, writer	晁補之 － 无咎
Chao Tuanyen, father of Puchih, friend	晁端彦 － 美叔
Chen Shiang (1017–1080), poet, friend, magistrate of Hangchow	陳 襄 － 述古
Chen Shihtao (1053–1101), disciple, poet	陳師道 － 履常
Chen Tsao, great friend	陳 慥 － 季常
Cheng Chiahui, friend during exile	鄭嘉會 － 靖老
Cheng Chihtsai, commissioner, brother-in-law	程之才 － 正輔

Li Chang (1027–1090), scholar, intimate
friend   李 常 － 公擇

Li Chih (*d.* after 1100, age 51), disciple,
memoir writer   李 廌 － 方叔

Li Chihyi, close associate, memoir writer   李之儀 － 端叔

Li Kunglin (Lungmien, 1049–after 1100),
great painter, friend   李公麟 － 伯時

Li Ting (Leeding, *d.* after 1100, age 62),
prosecutor of Su   李 定 － 資深

Liang Tao (1034–1097), high minister   梁 燾 － 況之

Liu Anshih (1048–1125), good censor   劉安世 － 器之

Liu Chih (1030–1097), Hopei political
leader   劉 摯 － 莘老

Liu Chin, friend, father of Liu Chungyuan   柳 瑾 － 子玉

Liu Chungyuan, husband of Su's cousin   柳仲遠

Liu Hung, son of Su's cousin   柳 閎 － 展如

Liu Pin (1022–1088), great friend and wit   劉 邠 － 貢父

Liu Shu (1032–1078), assistant editor of
Szema Kuang's "history", friend   劉 恕 － 道源

Lu Chiawen, trade dictator under Wang
Anshih   呂嘉問 － 望之

Lu Huei, censor   呂 誨 － 獻可

Lu Huichang (*d.* after1100, age 79), hench-
man of Wang Anshih   呂惠卿 － 吉甫

Lu Kungchu (1018–1089), great scholar,
prime minister   呂公著 － 晦叔

Lu Tafang (1027–1097), prime minister   呂大防 － 微叔

Lu Yu (1125–1210), poet   陸 游 － 務觀

Ma Mengteh (1036– ?), lifetime follower   馬夢得

Mei Yaochen (1002–1060), high minister   梅堯臣 － 聖俞

Mi Fei (1051–1107), outstanding painter,
friend   米 芾 － 元章

Ouyang Shiu (1007–1072), first scholar of
his time, master of Su   歐陽修 － 永叔

Ouyang Fei (1047–1113), son of Ouyang
Shiu, father-in-law of Tungpo's son,
Tai   歐陽棐 － 叔弼

Pan Ping, friend at Huangchow   潘 丙 － 彥明

Pan Talin, scholar, friend at Huangchow   潘大臨 － 邠老

Pu Tsungmeng (*d.* about 1094, age 65),
relative   蒲宗孟 － 傳正

Shao Yung (1011-1077), neo-Confucianist, friend of Szema Kuang　邵　雍 – 堯夫

Shao Powen (1057-1134), son of Shao Yung and important memoir writer　邵伯溫 – 子文

Shen Kua (1030-1094), learned writer　沈　适 – 存中

Shieh Chingwen, brother-in-law of Wang Anshih　謝景溫 – 師直

Shu Tan (Sudan, d. 1104) writer, enemy of Su　舒　亶 – 信道

Shü Tacheng, brother of Shü Tashou, friend　徐大正 – 得之

Shü Tashou, magistrate of Huangchow, good friend　徐大受 – 君猷

Su Cheh (Tseyu, 1039-1112), brother of Tungpo　蘇　轍 – 子由

Su Huan (1000-1062), uncle of Tungpo, elder brother of Su Shün, commissioner　蘇　渙 – 公羣

Su Kuo (1072-1123), third son of Tungpo　蘇　過 – 叔黨

Su Mai (1059-?), eldest son of Tungpo　蘇　邁 – 伯達

Su Shih (Tungpo, 1036-1101), poet　蘇　軾 – 子瞻

Su Shü (973-1047), grandfather of Tungpo　蘇　序 – 仲先

Su Shün (1009-1066), father of Tungpo　蘇　洵 – 明允

Su Sung (1020-1101), prime minister, friend　蘇　頌 – 子容

Su Tai (1070-?), second son of Tungpo　蘇　迨 – 仲豫

Sudan, see Shu Tan

Sun Chueh (1028-1090), close friend of Tungpo　孫　覺 – 莘老

Sung Minchiu (1019-1079), writer　宋敏求 – 次道

Szema Kuang (1019-1086), leader of opposition to Wang Anshih, historian, friend　司馬光 – 君實

Ten Yuanfa (1020-1090), close friend, scholar　滕元發 – 達道

Teng Kuan (Dunquan, d. age 58), unscrupulous official　鄧　綰 – 文約

Tsai Ching, prime minister, caused end of dynasty　蔡　京 – 元長

Tsai Chueh (d. about 1090, age 56), prime minister, wicked intriguer　蔡　確 – 持正

Tsai Pien (d. age 59), brother of Tsai Ching and son-in-law of Wang Anshih　蔡　卞 – 元度

Tsai Shiang (1012-1067), great calligraphist 蔡 襄 – 君謨

Tsanliao, monk, poet, friend 參 寥 (道潛)

Tseng Kung (1019-1083), great writer 曾 鞏 – 子固

Tseng Kungliang (998-1078), h i g h minister 曾公亮 – 敏仲

Tseng Pu, prime minister, husband of poetess "Madame Wei" 曾 布 – 子宣

Wang Ankuo (1028-1074), brother of Anshih, writer 王安國 – 平甫

Wang Anli (1034-1095), brother of Anshih 王安禮 – 和甫

Wang Anshih (1021-1086), poet, social reformer 王安石 – 介甫

Wang Chaoyun (1063-1096), concubine of Tungpo 王朝雲

Wang Chen (1049-1101), brother of Tungpo's second wife 王 箴 – 元直

Wang Chiyu, friend at Huangchow 王齊愈 – 文甫

Wang Chiung, brother of Wang Shih 王 迥 – 子高

Wang Fang (1044-1076), son of Wang Anshih 王 雱 – 元澤

Wang Fu (1039-1065), first wife of Tungpo 王 弗

Wang Junchi (1048-1093), second wife of Tungpo 王閏之 – 季璋

Wang Kuei (1019-1085), prime minister 王 珪 – 禹玉

Wang Kung, good friend 王 鞏 – 定國

Wang Mingching (1127- c. 1214), important memoir writer 王明清 – 仲言

Wang Shien, prince (d. after 1100), brother-in-law of Emperor Shentsung, painter, great friend 王 詵 – 晉卿

Wang Shih, son-in-law of Tseyu, tutor to children of Tungpo and Tseyu 王 適 – 子立

Wang Shihpeng (1112-1171), scholar, important commentator 王十朋 – 龜齡

Weilin, monk, friend 維 琳

Wen Tung (1019-1079), great bamboo painter, cousin 文 同 – 與可

Wen Yenpo (1006-1097), high minister 文彥博 – 寬夫

Wu Fuku (d. 1100), friend, Taoist 吳復古 – 子野

INDEX